Complete Works Of Thomas Paine

- Thomas Paine

Contents

About Thomas Paine 2

1 – RIGHTS OF MAN. 5

- PAINE'S PREFACE TO THE ENGLISH EDITION 8
- PAINE'S PREFACE TO THE FRENCH EDITION 9
- RIGHTS OF MAN. PART THE FIRST BEING AN ANSWER TO MR. BURKE'S ATTACK ON THE FRENCH REVOLUTION   10
- RIGHTS OF MAN. PART SECOND, COMBINING PRINCIPLE AND PRACTICE 44
- FRENCH TRANSLATOR'S PREFACE 44
- PREFACE 45
- RIGHTS OF MAN PART II: INTRODUCTION. 47
- CHAPTER I. OF SOCIETY AND CIVILISATION 48
- CHAPTER II. OF THE ORIGIN OF THE PRESENT OLD GOVERNMENTS 50
- CHAPTER III. OF THE OLD AND NEW SYSTEMS OF GOVERNMENT 50
- CHAPTER IV. OF CONSTITUTIONS 55
- CHAPTER V. WAYS AND MEANS OF IMPROVING THE CONDITION OF EUROPE 62
- APPENDIX 81
- THE AUTHOR'S NOTES FOR PART ONE AND PART TWO 83

2 – COMMON SENSE; 96

- **SUBJECTS** 96
- INTRODUCTION 97
- OF THE ORIGIN AND DESIGN OF GOVERNMENT IN GENERAL, WITH CONCISE REMARKS ON THE ENGLISH CONSTITUTION.   98
- OF MONARCHY AND HEREDITARY SUCCESSION. 100
- THOUGHTS ON THE PRESENT STATE OF AMERICAN AFFAIRS. 103
- OF THE PRESENT ABILITY OF AMERICA, WITH SOME MISCELLANEOUS REFLEXIONS. 109
- APPENDIX. 114
- Historical Context 119
- On Common Sense 121

3.1 – THE AGE OF REASON 122

- CHAPTER I – THE AUTHOR'S PROFESSION OF FAITH. 128
- CHAPTER II – OF MISSIONS AND REVELATIONS. 129
- CHAPTER III – CONCERNING THE CHARACTER OF JESUS CHRIST, AND HIS HISTORY. 130
- CHAPTER IV – OF THE BASES OF CHRISTIANITY. 131
- CHAPTER V – EXAMINATION IN DETAIL OF THE PRECEDING BASES. 131
- CHAPTER VI – OF THE TRUE THEOLOGY. 132
- CHAPTER VII – EXAMINATION OF THE OLD TESTAMENT. 132
- CHAPTER VIII – OF THE NEW TESTAMENT. 136
- CHAPTER IX – IN WHAT THE TRUE REVELATION CONSISTS. 138
- CHAPTER X – CONCERNING GOD, AND THE LIGHTS CAST ON HIS EXISTENCE AND ATTRIBUTES BY THE BIBLE.   139
- CHAPTER XI – OF THE THEOLOGY OF THE CHRISTIANS; AND THE TRUE THEOLOGY 141
- CHAPTER XII – THE EFFECTS OF CHRISTIANISM ON EDUCATION; PROPOSED 142
- CHAPTER XIII – COMPARISON OF CHRISTIANISM WITH THE RELIGIOUS IDEAS 145
- CHAPTER XIV – SYSTEM OF THE UNIVERSE. 148
- CHAPTER XV – ADVANTAGES OF THE EXISTENCE OF MANY WORLDS IN EACH SOLAR SYSTEM   149
- CHAPTER XVI – APPLICATION OF THE PRECEDING TO THE SYSTEM OF THE 150
- CHAPTER XVII – OF THE MEANS EMPLOYED IN ALL TIME, AND ALMOST 151

3.2 – THE AGE OF REASON – PART II 154

- PREFACE 154
- CHAPTER I – THE OLD TESTAMENT 156
- CHAPTER II – THE NEW TESTAMENT 176
- CHAPTER III – CONCLUSION 185

ABOUT THOMAS PAINE

Thomas Paine (born Thomas Pain (February 9, 1737 [O.S. January 29, 1736 – June 8, 1809) was an English-born American political activist, philosopher, political theorist and revolutionary. One of the Founding Fathers of the United States, he authored the two most influential pamphlets at the start of the American Revolution and inspired the patriots in 1776 to declare independence from Britain.

His ideas reflected Enlightenment-era ideals of transnational human rights.[3] Saul K. Padover described him as "a corsetmaker by trade, a journalist by profession, and a propagandist by inclination".

Born in Thetford in the English county of Norfolk, Paine migrated to the British American colonies in 1774 with the help of Benjamin Franklin, arriving just in time to participate in the American Revolution. Virtually every rebel read (or listened to a reading of) his powerful pamphlet Common Sense (1776), proportionally the all-time best-selling American title, which crystallized the rebellious demand for independence from Great Britain. His The American Crisis (1776–1783) was a pro-revolutionary pamphlet series. Common Sense was so influential that John Adams said: "Without the pen of the author of Common Sense, the sword of Washington would have been raised in vain".

Paine lived in France for most of the 1790s, becoming deeply involved in the French Revolution. He wrote Rights of Man (1791), in part a defense of the French Revolution against its critics. His attacks on Irish conservative writer Edmund Burke led to a trial and conviction in absentia in England in 1792 for the crime of seditious libel.

The British government of William Pitt the Younger, worried by the possibility that the French Revolution might spread to England, had begun suppressing works that espoused radical philosophies. Paine's work, which advocated the right of the people to overthrow their government, was duly targeted, with a writ for his arrest issued in early 1792. Paine fled to France in September where, rather immediately and despite not being able to speak French, he was elected to the French National Convention. The Girondists regarded him as an ally. Consequently, the Montagnards, especially Maximilien Robespierre, regarded him as an enemy.

In December 1793, he was arrested and was taken to Luxembourg Prison in Paris. While in prison, he continued to work on The Age of Reason (1793–1794). Future President James Monroe used his diplomatic connections to get Paine released in November 1794. He became notorious because of his pamphlets. The Age of Reason, in which he advocated deism, promoted reason and free thought and argued against institutionalized religion in general and Christian doctrine in particular. He published the pamphlet Agrarian Justice (1797), discussing the origins of property and introduced the concept of a guaranteed minimum income. In 1802, he returned to the U.S. where he died on June 8, 1809. Only six people attended his funeral as he had been ostracized for his ridicule of Christianity.

Ideas

Biographer Eric Foner identifies a utopian thread in Paine's thought, writing: "Through this new language he communicated a new vision—a utopian image of an egalitarian, republican society".

Paine's utopianism combined civic republicanism, belief in the inevitability of scientific and social progress and commitment to free markets and liberty generally. The multiple sources of Paine's political theory all pointed to a society based on the common good and individualism. Paine expressed a redemptive futurism or political messianism. Writing that his generation "would appear to the future as the Adam of a new world", Paine exemplified British utopianism.

Later, his encounters with the Indigenous peoples of the Americas made a deep impression. The ability of the Iroquois to live in harmony with nature while achieving a democratic decision-making process helped him refine his thinking on how to organize society.

Slavery

On March 8, 1775, one month after Paine became the editor of The Pennsylvania Magazine, the magazine published an anonymous article titled "African Slavery in America", the first prominent piece in the colonies proposing the emancipation of African-American slaves and the abolition of slavery.

Paine is often credited with writing the piece, on the basis of later testimony by Benjamin Rush, cosigner of the Declaration of Independence. Citing a lack of further evidence of Paine's authorship however, scholars Eric Foner and Alfred Owen Aldridge no longer consider this one of his works. By contrast, journalist John Nichols writes that Paine's "fervent objections to slavery" led to his exclusion from power during the early years of the Republic.

Agrarian Justice

His last pamphlet, Agrarian Justice, published in the winter of 1795, opposed to agrarian law and to agrarian monopoly and further developed his ideas in the Rights of Man about how land ownership separated the majority of people from their rightful, natural inheritance and means of independent survival. The U.S. Social Security Administration recognizes Agrarian Justice as the first American proposal for an old-age pension and basic income or citizen's dividend. Per Agrarian Justice:

In advocating the case of the persons thus dispossessed, it is a right, and not a charity ... [Government must] create a national fund, out of which there shall be paid to every person, when arrived at the age of twenty-one years, the sum of fifteen pounds sterling, as a compensation in part, for the loss of his or her natural inheritance, by the introduction of the system of landed property. And also, the sum of ten pounds per annum, during life, to every person now living, of the age of fifty years, and to all others as they shall arrive at that age.

Note that £10 and £15 would be worth about £800 and £1,200 ($1,200 and $2,000) when adjusted for inflation (2011 British pounds sterling).[98]

Lamb argues that Paine's analysis of property rights marks a distinct contribution to political theory. His theory of property defends a libertarian concern with private ownership that shows an egalitarian commitment. Paine's new justification of property sets him apart from previous theorists such as Hugo Grotius, Samuel von Pufendorf and John Locke. It demonstrates Paine's commitment to foundational liberal values of individual freedom and moral equality.

1 – RIGHTS OF MAN.

EDITOR'S INTRODUCTION.

WHEN Thomas Paine sailed from America for France, in April, 1787, he was perhaps as happy a man as any in the world. His most intimate friend, Jefferson, was Minister at Paris, and his friend Lafayette was the idol of France. His fame had preceded him, and he at once became, in Paris, the centre of the same circle of savants and philosophers that had surrounded Franklin. His main reason for proceeding at once to Paris was that he might submit to the Academy of Sciences his invention of an iron bridge, and with its favorable verdict he came to England, in September. He at once went to his aged mother at Thetford, leaving with a publisher (Ridgway), his "Prospects on the Rubicon." He next made arrangements to patent his bridge, and to construct at Rotherham the large model of it exhibited on Paddington Green, London. He was welcomed in England by leading statesmen, such as Lansdowne and Fox, and above all by Edmund Burke, who for some time had him as a guest at Beaconsfield, and drove him about in various parts of the country. He had not the slightest revolutionary purpose, either as regarded England or France. Towards Louis XVI. he felt only gratitude for the services he had rendered America, and towards George III. he felt no animosity whatever. His four months' sojourn in Paris had convinced him that there was approaching a reform of that country after the American model, except that the Crown would be preserved, a compromise he approved, provided the throne should not be hereditary. Events in France travelled more swiftly than he had anticipated, and Paine was summoned by Lafayette, Condorcet, and others, as an adviser in the formation of a new constitution.

Such was the situation immediately preceding the political and literary duel between Paine and Burke, which in the event turned out a tremendous war between Royalism and Republicanism in Europe. Paine was, both in France and in England, the inspirer of moderate counsels. Samuel Rogers relates that in early life he dined at a friend's house in London with Thomas Paine, when one of the toasts given was the "memory of Joshua,"—in allusion to the Hebrew leader's conquest of the kings of Canaan, and execution of them. Paine observed that he would not treat kings like Joshua. "I 'm of the Scotch parson's opinion," he said, "when he prayed against Louis XIV.—`Lord, shake him over the mouth of hell, but don't let him drop!'" Paine then gave as his toast, "The Republic of the World,"—which Samuel Rogers, aged twenty-nine, noted as a sublime idea. This was Paine's faith and hope, and with it he confronted the revolutionary storms which presently burst over France and England.

Until Burke's arraignment of France in his parliamentary speech (February 9, 1790), Paine had no doubt whatever that he would sympathize with the movement in France, and wrote to him from that country as if conveying glad tidings. Burke's "Reflections on the Revolution in France" appeared November 1, 1790, and Paine at once set himself to answer it. He was then staying at the Angel Inn, Islington. The inn has been twice rebuilt since that time, and from its contents there is preserved only a small image, which perhaps was meant to represent "Liberty,"—possibly brought from Paris by Paine as an ornament for his study. From the Angel he removed to a house in Harding Street, Fetter Lane. Rickman says Part First of "Rights of Man" was finished at Versailles, but probably this has reference to the preface only, as I cannot find Paine in France that year until April 8. The book had been printed by Johnson, in time for the opening of Parliament, in February; but this publisher became frightened after a few copies were out (there is one in the British Museum), and the work was transferred to J. S. Jordan, 166 Fleet Street, with a preface sent from Paris (not contained in Johnson's edition, nor in the American editions). The pamphlet, though sold at the same price as Burke's, three shillings, had a vast circulation, and Paine gave the proceeds to the Constitutional Societies which sprang up under his teachings in various parts of the country.

Soon after appeared Burke's "Appeal from the New to the Old Whigs." In this Burke quoted a good deal from "Rights of Man," but replied to it only with exclamation points, saying that the only answer such ideas merited was "criminal justice." Paine's Part Second followed, published February 17, 1792. In Part First Paine had mentioned a rumor that Burke was a masked pensioner (a charge that will be noticed in connection with its detailed statement in a further publication); and as Burke had been formerly arraigned in Parliament, while Paymaster, for a very questionable proceeding, this charge no doubt hurt a good deal. Although the government did not follow Burke's suggestion of a prosecution at that time, there is little doubt that it was he who induced the prosecution of Part Second. Before the trial came on, December 18, 1792, Paine was occupying his seat in the French Convention, and could only be outlawed.

Burke humorously remarked to a friend of Paine and himself, "We hunt in pairs." The severally representative character and influence of these two men in the revolutionary era, in France and England, deserve more adequate study than they have received. While Paine maintained freedom of discussion, Burke first proposed criminal prosecution for sentiments by no means libellous (such as Paine's Part First). While Paine was endeavoring to make the movement in France peaceful, Burke fomented the league of monarchs against France which maddened its people, and brought on the Reign of Terror. While Paine was endeavoring to preserve the French throne ("phantom" though he believed it), to prevent bloodshed, Burke was secretly writing to the Queen of France, entreating her not to compromise, and to "trust to the support of foreign armies" ("Histoire de France depuis 1789." Henri Martin, i., 151). While Burke thus helped to bring the King and Queen to the guillotine, Paine pleaded for their lives to the last moment. While Paine maintained the right of mankind to improve their condition, Burke held that "the awful Author of our being is the author of our place in the order of existence; and that, having disposed and marshalled us by a divine tactick, not according to our will, but according to his, he has, in and by that disposition, virtually subjected us to act the part which belongs to the place assigned us." Paine was a religious believer in eternal principles; Burke held that "political problems do not primarily concern truth or falsehood. They relate to good or evil. What in the result is likely to produce evil is politically false, that which is productive of good politically is true." Assuming thus the visionary's right to decide before the result what was "likely to produce evil," Burke vigorously sought to kindle war against the French Republic which might have developed itself peacefully, while Paine was striving for an international Congress in Europe in the interest of peace. Paine had faith in the people, and believed that, if allowed to choose representatives, they would select their best and wisest men; and that while reforming government the people would remain orderly, as they had generally remained in America during the transition from British rule to selfgovernment. Burke maintained that if the existing political order were broken up there would be no longer a people, but "a number of vague, loose individuals, and nothing more." "Alas!" he exclaims, "they little know how many a weary step is to be taken before they can form themselves into a mass, which has a true personality." For the sake of peace Paine wished the revolution to be peaceful as the advance of summer; he used every endeavor to reconcile English radicals to some modus vivendi with the existing order, as he was willing to retain Louis XVI. as head of the executive in France: Burke resisted every tendency of English statesmanship to reform at home, or to negotiate with the French Republic, and was mainly responsible for the King's death and the war that followed between England and France in February, 1793. Burke became a royal favorite, Paine was outlawed by a prosecution originally proposed by Burke. While Paine was demanding religious liberty, Burke was opposing the removal of penal statutes from Unitarians, on the ground that but for those statutes Paine might some day set up a church in England. When Burke was retiring on a large royal pension, Paine was in prison, through the devices of Burke's confederate, the American Minister in Paris. So the two men, as Burke said, "hunted in pairs."

So far as Burke attempts to affirm any principle he is fairly quoted in Paine's work, and nowhere misrepresented. As for Paine's own ideas, the reader should remember that "Rights of Man" was the earliest complete statement of republican principles. They were pronounced to be the fundamental principles of the American Republic by Jefferson, Madison, and Jackson,-the three Presidents who above all others represented the republican idea which Paine first allied with American Independence. Those who suppose that Paine did but reproduce the principles of Rousseau and Locke will find by careful study of his well-weighed language that such is not the case. Paine's political principles were evolved out of his early Quakerism. He was potential in George Fox. The belief that every human soul was the child of God, and capable of direct inspiration from the Father of all, without mediator or priestly intervention, or sacramental instrumentality, was fatal to all privilege and rank. The universal Fatherhood implied universal Brotherhood, or human equality. But the fate of the Quakers proved the necessity of protecting the individual spirit from oppression by the majority as well as by privileged classes. For this purpose Paine insisted on surrounding the individual right with the security of the Declaration of Rights, not to be invaded by any government; and would reduce government to an association limited in its operations to the defence of those rights which the individual is unable, alone, to maintain.

From the preceding chapter it will be seen that Part Second of "Rights of Man" was begun by Paine in the spring of 1791. At the close of that year, or early in 1792, he took up his abode with his friend Thomas "Clio" Rickman, at No. 7 Upper Marylebone Street. Rickman was a radical publisher; the house remains still a book-binding establishment, and seems little changed since Paine therein revised the proofs of Part Second on a table which Rickman marked with a plate, and which is now in possession of Mr. Edward Truelove. As the plate states, Paine wrote on the same table other works which appeared in England in 1792.

In 1795 D. I. Eaton published an edition of "Rights of Man," with a preface purporting to have been written by Paine while in Luxembourg prison. It is manifestly spurious. The genuine English and French prefaces are given.

RIGHTS OF MAN
Being An Answer To Mr. Burke's Attack On The French Revoloution

By Thomas Paine

Secretary For Foreign Affairs To Congress In The American War, And Author Of The Works Entitled "Common Sense" And "A Letter To Abbi Raynal"

DEDICATION

George Washington

President Of The United States Of America

Sir,

I present you a small treatise in defence of those principles of freedom which your exemplary virtue hath so eminently contributed to establish. That the Rights of Man may become as universal as your benevolence can wish, and that you may enjoy the happiness of seeing the New World regenerate the Old, is the prayer of

Sir,

Your much obliged, and

Obedient humble Servant,

Thomas Paine

PAINE'S PREFACE TO THE ENGLISH EDITION

From the part Mr. Burke took in the American Revolution, it was natural that I should consider him a friend to mankind; and as our acquaintance commenced on that ground, it would have been more agreeable to me to have had cause to continue in that opinion than to change it.

At the time Mr. Burke made his violent speech last winter in the English Parliament against the French Revolution and the National Assembly, I was in Paris, and had written to him but a short time before to inform him how prosperously matters were going on. Soon after this I saw his advertisement of the Pamphlet he intended to publish: As the attack was to be made in a language but little studied, and less understood in France, and as everything suffers by translation, I promised some of the friends of the Revolution in that country that whenever Mr. Burke's Pamphlet came forth, I would answer it. This appeared to me the more necessary to be done, when I saw the flagrant misrepresentations which Mr. Burke's Pamphlet contains; and that while it is an outrageous abuse on the French Revolution, and the principles of Liberty, it is an imposition on the rest of the world.

I am the more astonished and disappointed at this conduct in Mr. Burke, as (from the circumstances I am going to mention) I had formed other expectations.

I had seen enough of the miseries of war, to wish it might never more have existence in the world, and that some other mode might be found out to settle the differences that should occasionally arise in the neighbourhood of nations. This certainly might be done if Courts were disposed to set honesty about it, or if countries were enlightened enough not to be made the dupes of Courts. The people of America had been bred up in the same prejudices against France, which at that time characterised the people of England; but experience and an acquaintance with the French Nation have most effectually shown to the Americans the falsehood of those prejudices; and I do not believe that a more cordial and confidential intercourse exists between any two countries than between America and France.

When I came to France, in the spring of 1787, the Archbishop of Thoulouse was then Minister, and at that time highly esteemed. I became much acquainted with the private Secretary of that Minister, a man of an enlarged benevolent heart; and found that his sentiments and my own perfectly agreed with respect to the madness of war, and the wretched impolicy of two nations, like England and France, continually worrying each other, to no other end than that of a mutual increase of burdens and taxes. That I might be assured I had not misunderstood him, nor he me, I put the substance of our opinions into writing and sent it to him; subjoining a request, that if I should see among the people of England, any disposition to cultivate a better understanding between the two nations than had hitherto prevailed, how far I might be authorised to say that the same disposition prevailed on the part of France? He answered me by letter in the most unreserved manner, and that not for himself only, but for the Minister, with whose knowledge the letter was declared to be written.

I put this letter into the hands of Mr. Burke almost three years ago, and left it with him, where it still remains; hoping, and at the same time naturally expecting, from the opinion I had conceived of him, that he would find some opportunity of making good use of it, for the purpose of removing those errors and prejudices which two neighbouring nations, from the want of knowing each other, had entertained, to the injury of both.

When the French Revolution broke out, it certainly afforded to Mr. Burke an opportunity of doing some good, had he been disposed to it; instead of which, no sooner did he see the old prejudices wearing away, than he immediately began sowing the seeds of a new inveteracy, as if he were afraid that England and France would cease to be enemies. That there are men in all countries who get their living by war, and by keeping up the quarrels of Nations, is as shocking as it is true; but when those who are concerned in the government of a country, make it their study to sow discord and cultivate prejudices between Nations, it becomes the more unpardonable.

With respect to a paragraph in this work alluding to Mr. Burke's having a pension, the report has been some time in circulation, at least two months; and as a person is often the last to hear what concerns him the most to know, I have mentioned it, that Mr. Burke may have an opportunity of contradicting the rumour, if he thinks proper.

Thomas Paine

PAINE'S PREFACE TO THE FRENCH EDITION

The astonishment which the French Revolution has caused throughout Europe should be considered from two different points of view: first as it affects foreign peoples, secondly as it affects their governments.

The cause of the French people is that of all Europe, or rather of the whole world; but the governments of all those countries are by no means favorable to it. It is important that we should never lose sight of this distinction. We must not confuse the peoples with their governments; especially not the English people with its government.

The government of England is no friend of the revolution of France. Of this we have sufficient proofs in the thanks given by that weak and witless person, the Elector of Hanover, sometimes called the King of England, to Mr. Burke for the insults heaped on it in his book, and in the malevolent comments of the English Minister, Pitt, in his speeches in Parliament.

In spite of the professions of sincerest friendship found in the official correspondence of the English government with that of France, its conduct gives the lie to all its declarations, and shows us clearly that it is not a court to be trusted, but an insane court, plunging in all the quarrels and intrigues of Europe, in quest of a war to satisfy its folly and countenance its extravagance.

The English nation, on the contrary, is very favorably disposed towards the French Revolution, and to the progress of liberty in the whole world; and this feeling will become more general in England as the intrigues and artifices of its government are better known, and the principles of the revolution better understood. The French should know that most English newspapers are directly in the pay of government, or, if indirectly connected with it, always under its orders; and that those papers constantly distort and attack the revolution in France in order to deceive the nation. But, as it is impossible long to prevent the prevalence of truth, the daily falsehoods of those papers no longer have the desired effect.

To be convinced that the voice of truth has been stifled in England, the world needs only to be told that the government regards and prosecutes as a libel that which it should protect.*[1] This outrage on morality is called law, and judges are found wicked enough to inflict penalties on truth.

The English government presents, just now, a curious phenomenon. Seeing that the French and English nations are getting rid of the prejudices and false notions formerly entertained against each other, and which have cost them so much money, that government seems to be placarding its need of a foe; for unless it finds one somewhere, no pretext exists for the enormous revenue and taxation now deemed necessary.

Therefore it seeks in Russia the enemy it has lost in France, and appears to say to the universe, or to say to itself. "If nobody will be so kind as to become my foe, I shall need no more fleets nor armies, and shall be forced to reduce my taxes. The American war enabled me to double the taxes; the Dutch business to add more; the Nootka humbug gave me a pretext for raising three millions sterling more; but unless I can make an enemy of Russia the harvest from wars will end. I was the first to incite Turk against Russian, and now I hope to reap a fresh crop of taxes."

If the miseries of war, and the flood of evils it spreads over a country, did not check all inclination to mirth, and turn laughter into grief, the frantic conduct of the government of England would only excite ridicule. But it is impossible to banish from one's mind the images of suffering which the contemplation of such vicious policy presents. To reason with governments, as they have existed for ages, is to argue with brutes. It is only from the nations themselves that reforms can be expected. There ought not now to exist any doubt that the peoples of France, England, and America, enlightened and enlightening each other, shall henceforth be able, not merely to give the world an example of good government, but by their united influence enforce its practice.

(Translated from the French)

RIGHTS OF MAN. PART THE FIRST BEING AN ANSWER TO MR. BURKE'S ATTACK ON THE FRENCH REVOLUTION

Among the incivilities by which nations or individuals provoke and irritate each other, Mr. Burke's pamphlet on the French Revolution is an extraordinary instance. Neither the People of France, nor the National Assembly, were troubling themselves about the affairs of England, or the English Parliament; and that Mr. Burke should commence an unprovoked attack upon them, both in Parliament and in public, is a conduct that cannot be pardoned on the score of manners, nor justified on that of policy.

There is scarcely an epithet of abuse to be found in the English language, with which Mr. Burke has not loaded the French Nation and the National Assembly. Everything which rancour, prejudice, ignorance or knowledge could suggest, is poured forth in the copious fury of near four hundred pages. In the strain and on the plan Mr. Burke was writing, he might have written on to as many thousands. When the tongue or the pen is let loose in a frenzy of passion, it is the man, and not the subject, that becomes exhausted.

Hitherto Mr. Burke has been mistaken and disappointed in the opinions he had formed of the affairs of France; but such is the ingenuity of his hope, or the malignancy of his despair, that it furnishes him with new pretences to go on. There was a time when it was impossible to make Mr. Burke believe there would be any Revolution in France. His opinion then was, that the French had neither spirit to undertake it nor fortitude to support it; and now that there is one, he seeks an escape by condemning it.

Not sufficiently content with abusing the National Assembly, a great part of his work is taken up with abusing Dr. Price (one of the best-hearted men that lives) and the two societies in England known by the name of the Revolution Society and the Society for Constitutional Information.

Dr. Price had preached a sermon on the 4th of November, 1789, being the anniversary of what is called in England the Revolution, which took place 1688. Mr. Burke, speaking of this sermon, says: "The political Divine proceeds dogmatically to assert, that by the principles of the Revolution, the people of England have acquired three fundamental rights:

1. To choose our own governors.
2. To cashier them for misconduct.
3. To frame a government for ourselves."

Dr. Price does not say that the right to do these things exists in this or in that person, or in this or in that description of persons, but that it exists in the whole; that it is a right resident in the nation. Mr. Burke, on the contrary, denies that such a right exists in the nation, either in whole or in part, or that it exists anywhere; and, what is still more strange and marvellous, he says: "that the people of England utterly disclaim such a right, and that they will resist the practical assertion of it with their lives and fortunes." That men should take up arms and spend their lives and fortunes, not to maintain their rights, but to maintain they have not rights, is an entirely new species of discovery, and suited to the paradoxical genius of Mr. Burke.

The method which Mr. Burke takes to prove that the people of England have no such rights, and that such rights do not now exist in the nation, either in whole or in part, or anywhere at all, is of the same marvellous and monstrous kind with what he has already said; for his arguments are that the persons, or the generation of persons, in whom they did exist, are dead, and with them the right is dead also. To prove this, he quotes a declaration made by Parliament about a hundred years ago, to William and Mary, in these words: "The Lords Spiritual and Temporal, and Commons, do, in the name of the people aforesaid" (meaning the people of England then living) "most humbly and faithfully submit themselves, their heirs and posterities, for Ever." He quotes a clause of another Act of Parliament made in the same reign, the terms of which he says, "bind us" (meaning the people of their day), "our heirs and our posterity, to them, their heirs and posterity, to the end of time."

Mr. Burke conceives his point sufficiently established by producing those clauses, which he enforces by saying that they exclude the right of the nation for ever. And not yet content with making such declarations, repeated over and over again, he farther says, "that if the people of England possessed such a right before the Revolution" (which he acknowledges to have been the case, not only in England, but throughout Europe, at an early period), "yet that the English Nation did, at the time of the Revolution, most solemnly renounce and abdicate it, for themselves, and for all their posterity, for ever."

As Mr. Burke occasionally applies the poison drawn from his horrid principles, not only to the English nation, but to the French Revolution and the National Assembly, and charges that august, illuminated and illuminating body of men with the epithet of usurpers, I shall, sans ceremonie, place another system of principles in opposition to his.

The English Parliament of 1688 did a certain thing, which, for themselves and their constituents, they had a right to do, and which it appeared right should be done. But, in addition to this right, which they possessed by delegation, they set up another right by assumption, that of binding and controlling posterity to the end of time. The case, therefore, divides itself into two parts; the right which they possessed by delegation, and the right which they set up by assumption. The first is admitted; but with respect to the second, I reply: There never did, there never will, and there never can, exist a Parliament, or any description of men, or any generation of men, in any country, possessed of the right or the power of binding and controlling posterity to the "end of time," or of commanding for ever how the world shall be governed, or who shall govern it; and therefore all such clauses, acts or declarations by which the makers of them attempt to do what they have neither the right nor the power to do, nor the power to execute, are in themselves null and void. Every age and generation must be as free to act for itself in all cases as the age and generations which preceded it. The vanity and presumption of governing beyond the grave is the most ridiculous and insolent of all tyrannies. Man has no property in man; neither has any generation a property in the generations which are to follow. The Parliament or the people of 1688, or of any other period, had no more right to dispose of the people of the present day, or to bind or to control them in any shape whatever, than the parliament or the people of the present day have to dispose of, bind or control those who are to live a hundred or a thousand years hence. Every generation is, and must be, competent to all the purposes which its occasions require. It is the living, and not the dead, that are to be accommodated. When man ceases to be, his power and his wants cease with him; and having no longer any participation in the concerns of this world, he has no longer any authority in directing who shall be its governors, or how its government shall be organised, or how administered.

I am not contending for nor against any form of government, nor for nor against any party, here or elsewhere. That which a whole nation chooses to do it has a right to do. Mr. Burke says, No. Where, then, does the right exist? I am contending for the rights of the living, and against their being willed away and controlled and contracted for by the manuscript assumed authority of the dead, and Mr. Burke is contending for the authority of the dead over the rights and freedom of the living. There was a time when kings disposed of their crowns by will upon their death-beds, and consigned the people, like beasts of the field, to whatever successor they appointed. This is now so exploded as scarcely to be remembered, and so monstrous as hardly to be believed. But the Parliamentary clauses upon which Mr. Burke builds his political church are of the same nature.

The laws of every country must be analogous to some common principle. In England no parent or master, nor all the authority of Parliament, omnipotent as it has called itself, can bind or control the personal freedom even of an individual beyond the age of twenty-one years. On what ground of right, then, could the Parliament of 1688, or any other Parliament, bind all posterity for ever?

Those who have quitted the world, and those who have not yet arrived at it, are as remote from each other as the utmost stretch of mortal imagination can conceive. What possible obligation, then, can exist between them—what rule or principle can be laid down that of two nonentities, the one out of existence and the other not in, and who never can meet in this world, the one should control the other to the end of time?

In England it is said that money cannot be taken out of the pockets of the people without their consent. But who authorised, or who could authorise, the Parliament of 1688 to control and take away the freedom of posterity (who were not in existence to give or to withhold their consent) and limit and confine their right of acting in certain cases for ever?

A greater absurdity cannot present itself to the understanding of man than what Mr. Burke offers to his readers. He tells them, and he tells the world to come, that a certain body of men who existed a hundred years ago made a law, and that there does not exist in the nation, nor ever will, nor ever can, a power to alter it. Under how many subtilties or absurdities has the divine right to govern been imposed on the credulity of mankind? Mr. Burke has discovered a new one, and he has shortened his journey to Rome by appealing to the power of this infallible Parliament of former days, and he produces what it has done as of divine authority, for that power must certainly be more than human which no human power to the end of time can alter.

But Mr. Burke has done some service—not to his cause, but to his country—by bringing those clauses into public view. They serve to demonstrate how necessary it is at all times to watch against the attempted encroachment of power, and to prevent its running to excess. It is somewhat extraordinary that the offence for which James II. was expelled, that of setting up power by assumption, should be re-acted, under another shape and form, by the Parliament that expelled him. It shows that the Rights of Man were but imperfectly understood at the Revolution, for certain it is that the right which that Parliament set up by assumption (for by the delegation it had not, and could not have it, because none could give it) over the persons and freedom of posterity for ever was of the same tyrannical unfounded kind which James attempted to set up over the Parliament and the nation, and for which he was expelled. The only difference is (for in principle they differ not) that the one was an usurper over living, and the other over the unborn; and as the one has no better authority to stand upon than the other, both of them must be equally null and void, and of no effect.

From what, or from whence, does Mr. Burke prove the right of any human power to bind posterity for ever? He has produced his clauses, but he must produce also his proofs that such a right existed, and show how it existed. If it ever existed it must now exist, for whatever appertains to the nature of man cannot be annihilated by man. It is the nature of man to die, and he will continue to die as long as he continues to be born. But Mr. Burke has set up a sort of political Adam, in whom all posterity are bound for ever. He must, therefore, prove that his Adam possessed such a power, or such a right.

The weaker any cord is, the less will it bear to be stretched, and the worse is the policy to stretch it, unless it is intended to break it. Had anyone proposed the overthrow of Mr. Burke's positions, he would have proceeded as Mr. Burke has done. He would have magnified the authorities, on purpose to have called the right of them into question; and the instant the question of right was started, the authorities must have been given up.

It requires but a very small glance of thought to perceive that although laws made in one generation often continue in force through succeeding generations, yet they continue to derive their force from the consent of the living. A law not repealed continues in force, not because it cannot be repealed, but because it is not repealed; and the non-repealing passes for consent.

But Mr. Burke's clauses have not even this qualification in their favour. They become null, by attempting to become immortal. The nature of them precludes consent. They destroy the right which they might have, by grounding it on a right which they cannot have. Immortal power is not a human right, and therefore cannot be a right of Parliament. The Parliament of 1688 might as well have passed an act to have authorised themselves to live for ever, as to make their authority live for ever. All, therefore, that can be said of those clauses is that they are a formality of words, of as much import as if those who used them had addressed a congratulation to themselves, and in the oriental style of antiquity had said: O Parliament, live for ever!

The circumstances of the world are continually changing, and the opinions of men change also; and as government is for the living, and not for the dead, it is the living only that has any right in it. That which may be thought right and found convenient in one age may be thought wrong and found inconvenient in another. In such cases, who is to decide, the living or the dead?

As almost one hundred pages of Mr. Burke's book are employed upon these clauses, it will consequently follow that if the clauses themselves, so far as they set up an assumed usurped dominion over posterity for ever, are unauthoritative, and in their nature null and void; that all his voluminous inferences, and declamation drawn therefrom, or founded thereon, are null and void also; and on this ground I rest the matter.

We now come more particularly to the affairs of France. Mr. Burke's book has the appearance of being written as instruction to the French nation; but if I may permit myself the use of an extravagant metaphor, suited to the extravagance of the case, it is darkness attempting to illuminate light.

While I am writing this there are accidentally before me some proposals for a declaration of rights by the Marquis de la Fayette (I ask his pardon for using his former address, and do it only for distinction's sake) to the National Assembly, on the 11th of July, 1789, three days before the taking of the Bastille, and I cannot but remark with astonishment how opposite the sources are from which that gentleman and Mr. Burke draw their principles. Instead of referring to musty records and mouldy parchments to prove that the rights of the living are lost, "renounced and abdicated for ever," by those who are now no more, as Mr. Burke has done, M. de la Fayette applies to the living world, and emphatically says: "Call to mind the sentiments which nature has engraved on the heart of every citizen, and which take a new force when they are solemnly recognised by all:—For a nation to love liberty, it is sufficient that she knows it; and to be free, it is sufficient that she wills it." How dry, barren, and obscure is the source from which Mr. Burke labors! and how ineffectual, though gay with flowers, are all his declamation and his arguments compared with these clear, concise, and soul-animating sentiments! Few and short as they are, they lead on to a vast field of generous and manly thinking, and do not finish, like Mr. Burke's periods, with music in the ear, and nothing in the heart.

As I have introduced M. de la Fayette, I will take the liberty of adding an anecdote respecting his farewell address to the Congress of America in 1783, and which occurred fresh to my mind, when I saw Mr. Burke's thundering attack on the French Revolution. M. de la Fayette went to America at the early period of the war, and continued a volunteer in her service to the end. His conduct through the whole of that enterprise is one of the most extraordinary that is to be found in the history of a young man, scarcely twenty years of age. Situated in a country that was like the lap of sensual pleasure, and with the means of enjoying it, how few are there to be found who would exchange such a scene for the woods and wildernesses of America, and pass the flowery years of youth in unprofitable danger and hardship! but such is the fact. When the war ended, and he was on the point of taking his final departure, he presented himself to Congress, and contemplating in his affectionate farewell the Revolution he had seen, expressed himself in these words: "May this great monument raised to liberty serve as a lesson to the oppressor, and an example to the oppressed!" When this address came to the hands of Dr. Franklin, who was then in France, he applied to Count Vergennes to have it inserted in the French Gazette, but never could obtain his consent. The fact was that Count Vergennes was an aristocratical despot at home, and dreaded the example of the American Revolution in France, as certain other persons now dread the example of the French Revolution in England, and Mr. Burke's tribute of fear (for in this light his book must be considered) runs parallel with Count Vergennes' refusal. But to return more particularly to his work.

"We have seen," says Mr. Burke, "the French rebel against a mild and lawful monarch, with more fury, outrage, and insult, than any people has been known to rise against the most illegal usurper, or the most sanguinary tyrant." This is one among a thousand other instances, in which Mr. Burke shows that he is ignorant of the springs and principles of the French Revolution.

It was not against Louis XVI. but against the despotic principles of the Government, that the nation revolted. These principles had not their origin in him, but in the original establishment, many centuries back: and they were become too deeply rooted to be removed, and the Augean stables of parasites and plunderers too abominably filthy to be cleansed by anything short of a complete and universal Revolution. When it becomes necessary to do anything, the whole heart and soul should go into the measure, or not attempt it. That crisis was then arrived, and there remained no choice but to act with determined vigor, or not to act at all. The king was known to be the friend of the nation, and this circumstance was favorable to the enterprise. Perhaps no man bred up in the style of an absolute king, ever possessed a heart so little disposed to the exercise of that species of power as the present King of France. But the principles of the Government itself still remained the same. The Monarch and the Monarchy were distinct and separate things; and it was against the established despotism of the latter, and not against the person or principles of the former, that the revolt commenced, and the Revolution has been carried.

Mr. Burke does not attend to the distinction between men and principles, and, therefore, he does not see that a revolt may take place against the despotism of the latter, while there lies no charge of despotism against the former.

The natural moderation of Louis XVI. contributed nothing to alter the hereditary despotism of the monarchy. All the tyrannies of former reigns, acted under that hereditary despotism, were still liable to be revived in the hands of a successor. It was not the respite of a reign that would satisfy France, enlightened as she was then become. A casual discontinuance of the practice of despotism, is not a discontinuance of its principles: the former depends on the virtue of the individual who is in immediate possession of the power; the latter, on the virtue and fortitude of the nation. In the case of Charles I. and James II. of England, the revolt was against the personal despotism of the men; whereas in France, it was against the hereditary despotism of the established Government. But men who can consign over the rights of posterity for ever on the authority of a mouldy parchment, like Mr. Burke, are not qualified to judge of this Revolution. It takes in a field too vast for their views to explore, and proceeds with a mightiness of reason they cannot keep pace with.

But there are many points of view in which this Revolution may be considered. When despotism has established itself for ages in a country, as in France, it is not in the person of the king only that it resides. It has the appearance of being so in show, and in nominal authority; but it is not so in practice and in fact. It has its standard everywhere. Every office and department has its despotism, founded upon custom and usage. Every place has its Bastille, and every Bastille its despot. The original hereditary despotism resident in the person of the king, divides and sub-divides itself into a thousand shapes and forms, till at last the whole of it is acted by deputation. This was the case in France; and against this species of despotism, proceeding on through an endless labyrinth of office till the source of it is scarcely perceptible, there is no mode of redress. It strengthens itself by assuming the appearance of duty, and tyrannizes under the pretence of obeying.

When a man reflects on the condition which France was in from the nature of her government, he will see other causes for revolt than those which immediately connect themselves with the person or character of Louis XVI. There were, if I may so express it, a thousand despotisms to be reformed in France, which had grown up under the hereditary despotism of the monarchy, and became so rooted as to be in a great measure independent of it. Between the Monarchy, the Parliament, and the Church there was a rivalship of despotism; besides the feudal despotism operating locally, and the ministerial despotism operating everywhere. But Mr. Burke, by considering the king as the only possible object of a revolt, speaks as if France was a village, in which everything that passed must be known to its commanding officer, and no oppression could be acted but what he could immediately control. Mr. Burke might have been in the Bastille his whole life, as well under Louis XVI. as Louis XIV., and neither the one nor the other have known that such a man as Burke existed. The despotic principles of the government were the same in both reigns, though the dispositions of the men were as remote as tyranny and benevolence.

What Mr. Burke considers as a reproach to the French Revolution (that of bringing it forward under a reign more mild than the preceding ones) is one of its highest honors. The Revolutions that have taken place in other European countries, have been excited by personal hatred. The rage was against the man, and he became the victim. But, in the instance of France we see a

Revolution generated in the rational contemplation of the Rights of Man, and distinguishing from the beginning between persons and principles.

But Mr. Burke appears to have no idea of principles when he is contemplating Governments. "Ten years ago," says he, "I could have felicitated France on her having a Government, without inquiring what the nature of that Government was, or how it was administered." Is this the language of a rational man? Is it the language of a heart feeling as it ought to feel for the rights and happiness of the human race? On this ground, Mr. Burke must compliment all the Governments in the world, while the victims who suffer under them, whether sold into slavery, or tortured out of existence, are wholly forgotten. It is power, and not principles, that Mr. Burke venerates; and under this abominable depravity he is disqualified to judge between them. Thus much for his opinion as to the occasions of the French Revolution. I now proceed to other considerations.

I know a place in America called Point-no-Point, because as you proceed along the shore, gay and flowery as Mr. Burke's language, it continually recedes and presents itself at a distance before you; but when you have got as far as you can go, there is no point at all. Just thus it is with Mr. Burke's three hundred and sixty-six pages. It is therefore difficult to reply to him. But as the points he wishes to establish may be inferred from what he abuses, it is in his paradoxes that we must look for his arguments.

As to the tragic paintings by which Mr. Burke has outraged his own imagination, and seeks to work upon that of his readers, they are very well calculated for theatrical representation, where facts are manufactured for the sake of show, and accommodated to produce, through the weakness of sympathy, a weeping effect. But Mr. Burke should recollect that he is writing history, and not plays, and that his readers will expect truth, and not the spouting rant of high-toned exclamation.

When we see a man dramatically lamenting in a publication intended to be believed that "The age of chivalry is gone! that The glory of Europe is extinguished for ever! that The unbought grace of life (if anyone knows what it is), the cheap defence of nations, the nurse of manly sentiment and heroic enterprise is gone!" and all this because the Quixot age of chivalry nonsense is gone, what opinion can we form of his judgment, or what regard can we pay to his facts? In the rhapsody of his imagination he has discovered a world of wind mills, and his sorrows are that there are no Quixots to attack them. But if the age of aristocracy, like that of chivalry, should fall (and they had originally some connection) Mr. Burke, the trumpeter of the Order, may continue his parody to the end, and finish with exclaiming: "Othello's occupation's gone!"

Notwithstanding Mr. Burke's horrid paintings, when the French Revolution is compared with the Revolutions of other countries, the astonishment will be that it is marked with so few sacrifices; but this astonishment will cease when we reflect that principles, and not persons, were the meditated objects of destruction. The mind of the nation was acted upon by a higher stimulus than what the consideration of persons could inspire, and sought a higher conquest than could be produced by the downfall of an enemy. Among the few who fell there do not appear to be any that were intentionally singled out. They all of them had their fate in the circumstances of the moment, and were not pursued with that long, cold-blooded unabated revenge which pursued the unfortunate Scotch in the affair of 1745.

Through the whole of Mr. Burke's book I do not observe that the Bastille is mentioned more than once, and that with a kind of implication as if he were sorry it was pulled down, and wished it were built up again. "We have rebuilt Newgate," says he, "and tenanted the mansion; and we have prisons almost as strong as the Bastille for those who dare to libel the queens of France."*[2] As to what a madman like the person called Lord George Gordon might say, and to whom Newgate is rather a bedlam than a prison, it is unworthy a rational consideration. It was a madman that libelled, and that is sufficient apology; and it afforded an opportunity for confining him, which was the thing that was wished for. But certain it is that Mr. Burke, who does not call himself a madman (whatever other people may do), has libelled in the most unprovoked manner, and in the grossest style of the most vulgar abuse, the whole representative authority of France, and yet Mr. Burke takes his seat in the British House of Commons! From his violence and his grief, his silence on some points and his excess on others, it is difficult not to believe that Mr. Burke is sorry, extremely sorry, that arbitrary power, the power of the Pope and the Bastille, are pulled down.

Not one glance of compassion, not one commiserating reflection that I can find throughout his book, has he bestowed on those who lingered out the most wretched of lives, a life without hope in the most miserable of prisons. It is painful to behold a man employing his talents to corrupt himself. Nature has been kinder to Mr. Burke than he is to her. He is not affected by the reality of distress touching his heart, but by the showy resemblance of it striking his imagination. He pities the plumage, but forgets the dying bird. Accustomed to kiss the aristocratical hand that hath purloined him from himself, he degenerates into a composition of art, and the genuine soul of nature forsakes him. His hero or his heroine must be a tragedy-victim expiring in show, and not the real prisoner of misery, sliding into death in the silence of a dungeon.

As Mr. Burke has passed over the whole transaction of the Bastille (and his silence is nothing in his favour), and has entertained his readers with refections on supposed facts distorted into real falsehoods, I will give, since he has not, some account of the circumstances which preceded that transaction. They will serve to show that less mischief could scarcely have accompanied such an event when considered with the treacherous and hostile aggravations of the enemies of the Revolution.

The mind can hardly picture to itself a more tremendous scene than what the city of Paris exhibited at the time of taking the Bastille, and for two days before and after, nor perceive the possibility of its quieting so soon. At a distance this transaction has appeared only as an act of heroism standing on itself, and the close political connection it had with the Revolution is lost in the brilliancy of the achievement. But we are to consider it as the strength of the parties brought man to man, and contending for the issue. The Bastille was to be either the prize or the prison of the assailants. The downfall of it included the idea of the downfall of despotism, and this compounded image was become as figuratively united as Bunyan's Doubting Castle and Giant Despair.

The National Assembly, before and at the time of taking the Bastille, was sitting at Versailles, twelve miles distant from Paris. About a week before the rising of the Partisans, and their taking the Bastille, it was discovered that a plot was forming, at the head of which was the Count D'Artois, the king's youngest brother, for demolishing the National Assembly, seizing its members, and thereby crushing, by a coup de main, all hopes and prospects of forming a free government. For the sake of humanity, as well as freedom, it is well this plan did not succeed. Examples are not wanting to show how dreadfully vindictive and cruel are all old governments, when they are successful against what they call a revolt.

This plan must have been some time in contemplation; because, in order to carry it into execution, it was necessary to collect a large military force round Paris, and cut off the communication between that city and the National Assembly at Versailles. The troops destined for this service were chiefly the foreign troops in the pay of France, and who, for this particular purpose, were drawn from the distant provinces where they were then stationed. When they were collected to the amount of between twenty-five and thirty thousand, it was judged time to put the plan into execution. The ministry who were then in office, and who were friendly to the Revolution, were instantly dismissed and a new ministry formed of those who had concerted the project, among whom was Count de Broglio, and to his share was given the command of those troops. The character of this man as described to me in a letter which I communicated to Mr. Burke before he began to write his book, and from an authority which Mr. Burke well knows was good, was that of "a high-flying aristocrat, cool, and capable of every mischief."

While these matters were agitating, the National Assembly stood in the most perilous and critical situation that a body of men can be supposed to act in. They were the devoted victims, and they knew it. They had the hearts and wishes of their country on their side, but military authority they had none. The guards of Broglio surrounded the hall where the Assembly sat, ready, at the word of command, to seize their persons, as had been done the year before to the Parliament of Paris. Had the National Assembly deserted their trust, or had they exhibited signs of weakness or fear, their enemies had been encouraged and their country depressed. When the situation they stood in, the cause they were engaged in, and the crisis then ready to burst, which should determine their personal and political fate and that of their country, and probably of Europe, are taken into one view, none but a heart callous with prejudice or corrupted by dependence can avoid interesting itself in their success.

The Archbishop of Vienne was at this time President of the National Assembly—a person too old to undergo the scene that a few days or a few hours might bring forth. A man of more activity and bolder fortitude was necessary, and the National Assembly chose (under the form of a Vice-President, for the Presidency still resided in the Archbishop) M. de la Fayette; and this is the only instance of a Vice-President being chosen. It was at the moment that this storm was pending (July 11th) that a declaration of rights was brought forward by M. de la Fayette, and is the same which is alluded to earlier. It was hastily drawn up, and makes only a part of the more extensive declaration of rights agreed upon and adopted afterwards by the National Assembly. The particular reason for bringing it forward at this moment (M. de la Fayette has since informed me) was that, if the National Assembly should fall in the threatened destruction that then surrounded it, some trace of its principles might have the chance of surviving the wreck.

Everything now was drawing to a crisis. The event was freedom or slavery. On one side, an army of nearly thirty thousand men; on the other, an unarmed body of citizens—for the citizens of Paris, on whom the National Assembly must then immediately depend, were as unarmed and as undisciplined as the citizens of London are now. The French guards had given strong symptoms of their being attached to the national cause; but their numbers were small, not a tenth part of the force that Broglio commanded, and their officers were in the interest of Broglio.

Matters being now ripe for execution, the new ministry made their appearance in office. The reader will carry in his mind that the Bastille was taken the 14th July; the point of time I am now speaking of is the 12th. Immediately on the news of the change of ministry reaching Paris, in the afternoon, all the playhouses and places of entertainment, shops and houses, were shut up. The change of ministry was considered as the prelude of hostilities, and the opinion was rightly founded.

The foreign troops began to advance towards the city. The Prince de Lambesc, who commanded a body of German cavalry, approached by the Place of Louis Xv., which connects itself with some of the streets. In his march, he insulted and struck an old man with a sword. The French are remarkable for their respect to old age; and the insolence with which it appeared to be done, uniting with the general fermentation they were in, produced a powerful effect, and a cry of "To arms! to arms!" spread itself in a moment over the city.

Arms they had none, nor scarcely anyone who knew the use of them; but desperate resolution, when every hope is at stake, supplies, for a while, the want of arms. Near where the Prince de Lambesc was drawn up, were large piles of stones collected for building the new bridge, and with these the people attacked the cavalry. A party of French guards upon hearing the firing, rushed from their quarters and joined the people; and night coming on, the cavalry retreated.

The streets of Paris, being narrow, are favourable for defence, and the loftiness of the houses, consisting of many stories, from which great annoyance might be given, secured them against nocturnal enterprises; and the night was spent in providing themselves with every sort of weapon they could make or procure: guns, swords, blacksmiths' hammers, carpenters' axes, iron crows, pikes, halberts, pitchforks, spits, clubs, etc., etc. The incredible numbers in which they assembled the next morning, and the still more incredible resolution they exhibited, embarrassed and astonished their enemies. Little did the new ministry expect such a salute. Accustomed to slavery themselves, they had no idea that liberty was capable of such inspiration, or that a body of unarmed citizens would dare to face the military force of thirty thousand men. Every moment of this day was employed in collecting arms, concerting plans, and arranging themselves into the best order which such an instantaneous movement could afford. Broglio continued lying round the city, but made no further advances this day, and the succeeding night passed with as much tranquility as such a scene could possibly produce.

But defence only was not the object of the citizens. They had a cause at stake, on which depended their freedom or their slavery. They every moment expected an attack, or to hear of one made on the National Assembly; and in such a situation, the most prompt measures are sometimes the best. The object that now presented itself was the Bastille; and the eclat of carrying such a fortress in the face of such an army, could not fail to strike terror into the new ministry, who had scarcely yet had time to meet. By some intercepted correspondence this morning, it was discovered that the Mayor of Paris, M. Defflesselles, who appeared to be in the interest of the citizens, was betraying them; and from this discovery, there remained no doubt that Broglio would reinforce the Bastille the ensuing evening. It was therefore necessary to attack it that day; but before this could be done, it was first necessary to procure a better supply of arms than they were then possessed of.

There was, adjoining to the city a large magazine of arms deposited at the Hospital of the Invalids, which the citizens summoned to surrender; and as the place was neither defensible, nor attempted much defence, they soon succeeded. Thus supplied, they marched to attack the Bastille; a vast mixed multitude of all ages, and of all degrees, armed with all sorts of weapons. Imagination would fail in describing to itself the appearance of such a procession, and of the anxiety of the events which a few hours or a few minutes might produce. What plans the ministry were forming, were as unknown to the people within the city, as what the citizens were doing was unknown to the ministry; and what movements Broglio might make for the support or relief of the place, were to the citizens equally as unknown. All was mystery and hazard.

That the Bastille was attacked with an enthusiasm of heroism, such only as the highest animation of liberty could inspire, and carried in the space of a few hours, is an event which the world is fully possessed of. I am not undertaking the detail of the attack, but bringing into view the conspiracy against the nation which provoked it, and which fell with the Bastille. The prison to which the new ministry were dooming the National Assembly, in addition to its being the high altar and castle of despotism, became the proper object to begin with. This enterprise broke up the new ministry, who began now to fly from the ruin they had prepared for others. The troops of Broglio dispersed, and himself fled also.

Mr. Burke has spoken a great deal about plots, but he has never once spoken of this plot against the National Assembly, and the liberties of the nation; and that he might not, he has passed over all the circumstances that might throw it in his way. The exiles who have fled from France, whose case he so much interests himself in, and from whom he has had his lesson, fled in consequence of the miscarriage of this plot. No plot was formed against them; they were plotting against others; and those who fell, met, not unjustly, the punishment they were preparing to execute. But will Mr. Burke say that if this plot, contrived with the subtilty of an ambuscade, had succeeded, the successful party would have restrained their wrath so soon? Let the history of all governments answer the question.

Whom has the National Assembly brought to the scaffold? None. They were themselves the devoted victims of this plot, and they have not retaliated; why, then, are they charged with revenge they have not acted? In the tremendous breaking forth of a whole people, in which all degrees, tempers and characters are confounded, delivering themselves, by a miracle of exertion, from the destruction meditated against them, is it to be expected that nothing will happen? When men are sore with the sense of oppressions, and menaced with the prospects of new ones, is the calmness of philosophy or the palsy of insensibility to be looked for? Mr. Burke exclaims against outrage; yet the greatest is that which himself has committed. His book is a volume of outrage, not apologised for by the impulse of a moment, but cherished through a space of ten months; yet Mr. Burke had no provocation— no life, no interest, at stake.

More of the citizens fell in this struggle than of their opponents: but four or five persons were seized by the populace, and instantly put to death; the Governor of the Bastille, and the Mayor of Paris, who was detected in the act of betraying them; and afterwards Foulon, one of the new ministry, and Berthier, his son-in-law, who had accepted the office of intendant of Paris. Their heads were stuck upon spikes, and carried about the city; and it is upon this mode of punishment that Mr. Burke builds a great part of his tragic scene. Let us therefore examine how men came by the idea of punishing in this manner.

They learn it from the governments they live under; and retaliate the punishments they have been accustomed to behold. The heads stuck upon spikes, which remained for years upon Temple Bar, differed nothing in the horror of the scene from those carried about upon spikes at Paris; yet this was done by the English Government. It may perhaps be said that it signifies nothing to a man what is done to him after he is dead; but it signifies much to the living; it either tortures their feelings or hardens their hearts, and in either case it instructs them how to punish when power falls into their hands.

Lay then the axe to the root, and teach governments humanity. It is their sanguinary punishments which corrupt mankind. In England the punishment in certain cases is by hanging, drawing and quartering; the heart of the sufferer is cut out and held up to the view of the populace. In France, under the former Government, the punishments were not less barbarous. Who does not remember the execution of Damien, torn to pieces by horses? The effect of those cruel spectacles exhibited to the populace is to destroy tenderness or excite revenge; and by the base and false idea of governing men by terror, instead of reason, they become precedents. It is over the lowest class of mankind that government by terror is intended to operate, and it is on them that it operates to the worst effect. They have sense enough to feel they are the objects aimed at; and they inflict in their turn the examples of terror they have been instructed to practise.

There is in all European countries a large class of people of that description, which in England is called the "mob." Of this class were those who committed the burnings and devastations in London in 1780, and of this class were those who carried the heads on iron spikes in Paris. Foulon and Berthier were taken up in the country, and sent to Paris, to undergo their examination at the Hotel de Ville; for the National Assembly, immediately on the new ministry coming into office, passed a decree, which they communicated to the King and Cabinet, that they (the National Assembly) would hold the ministry, of which Foulon was one, responsible for the measures they were advising and pursuing; but the mob, incensed at the appearance of Foulon and Berthier, tore them from their conductors before they were carried to the Hotel de Ville, and executed them on the spot. Why then does Mr. Burke charge outrages of this kind on a whole people? As well may he charge the riots and outrages of 1780 on all the people of London, or those in Ireland on all his countrymen.

But everything we see or hear offensive to our feelings and derogatory to the human character should lead to other reflections than those of reproach. Even the beings who commit them have some claim to our consideration. How then is it that such vast classes of mankind as are distinguished by the appellation of the vulgar, or the ignorant mob, are so numerous in all old countries? The instant we ask ourselves this question, reflection feels an answer. They rise, as an unavoidable consequence, out of the ill construction of all old governments in Europe, England included with the rest. It is by distortedly exalting some men, that others are distortedly debased, till the whole is out of nature. A vast mass of mankind are degradedly thrown into the background of the human picture, to bring forward, with greater glare, the puppet-show of state and aristocracy. In the commencement of a revolution, those men are rather the followers of the camp than of the standard of liberty, and have yet to be instructed how to reverence it.

I give to Mr. Burke all his theatrical exaggerations for facts, and I then ask him if they do not establish the certainty of what I here lay down? Admitting them to be true, they show the necessity of the French Revolution, as much as any one thing he could have asserted. These outrages were not the effect of the principles of the Revolution, but of the degraded mind that existed before the Revolution, and which the Revolution is calculated to reform. Place them then to their proper cause, and take the reproach of them to your own side.

It is the honour of the National Assembly and the city of Paris that, during such a tremendous scene of arms and confusion, beyond the control of all authority, they have been able, by the influence of example and exhortation, to restrain so much. Never were more pains taken to instruct and enlighten mankind, and to make them see that their interest consisted in their virtue, and not in their revenge, than have been displayed in the Revolution of France. I now proceed to make some remarks on Mr. Burke's account of the expedition to Versailles, October the 5th and 6th. I can consider Mr. Burke's book in scarcely any other light than a dramatic performance; and he must, I think, have considered it in the same light himself, by the poetical liberties he has taken of omitting some facts, distorting others, and making the whole machinery bend to produce a stage effect. Of this kind is his account of the expedition to Versailles. He begins this account by omitting the only facts which as causes are known to be true; everything beyond these is conjecture, even in Paris; and he then works up a tale accommodated to his own passions and prejudices.

It is to be observed throughout Mr. Burke's book that he never speaks of plots against the Revolution; and it is from those plots that all the mischiefs have arisen. It suits his purpose to exhibit the consequences without their causes. It is one of the arts of the drama to do so. If the crimes of men were exhibited with their sufferings, stage effect would sometimes be lost, and the audience would be inclined to approve where it was intended they should commiserate.

After all the investigations that have been made into this intricate affair (the expedition to Versailles), it still remains enveloped in all that kind of mystery which ever accompanies events produced more from a concurrence of awkward circumstances than from fixed design. While the characters of men are forming, as is always the case in revolutions, there is a reciprocal suspicion, and a disposition to misinterpret each other; and even parties directly opposite in principle will sometimes concur in pushing forward the same movement with very different views, and with the hopes of its producing very different consequences. A great deal of this may be discovered in this embarrassed affair, and yet the issue of the whole was what nobody had in view. The only things certainly known are that considerable uneasiness was at this time excited at Paris by the delay of the King in not sanctioning and forwarding the decrees of the National Assembly, particularly that of the Declaration of the Rights of Man, and the decrees of the fourth of August, which contained the foundation principles on which the constitution was to be erected. The kindest, and perhaps the fairest conjecture upon this matter is, that some of the ministers intended to make remarks and observations upon certain parts of them before they were finally sanctioned and sent to the provinces; but be this as it may, the enemies of the Revolution derived hope from the delay, and the friends of the Revolution uneasiness.

During this state of suspense, the Garde du Corps, which was composed as such regiments generally are, of persons much connected with the Court, gave an entertainment at Versailles (October 1) to some foreign regiments then arrived; and when the entertainment was at the height, on a signal given, the Garde du Corps tore the national cockade from their hats, trampled it under foot, and replaced it with a counter-cockade prepared for the purpose. An indignity of this kind amounted to defiance. It was like declaring war; and if men will give challenges they must expect consequences. But all this Mr. Burke has carefully kept out of sight. He begins his account by saying: "History will record that on the morning of the 6th October, 1789, the King and Queen of France, after a day of confusion, alarm, dismay, and slaughter, lay down under the pledged security of public faith to indulge nature in a few hours of respite, and troubled melancholy repose." This is neither the sober style of history, nor the intention of it. It leaves everything to be guessed at and mistaken. One would at least think there had been a battle; and a battle there probably would have been had it not been for the moderating prudence of those whom Mr. Burke involves in his censures. By his keeping the Garde du Corps out of sight Mr. Burke has afforded himself the dramatic licence of putting the King and Queen in their places, as if the object of the expedition was against them. But to return to my account this conduct of the Garde du Corps, as might well be expected, alarmed and enraged the Partisans. The colors of the cause, and the cause itself, were become too united to mistake the intention of the insult, and the Partisans were determined to call the Garde du Corps to an account. There was certainly nothing of the cowardice of assassination in marching in the face of the day to demand satisfaction, if such a phrase may be used, of a body of armed men who had voluntarily given defiance. But the circumstance which serves to throw this affair into embarrassment is, that the enemies of the Revolution appear to have encouraged it as well as its friends. The one hoped to prevent a civil war by checking it in time, and the other to make one. The hopes of those opposed to the Revolution rested in making the King of their party, and getting him from Versailles to Metz, where they expected to collect a force and set up a standard. We have, therefore, two different objects presenting themselves at the same time, and to be accomplished by the same means: the one to chastise the Garde du Corps, which was the object of the Partisans; the other to render the confusion of such a scene an inducement to the King to set off for Metz.

On the 5th of October a very numerous body of women, and men in the disguise of women, collected around the Hotel de Ville or town-hall at Paris, and set off for Versailles. Their professed object was the Garde du Corps; but prudent men readily recollect that mischief is more easily begun than ended; and this impressed itself with the more force from the suspicions already stated, and the irregularity of such a cavalcade. As soon, therefore, as a sufficient force could be collected, M. de la Fayette, by orders from the civil authority of Paris, set off after them at the head of twenty thousand of the Paris militia. The Revolution could derive no benefit from confusion, and its opposers might. By an amiable and spirited manner of address he had hitherto been fortunate in calming disquietudes, and in this he was extraordinarily successful; to frustrate, therefore, the hopes of those who might seek to improve this scene into a sort of justifiable necessity for the King's quitting Versailles and withdrawing to Metz, and to prevent at the same time the consequences that might ensue between the Garde du Corps and this phalanx of men and women, he forwarded expresses to the King, that he was on his march to Versailles, by the orders of the civil authority of Paris, for the purpose of peace and protection, expressing at the same time the necessity of restraining the Garde du Corps from firing upon the people.*3

He arrived at Versailles between ten and eleven at night. The Garde du Corps was drawn up, and the people had arrived some time before, but everything had remained suspended. Wisdom and policy now consisted in changing a scene of danger into a happy event. M. de la Fayette became the mediator between the enraged parties; and the King, to remove the uneasiness which had arisen from the delay already stated, sent for the President of the National Assembly, and signed the Declaration of the Rights of Man, and such other parts of the constitution as were in readiness.

It was now about one in the morning. Everything appeared to be composed, and a general congratulation took place. By the beat of a drum a proclamation was made that the citizens of Versailles would give the hospitality of their houses to their fellow-citizens of Paris. Those who could not be accommodated in this manner remained in the streets, or took up their quarters in the churches; and at two o'clock the King and Queen retired.

In this state matters passed till the break of day, when a fresh disturbance arose from the censurable conduct of some of both parties, for such characters there will be in all such scenes. One of the Garde du Corps appeared at one of the windows of the palace, and the people who had remained during the night in the streets accosted him with reviling and provocative language. Instead of retiring, as in such a case prudence would have dictated, he presented his musket, fired, and killed one of the Paris militia. The peace being thus broken, the people rushed into the palace in quest of the offender. They attacked the quarters of the Garde du Corps within the palace, and pursued them throughout the avenues of it, and to the apartments of the King. On this tumult, not the Queen only, as Mr. Burke has represented it, but every person in the palace, was awakened and alarmed; and M.

de la Fayette had a second time to interpose between the parties, the event of which was that the Garde du Corps put on the national cockade, and the matter ended as by oblivion, after the loss of two or three lives.

During the latter part of the time in which this confusion was acting, the King and Queen were in public at the balcony, and neither of them concealed for safety's sake, as Mr. Burke insinuates. Matters being thus appeased, and tranquility restored, a general acclamation broke forth of Le Roi a Paris—Le Roi a Paris—The King to Paris. It was the shout of peace, and immediately accepted on the part of the King. By this measure all future projects of trapanning the King to Metz, and setting up the standard of opposition to the constitution, were prevented, and the suspicions extinguished. The King and his family reached Paris in the evening, and were congratulated on their arrival by M. Bailly, the Mayor of Paris, in the name of the citizens. Mr. Burke, who throughout his book confounds things, persons, and principles, as in his remarks on M. Bailly's address, confounded time also. He censures M. Bailly for calling it "un bon jour," a good day. Mr. Burke should have informed himself that this scene took up the space of two days, the day on which it began with every appearance of danger and mischief, and the day on which it terminated without the mischiefs that threatened; and that it is to this peaceful termination that M. Bailly alludes, and to the arrival of the King at Paris. Not less than three hundred thousand persons arranged themselves in the procession from Versailles to Paris, and not an act of molestation was committed during the whole march.

Mr. Burke on the authority of M. Lally Tollendal, a deserter from the National Assembly, says that on entering Paris, the people shouted "Tous les eveques a la lanterne." All Bishops to be hanged at the lanthorn or lamp-posts. It is surprising that nobody could hear this but Lally Tollendal, and that nobody should believe it but Mr. Burke. It has not the least connection with any part of the transaction, and is totally foreign to every circumstance of it. The Bishops had never been introduced before into any scene of Mr. Burke's drama: why then are they, all at once, and altogether, tout a coup, et tous ensemble, introduced now? Mr. Burke brings forward his Bishops and his lanthorn-like figures in a magic lanthorn, and raises his scenes by contrast instead of connection. But it serves to show, with the rest of his book what little credit ought to be given where even probability is set at defiance, for the purpose of defaming; and with this reflection, instead of a soliloquy in praise of chivalry, as Mr. Burke has done, I close the account of the expedition to Versailles.*4

I have now to follow Mr. Burke through a pathless wilderness of rhapsodies, and a sort of descant upon governments, in which he asserts whatever he pleases, on the presumption of its being believed, without offering either evidence or reasons for so doing.

Before anything can be reasoned upon to a conclusion, certain facts, principles, or data, to reason from, must be established, admitted, or denied. Mr. Burke with his usual outrage, abused the Declaration of the Rights of Man, published by the National Assembly of France, as the basis on which the constitution of France is built. This he calls "paltry and blurred sheets of paper about the rights of man." Does Mr. Burke mean to deny that man has any rights? If he does, then he must mean that there are no such things as rights anywhere, and that he has none himself; for who is there in the world but man? But if Mr. Burke means to admit that man has rights, the question then will be: What are those rights, and how man came by them originally?

The error of those who reason by precedents drawn from antiquity, respecting the rights of man, is that they do not go far enough into antiquity. They do not go the whole way. They stop in some of the intermediate stages of an hundred or a thousand years, and produce what was then done, as a rule for the present day. This is no authority at all. If we travel still farther into antiquity, we shall find a direct contrary opinion and practice prevailing; and if antiquity is to be authority, a thousand such authorities may be produced, successively contradicting each other; but if we proceed on, we shall at last come out right; we shall come to the time when man came from the hand of his Maker. What was he then? Man. Man was his high and only title, and a higher cannot be given him. But of titles I shall speak hereafter.

We are now got at the origin of man, and at the origin of his rights. As to the manner in which the world has been governed from that day to this, it is no farther any concern of ours than to make a proper use of the errors or the improvements which the history of it presents. Those who lived an hundred or a thousand years ago, were then moderns, as we are now. They had their ancients, and those ancients had others, and we also shall be ancients in our turn. If the mere name of antiquity is to govern in the affairs of life, the people who are to live an hundred or a thousand years hence, may as well take us for a precedent, as we make a precedent of those who lived an hundred or a thousand years ago. The fact is, that portions of antiquity, by proving everything, establish nothing. It is authority against authority all the way, till we come to the divine origin of the rights of man at the creation. Here our enquiries find a resting-place, and our reason finds a home. If a dispute about the rights of man had arisen at the distance of an hundred years from the creation, it is to this source of authority they must have referred, and it is to this same source of authority that we must now refer.

Though I mean not to touch upon any sectarian principle of religion, yet it may be worth observing, that the genealogy of Christ is traced to Adam. Why then not trace the rights of man to the creation of man? I will answer the question. Because there have been upstart governments, thrusting themselves between, and presumptuously working to un-make man.

If any generation of men ever possessed the right of dictating the mode by which the world should be governed for ever, it was the first generation that existed; and if that generation did it not, no succeeding generation can show any authority for doing it, nor can set any up. The illuminating and divine principle of the equal rights of man (for it has its origin from the Maker of man) relates, not only to the living individuals, but to generations of men succeeding each other. Every generation is equal in rights to generations which preceded it, by the same rule that every individual is born equal in rights with his contemporary.

Every history of the creation, and every traditionary account, whether from the lettered or unlettered world, however they may vary in their opinion or belief of certain particulars, all agree in establishing one point, the unity of man; by which I mean that men are all of one degree, and consequently that all men are born equal, and with equal natural right, in the same manner as if posterity had been continued by creation instead of generation, the latter being the only mode by which the former is carried forward; and consequently every child born into the world must be considered as deriving its existence from God. The world is as new to him as it was to the first man that existed, and his natural right in it is of the same kind.

The Mosaic account of the creation, whether taken as divine authority or merely historical, is full to this point, the unity or equality of man. The expression admits of no controversy. "And God said, Let us make man in our own image. In the image of God created he him; male and female created he them." The distinction of sexes is pointed out, but no other distinction is even implied. If this be not divine authority, it is at least historical authority, and shows that the equality of man, so far from being a modern doctrine, is the oldest upon record.

It is also to be observed that all the religions known in the world are founded, so far as they relate to man, on the unity of man, as being all of one degree. Whether in heaven or in hell, or in whatever state man may be supposed to exist hereafter, the good and the bad are the only distinctions. Nay, even the laws of governments are obliged to slide into this principle, by making degrees to consist in crimes and not in persons.

It is one of the greatest of all truths, and of the highest advantage to cultivate. By considering man in this light, and by instructing him to consider himself in this light, it places him in a close connection with all his duties, whether to his Creator or to the creation, of which he is a part; and it is only when he forgets his origin, or, to use a more fashionable phrase, his birth and family, that he becomes dissolute. It is not among the least of the evils of the present existing governments in all parts of Europe that man, considered as man, is thrown back to a vast distance from his Maker, and the artificial chasm filled up with a succession of barriers, or sort of turnpike gates, through which he has to pass. I will quote Mr. Burke's catalogue of barriers that he has set up between man and his Maker. Putting himself in the character of a herald, he says: "We fear God—we look with awe to kings—with affection to Parliaments with duty to magistrates—with reverence to priests, and with respect to nobility." Mr. Burke has forgotten to put in "'chivalry." He has also forgotten to put in Peter.

The duty of man is not a wilderness of turnpike gates, through which he is to pass by tickets from one to the other. It is plain and simple, and consists but of two points. His duty to God, which every man must feel; and with respect to his neighbor, to do as he would be done by. If those to whom power is delegated do well, they will be respected: if not, they will be despised; and with regard to those to whom no power is delegated, but who assume it, the rational world can know nothing of them.

Hitherto we have spoken only (and that but in part) of the natural rights of man. We have now to consider the civil rights of man, and to show how the one originates from the other. Man did not enter into society to become worse than he was before, nor to have fewer rights than he had before, but to have those rights better secured. His natural rights are the foundation of all his civil rights. But in order to pursue this distinction with more precision, it will be necessary to mark the different qualities of natural and civil rights.

A few words will explain this. Natural rights are those which appertain to man in right of his existence. Of this kind are all the intellectual rights, or rights of the mind, and also all those rights of acting as an individual for his own comfort and happiness, which are not injurious to the natural rights of others. Civil rights are those which appertain to man in right of his being a member of society. Every civil right has for its foundation some natural right pre-existing in the individual, but to the enjoyment of which his individual power is not, in all cases, sufficiently competent. Of this kind are all those which relate to security and protection.

From this short review it will be easy to distinguish between that class of natural rights which man retains after entering into society and those which he throws into the common stock as a member of society.

The natural rights which he retains are all those in which the Power to execute is as perfect in the individual as the right itself. Among this class, as is before mentioned, are all the intellectual rights, or rights of the mind; consequently religion is one of those rights. The natural rights which are not retained, are all those in which, though the right is perfect in the individual, the power to execute them is defective. They answer not his purpose. A man, by natural right, has a right to judge in his own cause; and so far as the right of the mind is concerned, he never surrenders it. But what availeth it him to judge, if he has not power to redress? He therefore deposits this right in the common stock of society, and takes the ann of society, of which he is a part, in preference and in addition to his own. Society grants him nothing. Every man is a proprietor in society, and draws on the capital as a matter of right.

From these premises two or three certain conclusions will follow:

First, That every civil right grows out of a natural right; or, in other words, is a natural right exchanged.

Secondly, That civil power properly considered as such is made up of the aggregate of that class of the natural rights of man, which becomes defective in the individual in point of power, and answers not his purpose, but when collected to a focus becomes competent to the Purpose of every one.

Thirdly, That the power produced from the aggregate of natural rights, imperfect in power in the individual, cannot be applied to invade the natural rights which are retained in the individual, and in which the power to execute is as perfect as the right itself.

We have now, in a few words, traced man from a natural individual to a member of society, and shown, or endeavoured to show, the quality of the natural rights retained, and of those which are exchanged for civil rights. Let us now apply these principles to governments.

In casting our eyes over the world, it is extremely easy to distinguish the governments which have arisen out of society, or out of the social compact, from those which have not; but to place this in a clearer light than what a single glance may afford, it will be proper to take a review of the several sources from which governments have arisen and on which they have been founded.

They may be all comprehended under three heads.

First, Superstition.

Secondly, Power.

Thirdly, The common interest of society and the common rights of man.

The first was a government of priestcraft, the second of conquerors, and the third of reason.

When a set of artful men pretended, through the medium of oracles, to hold intercourse with the Deity, as familiarly as they now march up the back-stairs in European courts, the world was completely under the government of superstition. The oracles were consulted, and whatever they were made to say became the law; and this sort of government lasted as long as this sort of superstition lasted.

After these a race of conquerors arose, whose government, like that of William the Conqueror, was founded in power, and the sword assumed the name of a sceptre. Governments thus established last as long as the power to support them lasts; but that they might avail themselves of every engine in their favor, they united fraud to force, and set up an idol which they called Divine Right, and which, in imitation of the Pope, who affects to be spiritual and temporal, and in contradiction to the Founder of the Christian religion, twisted itself afterwards into an idol of another shape, called Church and State. The key of St. Peter and the key of the Treasury became quartered on one another, and the wondering cheated multitude worshipped the invention.

When I contemplate the natural dignity of man, when I feel (for Nature has not been kind enough to me to blunt my feelings) for the honour and happiness of its character, I become irritated at the attempt to govern mankind by force and fraud, as if they were all knaves and fools, and can scarcely avoid disgust at those who are thus imposed upon.

We have now to review the governments which arise out of society, in contradistinction to those which arose out of superstition and conquest.

It has been thought a considerable advance towards establishing the principles of Freedom to say that Government is a compact between those who govern and those who are governed; but this cannot be true, because it is putting the effect before the cause; for as man must have existed before governments existed, there necessarily was a time when governments did not exist, and consequently there could originally exist no governors to form such a compact with.

The fact therefore must be that the individuals themselves, each in his own personal and sovereign right, entered into a compact with each other to produce a government: and this is the only mode in which governments have a right to arise, and the only principle on which they have a right to exist.

To possess ourselves of a clear idea of what government is, or ought to be, we must trace it to its origin. In doing this we shall easily discover that governments must have arisen either out of the people or over the people. Mr. Burke has made no distinction. He investigates nothing to its source, and therefore he confounds everything; but he has signified his intention of undertaking, at some future opportunity, a comparison between the constitution of England and France. As he thus renders it a subject of controversy by throwing the gauntlet, I take him upon his own ground. It is in high challenges that high truths have the right of appearing; and I accept it with the more readiness because it affords me, at the same time, an opportunity of pursuing the subject with respect to governments arising out of society.

But it will be first necessary to define what is meant by a Constitution. It is not sufficient that we adopt the word; we must fix also a standard signification to it.

A constitution is not a thing in name only, but in fact. It has not an ideal, but a real existence; and wherever it cannot be produced in a visible form, there is none. A constitution is a thing antecedent to a government, and a government is only the creature of a constitution. The constitution of a country is not the act of its government, but of the people constituting its government. It is the body of elements, to which you can refer, and quote article by article; and which contains the principles on which the government shall be established, the manner in which it shall be organised, the powers it shall have, the mode of elections, the duration of Parliaments, or by what other name such bodies may be called; the powers which the executive part of the government shall have; and in fine, everything that relates to the complete organisation of a civil government, and the principles on which it shall act, and by which it shall be bound. A constitution, therefore, is to a government what the laws made afterwards by that government are to a court of judicature. The court of judicature does not make the laws, neither can it alter them; it only acts in conformity to the laws made: and the government is in like manner governed by the constitution.

Can, then, Mr. Burke produce the English Constitution? If he cannot, we may fairly conclude that though it has been so much talked about, no such thing as a constitution exists, or ever did exist, and consequently that the people have yet a constitution to form.

Mr. Burke will not, I presume, deny the position I have already advanced—namely, that governments arise either out of the people or over the people. The English Government is one of those which arose out of a conquest, and not out of society, and consequently it arose over the people; and though it has been much modified from the opportunity of circumstances since the time of William the Conqueror, the country has never yet regenerated itself, and is therefore without a constitution.

I readily perceive the reason why Mr. Burke declined going into the comparison between the English and French constitutions, because he could not but perceive, when he sat down to the task, that no such a thing as a constitution existed on his side the question. His book is certainly bulky enough to have contained all he could say on this subject, and it would have been the best manner in which people could have judged of their separate merits. Why then has he declined the only thing that was worth while to write upon? It was the strongest ground he could take, if the advantages were on his side, but the weakest if they were not; and his declining to take it is either a sign that he could not possess it or could not maintain it.

Mr. Burke said, in a speech last winter in Parliament, "that when the National Assembly first met in three Orders (the Tiers Etat, the Clergy, and the Noblesse), France had then a good constitution." This shows, among numerous other instances, that Mr. Burke does not understand what a constitution is. The persons so met were not a constitution, but a convention, to make a constitution.

The present National Assembly of France is, strictly speaking, the personal social compact. The members of it are the delegates of the nation in its original character; future assemblies will be the delegates of the nation in its organised character. The authority of the present Assembly is different from what the authority of future Assemblies will be. The authority of the present one is to form a constitution; the authority of future assemblies will be to legislate according to the principles and forms prescribed in that constitution; and if experience should hereafter show that alterations, amendments, or additions are necessary, the constitution will point out the mode by which such things shall be done, and not leave it to the discretionary power of the future government.

A government on the principles on which constitutional governments arising out of society are established, cannot have the right of altering itself. If it had, it would be arbitrary. It might make itself what it pleased; and wherever such a right is set up, it shows there is no constitution. The act by which the English Parliament empowered itself to sit seven years, shows there is no constitution in England. It might, by the same self-authority, have sat any great number of years, or for life. The bill which the present Mr. Pitt brought into Parliament some years ago, to reform Parliament, was on the same erroneous principle. The right of reform is in the nation in its original character, and the constitutional method would be by a general convention elected for the purpose. There is, moreover, a paradox in the idea of vitiated bodies reforming themselves.

From these preliminaries I proceed to draw some comparisons. I have already spoken of the declaration of rights; and as I mean to be as concise as possible, I shall proceed to other parts of the French Constitution.

The constitution of France says that every man who pays a tax of sixty sous per annum (2s. 6d. English) is an elector. What article will Mr. Burke place against this? Can anything be more limited, and at the same time more capricious, than the qualification of electors is in England? Limited—because not one man in an hundred (I speak much within compass) is admitted to vote. Capricious—because the lowest character that can be supposed to exist, and who has not so much as the visible means of an honest livelihood, is an elector in some places: while in other places, the man who pays very large taxes, and has a known fair character, and the farmer who rents to the amount of three or four hundred pounds a year, with a property on that farm to three or four times that amount, is not admitted to be an elector. Everything is out of nature, as Mr. Burke says on another occasion, in this strange chaos, and all sorts of follies are blended with all sorts of crimes. William the Conqueror and his descendants parcelled out the country in this manner, and bribed some parts of it by what they call charters to hold the other parts of it the better subjected to their will. This is the reason why so many of those charters abound in Cornwall; the people were averse to the Government established at the Conquest, and the towns were garrisoned and bribed to enslave the country. All the old charters are the badges of this conquest, and it is from this source that the capriciousness of election arises.

The French Constitution says that the number of representatives for any place shall be in a ratio to the number of taxable inhabitants or electors. What article will Mr. Burke place against this? The county of York, which contains nearly a million of souls, sends two county members; and so does the county of Rutland, which contains not an hundredth part of that number. The old town of Sarum, which contains not three houses, sends two members; and the town of Manchester, which contains upward of sixty thousand souls, is not admitted to send any. Is there any principle in these things? It is admitted that all this is altered, but there is much to be done yet, before we have a fair representation of the people. Is there anything by which you can trace the marks of freedom, or discover those of wisdom? No wonder then Mr. Burke has declined the comparison, and endeavored to lead his readers from the point by a wild, unsystematical display of paradoxical rhapsodies.

The French Constitution says that the National Assembly shall be elected every two years. What article will Mr. Burke place against this? Why, that the nation has no right at all in the case; that the government is perfectly arbitrary with respect to this point; and he can quote for his authority the precedent of a former Parliament.

The French Constitution says there shall be no game laws, that the farmer on whose lands wild game shall be found (for it is by the produce of his lands they are fed) shall have a right to what he can take; that there shall be no monopolies of any kind—that all trades shall be free and every man free to follow any occupation by which he can procure an honest livelihood, and in any place, town, or city throughout the nation. What will Mr. Burke say to this? In England, game is made the property of those at whose expense it is not fed; and with respect to monopolies, the country is cut up into monopolies. Every chartered town is an aristocratical monopoly in itself, and the qualification of electors proceeds out of those chartered monopolies. Is this freedom? Is this what Mr. Burke means by a constitution?

In these chartered monopolies, a man coming from another part of the country is hunted from them as if he were a foreign enemy. An Englishman is not free of his own country; every one of those places presents a barrier in his way, and tells him he is not a freeman—that he has no rights. Within these monopolies are other monopolies. In a city, such for instance as Bath, which contains between twenty and thirty thousand inhabitants, the right of electing representatives to Parliament is monopolised by about thirty-one persons. And within these monopolies are still others. A man even of the same town, whose parents were not in circumstances to give him an occupation, is debarred, in many cases, from the natural right of acquiring one, be his genius or industry what it may.

Are these things examples to hold out to a country regenerating itself from slavery, like France? Certainly they are not, and certain am I, that when the people of England come to reflect upon them they will, like France, annihilate those badges of ancient oppression, those traces of a conquered nation. Had Mr. Burke possessed talents similar to the author of "On the Wealth of Nations." he would have comprehended all the parts which enter into, and, by assemblage, form a constitution. He would have reasoned from minutiae to magnitude. It is not from his prejudices only, but from the disorderly cast of his genius, that he is unfitted for the subject he writes upon. Even his genius is without a constitution. It is a genius at random, and not a genius constituted. But he must say something. He has therefore mounted in the air like a balloon, to draw the eyes of the multitude from the ground they stand upon.

Much is to be learned from the French Constitution. Conquest and tyranny transplanted themselves with William the Conqueror from Normandy into England, and the country is yet disfigured with the marks. May, then, the example of all France contribute to regenerate the freedom which a province of it destroyed!

The French Constitution says that to preserve the national representation from being corrupt, no member of the National Assembly shall be an officer of the government, a placeman or a pensioner. What will Mr. Burke place against this? I will whisper his answer: Loaves and Fishes. Ah! this government of loaves and fishes has more mischief in it than people have yet reflected on. The National Assembly has made the discovery, and it holds out the example to the world. Had governments agreed to quarrel on purpose to fleece their countries by taxes, they could not have succeeded better than they have done.

Everything in the English government appears to me the reverse of what it ought to be, and of what it is said to be. The Parliament, imperfectly and capriciously elected as it is, is nevertheless supposed to hold the national purse in trust for the nation; but in the manner in which an English Parliament is constructed it is like a man being both mortgagor and mortgagee, and in the case of misapplication of trust it is the criminal sitting in judgment upon himself. If those who vote the supplies are the same persons who receive the supplies when voted, and are to account for the expenditure of those supplies to those who voted them, it is themselves accountable to themselves, and the Comedy of Errors concludes with the pantomime of Hush. Neither the Ministerial party nor the Opposition will touch upon this case. The national purse is the common hack which each mounts upon. It is like what the country people call "Ride and tie—you ride a little way, and then I."*5 They order these things better in France.

The French Constitution says that the right of war and peace is in the nation. Where else should it reside but in those who are to pay the expense?

In England this right is said to reside in a metaphor shown at the Tower for sixpence or a shilling a piece: so are the lions; and it would be a step nearer to reason to say it resided in them, for any inanimate metaphor is no more than a hat or a cap. We can all see the absurdity of worshipping Aaron's molten calf, or Nebuchadnezzar's golden image; but why do men continue to practise themselves the absurdities they despise in others?

It may with reason be said that in the manner the English nation is represented it signifies not where the right resides, whether in the Crown or in the Parliament. War is the common harvest of all those who participate in the division and expenditure of public money, in all countries. It is the art of conquering at home; the object of it is an increase of revenue; and as revenue cannot be increased without taxes, a pretence must be made for expenditure. In reviewing the history of the English Government, its wars and its taxes, a bystander, not blinded by prejudice nor warped by interest, would declare that taxes were not raised to carry on wars, but that wars were raised to carry on taxes.

Mr. Burke, as a member of the House of Commons, is a part of the English Government; and though he professes himself an enemy to war, he abuses the French Constitution, which seeks to explode it. He holds up the English Government as a model, in all its parts, to France; but he should first know the remarks which the French make upon it. They contend in favor of their own, that the portion of liberty enjoyed in England is just enough to enslave a country more productively than by despotism, and that as the real object of all despotism is revenue, a government so formed obtains more than it could do either by direct despotism, or in a full state of freedom, and is, therefore on the ground of interest, opposed to both. They account also for the readiness which always appears in such governments for engaging in wars by remarking on the different motives which produced them. In despotic governments wars are the effect of pride; but in those governments in which they become the means of taxation, they acquire thereby a more permanent promptitude.

The French Constitution, therefore, to provide against both these evils, has taken away the power of declaring war from kings and ministers, and placed the right where the expense must fall.

When the question of the right of war and peace was agitating in the National Assembly, the people of England appeared to be much interested in the event, and highly to applaud the decision. As a principle it applies as much to one country as another. William the Conqueror, as a conqueror, held this power of war and peace in himself, and his descendants have ever since claimed it under him as a right.

Although Mr. Burke has asserted the right of the Parliament at the Revolution to bind and control the nation and posterity for ever, he denies at the same time that the Parliament or the nation had any right to alter what he calls the succession of the crown in anything but in part, or by a sort of modification. By his taking this ground he throws the case back to the Norman Conquest, and by thus running a line of succession springing from William the Conqueror to the present day, he makes it necessary to enquire who and what William the Conqueror was, and where he came from, and into the origin, history and nature of what are called prerogatives. Everything must have had a beginning, and the fog of time and antiquity should be penetrated to discover it. Let, then, Mr. Burke bring forward his William of Normandy, for it is to this origin that his argument goes. It also unfortunately happens, in running this line of succession, that another line parallel thereto presents itself, which is that if the succession runs in the line of the conquest, the nation runs in the line of being conquered, and it ought to rescue itself from this reproach.

But it will perhaps be said that though the power of declaring war descends in the heritage of the conquest, it is held in check by the right of Parliament to withhold the supplies. It will always happen when a thing is originally wrong that amendments do not make it right, and it often happens that they do as much mischief one way as good the other, and such is the case here, for if the one rashly declares war as a matter of right, and the other peremptorily withholds the supplies as a matter of right, the remedy becomes as bad, or worse, than the disease. The one forces the nation to a combat, and the other ties its hands; but the more probable issue is that the contest will end in a collusion between the parties, and be made a screen to both.

On this question of war, three things are to be considered. First, the right of declaring it: secondly, the expense of supporting it: thirdly, the mode of conducting it after it is declared. The French Constitution places the right where the expense must fall, and this union can only be in the nation. The mode of conducting it after it is declared, it consigns to the executive department. Were this the case in all countries, we should hear but little more of wars.

Before I proceed to consider other parts of the French Constitution, and by way of relieving the fatigue of argument, I will introduce an anecdote which I had from Dr. Franklin.

While the Doctor resided in France as Minister from America, during the war, he had numerous proposals made to him by projectors of every country and of every kind, who wished to go to the land that floweth with milk and honey, America; and among the rest, there was one who offered himself to be king. He introduced his proposal to the Doctor by letter, which is now in the hands of M. Beaumarchais, of Paris—stating, first, that as the Americans had dismissed or sent away*[6] their King, that they would want another. Secondly, that himself was a Norman. Thirdly, that he was of a more ancient family than the Dukes of Normandy, and of a more honorable descent, his line having never been bastardised. Fourthly, that there was already a precedent in England of kings coming out of Normandy, and on these grounds he rested his offer, enjoining that the Doctor would forward it to America. But as the Doctor neither did this, nor yet sent him an answer, the projector wrote a second letter, in which he did not, it is true, threaten to go over and conquer America, but only with great dignity proposed that if his offer was not accepted, an acknowledgment of about L30,000 might be made to him for his generosity! Now, as all arguments respecting succession must necessarily connect that succession with some beginning, Mr. Burke's arguments on this subject go to show that there is no English origin of kings, and that they are descendants of the Norman line in right of the Conquest. It may, therefore, be of service to his doctrine to make this story known, and to inform him, that in case of that natural extinction to which all mortality is subject, Kings may again be had from Normandy, on more reasonable terms than William the Conqueror; and consequently, that the good people of England, at the revolution of 1688, might have done much better, had such a generous Norman as this known their wants, and they had known his. The chivalric character which Mr. Burke so much admires, is certainly much easier to make a bargain with than a hard dealing Dutchman. But to return to the matters of the constitution: The French Constitution says, There shall be no titles; and, of consequence, all that class of equivocal generation which in some countries is called "aristocracy" and in others "nobility," is done away, and the peer is exalted into the Man.

Titles are but nicknames, and every nickname is a title. The thing is perfectly harmless in itself, but it marks a sort of foppery in the human character, which degrades it. It reduces man into the diminutive of man in things which are great, and the counterfeit of women in things which are little. It talks about its fine blue ribbon like a girl, and shows its new garter like a child. A certain writer, of some antiquity, says: "When I was a child, I thought as a child; but when I became a man, I put away childish things."

It is, properly, from the elevated mind of France that the folly of titles has fallen. It has outgrown the baby clothes of Count and Duke, and breeched itself in manhood. France has not levelled, it has exalted. It has put down the dwarf, to set up the man. The punyism of a senseless word like Duke, Count or Earl has ceased to please. Even those who possessed them have disowned the gibberish, and as they outgrew the rickets, have despised the rattle. The genuine mind of man, thirsting for its native home, society, contemns the gewgaws that separate him from it. Titles are like circles drawn by the magician's wand, to contract the sphere of man's felicity. He lives immured within the Bastille of a word, and surveys at a distance the envied life of man.

Is it, then, any wonder that titles should fall in France? Is it not a greater wonder that they should be kept up anywhere? What are they? What is their worth, and "what is their amount?" When we think or speak of a Judge or a General, we associate with it the ideas of office and character; we think of gravity in one and bravery in the other; but when we use the word merely as a title, no ideas associate with it. Through all the vocabulary of Adam there is not such an animal as a Duke or a Count; neither can we connect any certain ideas with the words. Whether they mean strength or weakness, wisdom or folly, a child or a man, or the rider or the horse, is all equivocal. What respect then can be paid to that which describes nothing, and which means nothing? Imagination has given figure and character to centaurs, satyrs, and down to all the fairy tribe; but titles baffle even the powers of fancy, and are a chimerical nondescript.

But this is not all. If a whole country is disposed to hold them in contempt, all their value is gone, and none will own them. It is common opinion only that makes them anything, or nothing, or worse than nothing. There is no occasion to take titles away, for they take themselves away when society concurs to ridicule them. This species of imaginary consequence has visibly declined in every part of Europe, and it hastens to its exit as the world of reason continues to rise. There was a time when the lowest class of what are called nobility was more thought of than the highest is now, and when a man in armour riding throughout Christendom in quest of adventures was more stared at than a modern Duke. The world has seen this folly fall, and it has fallen by being laughed at, and the farce of titles will follow its fate. The patriots of France have discovered in good time that rank and dignity in society must take a new ground. The old one has fallen through. It must now take the substantial ground of character, instead of the chimerical ground of titles; and they have brought their titles to the altar, and made of them a burnt-offering to Reason.

If no mischief had annexed itself to the folly of titles they would not have been worth a serious and formal destruction, such as the National Assembly have decreed them; and this makes it necessary to enquire farther into the nature and character of aristocracy.

That, then, which is called aristocracy in some countries and nobility in others arose out of the governments founded upon conquest. It was originally a military order for the purpose of supporting military government (for such were all governments founded in conquest); and to keep up a succession of this order for the purpose for which it was established, all the younger branches of those families were disinherited and the law of primogenitureship set up.

The nature and character of aristocracy shows itself to us in this law. It is the law against every other law of nature, and Nature herself calls for its destruction. Establish family justice, and aristocracy falls. By the aristocratical law of primogenitureship, in a family of six children five are exposed. Aristocracy has never more than one child. The rest are begotten to be devoured. They are thrown to the cannibal for prey, and the natural parent prepares the unnatural repast.

As everything which is out of nature in man affects, more or less, the interest of society, so does this. All the children which the aristocracy disowns (which are all except the eldest) are, in general, cast like orphans on a parish, to be provided for by the public, but at a greater charge. Unnecessary offices and places in governments and courts are created at the expense of the public to maintain them.

With what kind of parental reflections can the father or mother contemplate their younger offspring? By nature they are children, and by marriage they are heirs; but by aristocracy they are bastards and orphans. They are the flesh and blood of their parents in the one line, and nothing akin to them in the other. To restore, therefore, parents to their children, and children to their parents relations to each other, and man to society—and to exterminate the monster aristocracy, root and branch—the French Constitution has destroyed the law of Primogenitureship. Here then lies the monster; and Mr. Burke, if he pleases, may write its epitaph.

Hitherto we have considered aristocracy chiefly in one point of view. We have now to consider it in another. But whether we view it before or behind, or sideways, or any way else, domestically or publicly, it is still a monster.

In France aristocracy had one feature less in its countenance than what it has in some other countries. It did not compose a body of hereditary legislators. It was not "a corporation of aristocracy," for such I have heard M. de la Fayette describe an English House of Peers. Let us then examine the grounds upon which the French Constitution has resolved against having such a House in France.

Because, in the first place, as is already mentioned, aristocracy is kept up by family tyranny and injustice.

Secondly. Because there is an unnatural unfitness in an aristocracy to be legislators for a nation. Their ideas of distributive justice are corrupted at the very source. They begin life by trampling on all their younger brothers and sisters, and relations of every kind, and are taught and educated so to do. With what ideas of justice or honour can that man enter a house of legislation, who absorbs in his own person the inheritance of a whole family of children or doles out to them some pitiful portion with the insolence of a gift?

Thirdly. Because the idea of hereditary legislators is as inconsistent as that of hereditary judges, or hereditary juries; and as absurd as an hereditary mathematician, or an hereditary wise man; and as ridiculous as an hereditary poet laureate.

Fourthly. Because a body of men, holding themselves accountable to nobody, ought not to be trusted by anybody.

Fifthly. Because it is continuing the uncivilised principle of governments founded in conquest, and the base idea of man having property in man, and governing him by personal right.

Sixthly. Because aristocracy has a tendency to deteriorate the human species. By the universal economy of nature it is known, and by the instance of the Jews it is proved, that the human species has a tendency to degenerate, in any small number of persons, when separated from the general stock of society, and inter-marrying constantly with each other. It defeats even its pretended end, and becomes in time the opposite of what is noble in man. Mr. Burke talks of nobility; let him show what it is. The greatest characters the world have known have arisen on the democratic floor. Aristocracy has not been able to keep a proportionate pace with democracy. The artificial Noble shrinks into a dwarf before the Noble of Nature; and in the few instances of those (for there are some in all countries) in whom nature, as by a miracle, has survived in aristocracy, Those Men Despise It.—But it is time to proceed to a new subject.

The French Constitution has reformed the condition of the clergy. It has raised the income of the lower and middle classes, and taken from the higher. None are now less than twelve hundred livres (fifty pounds sterling), nor any higher than two or three thousand pounds. What will Mr. Burke place against this? Hear what he says.

He says: "That the people of England can see without pain or grudging, an archbishop precede a duke; they can see a Bishop of Durham, or a Bishop of Winchester in possession of L10,000 a-year; and cannot see why it is in worse hands than estates to a like amount, in the hands of this earl or that squire." And Mr. Burke offers this as an example to France.

As to the first part, whether the archbishop precedes the duke, or the duke the bishop, it is, I believe, to the people in general, somewhat like Sternhold and Hopkins, or Hopkins and Sternhold; you may put which you please first; and as I confess that I do not understand the merits of this case, I will not contest it with Mr. Burke.

But with respect to the latter, I have something to say. Mr. Burke has not put the case right. The comparison is out of order, by being put between the bishop and the earl or the squire. It ought to be put between the bishop and the curate, and then it will stand thus:—"The people of England can see without pain or grudging, a Bishop of Durham, or a Bishop of Winchester, in possession of ten thousand pounds a-year, and a curate on thirty or forty pounds a-year, or less." No, sir, they certainly do not see those things without great pain or grudging. It is a case that applies itself to every man's sense of justice, and is one among many that calls aloud for a constitution.

In France the cry of "the church! the church!" was repeated as often as in Mr. Burke's book, and as loudly as when the Dissenters' Bill was before the English Parliament; but the generality of the French clergy were not to be deceived by this cry any longer. They knew that whatever the pretence might be, it was they who were one of the principal objects of it. It was the cry of the high beneficed clergy, to prevent any regulation of income taking place between those of ten thousand pounds a-year and the parish priest. They therefore joined their case to those of every other oppressed class of men, and by this union obtained redress.

The French Constitution has abolished tythes, that source of perpetual discontent between the tythe-holder and the parishioner. When land is held on tythe, it is in the condition of an estate held between two parties; the one receiving one-tenth, and the other nine-tenths of the produce: and consequently, on principles of equity, if the estate can be improved, and made to produce by that improvement double or treble what it did before, or in any other ratio, the expense of such improvement ought to be borne in like proportion between the parties who are to share the produce. But this is not the case in tythes: the farmer bears the whole expense, and the tythe-holder takes a tenth of the improvement, in addition to the original tenth, and by this means gets the value of two-tenths instead of one. This is another case that calls for a constitution.

The French Constitution hath abolished or renounced Toleration and Intolerance also, and hath established Universal Right Of Conscience.

Toleration is not the opposite of Intolerance, but is the counterfeit of it. Both are despotisms. The one assumes to itself the right of withholding Liberty of Conscience, and the other of granting it. The one is the Pope armed with fire and faggot, and the other is the Pope selling or granting indulgences. The former is church and state, and the latter is church and traffic.

But Toleration may be viewed in a much stronger light. Man worships not himself, but his Maker; and the liberty of conscience which he claims is not for the service of himself, but of his God. In this case, therefore, we must necessarily have the associated idea of two things; the mortal who renders the worship, and the Immortal Being who is worshipped. Toleration, therefore, places itself, not between man and man, nor between church and church, nor between one denomination of religion and another, but between God and man; between the being who worships, and the Being who is worshipped; and by the same act of assumed authority which it tolerates man to pay his worship, it presumptuously and blasphemously sets itself up to tolerate the Almighty to receive it.

Were a bill brought into any Parliament, entitled, "An Act to tolerate or grant liberty to the Almighty to receive the worship of a Jew or Turk," or "to prohibit the Almighty from receiving it," all men would startle and call it blasphemy. There would be an uproar. The presumption of toleration in religious matters would then present itself unmasked; but the presumption is not the less because the name of "Man" only appears to those laws, for the associated idea of the worshipper and the worshipped cannot be separated. Who then art thou, vain dust and ashes! by whatever name thou art called, whether a King, a Bishop, a Church, or a State, a Parliament, or anything else, that obtrudest thine insignificance between the soul of man and its Maker? Mind thine own concerns. If he believes not as thou believest, it is a proof that thou believest not as he believes, and there is no earthly power can determine between you.

With respect to what are called denominations of religion, if every one is left to judge of its own religion, there is no such thing as a religion that is wrong; but if they are to judge of each other's religion, there is no such thing as a religion that is right; and therefore all the world is right, or all the world is wrong. But with respect to religion itself, without regard to names, and as directing itself from the universal family of mankind to the Divine object of all adoration, it is man bringing to his Maker the fruits of his heart; and though those fruits may differ from each other like the fruits of the earth, the grateful tribute of every one is accepted.

A Bishop of Durham, or a Bishop of Winchester, or the archbishop who heads the dukes, will not refuse a tythe-sheaf of wheat because it is not a cock of hay, nor a cock of hay because it is not a sheaf of wheat; nor a pig, because it is neither one nor the other; but these same persons, under the figure of an established church, will not permit their Maker to receive the varied tythes of man's devotion.

One of the continual choruses of Mr. Burke's book is "Church and State." He does not mean some one particular church, or some one particular state, but any church and state; and he uses the term as a general figure to hold forth the political doctrine of always uniting the church with the state in every country, and he censures the National Assembly for not having done this in France. Let us bestow a few thoughts on this subject.

All religions are in their nature kind and benign, and united with principles of morality. They could not have made proselytes at first by professing anything that was vicious, cruel, persecuting, or immoral. Like everything else, they had their beginning; and they proceeded by persuasion, exhortation, and example. How then is it that they lose their native mildness, and become morose and intolerant?

It proceeds from the connection which Mr. Burke recommends. By engendering the church with the state, a sort of mule-animal, capable only of destroying, and not of breeding up, is produced, called the Church established by Law. It is a stranger, even from its birth, to any parent mother, on whom it is begotten, and whom in time it kicks out and destroys.

The inquisition in Spain does not proceed from the religion originally professed, but from this mule-animal, engendered between the church and the state. The burnings in Smithfield proceeded from the same heterogeneous production; and it was the regeneration of this strange animal in England afterwards, that renewed rancour and irreligion among the inhabitants, and that drove the people called Quakers and Dissenters to America. Persecution is not an original feature in any religion; but it is alway the strongly-marked feature of all law-religions, or religions established by law. Take away the law-establishment, and every religion re-assumes its original benignity. In America, a catholic priest is a good citizen, a good character, and a good neighbour; an episcopalian minister is of the same description: and this proceeds independently of the men, from there being no law-establishment in America.

If also we view this matter in a temporal sense, we shall see the ill effects it has had on the prosperity of nations. The union of church and state has impoverished Spain. The revoking the edict of Nantes drove the silk manufacture from that country into England; and church and state are now driving the cotton manufacture from England to America and France. Let then Mr. Burke continue to preach his antipolitical doctrine of Church and State. It will do some good. The National Assembly will not follow his advice, but will benefit by his folly. It was by observing the ill effects of it in England, that America has been warned against it; and it is by experiencing them in France, that the National Assembly have abolished it, and, like America, have established Universal Right Of Conscience, And Universal Right Of Citizenship.*7

I will here cease the comparison with respect to the principles of the French Constitution, and conclude this part of the subject with a few observations on the organisation of the formal parts of the French and English governments.

The executive power in each country is in the hands of a person styled the King; but the French Constitution distinguishes between the King and the Sovereign: It considers the station of King as official, and places Sovereignty in the nation.

The representatives of the nation, who compose the National Assembly, and who are the legislative power, originate in and from the people by election, as an inherent right in the people.—In England it is otherwise; and this arises from the original establishment of what is called its monarchy; for, as by the conquest all the rights of the people or the nation were absorbed into the hands of the Conqueror, and who added the title of King to that of Conqueror, those same matters which in France are now held as rights in the people, or in the nation, are held in England as grants from what is called the crown. The Parliament in England, in both its branches, was erected by patents from the descendants of the Conqueror. The House of Commons did not originate as a matter of right in the people to delegate or elect, but as a grant or boon.

By the French Constitution the nation is always named before the king. The third article of the declaration of rights says: "The nation is essentially the source (or fountain) of all sovereignty." Mr. Burke argues that in England a king is the fountain—that he is the fountain of all honour. But as this idea is evidently descended from the conquest I shall make no other remark upon it, than that it is the nature of conquest to turn everything upside down; and as Mr. Burke will not be refused the privilege of speaking twice, and as there are but two parts in the figure, the fountain and the spout, he will be right the second time.

The French Constitution puts the legislative before the executive, the law before the king; la loi, le roi. This also is in the natural order of things, because laws must have existence before they can have execution.

A king in France does not, in addressing himself to the National Assembly, say, "My Assembly," similar to the phrase used in England of my "Parliament"; neither can he use it consistently with the constitution, nor could it be admitted. There may be propriety in the use of it in England, because as is before mentioned, both Houses of Parliament originated from what is called the crown by patent or boon—and not from the inherent rights of the people, as the National Assembly does in France, and whose name designates its origin.

The President of the National Assembly does not ask the King to grant to the Assembly liberty of speech, as is the case with the English House of Commons. The constitutional dignity of the National Assembly cannot debase itself. Speech is, in the first place, one of the natural rights of man always retained; and with respect to the National Assembly the use of it is their duty, and the nation is their authority. They were elected by the greatest body of men exercising the right of election the European world ever saw. They sprung not from the filth of rotten boroughs, nor are they the vassal representatives of aristocratical ones. Feeling the proper dignity of their character they support it. Their Parliamentary language, whether for or against a question, is free, bold and manly, and extends to all the parts and circumstances of the case. If any matter or subject respecting the executive department or the person who presides in it (the king) comes before them it is debated on with the spirit of men, and in the language of gentlemen; and their answer or their address is returned in the same style. They stand not aloof with the gaping vacuity of vulgar ignorance, nor bend with the cringe of sycophantic insignificance. The graceful pride of truth knows no extremes, and preserves, in every latitude of life, the right-angled character of man.

Let us now look to the other side of the question. In the addresses of the English Parliaments to their kings we see neither the intrepid spirit of the old Parliaments of France, nor the serene dignity of the present National Assembly; neither do we see in them anything of the style of English manners, which border somewhat on bluntness. Since then they are neither of foreign extraction, nor naturally of English production, their origin must be sought for elsewhere, and that origin is the Norman Conquest. They are evidently of the vassalage class of manners, and emphatically mark the prostrate distance that exists in no other condition of men than between the conqueror and the conquered. That this vassalage idea and style of speaking was not got rid of even at the Revolution of 1688, is evident from the declaration of Parliament to William and Mary in these words: "We do most humbly and faithfully submit ourselves, our heirs and posterities, for ever." Submission is wholly a vassalage term, repugnant to the dignity of freedom, and an echo of the language used at the Conquest.

As the estimation of all things is given by comparison, the Revolution of 1688, however from circumstances it may have been exalted beyond its value, will find its level. It is already on the wane, eclipsed by the enlarging orb of reason, and the luminous revolutions of America and France. In less than another century it will go, as well as Mr. Burke's labours, "to the family vault of all the Capulets." Mankind will then scarcely believe that a country calling itself free would send to Holland for a man, and clothe him with power on purpose to put themselves in fear of him, and give him almost a million sterling a year for leave to submit themselves and their posterity, like bondmen and bondwomen, for ever.

But there is a truth that ought to be made known; I have had the opportunity of seeing it; which is, that notwithstanding appearances, there is not any description of men that despise monarchy so much as courtiers. But they well know, that if it were seen by others, as it is seen by them, the juggle could not be kept up; they are in the condition of men who get their living by a show, and to whom the folly of that show is so familiar that they ridicule it; but were the audience to be made as wise in this respect as themselves, there would be an end to the show and the profits with it. The difference between a republican and a courtier with respect to monarchy, is that the one opposes monarchy, believing it to be something; and the other laughs at it, knowing it to be nothing.

As I used sometimes to correspond with Mr. Burke believing him then to be a man of sounder principles than his book shows him to be, I wrote to him last winter from Paris, and gave him an account how prosperously matters were going on. Among other subjects in that letter, I referred to the happy situation the National Assembly were placed in; that they had taken ground on which their moral duty and their political interest were united. They have not to hold out a language which they do not themselves believe, for the fraudulent purpose of making others believe it. Their station requires no artifice to support it, and can only be maintained by enlightening mankind. It is not their interest to cherish ignorance, but to dispel it. They are not in the case of a ministerial or an opposition party in England, who, though they are opposed, are still united to keep up the common mystery. The National Assembly must throw open a magazine of light. It must show man the proper character of man; and the nearer it can bring him to that standard, the stronger the National Assembly becomes.

In contemplating the French Constitution, we see in it a rational order of things. The principles harmonise with the forms, and both with their origin. It may perhaps be said as an excuse for bad forms, that they are nothing more than forms; but this is a mistake. Forms grow out of principles, and operate to continue the principles they grow from. It is impossible to practise a bad form on anything but a bad principle. It cannot be ingrafted on a good one; and wherever the forms in any government are bad, it is a certain indication that the principles are bad also.

I will here finally close this subject. I began it by remarking that Mr. Burke had voluntarily declined going into a comparison of the English and French Constitutions. He apologises (in page 241) for not doing it, by saying that he had not time. Mr. Burke's book was upwards of eight months in hand, and is extended to a volume of three hundred and sixty-six pages. As his omission does injury to his cause, his apology makes it worse; and men on the English side of the water will begin to consider, whether there is not some radical defect in what is called the English constitution, that made it necessary for Mr. Burke to suppress the comparison, to avoid bringing it into view.

As Mr. Burke has not written on constitutions so neither has he written on the French Revolution. He gives no account of its commencement or its progress. He only expresses his wonder. "It looks," says he, "to me, as if I were in a great crisis, not of the affairs of France alone, but of all Europe, perhaps of more than Europe. All circumstances taken together, the French Revolution is the most astonishing that has hitherto happened in the world."

As wise men are astonished at foolish things, and other people at wise ones, I know not on which ground to account for Mr. Burke's astonishment; but certain it is, that he does not understand the French Revolution. It has apparently burst forth like a creation from a chaos, but it is no more than the consequence of a mental revolution priorily existing in France. The mind of the nation had changed beforehand, and the new order of things has naturally followed the new order of thoughts. I will here, as concisely as I can, trace out the growth of the French Revolution, and mark the circumstances that have contributed to produce it.

The despotism of Louis XIV., united with the gaiety of his Court, and the gaudy ostentation of his character, had so humbled, and at the same time so fascinated the mind of France, that the people appeared to have lost all sense of their own dignity, in contemplating that of their Grand Monarch; and the whole reign of Louis XV., remarkable only for weakness and effeminacy, made no other alteration than that of spreading a sort of lethargy over the nation, from which it showed no disposition to rise.

The only signs which appeared to the spirit of Liberty during those periods, are to be found in the writings of the French philosophers. Montesquieu, President of the Parliament of Bordeaux, went as far as a writer under a despotic government could well proceed; and being obliged to divide himself between principle and prudence, his mind often appears under a veil, and we ought to give him credit for more than he has expressed.

Voltaire, who was both the flatterer and the satirist of despotism, took another line. His forte lay in exposing and ridiculing the superstitions which priest-craft, united with state-craft, had interwoven with governments. It was not from the purity of his principles, or his love of mankind (for satire and philanthropy are not naturally concordant), but from his strong capacity of seeing folly in its true shape, and his irresistible propensity to expose it, that he made those attacks. They were, however, as formidable as if the motive had been virtuous; and he merits the thanks rather than the esteem of mankind.

On the contrary, we find in the writings of Rousseau, and the Abbe Raynal, a loveliness of sentiment in favour of liberty, that excites respect, and elevates the human faculties; but having raised this animation, they do not direct its operation, and leave the mind in love with an object, without describing the means of possessing it.

The writings of Quesnay, Turgot, and the friends of those authors, are of the serious kind; but they laboured under the same disadvantage with Montesquieu; their writings abound with moral maxims of government, but are rather directed to economise and reform the administration of the government, than the government itself.

But all those writings and many others had their weight; and by the different manner in which they treated the subject of government, Montesquieu by his judgment and knowledge of laws, Voltaire by his wit, Rousseau and Raynal by their animation, and Quesnay and Turgot by their moral maxims and systems of economy, readers of every class met with something to their taste, and a spirit of political inquiry began to diffuse itself through the nation at the time the dispute between England and the then colonies of America broke out.

In the war which France afterwards engaged in, it is very well known that the nation appeared to be before-hand with the French ministry. Each of them had its view; but those views were directed to different objects; the one sought liberty, and the other retaliation on England. The French officers and soldiers who after this went to America, were eventually placed in the school of Freedom, and learned the practice as well as the principles of it by heart.

As it was impossible to separate the military events which took place in America from the principles of the American Revolution, the publication of those events in France necessarily connected themselves with the principles which produced them. Many of the facts were in themselves principles; such as the declaration of American Independence, and the treaty of alliance between France and America, which recognised the natural rights of man, and justified resistance to oppression.

The then Minister of France, Count Vergennes, was not the friend of America; and it is both justice and gratitude to say, that it was the Queen of France who gave the cause of America a fashion at the French Court. Count Vergennes was the personal and social friend of Dr. Franklin; and the Doctor had obtained, by his sensible gracefulness, a sort of influence over him; but with respect to principles Count Vergennes was a despot.

The situation of Dr. Franklin, as Minister from America to France, should be taken into the chain of circumstances. The diplomatic character is of itself the narrowest sphere of society that man can act in. It forbids intercourse by the reciprocity of suspicion; and a diplomatic is a sort of unconnected atom, continually repelling and repelled. But this was not the case with Dr. Franklin. He was not the diplomatic of a Court, but of Man. His character as a philosopher had been long established, and his circle of society in France was universal.

Count Vergennes resisted for a considerable time the publication in France of American constitutions, translated into the French language: but even in this he was obliged to give way to public opinion, and a sort of propriety in admitting to appear what he had undertaken to defend. The American constitutions were to liberty what a grammar is to language: they define its parts of speech, and practically construct them into syntax.

The peculiar situation of the then Marquis de la Fayette is another link in the great chain. He served in America as an American officer under a commission of Congress, and by the universality of his acquaintance was in close friendship with the civil government of America, as well as with the military line. He spoke the language of the country, entered into the discussions on the principles of government, and was always a welcome friend at any election.

When the war closed, a vast reinforcement to the cause of Liberty spread itself over France, by the return of the French officers and soldiers. A knowledge of the practice was then joined to the theory; and all that was wanting to give it real existence was opportunity. Man cannot, properly speaking, make circumstances for his purpose, but he always has it in his power to improve them when they occur, and this was the case in France.

M. Neckar was displaced in May, 1781; and by the ill-management of the finances afterwards, and particularly during the extravagant administration of M. Calonne, the revenue of France, which was nearly twenty-four millions sterling per year, was become unequal to the expenditure, not because the revenue had decreased, but because the expenses had increased; and this was a circumstance which the nation laid hold of to bring forward a Revolution. The English Minister, Mr. Pitt, has frequently alluded to the state of the French finances in his budgets, without understanding the subject. Had the French Parliaments been as ready to register edicts for new taxes as an English Parliament is to grant them, there had been no derangement in the finances, nor yet any Revolution; but this will better explain itself as I proceed.

It will be necessary here to show how taxes were formerly raised in France. The King, or rather the Court or Ministry acting under the use of that name, framed the edicts for taxes at their own discretion, and sent them to the Parliaments to be registered; for until they were registered by the Parliaments they were not operative. Disputes had long existed between the Court and the Parliaments with respect to the extent of the Parliament's authority on this head. The Court insisted that the authority of Parliaments went no farther than to remonstrate or show reasons against the tax, reserving to itself the right of determining whether the reasons were well or ill-founded; and in consequence thereof, either to withdraw the edict as a matter of choice, or to order it to be unregistered as a matter of authority. The Parliaments on their part insisted that they had not only a right to remonstrate, but to reject; and on this ground they were always supported by the nation.

But to return to the order of my narrative. M. Calonne wanted money: and as he knew the sturdy disposition of the Parliaments with respect to new taxes, he ingeniously sought either to approach them by a more gentle means than that of direct authority, or to get over their heads by a manoeuvre; and for this purpose he revived the project of assembling a body of men from the several provinces, under the style of an "Assembly of the Notables," or men of note, who met in 1787, and who were either to recommend taxes to the Parliaments, or to act as a Parliament themselves. An Assembly under this name had been called in 1617.

As we are to view this as the first practical step towards the Revolution, it will be proper to enter into some particulars respecting it. The Assembly of the Notables has in some places been mistaken for the States-General, but was wholly a different body, the States-General being always by election. The persons who composed the Assembly of the Notables were all nominated by the king, and consisted of one hundred and forty members. But as M. Calonne could not depend upon a majority of this Assembly in his favour, he very ingeniously arranged them in such a manner as to make forty-four a majority of one hundred and forty; to effect this he disposed of them into seven separate committees, of twenty members each. Every general question was to be decided, not by a majority of persons, but by a majority of committee, and as eleven votes would make a majority in a committee, and four committees a majority of seven, M. Calonne had good reason to conclude that as forty-four would determine any general question he could not be outvoted. But all his plans deceived him, and in the event became his overthrow.

The then Marquis de la Fayette was placed in the second committee, of which the Count D'Artois was president, and as money matters were the object, it naturally brought into view every circumstance connected with it. M. de la Fayette made a verbal charge against Calonne for selling crown lands to the amount of two millions of livres, in a manner that appeared to be unknown to the king. The Count D'Artois (as if to intimidate, for the Bastille was then in being) asked the Marquis if he would render the charge in writing? He replied that he would. The Count D'Artois did not demand it, but brought a message from the king to that purport. M. de la Fayette then delivered in his charge in writing, to be given to the king, undertaking to support it. No farther proceedings were had upon this affair, but M. Calonne was soon after dismissed by the king and set off to England.

As M. de la Fayette, from the experience of what he had seen in America, was better acquainted with the science of civil government than the generality of the members who composed the Assembly of the Notables could then be, the brunt of the business fell considerably to his share. The plan of those who had a constitution in view was to contend with the Court on the ground of taxes, and some of them openly professed their object. Disputes frequently arose between Count D'Artois and M. de la Fayette upon various subjects. With respect to the arrears already incurred the latter proposed to remedy them by accommodating the expenses to the revenue instead of the revenue to the expenses; and as objects of reform he proposed to abolish the Bastille and all the State prisons throughout the nation (the keeping of which was attended with great expense), and to suppress Lettres de Cachet; but those matters were not then much attended to, and with respect to Lettres de Cachet, a majority of the Nobles appeared to be in favour of them.

On the subject of supplying the Treasury by new taxes the Assembly declined taking the matter on themselves, concurring in the opinion that they had not authority. In a debate on this subject M. de la Fayette said that raising money by taxes could only be done by a National Assembly, freely elected by the people, and acting as their representatives. Do you mean, said the Count D'Artois, the States-General? M. de la Fayette replied that he did. Will you, said the Count D'Artois, sign what you say to be given to the king? The other replied that he would not only do this but that he would go farther, and say that the effectual mode would be for the king to agree to the establishment of a constitution.

As one of the plans had thus failed, that of getting the Assembly to act as a Parliament, the other came into view, that of recommending. On this subject the Assembly agreed to recommend two new taxes to be unregistered by the Parliament: the one a stamp-tax and the other a territorial tax, or sort of land-tax. The two have been estimated at about five millions sterling per annum. We have now to turn our attention to the Parliaments, on whom the business was again devolving.

The Archbishop of Thoulouse (since Archbishop of Sens, and now a Cardinal), was appointed to the administration of the finances soon after the dismission of Calonne. He was also made Prime Minister, an office that did not always exist in France. When this office did not exist, the chief of each of the principal departments transacted business immediately with the King, but when a Prime Minister was appointed they did business only with him. The Archbishop arrived to more state authority than any minister since the Duke de Choiseul, and the nation was strongly disposed in his favour; but by a line of conduct scarcely to be accounted for he perverted every opportunity, turned out a despot, and sunk into disgrace, and a Cardinal.

The Assembly of the Notables having broken up, the minister sent the edicts for the two new taxes recommended by the Assembly to the Parliaments to be unregistered. They of course came first before the Parliament of Paris, who returned for answer: "that with such a revenue as the nation then supported the name of taxes ought not to be mentioned but for the purpose of reducing them"; and threw both the edicts out.*8 On this refusal the Parliament was ordered to Versailles, where, in the usual form, the King held what under the old government was called a Bed of justice; and the two edicts were unregistered in presence of the Parliament by an order of State, in the manner mentioned, earlier. On this the Parliament immediately returned to Paris, renewed their session in form, and ordered the enregistering to be struck out, declaring that everything done at Versailles was illegal. All the members of the Parliament were then served with Lettres de Cachet, and exiled to Troyes; but as they continued as inflexible in exile as before, and as vengeance did not supply the place of taxes, they were after a short time recalled to Paris.

The edicts were again tendered to them, and the Count D'Artois undertook to act as representative of the King. For this purpose he came from Versailles to Paris, in a train of procession; and the Parliament were assembled to receive him. But show and parade had lost their influence in France; and whatever ideas of importance he might set off with, he had to return with those of mortification and disappointment. On alighting from his carriage to ascend the steps of the Parliament House, the crowd (which was numerously collected) threw out trite expressions, saying: "This is Monsieur D'Artois, who wants more of our money to spend." The marked disapprobation which he saw impressed him with apprehensions, and the word Aux armes! (To arms!) was given out by the officer of the guard who attended him. It was so loudly vociferated, that it echoed through the avenues of the house, and produced a temporary confusion. I was then standing in one of the apartments through which he had to pass, and could not avoid reflecting how wretched was the condition of a disrespected man.

He endeavoured to impress the Parliament by great words, and opened his authority by saying, "The King, our Lord and Master." The Parliament received him very coolly, and with their usual determination not to register the taxes: and in this manner the interview ended.

After this a new subject took place: In the various debates and contests which arose between the Court and the Parliaments on the subject of taxes, the Parliament of Paris at last declared that although it had been customary for Parliaments to enregister edicts for taxes as a matter of convenience, the right belonged only to the States-General; and that, therefore, the Parliament could no longer with propriety continue to debate on what it had not authority to act. The King after this came to Paris and held a meeting with the Parliament, in which he continued from ten in the morning till about six in the evening, and, in a manner that appeared to proceed from him as if unconsulted upon with the Cabinet or Ministry, gave his word to the Parliament that the States-General should be convened.

But after this another scene arose, on a ground different from all the former. The Minister and the Cabinet were averse to calling the States-General. They well knew that if the States-General were assembled, themselves must fall; and as the King had not mentioned any time, they hit on a project calculated to elude, without appearing to oppose.

For this purpose, the Court set about making a sort of constitution itself. It was principally the work of M. Lamoignon, the Keeper of the Seals, who afterwards shot himself. This new arrangement consisted in establishing a body under the name of a Cour Pleniere, or Full Court, in which were invested all the powers that the Government might have occasion to make use of. The persons composing this Court were to be nominated by the King; the contended right of taxation was given up on the part of the King, and a new criminal code of laws and law proceedings was substituted in the room of the former. The thing, in many points, contained better principles than those upon which the Government had hitherto been administered; but with respect to the Cour Pleniere, it was no other than a medium through which despotism was to pass, without appearing to act directly from itself.

The Cabinet had high expectations from their new contrivance. The people who were to compose the Cour Pleniere were already nominated; and as it was necessary to carry a fair appearance, many of the best characters in the nation were appointed among the number. It was to commence on May 8, 1788; but an opposition arose to it on two grounds the one as to principle, the other as to form.

On the ground of Principle it was contended that Government had not a right to alter itself, and that if the practice was once admitted it would grow into a principle and be made a precedent for any future alterations the Government might wish to establish: that the right of altering the Government was a national right, and not a right of Government. And on the ground of form it was contended that the Cour Pleniere was nothing more than a larger Cabinet.

The then Duke de la Rochefoucault, Luxembourg, De Noailles, and many others, refused to accept the nomination, and strenuously opposed the whole plan. When the edict for establishing this new court was sent to the Parliaments to be unregistered and put into execution, they resisted also. The Parliament of Paris not only refused, but denied the authority; and the contest renewed itself between the Parliament and the Cabinet more strongly than ever. While the Parliament were sitting in debate on this subject, the Ministry ordered a regiment of soldiers to surround the House and form a blockade. The members sent out for beds and provisions, and lived as in a besieged citadel: and as this had no effect, the commanding officer was ordered to enter the Parliament House and seize them, which he did, and some of the principal members were shut up in different prisons. About the same time a deputation of persons arrived from the province of Brittany to remonstrate against the establishment of the Cour Pleniere, and those the archbishop sent to the Bastille. But the spirit of the nation was not to be overcome, and it was so fully sensible of the strong ground it had taken—that of withholding taxes—that it contented itself with keeping up a sort of quiet resistance, which effectually overthrew all the plans at that time formed against it. The project of the Cour Pleniere was at last obliged to be given up, and the Prime Minister not long afterwards followed its fate, and M. Neckar was recalled into office.

The attempt to establish the Cour Pleniere had an effect upon the nation which itself did not perceive. It was a sort of new form of government that insensibly served to put the old one out of sight and to unhinge it from the superstitious authority of antiquity. It was Government dethroning Government; and the old one, by attempting to make a new one, made a chasm.

The failure of this scheme renewed the subject of convening the State-General; and this gave rise to a new series of politics. There was no settled form for convening the States-General: all that it positively meant was a deputation from what was then called the Clergy, the Noblesse, and the Commons; but their numbers or their proportions had not been always the same. They had been convened only on extraordinary occasions, the last of which was in 1614; their numbers were then in equal proportions, and they voted by orders.

It could not well escape the sagacity of M. Neckar, that the mode of 1614 would answer neither the purpose of the then government nor of the nation. As matters were at that time circumstanced it would have been too contentious to agree upon anything. The debates would have been endless upon privileges and exemptions, in which neither the wants of the Government nor the wishes of the nation for a Constitution would have been attended to. But as he did not choose to take the decision upon himself, he summoned again the Assembly of the Notables and referred it to them. This body was in general interested in the decision, being chiefly of aristocracy and high-paid clergy, and they decided in favor of the mode of 1614. This decision was against the sense of the Nation, and also against the wishes of the Court; for the aristocracy opposed itself to both and contended for privileges independent of either. The subject was then taken up by the Parliament, who recommended that the number of the Commons should be equal to the other two: and they should all sit in one house and vote in one body. The number finally determined on was 1,200; 600 to be chosen by the Commons (and this was less than their proportion ought to have been when their worth and consequence is considered on a national scale), 300 by the Clergy, and 300 by the Aristocracy; but with respect to the mode of assembling themselves, whether together or apart, or the manner in which they should vote, those matters were referred.*9

The election that followed was not a contested election, but an animated one. The candidates were not men, but principles. Societies were formed in Paris, and committees of correspondence and communication established throughout the nation, for the purpose of enlightening the people, and explaining to them the principles of civil government; and so orderly was the election conducted, that it did not give rise even to the rumour of tumult.

The States-General were to meet at Versailles in April 1789, but did not assemble till May. They situated themselves in three separate chambers, or rather the Clergy and Aristocracy withdrew each into a separate chamber. The majority of the Aristocracy claimed what they called the privilege of voting as a separate body, and of giving their consent or their negative in that manner; and many of the bishops and the high-beneficed clergy claimed the same privilege on the part of their Order.

The Tiers Etat (as they were then called) disowned any knowledge of artificial orders and artificial privileges; and they were not only resolute on this point, but somewhat disdainful. They began to consider the Aristocracy as a kind of fungus growing out of the corruption of society, that could not be admitted even as a branch of it; and from the disposition the Aristocracy had shown by upholding Lettres de Cachet, and in sundry other instances, it was manifest that no constitution could be formed by admitting men in any other character than as National Men.

After various altercations on this head, the Tiers Etat or Commons (as they were then called) declared themselves (on a motion made for that purpose by the Abbe Sieyes) "The Representative Of The Nation; and that the two Orders could be considered but as deputies of corporations, and could only have a deliberate voice when they assembled in a national character with the national representatives." This proceeding extinguished the style of Etats Generaux, or States-General, and erected it into the style it now bears, that of L'Assemblee Nationale, or National Assembly.

This motion was not made in a precipitate manner. It was the result of cool deliberation, and concerned between the national representatives and the patriotic members of the two chambers, who saw into the folly, mischief, and injustice of artificial privileged distinctions. It was become evident, that no constitution, worthy of being called by that name, could be established on anything less than a national ground. The Aristocracy had hitherto opposed the despotism of the Court, and affected the language of patriotism; but it opposed it as its rival (as the English Barons opposed King John) and it now opposed the nation from the same motives.

On carrying this motion, the national representatives, as had been concerted, sent an invitation to the two chambers, to unite with them in a national character, and proceed to business. A majority of the clergy, chiefly of the parish priests, withdrew from the clerical chamber, and joined the nation; and forty-five from the other chamber joined in like manner. There is a sort of secret history belonging to this last circumstance, which is necessary to its explanation; it was not judged prudent that all the patriotic members of the chamber styling itself the Nobles, should quit it at once; and in consequence of this arrangement, they drew off by degrees, always leaving some, as well to reason the case, as to watch the suspected. In a little time the numbers increased from forty-five to eighty, and soon after to a greater number; which, with the majority of the clergy, and the whole of the national representatives, put the malcontents in a very diminutive condition.

The King, who, very different from the general class called by that name, is a man of a good heart, showed himself disposed to recommend a union of the three chambers, on the ground the National Assembly had taken; but the malcontents exerted themselves to prevent it, and began now to have another project in view. Their numbers consisted of a majority of the aristocratical chamber, and the minority of the clerical chamber, chiefly of bishops and high-beneficed clergy; and these men were determined to put everything to issue, as well by strength as by stratagem. They had no objection to a constitution; but it must be such a one as themselves should dictate, and suited to their own views and particular situations. On the other hand, the Nation disowned knowing anything of them but as citizens, and was determined to shut out all such up-start pretensions. The more aristocracy appeared, the more it was despised; there was a visible imbecility and want of intellects in the majority, a sort of je ne sais quoi, that while it affected to be more than citizen, was less than man. It lost ground from contempt more than from hatred; and was rather jeered at as an ass, than dreaded as a lion. This is the general character of aristocracy, or what are called Nobles or Nobility, or rather No-ability, in all countries.

The plan of the malcontents consisted now of two things; either to deliberate and vote by chambers (or orders), more especially on all questions respecting a Constitution (by which the aristocratical chamber would have had a negative on any article of the Constitution); or, in case they could not accomplish this object, to overthrow the National Assembly entirely.

To effect one or other of these objects they began to cultivate a friendship with the despotism they had hitherto attempted to rival, and the Count D'Artois became their chief. The king (who has since declared himself deceived into their measures) held, according to the old form, a Bed of Justice, in which he accorded to the deliberation and vote par tete (by head) upon several subjects; but reserved the deliberation and vote upon all questions respecting a constitution to the three chambers separately. This declaration of the king was made against the advice of M. Neckar, who now began to perceive that he was growing out of fashion at Court, and that another minister was in contemplation.

As the form of sitting in separate chambers was yet apparently kept up, though essentially destroyed, the national representatives immediately after this declaration of the King resorted to their own chambers to consult on a protest against it; and the minority of the chamber (calling itself the Nobles), who had joined the national cause, retired to a private house to consult in like manner. The malcontents had by this time concerted their measures with the court, which the Count D'Artois undertook to conduct; and as they saw from the discontent which the declaration excited, and the opposition making against it, that they could not obtain a control over the intended constitution by a separate vote, they prepared themselves for their final object—that of conspiring against the National Assembly, and overthrowing it.

The next morning the door of the chamber of the National Assembly was shut against them, and guarded by troops; and the members were refused admittance. On this they withdrew to a tennis-ground in the neighbourhood of Versailles, as the most convenient place they could find, and, after renewing their session, took an oath never to separate from each other, under any circumstance whatever, death excepted, until they had established a constitution. As the experiment of shutting up the house had no other effect than that of producing a closer connection in the members, it was opened again the next day, and the public business recommenced in the usual place.

We are now to have in view the forming of the new ministry, which was to accomplish the overthrow of the National Assembly. But as force would be necessary, orders were issued to assemble thirty thousand troops, the command of which was given to

Broglio, one of the intended new ministry, who was recalled from the country for this purpose. But as some management was necessary to keep this plan concealed till the moment it should be ready for execution, it is to this policy that a declaration made by Count D'Artois must be attributed, and which is here proper to be introduced.

It could not but occur while the malcontents continued to resort to their chambers separate from the National Assembly, more jealousy would be excited than if they were mixed with it, and that the plot might be suspected. But as they had taken their ground, and now wanted a pretence for quitting it, it was necessary that one should be devised. This was effectually accomplished by a declaration made by the Count D'Artois: "That if they took not a Part in the National Assembly, the life of the king would be endangered": on which they quitted their chambers, and mixed with the Assembly, in one body.

At the time this declaration was made, it was generally treated as a piece of absurdity in Count D'Artois calculated merely to relieve the outstanding members of the two chambers from the diminutive situation they were put in; and if nothing more had followed, this conclusion would have been good. But as things best explain themselves by their events, this apparent union was only a cover to the machinations which were secretly going on; and the declaration accommodated itself to answer that purpose. In a little time the National Assembly found itself surrounded by troops, and thousands more were daily arriving. On this a very strong declaration was made by the National Assembly to the King, remonstrating on the impropriety of the measure, and demanding the reason. The King, who was not in the secret of this business, as himself afterwards declared, gave substantially for answer, that he had no other object in view than to preserve the public tranquility, which appeared to be much disturbed.

But in a few days from this time the plot unravelled itself M. Neckar and the ministry were displaced, and a new one formed of the enemies of the Revolution; and Broglio, with between twenty-five and thirty thousand foreign troops, was arrived to support them. The mask was now thrown off, and matters were come to a crisis. The event was that in a space of three days the new ministry and their abettors found it prudent to fly the nation; the Bastille was taken, and Broglio and his foreign troops dispersed, as is already related in the former part of this work.

There are some curious circumstances in the history of this short-lived ministry, and this short-lived attempt at a counter-revolution. The Palace of Versailles, where the Court was sitting, was not more than four hundred yards distant from the hall where the National Assembly was sitting. The two places were at this moment like the separate headquarters of two combatant armies; yet the Court was as perfectly ignorant of the information which had arrived from Paris to the National Assembly, as if it had resided at an hundred miles distance. The then Marquis de la Fayette, who (as has been already mentioned) was chosen to preside in the National Assembly on this particular occasion, named by order of the Assembly three successive deputations to the king, on the day and up to the evening on which the Bastille was taken, to inform and confer with him on the state of affairs; but the ministry, who knew not so much as that it was attacked, precluded all communication, and were solacing themselves how dextrously they had succeeded; but in a few hours the accounts arrived so thick and fast that they had to start from their desks and run. Some set off in one disguise, and some in another, and none in their own character. Their anxiety now was to outride the news, lest they should be stopt, which, though it flew fast, flew not so fast as themselves.

It is worth remarking that the National Assembly neither pursued those fugitive conspirators, nor took any notice of them, nor sought to retaliate in any shape whatever. Occupied with establishing a constitution founded on the Rights of Man and the Authority of the People, the only authority on which Government has a right to exist in any country, the National Assembly felt none of those mean passions which mark the character of impertinent governments, founding themselves on their own authority, or on the absurdity of hereditary succession. It is the faculty of the human mind to become what it contemplates, and to act in unison with its object.

The conspiracy being thus dispersed, one of the first works of the National Assembly, instead of vindictive proclamations, as has been the case with other governments, was to publish a declaration of the Rights of Man, as the basis on which the new constitution was to be built, and which is here subjoined:

Declaration

Of The

Rights Of Man And Of Citizens

By The National Assembly Of France

The representatives of the people of France, formed into a National Assembly, considering that ignorance, neglect, or contempt of human rights, are the sole causes of public misfortunes and corruptions of Government, have resolved to set forth in a solemn declaration, these natural, imprescriptible, and inalienable rights: that this declaration being constantly present to the minds of the members of the body social, they may be forever kept attentive to their rights and their duties; that the acts of the legislative and executive powers of Government, being capable of being every moment compared with the end of political institutions, may be more respected; and also, that the future claims of the citizens, being directed by simple and incontestable principles, may always tend to the maintenance of the Constitution, and the general happiness.

For these reasons the National Assembly doth recognize and declare, in the presence of the Supreme Being, and with the hope of his blessing and favour, the following sacred rights of men and of citizens:

One: Men are born, and always continue, free and equal in respect of their Rights. Civil distinctions, therefore, can be founded only on Public Utility.

Two: The end of all Political associations is the Preservation of the Natural and Imprescriptible Rights of Man; and these rights are Liberty, Property, Security, and Resistance of Oppression.

Three: The Nation is essentially the source of all Sovereignty; nor can any individual, or any body of Men, be entitled to any authority which is not expressly derived from it.

Four: Political Liberty consists in the power of doing whatever does not Injure another. The exercise of the Natural Rights of every Man, has no other limits than those which are necessary to secure to every other Man the Free exercise of the same Rights; and these limits are determinable only by the Law.

Five: The Law ought to Prohibit only actions hurtful to Society. What is not Prohibited by the Law should not be hindered; nor should anyone be compelled to that which the Law does not Require.

Six: the Law is an expression of the Will of the Community. All Citizens have a right to concur, either personally or by their Representatives, in its formation. It Should be the same to all, whether it protects or punishes; and all being equal in its sight, are equally eligible to all Honours, Places, and employments, according to their different abilities, without any other distinction than that created by their Virtues and talents.

Seven: No Man should be accused, arrested, or held in confinement, except in cases determined by the Law, and according to the forms which it has prescribed. All who promote, solicit, execute, or cause to be executed, arbitrary orders, ought to be punished, and every Citizen called upon, or apprehended by virtue of the Law, ought immediately to obey, and renders himself culpable by resistance.

Eight: The Law ought to impose no other penalties but such as are absolutely and evidently necessary; and no one ought to be punished, but in virtue of a Law promulgated before the offence, and Legally applied.

Nine: Every Man being presumed innocent till he has been convicted, whenever his detention becomes indispensable, all rigour to him, more than is necessary to secure his person, ought to be provided against by the Law.

Ten: No Man ought to be molested on account of his opinions, not even on account of his Religious opinions, provided his avowal of them does not disturb the Public Order established by the Law.

Eleven: The unrestrained communication of thoughts and opinions being one of the Most Precious Rights of Man, every Citizen may speak, write, and publish freely, provided he is responsible for the abuse of this Liberty, in cases determined by the Law.

Twelve: A Public force being necessary to give security to the Rights of Men and of Citizens, that force is instituted for the benefit of the Community and not for the particular benefit of the persons to whom it is intrusted.

Thirteen: A common contribution being necessary for the support of the Public force, and for defraying the other expenses of Government, it ought to be divided equally among the Members of the Community, according to their abilities.

Fourteen: every Citizen has a Right, either by himself or his Representative, to a free voice in determining the necessity of Public Contributions, the appropriation of them, and their amount, mode of assessment, and duration.

Fifteen: every Community has a Right to demand of all its agents an account of their conduct.

Sixteen: every Community in which a Separation of Powers and a Security of Rights is not Provided for, wants a Constitution.

Seventeen: The Right to Property being inviolable and sacred, no one ought to be deprived of it, except in cases of evident Public necessity, legally ascertained, and on condition of a previous just Indemnity.

OBSERVATIONS ON THE DECLARATION OF RIGHTS

The first three articles comprehend in general terms the whole of a Declaration of Rights, all the succeeding articles either originate from them or follow as elucidations. The 4th, 5th, and 6th define more particularly what is only generally expressed in the 1st, 2nd, and 3rd.

The 7th, 8th, 9th, 10th, and 11th articles are declaratory of principles upon which laws shall be constructed, conformable to rights already declared. But it is questioned by some very good people in France, as well as in other countries, whether the 10th article sufficiently guarantees the right it is intended to accord with; besides which it takes off from the divine dignity of religion, and weakens its operative force upon the mind, to make it a subject of human laws. It then presents itself to man like light intercepted by a cloudy medium, in which the source of it is obscured from his sight, and he sees nothing to reverence in the dusky ray.*10

The remaining articles, beginning with the twelfth, are substantially contained in the principles of the preceding articles; but in the particular situation in which France then was, having to undo what was wrong, as well as to set up what was right, it was proper to be more particular than what in another condition of things would be necessary.

While the Declaration of Rights was before the National Assembly some of its members remarked that if a declaration of rights were published it should be accompanied by a Declaration of Duties. The observation discovered a mind that reflected, and it only erred by not reflecting far enough. A Declaration of Rights is, by reciprocity, a Declaration of Duties also. Whatever is my right as a man is also the right of another; and it becomes my duty to guarantee as well as to possess.

The three first articles are the base of Liberty, as well individual as national; nor can any country be called free whose government does not take its beginning from the principles they contain, and continue to preserve them pure; and the whole of the Declaration of Rights is of more value to the world, and will do more good, than all the laws and statutes that have yet been promulgated.

In the declaratory exordium which prefaces the Declaration of Rights we see the solemn and majestic spectacle of a nation opening its commission, under the auspices of its Creator, to establish a Government, a scene so new, and so transcendantly unequalled by anything in the European world, that the name of a Revolution is diminutive of its character, and it rises into a Regeneration of man. What are the present Governments of Europe but a scene of iniquity and oppression? What is that of England? Do not its own inhabitants say it is a market where every man has his price, and where corruption is common traffic at the expense of a deluded people? No wonder, then, that the French Revolution is traduced. Had it confined itself merely to the destruction of flagrant despotism perhaps Mr. Burke and some others had been silent. Their cry now is, "It has gone too far"— that is, it has gone too far for them. It stares corruption in the face, and the venal tribe are all alarmed. Their fear discovers itself in their outrage, and they are but publishing the groans of a wounded vice. But from such opposition the French Revolution, instead of suffering, receives an homage. The more it is struck the more sparks it will emit; and the fear is it will not be struck enough. It has nothing to dread from attacks; truth has given it an establishment, and time will record it with a name as lasting as his own.

Having now traced the progress of the French Revolution through most of its principal stages, from its commencement to the taking of the Bastille, and its establishment by the Declaration of Rights, I will close the subject with the energetic apostrophe of M. de la Fayette, "May this great monument, raised to Liberty, serve as a lesson to the oppressor, and an example to the oppressed!"*11

MISCELLANEOUS CHAPTER

To prevent interrupting the argument in the preceding part of this work, or the narrative that follows it, I reserved some observations to be thrown together in a Miscellaneous Chapter; by which variety might not be censured for confusion. Mr. Burke's book is all Miscellany. His intention was to make an attack on the French Revolution; but instead of proceeding with an orderly arrangement, he has stormed it with a mob of ideas tumbling over and destroying one another.

But this confusion and contradiction in Mr. Burke's Book is easily accounted for.—When a man in a wrong cause attempts to steer his course by anything else than some polar truth or principle, he is sure to be lost. It is beyond the compass of his capacity to keep all the parts of an argument together, and make them unite in one issue, by any other means than having this guide always in view. Neither memory nor invention will supply the want of it. The former fails him, and the latter betrays him.

Notwithstanding the nonsense, for it deserves no better name, that Mr. Burke has asserted about hereditary rights, and hereditary succession, and that a Nation has not a right to form a Government of itself; it happened to fall in his way to give some account of what Government is. "Government," says he, "is a contrivance of human wisdom."

Admitting that government is a contrivance of human wisdom, it must necessarily follow, that hereditary succession, and hereditary rights (as they are called), can make no part of it, because it is impossible to make wisdom hereditary; and on the other hand, that cannot be a wise contrivance, which in its operation may commit the government of a nation to the wisdom of an idiot. The ground which Mr. Burke now takes is fatal to every part of his cause. The argument changes from hereditary rights to hereditary wisdom; and the question is, Who is the wisest man? He must now show that every one in the line of hereditary succession was a Solomon, or his title is not good to be a king. What a stroke has Mr. Burke now made! To use a sailor's phrase, he has swabbed the deck, and scarcely left a name legible in the list of Kings; and he has mowed down and thinned the House of Peers, with a scythe as formidable as Death and Time.

But Mr. Burke appears to have been aware of this retort; and he has taken care to guard against it, by making government to be not only a contrivance of human wisdom, but a monopoly of wisdom. He puts the nation as fools on one side, and places his government of wisdom, all wise men of Gotham, on the other side; and he then proclaims, and says that "Men have a Right that their Wants should be provided for by this wisdom." Having thus made proclamation, he next proceeds to explain to them what their wants are, and also what their rights are. In this he has succeeded dextrously, for he makes their wants to be a want of wisdom; but as this is cold comfort, he then informs them, that they have a right (not to any of the wisdom) but to be governed by it; and in order to impress them with a solemn reverence for this monopoly-government of wisdom, and of its vast capacity for all purposes, possible or impossible, right or wrong, he proceeds with astrological mysterious importance, to tell to them its powers in these words: "The rights of men in government are their advantages; and these are often in balance between differences of good; and in compromises sometimes between good and evil, and sometimes between evil and evil. Political reason is a computing principle; adding—subtracting—multiplying—and dividing, morally and not metaphysically or mathematically, true moral denominations."

As the wondering audience, whom Mr. Burke supposes himself talking to, may not understand all this learned jargon, I will undertake to be its interpreter. The meaning, then, good people, of all this, is: That government is governed by no principle whatever; that it can make evil good, or good evil, just as it pleases. In short, that government is arbitrary power.

But there are some things which Mr. Burke has forgotten. First, he has not shown where the wisdom originally came from: and secondly, he has not shown by what authority it first began to act. In the manner he introduces the matter, it is either government stealing wisdom, or wisdom stealing government. It is without an origin, and its powers without authority. In short, it is usurpation.

Whether it be from a sense of shame, or from a consciousness of some radical defect in a government necessary to be kept out of sight, or from both, or from any other cause, I undertake not to determine, but so it is, that a monarchical reasoner never traces government to its source, or from its source. It is one of the shibboleths by which he may be known. A thousand years hence, those who shall live in America or France, will look back with contemplative pride on the origin of their government, and say, This was the work of our glorious ancestors! But what can a monarchical talker say? What has he to exult in? Alas he has nothing. A certain something forbids him to look back to a beginning, lest some robber, or some Robin Hood, should rise from the long obscurity of time and say, I am the origin. Hard as Mr. Burke laboured at the Regency Bill and Hereditary Succession two years ago, and much as he dived for precedents, he still had not boldness enough to bring up William of Normandy, and say, There is the head of the list! there is the fountain of honour! the son of a prostitute, and the plunderer of the English nation.

The opinions of men with respect to government are changing fast in all countries. The Revolutions of America and France have thrown a beam of light over the world, which reaches into man. The enormous expense of governments has provoked people to think, by making them feel; and when once the veil begins to rend, it admits not of repair. Ignorance is of a peculiar nature: once dispelled, it is impossible to re-establish it. It is not originally a thing of itself, but is only the absence of knowledge; and though man may be kept ignorant, he cannot be made ignorant. The mind, in discovering truth, acts in the same manner as it acts through the eye in discovering objects; when once any object has been seen, it is impossible to put the mind back to the same condition it was in before it saw it. Those who talk of a counter-revolution in France, show how little they understand of man. There does not exist in the compass of language an arrangement of words to express so much as the means of effecting a counter-revolution. The means must be an obliteration of knowledge; and it has never yet been discovered how to make man unknow his knowledge, or unthink his thoughts.

Mr. Burke is labouring in vain to stop the progress of knowledge; and it comes with the worse grace from him, as there is a certain transaction known in the city which renders him suspected of being a pensioner in a fictitious name. This may account for some strange doctrine he has advanced in his book, which though he points it at the Revolution Society, is effectually directed against the whole nation.

"The King of England," says he, "holds his crown (for it does not belong to the Nation, according to Mr. Burke) in contempt of the choice of the Revolution Society, who have not a single vote for a king among them either individually or collectively; and his Majesty's heirs each in their time and order, will come to the Crown with the same contempt of their choice, with which his Majesty has succeeded to that which he now wears."

As to who is King in England, or elsewhere, or whether there is any King at all, or whether the people choose a Cherokee chief, or a Hessian hussar for a King, it is not a matter that I trouble myself about—be that to themselves; but with respect to the doctrine, so far as it relates to the Rights of Men and Nations, it is as abominable as anything ever uttered in the most enslaved country under heaven. Whether it sounds worse to my ear, by not being accustomed to hear such despotism, than what it does to another person, I am not so well a judge of; but of its abominable principle I am at no loss to judge.

It is not the Revolution Society that Mr. Burke means; it is the Nation, as well in its original as in its representative character; and he has taken care to make himself understood, by saying that they have not a vote either collectively or individually. The Revolution Society is composed of citizens of all denominations, and of members of both the Houses of Parliament; and consequently, if there is not a right to a vote in any of the characters, there can be no right to any either in the nation or in its Parliament. This ought to be a caution to every country how to import foreign families to be kings. It is somewhat curious to observe, that although the people of England had been in the habit of talking about kings, it is always a Foreign House of Kings; hating Foreigners yet governed by them.—It is now the House of Brunswick, one of the petty tribes of Germany.

It has hitherto been the practice of the English Parliaments to regulate what was called the succession (taking it for granted that the Nation then continued to accord to the form of annexing a monarchical branch of its government; for without this the Parliament could not have had authority to have sent either to Holland or to Hanover, or to impose a king upon the nation against its will). And this must be the utmost limit to which Parliament can go upon this case; but the right of the Nation goes to the whole case, because it has the right of changing its whole form of government. The right of a Parliament is only a right in trust, a right by delegation, and that but from a very small part of the Nation; and one of its Houses has not even this. But the right of the Nation is an original right, as universal as taxation. The nation is the paymaster of everything, and everything must conform to its general will.

I remember taking notice of a speech in what is called the English House of Peers, by the then Earl of Shelburne, and I think it was at the time he was Minister, which is applicable to this case. I do not directly charge my memory with every particular; but the words and the purport, as nearly as I remember, were these: "That the form of a Government was a matter wholly at the will of the Nation at all times, that if it chose a monarchical form, it had a right to have it so; and if it afterwards chose to be a Republic, it had a right to be a Republic, and to say to a King, 'We have no longer any occasion for you.'"

When Mr. Burke says that "His Majesty's heirs and successors, each in their time and order, will come to the crown with the same content of their choice with which His Majesty had succeeded to that he wears," it is saying too much even to the humblest individual in the country; part of whose daily labour goes towards making up the million sterling a-year, which the country gives the person it styles a king. Government with insolence is despotism; but when contempt is added it becomes worse; and to pay for contempt is the excess of slavery. This species of government comes from Germany; and reminds me of what one of the Brunswick soldiers told me, who was taken prisoner by, the Americans in the late war: "Ah!" said he, "America is a fine free country, it is worth the people's fighting for; I know the difference by knowing my own: in my country, if the prince says eat straw, we eat straw." God help that country, thought I, be it England or elsewhere, whose liberties are to be protected by German principles of government, and Princes of Brunswick!

As Mr. Burke sometimes speaks of England, sometimes of France, and sometimes of the world, and of government in general, it is difficult to answer his book without apparently meeting him on the same ground. Although principles of Government are general subjects, it is next to impossible, in many cases, to separate them from the idea of place and circumstance, and the more so when circumstances are put for arguments, which is frequently the case with Mr. Burke.

In the former part of his book, addressing himself to the people of France, he says: "No experience has taught us (meaning the English), that in any other course or method than that of a hereditary crown, can our liberties be regularly perpetuated and preserved sacred as our hereditary right." I ask Mr. Burke, who is to take them away? M. de la Fayette, in speaking to France, says: "For a Nation to be free, it is sufficient that she wills it." But Mr. Burke represents England as wanting capacity to take care of itself, and that its liberties must be taken care of by a King holding it in "contempt." If England is sunk to this, it is preparing itself to eat straw, as in Hanover, or in Brunswick. But besides the folly of the declaration, it happens that the facts are all against Mr. Burke. It was by the government being hereditary, that the liberties of the people were endangered. Charles I. and James II. are instances of this truth; yet neither of them went so far as to hold the Nation in contempt.

As it is sometimes of advantage to the people of one country to hear what those of other countries have to say respecting it, it is possible that the people of France may learn something from Mr. Burke's book, and that the people of England may also learn something from the answers it will occasion. When Nations fall out about freedom, a wide field of debate is opened. The argument commences with the rights of war, without its evils, and as knowledge is the object contended for, the party that sustains the defeat obtains the prize.

Mr. Burke talks about what he calls an hereditary crown, as if it were some production of Nature; or as if, like Time, it had a power to operate, not only independently, but in spite of man; or as if it were a thing or a subject universally consented to. Alas! it has none of those properties, but is the reverse of them all. It is a thing in imagination, the propriety of which is more than doubted, and the legality of which in a few years will be denied.

But, to arrange this matter in a clearer view than what general expression can heads under which (what is called) an hereditary crown, or more properly speaking, an hereditary succession to the Government of a Nation, can be considered; which are:

First, The right of a particular Family to establish itself.

Secondly, The right of a Nation to establish a particular Family.

With respect to the first of these heads, that of a Family establishing itself with hereditary powers on its own authority, and independent of the consent of a Nation, all men will concur in calling it despotism; and it would be trespassing on their understanding to attempt to prove it.

But the second head, that of a Nation establishing a particular Family with hereditary powers, does not present itself as despotism on the first reflection; but if men will permit it a second reflection to take place, and carry that reflection forward but one remove out of their own persons to that of their offspring, they will then see that hereditary succession becomes in its consequences the same despotism to others, which they reprobated for themselves. It operates to preclude the consent of the succeeding generations; and the preclusion of consent is despotism. When the person who at any time shall be in possession of a Government, or those who stand in succession to him, shall say to a Nation, I hold this power in "contempt" of you, it signifies not on what authority he pretends to say it. It is no relief, but an aggravation to a person in slavery, to reflect that he was sold by his parent; and as that which heightens the criminality of an act cannot be produced to prove the legality of it, hereditary succession cannot be established as a legal thing.

In order to arrive at a more perfect decision on this head, it will be proper to consider the generation which undertakes to establish a Family with hereditary powers, apart and separate from the generations which are to follow; and also to consider the character in which the first generation acts with respect to succeeding generations.

The generation which first selects a person, and puts him at the head of its Government, either with the title of King, or any other distinction, acts on its own choice, be it wise or foolish, as a free agent for itself The person so set up is not hereditary, but selected and appointed; and the generation who sets him up, does not live under a hereditary government, but under a government of its own choice and establishment. Were the generation who sets him up, and the person so set up, to live for ever, it never could become hereditary succession; and of consequence hereditary succession can only follow on the death of the first parties.

As, therefore, hereditary succession is out of the question with respect to the first generation, we have now to consider the character in which that generation acts with respect to the commencing generation, and to all succeeding ones.

It assumes a character, to which it has neither right nor title. It changes itself from a Legislator to a Testator, and effects to make its Will, which is to have operation after the demise of the makers, to bequeath the Government; and it not only attempts to bequeath, but to establish on the succeeding generation, a new and different form of Government under which itself lived. Itself, as already observed, lived not under a hereditary Government but under a Government of its own choice and establishment; and it now attempts, by virtue of a will and testament (and which it has not authority to make), to take from the commencing generation, and all future ones, the rights and free agency by which itself acted.

But, exclusive of the right which any generation has to act collectively as a testator, the objects to which it applies itself in this case, are not within the compass of any law, or of any will or testament.

The rights of men in society, are neither devisable or transferable, nor annihilable, but are descendable only, and it is not in the power of any generation to intercept finally, and cut off the descent. If the present generation, or any other, are disposed to be slaves, it does not lessen the right of the succeeding generation to be free. Wrongs cannot have a legal descent. When Mr. Burke attempts to maintain that the English nation did at the Revolution of 1688, most solemnly renounce and abdicate their rights for themselves, and for all their posterity for ever, he speaks a language that merits not reply, and which can only excite contempt for his prostitute principles, or pity for his ignorance.

In whatever light hereditary succession, as growing out of the will and testament of some former generation, presents itself, it is an absurdity. A cannot make a will to take from B the property of B, and give it to C; yet this is the manner in which (what is called) hereditary succession by law operates. A certain former generation made a will, to take away the rights of the commencing generation, and all future ones, and convey those rights to a third person, who afterwards comes forward, and tells them, in Mr. Burke's language, that they have no rights, that their rights are already bequeathed to him and that he will govern in contempt of them. From such principles, and such ignorance, good Lord deliver the world!

But, after all, what is this metaphor called a crown, or rather what is monarchy? Is it a thing, or is it a name, or is it a fraud? Is it a "contrivance of human wisdom," or of human craft to obtain money from a nation under specious pretences? Is it a thing necessary to a nation? If it is, in what does that necessity consist, what service does it perform, what is its business, and what are its merits? Does the virtue consist in the metaphor, or in the man? Doth the goldsmith that makes the crown, make the virtue also? Doth it operate like Fortunatus's wishing-cap, or Harlequin's wooden sword? Doth it make a man a conjurer? In fine, what is it? It appears to be something going much out of fashion, falling into ridicule, and rejected in some countries, both as unnecessary and expensive. In America it is considered as an absurdity; and in France it has so far declined, that the goodness of the man, and the respect for his personal character, are the only things that preserve the appearance of its existence.

If government be what Mr. Burke describes it, "a contrivance of human wisdom" I might ask him, if wisdom was at such a low ebb in England, that it was become necessary to import it from Holland and from Hanover? But I will do the country the justice to say, that was not the case; and even if it was it mistook the cargo. The wisdom of every country, when properly exerted, is sufficient for all its purposes; and there could exist no more real occasion in England to have sent for a Dutch Stadtholder, or a German Elector, than there was in America to have done a similar thing. If a country does not understand its own affairs, how is a foreigner to understand them, who knows neither its laws, its manners, nor its language? If there existed a man so transcendently wise above all others, that his wisdom was necessary to instruct a nation, some reason might be offered for monarchy; but when we cast our eyes about a country, and observe how every part understands its own affairs; and when we look around the world, and see that of all men in it, the race of kings are the most insignificant in capacity, our reason cannot fail to ask us—What are those men kept for?

If there is anything in monarchy which we people of America do not understand, I wish Mr. Burke would be so kind as to inform us. I see in America, a government extending over a country ten times as large as England, and conducted with regularity, for a fortieth part of the expense which Government costs in England. If I ask a man in America if he wants a King, he retorts, and asks me if I take him for an idiot? How is it that this difference happens? are we more or less wise than others? I see in America the generality of people living in a style of plenty unknown in monarchical countries; and I see that the principle of its government, which is that of the equal Rights of Man, is making a rapid progress in the world.

If monarchy is a useless thing, why is it kept up anywhere? and if a necessary thing, how can it be dispensed with? That civil government is necessary, all civilized nations will agree; but civil government is republican government. All that part of the government of England which begins with the office of constable, and proceeds through the department of magistrate, quarter-sessions, and general assize, including trial by jury, is republican government. Nothing of monarchy appears in any part of it, except in the name which William the Conqueror imposed upon the English, that of obliging them to call him "Their Sovereign Lord the King."

It is easy to conceive that a band of interested men, such as Placemen, Pensioners, Lords of the bed-chamber, Lords of the kitchen, Lords of the necessary-house, and the Lord knows what besides, can find as many reasons for monarchy as their salaries, paid at the expense of the country, amount to; but if I ask the farmer, the manufacturer, the merchant, the tradesman, and down through all the occupations of life to the common labourer, what service monarchy is to him? he can give me no answer. If I ask him what monarchy is, he believes it is something like a sinecure.

Notwithstanding the taxes of England amount to almost seventeen millions a year, said to be for the expenses of Government, it is still evident that the sense of the Nation is left to govern itself, and does govern itself, by magistrates and juries, almost at its own charge, on republican principles, exclusive of the expense of taxes. The salaries of the judges are almost the only charge that is paid out of the revenue. Considering that all the internal government is executed by the people, the taxes of England ought to be the lightest of any nation in Europe; instead of which, they are the contrary. As this cannot be accounted for on the score of civil government, the subject necessarily extends itself to the monarchical part.

When the people of England sent for George the First (and it would puzzle a wiser man than Mr. Burke to discover for what he could be wanted, or what service he could render), they ought at least to have conditioned for the abandonment of Hanover. Besides the endless German intrigues that must follow from a German Elector being King of England, there is a natural impossibility of uniting in the same person the principles of Freedom and the principles of Despotism, or as it is usually called in England Arbitrary Power. A German Elector is in his electorate a despot; how then could it be expected that he should be attached to principles of liberty in one country, while his interest in another was to be supported by despotism? The union cannot exist; and it might easily have been foreseen that German Electors would make German Kings, or in Mr. Burke's words, would assume government with "contempt." The English have been in the habit of considering a King of England only in the character in which he appears to them; whereas the same person, while the connection lasts, has a home-seat in another country, the interest of which is different to their own, and the principles of the governments in opposition to each other. To such a person England will appear as a town-residence, and the Electorate as the estate. The English may wish, as I believe they do, success to the principles of liberty in France, or in Germany; but a German Elector trembles for the fate of despotism in his electorate; and the Duchy of Mecklenburgh, where the present Queen's family governs, is under the same wretched state of arbitrary power, and the people in slavish vassalage.

There never was a time when it became the English to watch continental intrigues more circumspectly than at the present moment, and to distinguish the politics of the Electorate from the politics of the Nation. The Revolution of France has entirely changed the ground with respect to England and France, as nations; but the German despots, with Prussia at their head, are combining against liberty; and the fondness of Mr. Pitt for office, and the interest which all his family connections have obtained, do not give sufficient security against this intrigue.

As everything which passes in the world becomes matter for history, I will now quit this subject, and take a concise review of the state of parties and politics in England, as Mr. Burke has done in France.

Whether the present reign commenced with contempt, I leave to Mr. Burke: certain, however, it is, that it had strongly that appearance. The animosity of the English nation, it is very well remembered, ran high; and, had the true principles of Liberty been as well understood then as they now promise to be, it is probable the Nation would not have patiently submitted to so much. George the First and Second were sensible of a rival in the remains of the Stuarts; and as they could not but consider themselves as standing on their good behaviour, they had prudence to keep their German principles of government to themselves; but as the Stuart family wore away, the prudence became less necessary.

The contest between rights, and what were called prerogatives, continued to heat the nation till some time after the conclusion of the American War, when all at once it fell a calm—Execration exchanged itself for applause, and Court popularity sprung up like a mushroom in a night.

To account for this sudden transition, it is proper to observe that there are two distinct species of popularity; the one excited by merit, and the other by resentment. As the Nation had formed itself into two parties, and each was extolling the merits of its parliamentary champions for and against prerogative, nothing could operate to give a more general shock than an immediate coalition of the champions themselves. The partisans of each being thus suddenly left in the lurch, and mutually heated with disgust at the measure, felt no other relief than uniting in a common execration against both. A higher stimulus or resentment being thus excited than what the contest on prerogatives occasioned, the nation quitted all former objects of rights and wrongs, and sought only that of gratification. The indignation at the Coalition so effectually superseded the indignation against the Court as to extinguish it; and without any change of principles on the part of the Court, the same people who had reprobated its despotism united with it to revenge themselves on the Coalition Parliament. The case was not, which they liked best, but which they hated most; and the least hated passed for love. The dissolution of the Coalition Parliament, as it afforded the means of gratifying the resentment of the Nation, could not fail to be popular; and from hence arose the popularity of the Court.

Transitions of this kind exhibit a Nation under the government of temper, instead of a fixed and steady principle; and having once committed itself, however rashly, it feels itself urged along to justify by continuance its first proceeding. Measures which at other times it would censure it now approves, and acts persuasion upon itself to suffocate its judgment.

On the return of a new Parliament, the new Minister, Mr. Pitt, found himself in a secure majority; and the Nation gave him credit, not out of regard to himself, but because it had resolved to do it out of resentment to another. He introduced himself to public notice by a proposed Reform of Parliament, which in its operation would have amounted to a public justification of corruption. The Nation was to be at the expense of buying up the rotten boroughs, whereas it ought to punish the persons who deal in the traffic.

Passing over the two bubbles of the Dutch business and the million a-year to sink the national debt, the matter which most presents itself, is the affair of the Regency. Never, in the course of my observation, was delusion more successfully acted, nor a nation more completely deceived. But, to make this appear, it will be necessary to go over the circumstances.

Mr. Fox had stated in the House of Commons, that the Prince of Wales, as heir in succession, had a right in himself to assume the Government. This was opposed by Mr. Pitt; and, so far as the opposition was confined to the doctrine, it was just. But the principles which Mr. Pitt maintained on the contrary side were as bad, or worse in their extent, than those of Mr. Fox; because they went to establish an aristocracy over the nation, and over the small representation it has in the House of Commons. Wheth.er the English form of Government be good or bad, is not in this case the question; but, taking it as it stands, without regard to its merits or demerits, Mr. Pitt was farther from the point than Mr. Fox. It is supposed to consist of three parts:—while therefore the Nation is disposed to continue this form, the parts have a national standing, independent of each other, and are not the creatures of each other. Had Mr. Fox passed through Parliament, and said that the person alluded to claimed on the ground of the Nation, Mr. Pitt must then have contended what he called the right of the Parliament against the right of the Nation. By the appearance which the contest made, Mr. Fox took the hereditary ground, and Mr. Pitt the Parliamentary ground; but the fact is, they both took hereditary ground, and Mr. Pitt took the worst of the two. What is called the Parliament is made up of two Houses, one of which is more hereditary, and more beyond the control of the Nation than what the Crown (as it is called) is supposed to be. It is an hereditary aristocracy, assuming and asserting indefeasible, irrevocable rights and authority, wholly independent of the Nation. Where, then, was the merited popularity of exalting this hereditary power over another hereditary power less independent of the Nation than what itself assumed to be, and of absorbing the rights of the Nation into a House over which it has neither election nor control?

The general impulse of the Nation was right; but it acted without reflection. It approved the opposition made to the right set up by Mr. Fox, without perceiving that Mr. Pitt was supporting another indefeasible right more remote from the Nation, in opposition to it.

With respect to the House of Commons, it is elected but by a small part of the Nation; but were the election as universal as taxation, which it ought to be, it would still be only the organ of the Nation, and cannot possess inherent rights.—When the National Assembly of France resolves a matter, the resolve is made in right of the Nation; but Mr. Pitt, on all national questions, so far as they refer to the House of Commons, absorbs the rights of the Nation into the organ, and makes the organ into a Nation, and the Nation itself into a cypher.

In a few words, the question on the Regency was a question of a million a-year, which is appropriated to the executive department: and Mr. Pitt could not possess himself of any management of this sum, without setting up the supremacy of Parliament; and when this was accomplished, it was indifferent who should be Regent, as he must be Regent at his own cost. Among the curiosities which this contentious debate afforded, was that of making the Great Seal into a King, the affixing of which to an act was to be royal authority. If, therefore, Royal Authority is a Great Seal, it consequently is in itself nothing; and a good Constitution would be of infinitely more value to the Nation than what the three Nominal Powers, as they now stand, are worth.

The continual use of the word Constitution in the English Parliament shows there is none; and that the whole is merely a form of government without a Constitution, and constituting itself with what powers it pleases. If there were a Constitution, it certainly could be referred to; and the debate on any constitutional point would terminate by producing the Constitution. One member says this is Constitution, and another says that is Constitution—To-day it is one thing; and to-morrow something else—while the maintaining of the debate proves there is none. Constitution is now the cant word of Parliament, tuning itself to the ear of the Nation. Formerly it was the universal supremacy of Parliament—the omnipotence of Parliament: But since the progress of Liberty in France, those phrases have a despotic harshness in their note; and the English Parliament have catched the fashion from the National Assembly, but without the substance, of speaking of Constitution.

As the present generation of the people in England did not make the Government, they are not accountable for any of its defects; but, that sooner or later, it must come into their hands to undergo a constitutional reformation, is as certain as that the same thing has happened in France. If France, with a revenue of nearly twenty-four millions sterling, with an extent of rich and fertile country above four times larger than England, with a population of twenty-four millions of inhabitants to support taxation, with upwards of ninety millions sterling of gold and silver circulating in the nation, and with a debt less than the present debt of England—still found it necessary, from whatever cause, to come to a settlement of its affairs, it solves the problem of funding for both countries.

It is out of the question to say how long what is called the English constitution has lasted, and to argue from thence how long it is to last; the question is, how long can the funding system last? It is a thing but of modern invention, and has not yet continued beyond the life of a man; yet in that short space it has so far accumulated, that, together with the current expenses, it requires an amount of taxes at least equal to the whole landed rental of the nation in acres to defray the annual expenditure. That a government could not have always gone on by the same system which has been followed for the last seventy years, must be evident to every man; and for the same reason it cannot always go on.

The funding system is not money; neither is it, properly speaking, credit. It, in effect, creates upon paper the sum which it appears to borrow, and lays on a tax to keep the imaginary capital alive by the payment of interest and sends the annuity to market, to be sold for paper already in circulation. If any credit is given, it is to the disposition of the people to pay the tax, and not to the government, which lays it on. When this disposition expires, what is supposed to be the credit of Government expires with it. The instance of France under the former Government shows that it is impossible to compel the payment of taxes by force, when a whole nation is determined to take its stand upon that ground.

Mr. Burke, in his review of the finances of France, states the quantity of gold and silver in France, at about eighty-eight millions sterling. In doing this, he has, I presume, divided by the difference of exchange, instead of the standard of twenty-four livres to a pound sterling; for M. Neckar's statement, from which Mr. Burke's is taken, is two thousand two hundred millions of livres, which is upwards of ninety-one millions and a half sterling.

M. Neckar in France, and Mr. George Chalmers at the Office of Trade and Plantation in England, of which Lord Hawkesbury is president, published nearly about the same time (1786) an account of the quantity of money in each nation, from the returns of the Mint of each nation. Mr. Chalmers, from the returns of the English Mint at the Tower of London, states the quantity of money in England, including Scotland and Ireland, to be twenty millions sterling.*12

M. Neckar*13 says that the amount of money in France, recoined from the old coin which was called in, was two thousand five hundred millions of livres (upwards of one hundred and four millions sterling); and, after deducting for waste, and what may be in the West Indies and other possible circumstances, states the circulation quantity at home to be ninety-one millions and a half sterling; but, taking it as Mr. Burke has put it, it is sixty-eight millions more than the national quantity in England.

That the quantity of money in France cannot be under this sum, may at once be seen from the state of the French Revenue, without referring to the records of the French Mint for proofs. The revenue of France, prior to the Revolution, was nearly twenty-four millions sterling; and as paper had then no existence in France the whole revenue was collected upon gold and silver; and it would have been impossible to have collected such a quantity of revenue upon a less national quantity than M. Neckar has stated. Before the establishment of paper in England, the revenue was about a fourth part of the national amount of gold and silver, as may be known by referring to the revenue prior to King William, and the quantity of money stated to be in the nation at that time, which was nearly as much as it is now.

It can be of no real service to a nation, to impose upon itself, or to permit itself to be imposed upon; but the prejudices of some, and the imposition of others, have always represented France as a nation possessing but little money—whereas the quantity is not only more than four times what the quantity is in England, but is considerably greater on a proportion of numbers. To account for this deficiency on the part of England, some reference should be had to the English system of funding. It operates to multiply paper, and to substitute it in the room of money, in various shapes; and the more paper is multiplied, the more opportunities are offered to export the specie; and it admits of a possibility (by extending it to small notes) of increasing paper till there is no money left.

I know this is not a pleasant subject to English readers; but the matters I am going to mention, are so important in themselves, as to require the attention of men interested in money transactions of a public nature. There is a circumstance stated by M. Neckar, in his treatise on the administration of the finances, which has never been attended to in England, but which forms the only basis whereon to estimate the quantity of money (gold and silver) which ought to be in every nation in Europe, to preserve a relative proportion with other nations.

Lisbon and Cadiz are the two ports into which (money) gold and silver from South America are imported, and which afterwards divide and spread themselves over Europe by means of commerce, and increase the quantity of money in all parts of Europe. If, therefore, the amount of the annual importation into Europe can be known, and the relative proportion of the foreign commerce of the several nations by which it can be distributed can be ascertained, they give a rule sufficiently true, to ascertain the quantity of money which ought to be found in any nation, at any given time.

M. Neckar shows from the registers of Lisbon and Cadiz, that the importation of gold and silver into Europe, is five millions sterling annually. He has not taken it on a single year, but on an average of fifteen succeeding years, from 1763 to 1777, both inclusive; in which time, the amount was one thousand eight hundred million livres, which is seventy-five millions sterling.*14

From the commencement of the Hanover succession in 1714 to the time Mr. Chalmers published, is seventy-two years; and the quantity imported into Europe, in that time, would be three hundred and sixty millions sterling.

If the foreign commerce of Great Britain be stated at a sixth part of what the whole foreign commerce of Europe amounts to (which is probably an inferior estimation to what the gentlemen at the Exchange would allow) the proportion which Britain should draw by commerce of this sum, to keep herself on a proportion with the rest of Europe, would be also a sixth part which is sixty millions sterling; and if the same allowance for waste and accident be made for England which M. Neckar makes for France, the quantity remaining after these deductions would be fifty-two millions; and this sum ought to have been in the nation (at the time Mr. Chalmers published), in addition to the sum which was in the nation at the commencement of the Hanover succession, and to have made in the whole at least sixty-six millions sterling; instead of which there were but twenty millions, which is forty-six millions below its proportionate quantity.

As the quantity of gold and silver imported into Lisbon and Cadiz is more exactly ascertained than that of any commodity imported into England, and as the quantity of money coined at the Tower of London is still more positively known, the leading facts do not admit of controversy. Either, therefore, the commerce of England is unproductive of profit, or the gold and silver which it brings in leak continually away by unseen means at the average rate of about three-quarters of a million a year, which, in the course of seventy-two years, accounts for the deficiency; and its absence is supplied by paper.*15

The Revolution of France is attended with many novel circumstances, not only in the political sphere, but in the circle of money transactions. Among others, it shows that a government may be in a state of insolvency and a nation rich. So far as the fact is confined to the late Government of France, it was insolvent; because the nation would no longer support its extravagance, and therefore it could no longer support itself—but with respect to the nation all the means existed. A government may be said to be insolvent every time it applies to the nation to discharge its arrears. The insolvency of the late Government of France and the present of England differed in no other respect than as the dispositions of the people differ. The people of France refused their aid to the old Government; and the people of England submit to taxation without inquiry. What is called the Crown in England has been insolvent several times; the last of which, publicly known, was in May, 1777, when it applied to the nation to discharge upwards of L600,000 private debts, which otherwise it could not pay.

It was the error of Mr. Pitt, Mr. Burke, and all those who were unacquainted with the affairs of France to confound the French nation with the French Government. The French nation, in effect, endeavoured to render the late Government insolvent for the purpose of taking government into its own hands: and it reserved its means for the support of the new Government. In a country of such vast extent and population as France the natural means cannot be wanting, and the political means appear the instant the nation is disposed to permit them. When Mr. Burke, in a speech last winter in the British Parliament, "cast his eyes over the map of Europe, and saw a chasm that once was France," he talked like a dreamer of dreams. The same natural France existed as before, and all the natural means existed with it. The only chasm was that the extinction of despotism had left, and which was to be filled up with the Constitution more formidable in resources than the power which had expired.

Although the French Nation rendered the late Government insolvent, it did not permit the insolvency to act towards the creditors; and the creditors, considering the Nation as the real pay-master, and the Government only as the agent, rested themselves on the nation, in preference to the Government. This appears greatly to disturb Mr. Burke, as the precedent is fatal to the policy by which governments have supposed themselves secure. They have contracted debts, with a view of attaching what is called the monied interest of a Nation to their support; but the example in France shows that the permanent security of the creditor is in the Nation, and not in the Government; and that in all possible revolutions that may happen in Governments, the means are always with the Nation, and the Nation always in existence. Mr. Burke argues that the creditors ought to have abided the fate of the Government which they trusted; but the National Assembly considered them as the creditors of the Nation, and not of the Government—of the master, and not of the steward.

Notwithstanding the late government could not discharge the current expenses, the present government has paid off a great part of the capital. This has been accomplished by two means; the one by lessening the expenses of government, and the other by the sale of the monastic and ecclesiastical landed estates. The devotees and penitent debauchees, extortioners and misers of former days, to ensure themselves a better world than that they were about to leave, had bequeathed immense property in trust to the priesthood for pious uses; and the priesthood kept it for themselves. The National Assembly has ordered it to be sold for the good of the whole nation, and the priesthood to be decently provided for.

In consequence of the revolution, the annual interest of the debt of France will be reduced at least six millions sterling, by paying off upwards of one hundred millions of the capital; which, with lessening the former expenses of government at least three millions, will place France in a situation worthy the imitation of Europe.

Upon a whole review of the subject, how vast is the contrast! While Mr. Burke has been talking of a general bankruptcy in France, the National Assembly has been paying off the capital of its debt; and while taxes have increased near a million a year in England, they have lowered several millions a year in France. Not a word has either Mr. Burke or Mr. Pitt said about the French affairs, or the state of the French finances, in the present Session of Parliament. The subject begins to be too well understood, and imposition serves no longer.

There is a general enigma running through the whole of Mr. Burke's book. He writes in a rage against the National Assembly; but what is he enraged about? If his assertions were as true as they are groundless, and that France by her Revolution, had annihilated her power, and become what he calls a chasm, it might excite the grief of a Frenchman (considering himself as a national man), and provoke his rage against the National Assembly; but why should it excite the rage of Mr. Burke? Alas! it is not the nation of France that Mr. Burke means, but the Court; and every Court in Europe, dreading the same fate, is in mourning. He writes neither in the character of a Frenchman nor an Englishman, but in the fawning character of that creature known in all countries, and a friend to none—a courtier. Whether it be the Court of Versailles, or the Court of St. James, or Carlton-House, or the Court in expectation, signifies not; for the caterpillar principle of all Courts and Courtiers are alike. They form a common policy throughout Europe, detached and separate from the interest of Nations: and while they appear to quarrel, they agree to plunder. Nothing can be more terrible to a Court or Courtier than the Revolution of France. That which is a blessing to Nations is bitterness to them: and as their existence depends on the duplicity of a country, they tremble at the approach of principles, and dread the precedent that threatens their overthrow.

CONCLUSION

Reason and Ignorance, the opposites of each other, influence the great bulk of mankind. If either of these can be rendered sufficiently extensive in a country, the machinery of Government goes easily on. Reason obeys itself; and Ignorance submits to whatever is dictated to it.

The two modes of the Government which prevail in the world, are:

First, Government by election and representation.

Secondly, Government by hereditary succession.

The former is generally known by the name of republic; the latter by that of monarchy and aristocracy.

Those two distinct and opposite forms erect themselves on the two distinct and opposite bases of Reason and Ignorance.—As the exercise of Government requires talents and abilities, and as talents and abilities cannot have hereditary descent, it is evident that hereditary succession requires a belief from man to which his reason cannot subscribe, and which can only be established upon his ignorance; and the more ignorant any country is, the better it is fitted for this species of Government.

On the contrary, Government, in a well-constituted republic, requires no belief from man beyond what his reason can give. He sees the rationale of the whole system, its origin and its operation; and as it is best supported when best understood, the human faculties act with boldness, and acquire, under this form of government, a gigantic manliness.

As, therefore, each of those forms acts on a different base, the one moving freely by the aid of reason, the other by ignorance; we have next to consider, what it is that gives motion to that species of Government which is called mixed Government, or, as it is sometimes ludicrously styled, a Government of this, that and t' other.

The moving power in this species of Government is, of necessity, Corruption. However imperfect election and representation may be in mixed Governments, they still give exercise to a greater portion of reason than is convenient to the hereditary Part; and therefore it becomes necessary to buy the reason up. A mixed Government is an imperfect everything, cementing and soldering the discordant parts together by corruption, to act as a whole. Mr. Burke appears highly disgusted that France, since she had resolved on a revolution, did not adopt what he calls "A British Constitution"; and the regretful manner in which he expresses himself on this occasion implies a suspicion that the British Constitution needed something to keep its defects in countenance.

In mixed Governments there is no responsibility: the parts cover each other till responsibility is lost; and the corruption which moves the machine, contrives at the same time its own escape. When it is laid down as a maxim, that a King can do no wrong, it places him in a state of similar security with that of idiots and persons insane, and responsibility is out of the question with respect to himself. It then descends upon the Minister, who shelters himself under a majority in Parliament, which, by places, pensions, and corruption, he can always command; and that majority justifies itself by the same authority with which it protects the Minister. In this rotatory motion, responsibility is thrown off from the parts, and from the whole.

When there is a Part in a Government which can do no wrong, it implies that it does nothing; and is only the machine of another power, by whose advice and direction it acts. What is supposed to be the King in the mixed Governments, is the Cabinet; and as the Cabinet is always a part of the Parliament, and the members justifying in one character what they advise and act in another, a mixed Government becomes a continual enigma; entailing upon a country by the quantity of corruption necessary to solder the parts, the expense of supporting all the forms of government at once, and finally resolving itself into a Government by Committee; in which the advisers, the actors, the approvers, the justifiers, the persons responsible, and the persons not responsible, are the same persons.

By this pantomimical contrivance, and change of scene and character, the parts help each other out in matters which neither of them singly would assume to act. When money is to be obtained, the mass of variety apparently dissolves, and a profusion of parliamentary praises passes between the parts. Each admires with astonishment, the wisdom, the liberality, the disinterestedness of the other: and all of them breathe a pitying sigh at the burthens of the Nation.

But in a well-constituted republic, nothing of this soldering, praising, and pitying, can take place; the representation being equal throughout the country, and complete in itself, however it may be arranged into legislative and executive, they have all one and the same natural source. The parts are not foreigners to each other, like democracy, aristocracy, and monarchy. As there are no discordant distinctions, there is nothing to corrupt by compromise, nor confound by contrivance. Public measures appeal of themselves to the understanding of the Nation, and, resting on their own merits, disown any flattering applications to vanity. The continual whine of lamenting the burden of taxes, however successfully it may be practised in mixed Governments, is inconsistent with the sense and spirit of a republic. If taxes are necessary, they are of course advantageous; but if they require an apology, the apology itself implies an impeachment. Why, then, is man thus imposed upon, or why does he impose upon himself?

When men are spoken of as kings and subjects, or when Government is mentioned under the distinct and combined heads of monarchy, aristocracy, and democracy, what is it that reasoning man is to understand by the terms? If there really existed in the world two or more distinct and separate elements of human power, we should then see the several origins to which those terms would descriptively apply; but as there is but one species of man, there can be but one element of human power; and that element is man himself. Monarchy, aristocracy, and democracy, are but creatures of imagination; and a thousand such may be contrived as well as three.

From the Revolutions of America and France, and the symptoms that have appeared in other countries, it is evident that the opinion of the world is changing with respect to systems of Government, and that revolutions are not within the compass of political calculations. The progress of time and circumstances, which men assign to the accomplishment of great changes, is too mechanical to measure the force of the mind, and the rapidity of reflection, by which revolutions are generated: All the old governments have received a shock from those that already appear, and which were once more improbable, and are a greater subject of wonder, than a general revolution in Europe would be now.

When we survey the wretched condition of man, under the monarchical and hereditary systems of Government, dragged from his home by one power, or driven by another, and impoverished by taxes more than by enemies, it becomes evident that those systems are bad, and that a general revolution in the principle and construction of Governments is necessary.

What is government more than the management of the affairs of a Nation? It is not, and from its nature cannot be, the property of any particular man or family, but of the whole community, at whose expense it is supported; and though by force and contrivance it has been usurped into an inheritance, the usurpation cannot alter the right of things. Sovereignty, as a matter of right, appertains to the Nation only, and not to any individual; and a Nation has at all times an inherent indefeasible right to abolish any form of Government it finds inconvenient, and to establish such as accords with its interest, disposition and happiness. The romantic and barbarous distinction of men into Kings and subjects, though it may suit the condition of courtiers, cannot that of citizens; and is exploded by the principle upon which Governments are now founded. Every citizen is a member of the Sovereignty, and, as such, can acknowledge no personal subjection; and his obedience can be only to the laws.

When men think of what Government is, they must necessarily suppose it to possess a knowledge of all the objects and matters upon which its authority is to be exercised. In this view of Government, the republican system, as established by America and France, operates to embrace the whole of a Nation; and the knowledge necessary to the interest of all the parts, is to be found in the center, which the parts by representation form: But the old Governments are on a construction that excludes knowledge as well as happiness; government by Monks, who knew nothing of the world beyond the walls of a Convent, is as consistent as government by Kings.

What were formerly called Revolutions, were little more than a change of persons, or an alteration of local circumstances. They rose and fell like things of course, and had nothing in their existence or their fate that could influence beyond the spot that produced them. But what we now see in the world, from the Revolutions of America and France, are a renovation of the natural order of things, a system of principles as universal as truth and the existence of man, and combining moral with political happiness and national prosperity.

"I. Men are born, and always continue, free and equal in respect of their rights. Civil distinctions, therefore, can be founded only on public utility.

"II. The end of all political associations is the preservation of the natural and imprescriptible rights of man; and these rights are liberty, property, security, and resistance of oppression.

"III. The nation is essentially the source of all sovereignty; nor can any Individual, or Any Body Of Men, be entitled to any authority which is not expressly derived from it."

In these principles, there is nothing to throw a Nation into confusion by inflaming ambition. They are calculated to call forth wisdom and abilities, and to exercise them for the public good, and not for the emolument or aggrandisement of particular descriptions of men or families. Monarchical sovereignty, the enemy of mankind, and the source of misery, is abolished; and the sovereignty itself is restored to its natural and original place, the Nation. Were this the case throughout Europe, the cause of wars would be taken away.

It is attributed to Henry the Fourth of France, a man of enlarged and benevolent heart, that he proposed, about the year 1610, a plan for abolishing war in Europe. The plan consisted in constituting an European Congress, or as the French authors style it, a Pacific Republic; by appointing delegates from the several Nations who were to act as a Court of arbitration in any disputes that might arise between nation and nation.

Had such a plan been adopted at the time it was proposed, the taxes of England and France, as two of the parties, would have been at least ten millions sterling annually to each Nation less than they were at the commencement of the French Revolution.

To conceive a cause why such a plan has not been adopted (and that instead of a Congress for the purpose of preventing war, it has been called only to terminate a war, after a fruitless expense of several years) it will be necessary to consider the interest of Governments as a distinct interest to that of Nations.

Whatever is the cause of taxes to a Nation, becomes also the means of revenue to Government. Every war terminates with an addition of taxes, and consequently with an addition of revenue; and in any event of war, in the manner they are now commenced and concluded, the power and interest of Governments are increased. War, therefore, from its productiveness, as it easily furnishes the pretence of necessity for taxes and appointments to places and offices, becomes a principal part of the system of old Governments; and to establish any mode to abolish war, however advantageous it might be to Nations, would be to take from such Government the most lucrative of its branches. The frivolous matters upon which war is made, show the disposition and avidity of Governments to uphold the system of war, and betray the motives upon which they act.

Why are not Republics plunged into war, but because the nature of their Government does not admit of an interest distinct from that of the Nation? Even Holland, though an ill-constructed Republic, and with a commerce extending over the world, existed nearly a century without war: and the instant the form of Government was changed in France, the republican principles of peace and domestic prosperity and economy arose with the new Government; and the same consequences would follow the cause in other Nations.

As war is the system of Government on the old construction, the animosity which Nations reciprocally entertain, is nothing more than what the policy of their Governments excites to keep up the spirit of the system. Each Government accuses the other of perfidy, intrigue, and ambition, as a means of heating the imagination of their respective Nations, and incensing them to hostilities. Man is not the enemy of man, but through the medium of a false system of Government. Instead, therefore, of exclaiming against the ambition of Kings, the exclamation should be directed against the principle of such Governments; and instead of seeking to reform the individual, the wisdom of a Nation should apply itself to reform the system.

Whether the forms and maxims of Governments which are still in practice, were adapted to the condition of the world at the period they were established, is not in this case the question. The older they are, the less correspondence can they have with the present state of things. Time, and change of circumstances and opinions, have the same progressive effect in rendering modes of Government obsolete as they have upon customs and manners.—Agriculture, commerce, manufactures, and the tranquil arts, by which the prosperity of Nations is best promoted, require a different system of Government, and a different species of knowledge to direct its operations, than what might have been required in the former condition of the world.

As it is not difficult to perceive, from the enlightened state of mankind, that hereditary Governments are verging to their decline, and that Revolutions on the broad basis of national sovereignty and Government by representation, are making their way in Europe, it would be an act of wisdom to anticipate their approach, and produce Revolutions by reason and accommodation, rather than commit them to the issue of convulsions.

From what we now see, nothing of reform in the political world ought to be held improbable. It is an age of Revolutions, in which everything may be looked for. The intrigue of Courts, by which the system of war is kept up, may provoke a confederation of Nations to abolish it: and an European Congress to patronise the progress of free Government, and promote the civilisation of Nations with each other, is an event nearer in probability, than once were the revolutions and alliance of France and America.

END OF PART I.

* * *

RIGHTS OF MAN. PART SECOND, COMBINING PRINCIPLE AND PRACTICE.

By Thomas Paine.

FRENCH TRANSLATOR'S PREFACE.

(1792)

THE work of which we offer a translation to the public has created the greatest sensation in England. Paine, that man of freedom, who seems born to preach "Common Sense" to the whole world with the same success as in America, explains in it to the people of England the theory of the practice of the Rights of Man.

Owing to the prejudices that still govern that nation, the author has been obliged to condescend to answer Mr. Burke. He has done so more especially in an extended preface which is nothing but a piece of very tedious controversy, in which he shows himself very sensitive to criticisms that do not really affect him. To translate it seemed an insult to the free French people, and similar reasons have led the editors to suppress also a dedicatory epistle addressed by Paine to Lafayette.

The French can no longer endure dedicatory epistles. A man should write privately to those he esteems: when he publishes a book his thoughts should be offered to the public alone. Paine, that uncorrupted friend of freedom, believed too in the sincerity of Lafayette. So easy is it to deceive men of single-minded purpose! Bred at a distance from courts, that austere American does not seem any more on his guard against the artful ways and speech of courtiers than some Frenchmen who resemble him.

TO

    M. DE LA FAYETTE

After an acquaintance of nearly fifteen years in difficult situations in America, and various consultations in Europe, I feel a pleasure in presenting to you this small treatise, in gratitude for your services to my beloved America, and as a testimony of my esteem for the virtues, public and private, which I know you to possess.

The only point upon which I could ever discover that we differed was not as to principles of government, but as to time. For my own part I think it equally as injurious to good principles to permit them to linger, as to push them on too fast. That which you suppose accomplishable in fourteen or fifteen years, I may believe practicable in a much shorter period. Mankind, as it appears to me, are always ripe enough to understand their true interest, provided it be presented clearly to their understanding, and that in a manner not to create suspicion by anything like self-design, nor offend by assuming too much. Where we would wish to reform we must not reproach.

When the American revolution was established I felt a disposition to sit serenely down and enjoy the calm. It did not appear to me that any object could afterwards arise great enough to make me quit tranquility and feel as I had felt before. But when principle, and not place, is the energetic cause of action, a man, I find, is everywhere the same.

I am now once more in the public world; and as I have not a right to contemplate on so many years of remaining life as you have, I have resolved to labour as fast as I can; and as I am anxious for your aid and your company, I wish you to hasten your principles and overtake me.

If you make a campaign the ensuing spring, which it is most probable there will be no occasion for, I will come and join you. Should the campaign commence, I hope it will terminate in the extinction of German despotism, and in establishing the freedom of all Germany. When France shall be surrounded with revolutions she will be in peace and safety, and her taxes, as well as those of Germany, will consequently become less.

Your sincere,

Affectionate Friend,

Thomas Paine

London, Feb. 9, 1792

PREFACE

When I began the chapter entitled the "Conclusion" in the former part of the RIGHTS OF MAN, published last year, it was my intention to have extended it to a greater length; but in casting the whole matter in my mind, which I wish to add, I found that it must either make the work too bulky, or contract my plan too much. I therefore brought it to a close as soon as the subject would admit, and reserved what I had further to say to another opportunity.

Several other reasons contributed to produce this determination. I wished to know the manner in which a work, written in a style of thinking and expression different to what had been customary in England, would be received before I proceeded farther. A great field was opening to the view of mankind by means of the French Revolution. Mr. Burke's outrageous opposition thereto brought the controversy into England. He attacked principles which he knew (from information) I would contest with him, because they are principles I believe to be good, and which I have contributed to establish, and conceive myself bound to defend. Had he not urged the controversy, I had most probably been a silent man.

Another reason for deferring the remainder of the work was, that Mr. Burke promised in his first publication to renew the subject at another opportunity, and to make a comparison of what he called the English and French Constitutions. I therefore held myself in reserve for him. He has published two works since, without doing this: which he certainly would not have omitted, had the comparison been in his favour.

In his last work, his "Appeal from the New to the Old Whigs," he has quoted about ten pages from the RIGHTS OF MAN, and having given himself the trouble of doing this, says he "shall not attempt in the smallest degree to refute them," meaning the principles therein contained. I am enough acquainted with Mr. Burke to know that he would if he could. But instead of contesting them, he immediately after consoles himself with saying that "he has done his part."—He has not done his part. He has not performed his promise of a comparison of constitutions. He started the controversy, he gave the challenge, and has fled from it; and he is now a case in point with his own opinion that "the age of chivalry is gone!"

The title, as well as the substance of his last work, his "Appeal," is his condemnation. Principles must stand on their own merits, and if they are good they certainly will. To put them under the shelter of other men's authority, as Mr. Burke has done, serves to bring them into suspicion. Mr. Burke is not very fond of dividing his honours, but in this case he is artfully dividing the disgrace.

But who are those to whom Mr. Burke has made his appeal? A set of childish thinkers, and half-way politicians born in the last century, men who went no farther with any principle than as it suited their purposes as a party; the nation was always left out of the question; and this has been the character of every party from that day to this. The nation sees nothing of such works, or such politics, worthy its attention. A little matter will move a party, but it must be something great that moves a nation.

Though I see nothing in Mr. Burke's "Appeal" worth taking much notice of, there is, however, one expression upon which I shall offer a few remarks. After quoting largely from the RIGHTS OF MAN, and declining to contest the principles contained in that work, he says: "This will most probably be done (if such writings shall be thought to deserve any other refutation than that of criminal justice) by others, who may think with Mr. Burke and with the same zeal."

In the first place, it has not yet been done by anybody. Not less, I believe, than eight or ten pamphlets intended as answers to the former part of the RIGHTS OF MAN have been published by different persons, and not one of them to my knowledge, has extended to a second edition, nor are even the titles of them so much as generally remembered. As I am averse to unnecessary multiplying publications, I have answered none of them. And as I believe that a man may write himself out of reputation when nobody else can do it, I am careful to avoid that rock.

But as I would decline unnecessary publications on the one hand, so would I avoid everything that might appear like sullen pride on the other. If Mr. Burke, or any person on his side the question, will produce an answer to the RIGHTS OF MAN that shall extend to a half, or even to a fourth part of the number of copies to which the Rights Of Man extended, I will reply to his work. But until this be done, I shall so far take the sense of the public for my guide (and the world knows I am not a flatterer) that what they do not think worth while to read, is not worth mine to answer. I suppose the number of copies to which the first part of the RIGHTS OF MAN extended, taking England, Scotland, and Ireland, is not less than between forty and fifty thousand.

I now come to remark on the remaining part of the quotation I have made from Mr. Burke.

"If," says he, "such writings shall be thought to deserve any other refutation than that of criminal justice."

Pardoning the pun, it must be criminal justice indeed that should condemn a work as a substitute for not being able to refute it. The greatest condemnation that could be passed upon it would be a refutation. But in proceeding by the method Mr. Burke alludes to, the condemnation would, in the final event, pass upon the criminality of the process and not upon the work, and in this case, I had rather be the author, than be either the judge or the jury that should condemn it.

But to come at once to the point. I have differed from some professional gentlemen on the subject of prosecutions, and I since find they are falling into my opinion, which I will here state as fully, but as concisely as I can.

I will first put a case with respect to any law, and then compare it with a government, or with what in England is, or has been, called a constitution.

It would be an act of despotism, or what in England is called arbitrary power, to make a law to prohibit investigating the principles, good or bad, on which such a law, or any other is founded.

If a law be bad it is one thing to oppose the practice of it, but it is quite a different thing to expose its errors, to reason on its defects, and to show cause why it should be repealed, or why another ought to be substituted in its place. I have always held it an opinion (making it also my practice) that it is better to obey a bad law, making use at the same time of every argument to show its errors and procure its repeal, than forcibly to violate it; because the precedent of breaking a bad law might weaken the force, and lead to a discretionary violation, of those which are good.

The case is the same with respect to principles and forms of government, or to what are called constitutions and the parts of which they are, composed.

It is for the good of nations and not for the emolument or aggrandisement of particular individuals, that government ought to be established, and that mankind are at the expense of supporting it. The defects of every government and constitution both as to principle and form, must, on a parity of reasoning, be as open to discussion as the defects of a law, and it is a duty which every man owes to society to point them out. When those defects, and the means of remedying them, are generally seen by a nation, that nation will reform its government or its constitution in the one case, as the government repealed or reformed the law in the other. The operation of government is restricted to the making and the administering of laws; but it is to a nation that the right of forming or reforming, generating or regenerating constitutions and governments belong; and consequently those subjects, as subjects of investigation, are always before a country as a matter of right, and cannot, without invading the general rights of that country, be made subjects for prosecution. On this ground I will meet Mr. Burke whenever he please. It is better that the whole argument should come out than to seek to stifle it. It was himself that opened the controversy, and he ought not to desert it.

I do not believe that monarchy and aristocracy will continue seven years longer in any of the enlightened countries in Europe. If better reasons can be shown for them than against them, they will stand; if the contrary, they will not. Mankind are not now to be told they shall not think, or they shall not read; and publications that go no farther than to investigate principles of government, to invite men to reason and to reflect, and to show the errors and excellences of different systems, have a right to appear. If they do not excite attention, they are not worth the trouble of a prosecution; and if they do, the prosecution will amount to nothing, since it cannot amount to a prohibition of reading. This would be a sentence on the public, instead of the author, and would also be the most effectual mode of making or hastening revolution.

On all cases that apply universally to a nation, with respect to systems of government, a jury of twelve men is not competent to decide. Where there are no witnesses to be examined, no facts to be proved, and where the whole matter is before the whole public, and the merits or demerits of it resting on their opinion; and where there is nothing to be known in a court, but what every body knows out of it, every twelve men is equally as good a jury as the other, and would most probably reverse each other's verdict; or, from the variety of their opinions, not be able to form one. It is one case, whether a nation approve a work, or a plan; but it is quite another case, whether it will commit to any such jury the power of determining whether that nation have a right to, or shall reform its government or not. I mention those cases that Mr. Burke may see I have not written on Government without reflecting on what is Law, as well as on what are Rights.—The only effectual jury in such cases would be a convention of the whole nation fairly elected; for in all such cases the whole nation is the vicinage. If Mr. Burke will propose such a jury, I will waive all privileges of being the citizen of another country, and, defending its principles, abide the issue, provided he will do the same; for my opinion is, that his work and his principles would be condemned instead of mine.

As to the prejudices which men have from education and habit, in favour of any particular form or system of government, those prejudices have yet to stand the test of reason and reflection. In fact, such prejudices are nothing. No man is prejudiced in favour of a thing, knowing it to be wrong. He is attached to it on the belief of its being right; and when he sees it is not so, the prejudice will be gone. We have but a defective idea of what prejudice is. It might be said, that until men think for themselves the whole is prejudice, and not opinion; for that only is opinion which is the result of reason and reflection. I offer this remark, that Mr. Burke may not confide too much in what have been the customary prejudices of the country.

I do not believe that the people of England have ever been fairly and candidly dealt by. They have been imposed upon by parties, and by men assuming the character of leaders. It is time that the nation should rise above those trifles. It is time to dismiss that inattention which has so long been the encouraging cause of stretching taxation to excess. It is time to dismiss all those songs and toasts which are calculated to enslave, and operate to suffocate reflection. On all such subjects men have but to think, and they will neither act wrong nor be misled. To say that any people are not fit for freedom, is to make poverty their choice, and to say they had rather be loaded with taxes than not. If such a case could be proved, it would equally prove that those who govern are not fit to govern them, for they are a part of the same national mass.

But admitting governments to be changed all over Europe; it certainly may be done without convulsion or revenge. It is not worth making changes or revolutions, unless it be for some great national benefit: and when this shall appear to a nation, the danger will be, as in America and France, to those who oppose; and with this reflection I close my Preface.

THOMAS PAINE

London, Feb. 9, 1792

RIGHTS OF MAN PART II:INTRODUCTION.

What Archimedes said of the mechanical powers, may be applied to Reason and Liberty. "Had we," said he, "a place to stand upon, we might raise the world."

The revolution of America presented in politics what was only theory in mechanics. So deeply rooted were all the governments of the old world, and so effectually had the tyranny and the antiquity of habit established itself over the mind, that no beginning could be made in Asia, Africa, or Europe, to reform the political condition of man. Freedom had been hunted round the globe; reason was considered as rebellion; and the slavery of fear had made men afraid to think.

But such is the irresistible nature of truth, that all it asks,—and all it wants,—is the liberty of appearing. The sun needs no inscription to distinguish him from darkness; and no sooner did the American governments display themselves to the world, than despotism felt a shock and man began to contemplate redress.

The independence of America, considered merely as a separation from England, would have been a matter but of little importance, had it not been accompanied by a revolution in the principles and practice of governments. She made a stand, not for herself only, but for the world, and looked beyond the advantages herself could receive. Even the Hessian, though hired to fight against her, may live to bless his defeat; and England, condemning the viciousness of its government, rejoice in its miscarriage.

As America was the only spot in the political world where the principle of universal reformation could begin, so also was it the best in the natural world. An assemblage of circumstances conspired, not only to give birth, but to add gigantic maturity to its principles. The scene which that country presents to the eye of a spectator, has something in it which generates and encourages great ideas. Nature appears to him in magnitude. The mighty objects he beholds, act upon his mind by enlarging it, and he partakes of the greatness he contemplates.—Its first settlers were emigrants from different European nations, and of diversified professions of religion, retiring from the governmental persecutions of the old world, and meeting in the new, not as enemies, but as brothers. The wants which necessarily accompany the cultivation of a wilderness produced among them a state of society, which countries long harassed by the quarrels and intrigues of governments, had neglected to cherish. In such a situation man becomes what he ought. He sees his species, not with the inhuman idea of a natural enemy, but as kindred; and the example shows to the artificial world, that man must go back to Nature for information.

From the rapid progress which America makes in every species of improvement, it is rational to conclude that, if the governments of Asia, Africa, and Europe had begun on a principle similar to that of America, or had not been very early corrupted therefrom, those countries must by this time have been in a far superior condition to what they are. Age after age has passed away, for no other purpose than to behold their wretchedness. Could we suppose a spectator who knew nothing of the world, and who was put into it merely to make his observations, he would take a great part of the old world to be new, just struggling with the difficulties and hardships of an infant settlement. He could not suppose that the hordes of miserable poor with which old countries abound could be any other than those who had not yet had time to provide for themselves. Little would he think they were the consequence of what in such countries they call government.

If, from the more wretched parts of the old world, we look at those which are in an advanced stage of improvement we still find the greedy hand of government thrusting itself into every corner and crevice of industry, and grasping the spoil of the multitude. Invention is continually exercised to furnish new pretences for revenue and taxation. It watches prosperity as its prey, and permits none to escape without a tribute.

As revolutions have begun (and as the probability is always greater against a thing beginning, than of proceeding after it has begun), it is natural to expect that other revolutions will follow. The amazing and still increasing expenses with which old governments are conducted, the numerous wars they engage in or provoke, the embarrassments they throw in the way of universal civilisation and commerce, and the oppression and usurpation acted at home, have wearied out the patience, and exhausted the property of the world. In such a situation, and with such examples already existing, revolutions are to be looked for. They are become subjects of universal conversation, and may be considered as the Order of the day.

If systems of government can be introduced less expensive and more productive of general happiness than those which have existed, all attempts to oppose their progress will in the end be fruitless. Reason, like time, will make its own way, and prejudice will fall in a combat with interest. If universal peace, civilisation, and commerce are ever to be the happy lot of man, it cannot be accomplished but by a revolution in the system of governments. All the monarchical governments are military. War is their trade, plunder and revenue their objects. While such governments continue, peace has not the absolute security of a day. What is the history of all monarchical governments but a disgustful picture of human wretchedness, and the accidental respite of a few years' repose? Wearied with war, and tired with human butchery, they sat down to rest, and called it peace. This certainly is not the condition that heaven intended for man; and if this be monarchy, well might monarchy be reckoned among the sins of the Jews.

The revolutions which formerly took place in the world had nothing in them that interested the bulk of mankind. They extended only to a change of persons and measures, but not of principles, and rose or fell among the common transactions of the moment. What we now behold may not improperly be called a "counter-revolution." Conquest and tyranny, at some earlier period, dispossessed man of his rights, and he is now recovering them. And as the tide of all human affairs has its ebb and flow in directions contrary to each other, so also is it in this. Government founded on a moral theory, on a system of universal peace, on the indefeasible hereditary Rights of Man, is now revolving from west to east by a stronger impulse than the government of the sword revolved from east to west. It interests not particular individuals, but nations in its progress, and promises a new era to the human race.

The danger to which the success of revolutions is most exposed is that of attempting them before the principles on which they proceed, and the advantages to result from them, are sufficiently seen and understood. Almost everything appertaining to the circumstances of a nation, has been absorbed and confounded under the general and mysterious word government. Though it avoids taking to its account the errors it commits, and the mischiefs it occasions, it fails not to arrogate to itself whatever has the appearance of prosperity. It robs industry of its honours, by pedantically making itself the cause of its effects; and purloins from the general character of man, the merits that appertain to him as a social being.

It may therefore be of use in this day of revolutions to discriminate between those things which are the effect of government, and those which are not. This will best be done by taking a review of society and civilisation, and the consequences resulting therefrom, as things distinct from what are called governments. By beginning with this investigation, we shall be able to assign effects to their proper causes and analyse the mass of common errors.

CHAPTER I. OF SOCIETY AND CIVILISATION

Great part of that order which reigns among mankind is not the effect of government. It has its origin in the principles of society and the natural constitution of man. It existed prior to government, and would exist if the formality of government was abolished. The mutual dependence and reciprocal interest which man has upon man, and all the parts of civilised community upon each other, create that great chain of connection which holds it together. The landholder, the farmer, the manufacturer, the merchant, the tradesman, and every occupation, prospers by the aid which each receives from the other, and from the whole. Common interest regulates their concerns, and forms their law; and the laws which common usage ordains, have a greater influence than the laws of government. In fine, society performs for itself almost everything which is ascribed to government.

To understand the nature and quantity of government proper for man, it is necessary to attend to his character. As Nature created him for social life, she fitted him for the station she intended. In all cases she made his natural wants greater than his individual powers. No one man is capable, without the aid of society, of supplying his own wants, and those wants, acting upon every individual, impel the whole of them into society, as naturally as gravitation acts to a centre.

But she has gone further. She has not only forced man into society by a diversity of wants which the reciprocal aid of each other can supply, but she has implanted in him a system of social affections, which, though not necessary to his existence, are essential to his happiness. There is no period in life when this love for society ceases to act. It begins and ends with our being.

If we examine with attention into the composition and constitution of man, the diversity of his wants, and the diversity of talents in different men for reciprocally accommodating the wants of each other, his propensity to society, and consequently to preserve the advantages resulting from it, we shall easily discover, that a great part of what is called government is mere imposition.

Government is no farther necessary than to supply the few cases to which society and civilisation are not conveniently competent; and instances are not wanting to show, that everything which government can usefully add thereto, has been performed by the common consent of society, without government.

For upwards of two years from the commencement of the American War, and to a longer period in several of the American States, there were no established forms of government. The old governments had been abolished, and the country was too much occupied in defence to employ its attention in establishing new governments; yet during this interval order and harmony were preserved as inviolate as in any country in Europe. There is a natural aptness in man, and more so in society, because it embraces a greater variety of abilities and resource, to accommodate itself to whatever situation it is in. The instant formal government is abolished, society begins to act: a general association takes place, and common interest produces common security.

So far is it from being true, as has been pretended, that the abolition of any formal government is the dissolution of society, that it acts by a contrary impulse, and brings the latter the closer together. All that part of its organisation which it had committed to its government, devolves again upon itself, and acts through its medium. When men, as well from natural instinct as from reciprocal benefits, have habituated themselves to social and civilised life, there is always enough of its principles in practice to carry them through any changes they may find necessary or convenient to make in their government. In short, man is so naturally a creature of society that it is almost impossible to put him out of it.

Formal government makes but a small part of civilised life; and when even the best that human wisdom can devise is established, it is a thing more in name and idea than in fact. It is to the great and fundamental principles of society and civilisation—to the common usage universally consented to, and mutually and reciprocally maintained—to the unceasing circulation of interest, which, passing through its million channels, invigorates the whole mass of civilised man—it is to these things, infinitely more than to anything which even the best instituted government can perform, that the safety and prosperity of the individual and of the whole depends.

The more perfect civilisation is, the less occasion has it for government, because the more does it regulate its own affairs, and govern itself; but so contrary is the practice of old governments to the reason of the case, that the expenses of them increase in the proportion they ought to diminish. It is but few general laws that civilised life requires, and those of such common usefulness, that whether they are enforced by the forms of government or not, the effect will be nearly the same. If we consider what the principles are that first condense men into society, and what are the motives that regulate their mutual intercourse afterwards, we shall find, by the time we arrive at what is called government, that nearly the whole of the business is performed by the natural operation of the parts upon each other.

Man, with respect to all those matters, is more a creature of consistency than he is aware, or than governments would wish him to believe. All the great laws of society are laws of nature. Those of trade and commerce, whether with respect to the intercourse of individuals or of nations, are laws of mutual and reciprocal interest. They are followed and obeyed, because it is the interest of the parties so to do, and not on account of any formal laws their governments may impose or interpose.

But how often is the natural propensity to society disturbed or destroyed by the operations of government! When the latter, instead of being ingrafted on the principles of the former, assumes to exist for itself, and acts by partialities of favour and oppression, it becomes the cause of the mischiefs it ought to prevent.

If we look back to the riots and tumults which at various times have happened in England, we shall find that they did not proceed from the want of a government, but that government was itself the generating cause; instead of consolidating society it divided it; it deprived it of its natural cohesion, and engendered discontents and disorders which otherwise would not have existed. In those associations which men promiscuously form for the purpose of trade, or of any concern in which government is totally out of the question, and in which they act merely on the principles of society, we see how naturally the various parties unite; and this shows, by comparison, that governments, so far from being always the cause or means of order, are often the destruction of it. The riots of 1780 had no other source than the remains of those prejudices which the government itself had encouraged. But with respect to England there are also other causes.

Excess and inequality of taxation, however disguised in the means, never fail to appear in their effects. As a great mass of the community are thrown thereby into poverty and discontent, they are constantly on the brink of commotion; and deprived, as they unfortunately are, of the means of information, are easily heated to outrage. Whatever the apparent cause of any riots may be, the real one is always want of happiness. It shows that something is wrong in the system of government that injures the felicity by which society is to be preserved.

But as a fact is superior to reasoning, the instance of America presents itself to confirm these observations. If there is a country in the world where concord, according to common calculation, would be least expected, it is America. Made up as it is of people from different nations,*16 accustomed to different forms and habits of government, speaking different languages, and more different in their modes of worship, it would appear that the union of such a people was impracticable; but by the simple operation of constructing government on the principles of society and the rights of man, every difficulty retires, and all the parts are brought into cordial unison. There the poor are not oppressed, the rich are not privileged. Industry is not mortified by the splendid extravagance of a court rioting at its expense. Their taxes are few, because their government is just: and as there is nothing to render them wretched, there is nothing to engender riots and tumults.

A metaphysical man, like Mr. Burke, would have tortured his invention to discover how such a people could be governed. He would have supposed that some must be managed by fraud, others by force, and all by some contrivance; that genius must be hired to impose upon ignorance, and show and parade to fascinate the vulgar. Lost in the abundance of his researches, he would have resolved and re-resolved, and finally overlooked the plain and easy road that lay directly before him.

One of the great advantages of the American Revolution has been, that it led to a discovery of the principles, and laid open the imposition, of governments. All the revolutions till then had been worked within the atmosphere of a court, and never on the grand floor of a nation. The parties were always of the class of courtiers; and whatever was their rage for reformation, they carefully preserved the fraud of the profession.

In all cases they took care to represent government as a thing made up of mysteries, which only themselves understood; and they hid from the understanding of the nation the only thing that was beneficial to know, namely, That government is nothing more than a national association adding on the principles of society.

Having thus endeavoured to show that the social and civilised state of man is capable of performing within itself almost everything necessary to its protection and government, it will be proper, on the other hand, to take a review of the present old governments, and examine whether their principles and practice are correspondent thereto.

CHAPTER II. OF THE ORIGIN OF THE PRESENT OLD GOVERNMENTS

It is impossible that such governments as have hitherto existed in the world, could have commenced by any other means than a total violation of every principle sacred and moral. The obscurity in which the origin of all the present old governments is buried, implies the iniquity and disgrace with which they began. The origin of the present government of America and France will ever be remembered, because it is honourable to record it; but with respect to the rest, even Flattery has consigned them to the tomb of time, without an inscription.

It could have been no difficult thing in the early and solitary ages of the world, while the chief employment of men was that of attending flocks and herds, for a banditti of ruffians to overrun a country, and lay it under contributions. Their power being thus established, the chief of the band contrived to lose the name of Robber in that of Monarch; and hence the origin of Monarchy and Kings.

The origin of the Government of England, so far as relates to what is called its line of monarchy, being one of the latest, is perhaps the best recorded. The hatred which the Norman invasion and tyranny begat, must have been deeply rooted in the nation, to have outlived the contrivance to obliterate it. Though not a courtier will talk of the curfew-bell, not a village in England has forgotten it.

Those bands of robbers having parcelled out the world, and divided it into dominions, began, as is naturally the case, to quarrel with each other. What at first was obtained by violence was considered by others as lawful to be taken, and a second plunderer succeeded the first. They alternately invaded the dominions which each had assigned to himself, and the brutality with which they treated each other explains the original character of monarchy. It was ruffian torturing ruffian. The conqueror considered the conquered, not as his prisoner, but his property. He led him in triumph rattling in chains, and doomed him, at pleasure, to slavery or death. As time obliterated the history of their beginning, their successors assumed new appearances, to cut off the entail of their disgrace, but their principles and objects remained the same. What at first was plunder, assumed the softer name of revenue; and the power originally usurped, they affected to inherit.

From such beginning of governments, what could be expected but a continued system of war and extortion? It has established itself into a trade. The vice is not peculiar to one more than to another, but is the common principle of all. There does not exist within such governments sufficient stamina whereon to engraft reformation; and the shortest and most effectual remedy is to begin anew on the ground of the nation.

What scenes of horror, what perfection of iniquity, present themselves in contemplating the character and reviewing the history of such governments! If we would delineate human nature with a baseness of heart and hypocrisy of countenance that reflection would shudder at and humanity disown, it is kings, courts and cabinets that must sit for the portrait. Man, naturally as he is, with all his faults about him, is not up to the character.

Can we possibly suppose that if governments had originated in a right principle, and had not an interest in pursuing a wrong one, the world could have been in the wretched and quarrelsome condition we have seen it? What inducement has the farmer, while following the plough, to lay aside his peaceful pursuit, and go to war with the farmer of another country? or what inducement has the manufacturer? What is dominion to them, or to any class of men in a nation? Does it add an acre to any man's estate, or raise its value? Are not conquest and defeat each of the same price, and taxes the never-failing consequence?— Though this reasoning may be good to a nation, it is not so to a government. War is the Pharo-table of governments, and nations the dupes of the game.

If there is anything to wonder at in this miserable scene of governments more than might be expected, it is the progress which the peaceful arts of agriculture, manufacture and commerce have made beneath such a long accumulating load of discouragement and oppression. It serves to show that instinct in animals does not act with stronger impulse than the principles of society and civilisation operate in man. Under all discouragements, he pursues his object, and yields to nothing but impossibilities.

CHAPTER III. OF THE OLD AND NEW SYSTEMS OF GOVERNMENT

Nothing can appear more contradictory than the principles on which the old governments began, and the condition to which society, civilisation and commerce are capable of carrying mankind. Government, on the old system, is an assumption of power, for the aggrandisement of itself; on the new, a delegation of power for the common benefit of society. The former supports itself by keeping up a system of war; the latter promotes a system of peace, as the true means of enriching a nation. The one encourages national prejudices; the other promotes universal society, as the means of universal commerce. The one measures its prosperity, by the quantity of revenue it extorts; the other proves its excellence, by the small quantity of taxes it requires.

Mr. Burke has talked of old and new whigs. If he can amuse himself with childish names and distinctions, I shall not interrupt his pleasure. It is not to him, but to the Abbe Sieyes, that I address this chapter. I am already engaged to the latter gentleman to discuss the subject of monarchical government; and as it naturally occurs in comparing the old and new systems, I make this the opportunity of presenting to him my observations. I shall occasionally take Mr. Burke in my way.

Though it might be proved that the system of government now called the New, is the most ancient in principle of all that have existed, being founded on the original, inherent Rights of Man: yet, as tyranny and the sword have suspended the exercise of those rights for many centuries past, it serves better the purpose of distinction to call it the new, than to claim the right of calling it the old.

The first general distinction between those two systems, is, that the one now called the old is hereditary, either in whole or in part; and the new is entirely representative. It rejects all hereditary government:

First, As being an imposition on mankind.

Secondly, As inadequate to the purposes for which government is necessary.

With respect to the first of these heads—It cannot be proved by what right hereditary government could begin; neither does there exist within the compass of mortal power a right to establish it. Man has no authority over posterity in matters of personal right; and, therefore, no man, or body of men, had, or can have, a right to set up hereditary government. Were even ourselves to come again into existence, instead of being succeeded by posterity, we have not now the right of taking from ourselves the rights which would then be ours. On what ground, then, do we pretend to take them from others?

All hereditary government is in its nature tyranny. An heritable crown, or an heritable throne, or by what other fanciful name such things may be called, have no other significant explanation than that mankind are heritable property. To inherit a government, is to inherit the people, as if they were flocks and herds.

With respect to the second head, that of being inadequate to the purposes for which government is necessary, we have only to consider what government essentially is, and compare it with the circumstances to which hereditary succession is subject.

Government ought to be a thing always in full maturity. It ought to be so constructed as to be superior to all the accidents to which individual man is subject; and, therefore, hereditary succession, by being subject to them all, is the most irregular and imperfect of all the systems of government.

We have heard the Rights of Man called a levelling system; but the only system to which the word levelling is truly applicable, is the hereditary monarchical system. It is a system of mental levelling. It indiscriminately admits every species of character to the same authority. Vice and virtue, ignorance and wisdom, in short, every quality good or bad, is put on the same level. Kings succeed each other, not as rationals, but as animals. It signifies not what their mental or moral characters are. Can we then be surprised at the abject state of the human mind in monarchical countries, when the government itself is formed on such an abject levelling system?—It has no fixed character. To-day it is one thing; to-morrow it is something else. It changes with the temper of every succeeding individual, and is subject to all the varieties of each. It is government through the medium of passions and accidents. It appears under all the various characters of childhood, decrepitude, dotage, a thing at nurse, in leading-strings, or in crutches. It reverses the wholesome order of nature. It occasionally puts children over men, and the conceits of nonage over wisdom and experience. In short, we cannot conceive a more ridiculous figure of government, than hereditary succession, in all its cases, presents.

Could it be made a decree in nature, or an edict registered in heaven, and man could know it, that virtue and wisdom should invariably appertain to hereditary succession, the objection to it would be removed; but when we see that nature acts as if she disowned and sported with the hereditary system; that the mental character of successors, in all countries, is below the average of human understanding; that one is a tyrant, another an idiot, a third insane, and some all three together, it is impossible to attach confidence to it, when reason in man has power to act.

It is not to the Abbe Sieyes that I need apply this reasoning; he has already saved me that trouble by giving his own opinion upon the case. "If it be asked," says he, "what is my opinion with respect to hereditary right, I answer without hesitation, That in good theory, an hereditary transmission of any power of office, can never accord with the laws of a true representation. Hereditaryship is, in this sense, as much an attaint upon principle, as an outrage upon society. But let us," continues he, "refer to the history of all elective monarchies and principalities: is there one in which the elective mode is not worse than the hereditary succession?"

As to debating on which is the worst of the two, it is admitting both to be bad; and herein we are agreed. The preference which the Abbe has given, is a condemnation of the thing that he prefers. Such a mode of reasoning on such a subject is inadmissible, because it finally amounts to an accusation upon Providence, as if she had left to man no other choice with respect to government than between two evils, the best of which he admits to be "an attaint upon principle, and an outrage upon society."

Passing over, for the present, all the evils and mischiefs which monarchy has occasioned in the world, nothing can more effectually prove its uselessness in a state of civil government, than making it hereditary. Would we make any office hereditary that required wisdom and abilities to fill it? And where wisdom and abilities are not necessary, such an office, whatever it may be, is superfluous or insignificant.

Hereditary succession is a burlesque upon monarchy. It puts it in the most ridiculous light, by presenting it as an office which any child or idiot may fill. It requires some talents to be a common mechanic; but to be a king requires only the animal figure of man—a sort of breathing automaton. This sort of superstition may last a few years more, but it cannot long resist the awakened reason and interest of man.

As to Mr. Burke, he is a stickler for monarchy, not altogether as a pensioner, if he is one, which I believe, but as a political man. He has taken up a contemptible opinion of mankind, who, in their turn, are taking up the same of him. He considers them as a herd of beings that must be governed by fraud, effigy, and show; and an idol would be as good a figure of monarchy with him, as a man. I will, however, do him the justice to say that, with respect to America, he has been very complimentary. He always contended, at least in my hearing, that the people of America were more enlightened than those of England, or of any country in Europe; and that therefore the imposition of show was not necessary in their governments.

Though the comparison between hereditary and elective monarchy, which the Abbe has made, is unnecessary to the case, because the representative system rejects both: yet, were I to make the comparison, I should decide contrary to what he has done.

The civil wars which have originated from contested hereditary claims, are more numerous, and have been more dreadful, and of longer continuance, than those which have been occasioned by election. All the civil wars in France arose from the hereditary system; they were either produced by hereditary claims, or by the imperfection of the hereditary form, which admits of regencies or monarchy at nurse. With respect to England, its history is full of the same misfortunes. The contests for succession between the houses of York and Lancaster lasted a whole century; and others of a similar nature have renewed themselves since that period. Those of 1715 and 1745 were of the same kind. The succession war for the crown of Spain embroiled almost half Europe. The disturbances of Holland are generated from the hereditaryship of the Stadtholder. A government calling itself free, with an hereditary office, is like a thorn in the flesh, that produces a fermentation which endeavours to discharge it.

But I might go further, and place also foreign wars, of whatever kind, to the same cause. It is by adding the evil of hereditary succession to that of monarchy, that a permanent family interest is created, whose constant objects are dominion and revenue. Poland, though an elective monarchy, has had fewer wars than those which are hereditary; and it is the only government that has made a voluntary essay, though but a small one, to reform the condition of the country.

Having thus glanced at a few of the defects of the old, or hereditary systems of government, let us compare it with the new, or representative system.

The representative system takes society and civilisation for its basis; nature, reason, and experience, for its guide.

Experience, in all ages, and in all countries, has demonstrated that it is impossible to control Nature in her distribution of mental powers. She gives them as she pleases. Whatever is the rule by which she, apparently to us, scatters them among mankind, that rule remains a secret to man. It would be as ridiculous to attempt to fix the hereditaryship of human beauty, as of wisdom. Whatever wisdom constituently is, it is like a seedless plant; it may be reared when it appears, but it cannot be voluntarily produced. There is always a sufficiency somewhere in the general mass of society for all purposes; but with respect to the parts of society, it is continually changing its place. It rises in one to-day, in another to-morrow, and has most probably visited in rotation every family of the earth, and again withdrawn.

As this is in the order of nature, the order of government must necessarily follow it, or government will, as we see it does, degenerate into ignorance. The hereditary system, therefore, is as repugnant to human wisdom as to human rights; and is as absurd as it is unjust.

As the republic of letters brings forward the best literary productions, by giving to genius a fair and universal chance; so the representative system of government is calculated to produce the wisest laws, by collecting wisdom from where it can be found. I smile to myself when I contemplate the ridiculous insignificance into which literature and all the sciences would sink, were they made hereditary; and I carry the same idea into governments. An hereditary governor is as inconsistent as an hereditary author. I know not whether Homer or Euclid had sons; but I will venture an opinion that if they had, and had left their works unfinished, those sons could not have completed them.

Do we need a stronger evidence of the absurdity of hereditary government than is seen in the descendants of those men, in any line of life, who once were famous? Is there scarcely an instance in which there is not a total reverse of the character? It appears as if the tide of mental faculties flowed as far as it could in certain channels, and then forsook its course, and arose in others. How irrational then is the hereditary system, which establishes channels of power, in company with which wisdom refuses to flow! By continuing this absurdity, man is perpetually in contradiction with himself; he accepts, for a king, or a chief magistrate, or a legislator, a person whom he would not elect for a constable.

It appears to general observation, that revolutions create genius and talents; but those events do no more than bring them forward. There is existing in man, a mass of sense lying in a dormant state, and which, unless something excites it to action, will descend with him, in that condition, to the grave. As it is to the advantage of society that the whole of its faculties should be employed, the construction of government ought to be such as to bring forward, by a quiet and regular operation, all that extent of capacity which never fails to appear in revolutions.

This cannot take place in the insipid state of hereditary government, not only because it prevents, but because it operates to benumb. When the mind of a nation is bowed down by any political superstition in its government, such as hereditary succession is, it loses a considerable portion of its powers on all other subjects and objects. Hereditary succession requires the same obedience to ignorance, as to wisdom; and when once the mind can bring itself to pay this indiscriminate reverence, it descends below the stature of mental manhood. It is fit to be great only in little things. It acts a treachery upon itself, and suffocates the sensations that urge the detection.

Though the ancient governments present to us a miserable picture of the condition of man, there is one which above all others exempts itself from the general description. I mean the democracy of the Athenians. We see more to admire, and less to condemn, in that great, extraordinary people, than in anything which history affords.

Mr. Burke is so little acquainted with constituent principles of government, that he confounds democracy and representation together. Representation was a thing unknown in the ancient democracies. In those the mass of the people met and enacted laws (grammatically speaking) in the first person. Simple democracy was no other than the common hall of the ancients. It signifies the form, as well as the public principle of the government. As those democracies increased in population, and the territory extended, the simple democratical form became unwieldy and impracticable; and as the system of representation was not known, the consequence was, they either degenerated convulsively into monarchies, or became absorbed into such as then existed. Had the system of representation been then understood, as it now is, there is no reason to believe that those forms of government, now called monarchical or aristocratical, would ever have taken place. It was the want of some method to consolidate the parts of society, after it became too populous, and too extensive for the simple democratical form, and also the lax and solitary condition of shepherds and herdsmen in other parts of the world, that afforded opportunities to those unnatural modes of government to begin.

As it is necessary to clear away the rubbish of errors, into which the subject of government has been thrown, I will proceed to remark on some others.

It has always been the political craft of courtiers and court-governments, to abuse something which they called republicanism; but what republicanism was, or is, they never attempt to explain. Let us examine a little into this case.

The only forms of government are the democratical, the aristocratical, the monarchical, and what is now called the representative.

What is called a republic is not any particular form of government. It is wholly characteristical of the purport, matter or object for which government ought to be instituted, and on which it is to be employed, Res-Publica, the public affairs, or the public good; or, literally translated, the public thing. It is a word of a good original, referring to what ought to be the character and business of government; and in this sense it is naturally opposed to the word monarchy, which has a base original signification. It means arbitrary power in an individual person; in the exercise of which, himself, and not the res-publica, is the object.

Every government that does not act on the principle of a Republic, or in other words, that does not make the res-publica its whole and sole object, is not a good government. Republican government is no other than government established and conducted for the interest of the public, as well individually as collectively. It is not necessarily connected with any particular form, but it most naturally associates with the representative form, as being best calculated to secure the end for which a nation is at the expense of supporting it.

Various forms of government have affected to style themselves a republic. Poland calls itself a republic, which is an hereditary aristocracy, with what is called an elective monarchy. Holland calls itself a republic, which is chiefly aristocratical, with an hereditary stadtholdership. But the government of America, which is wholly on the system of representation, is the only real Republic, in character and in practice, that now exists. Its government has no other object than the public business of the nation, and therefore it is properly a republic; and the Americans have taken care that This, and no other, shall always be the object of their government, by their rejecting everything hereditary, and establishing governments on the system of representation only. Those who have said that a republic is not a form of government calculated for countries of great extent, mistook, in the first place, the business of a government, for a form of government; for the res-publica equally appertains to every extent of territory and population. And, in the second place, if they meant anything with respect to form, it was the simple democratical form, such as was the mode of government in the ancient democracies, in which there was no representation. The case, therefore, is not, that a republic cannot be extensive, but that it cannot be extensive on the simple democratical form; and the question naturally presents itself, What is the best form of government for conducting the Res-Publica, or the Public Business of a nation, after it becomes too extensive and populous for the simple democratical form? It cannot be monarchy, because monarchy is subject to an objection of the same amount to which the simple democratical form was subject.

It is possible that an individual may lay down a system of principles, on which government shall be constitutionally established to any extent of territory. This is no more than an operation of the mind, acting by its own powers. But the practice upon those principles, as applying to the various and numerous circumstances of a nation, its agriculture, manufacture, trade, commerce, etc., etc., a knowledge of a different kind, and which can be had only from the various parts of society. It is an assemblage of practical knowledge, which no individual can possess; and therefore the monarchical form is as much limited, in useful practice, from the incompetency of knowledge, as was the democratical form, from the multiplicity of population. The one degenerates, by extension, into confusion; the other, into ignorance and incapacity, of which all the great monarchies are an evidence. The monarchical form, therefore, could not be a substitute for the democratical, because it has equal inconveniences.

Much less could it when made hereditary. This is the most effectual of all forms to preclude knowledge. Neither could the high democratical mind have voluntarily yielded itself to be governed by children and idiots, and all the motley insignificance of character, which attends such a mere animal system, the disgrace and the reproach of reason and of man.

As to the aristocratical form, it has the same vices and defects with the monarchical, except that the chance of abilities is better from the proportion of numbers, but there is still no security for the right use and application of them.*[17]

Referring them to the original simple democracy, it affords the true data from which government on a large scale can begin. It is incapable of extension, not from its principle, but from the inconvenience of its form; and monarchy and aristocracy, from their incapacity. Retaining, then, democracy as the ground, and rejecting the corrupt systems of monarchy and aristocracy, the representative system naturally presents itself; remedying at once the defects of the simple democracy as to form, and the incapacity of the other two with respect to knowledge.

Simple democracy was society governing itself without the aid of secondary means. By ingrafting representation upon democracy, we arrive at a system of government capable of embracing and confederating all the various interests and every extent of territory and population; and that also with advantages as much superior to hereditary government, as the republic of letters is to hereditary literature.

It is on this system that the American government is founded. It is representation ingrafted upon democracy. It has fixed the form by a scale parallel in all cases to the extent of the principle. What Athens was in miniature America will be in magnitude. The one was the wonder of the ancient world; the other is becoming the admiration of the present. It is the easiest of all the forms of government to be understood and the most eligible in practice; and excludes at once the ignorance and insecurity of the hereditary mode, and the inconvenience of the simple democracy.

It is impossible to conceive a system of government capable of acting over such an extent of territory, and such a circle of interests, as is immediately produced by the operation of representation. France, great and populous as it is, is but a spot in the capaciousness of the system. It is preferable to simple democracy even in small territories. Athens, by representation, would have outrivalled her own democracy.

That which is called government, or rather that which we ought to conceive government to be, is no more than some common center in which all the parts of society unite. This cannot be accomplished by any method so conducive to the various interests of the community, as by the representative system. It concentrates the knowledge necessary to the interest of the parts, and of the whole. It places government in a state of constant maturity. It is, as has already been observed, never young, never old. It is subject neither to nonage, nor dotage. It is never in the cradle, nor on crutches. It admits not of a separation between knowledge and power, and is superior, as government always ought to be, to all the accidents of individual man, and is therefore superior to what is called monarchy.

A nation is not a body, the figure of which is to be represented by the human body; but is like a body contained within a circle, having a common center, in which every radius meets; and that center is formed by representation. To connect representation with what is called monarchy, is eccentric government. Representation is of itself the delegated monarchy of a nation, and cannot debase itself by dividing it with another.

Mr. Burke has two or three times, in his parliamentary speeches, and in his publications, made use of a jingle of words that convey no ideas. Speaking of government, he says, "It is better to have monarchy for its basis, and republicanism for its corrective, than republicanism for its basis, and monarchy for its corrective."—If he means that it is better to correct folly with wisdom, than wisdom with folly, I will no otherwise contend with him, than that it would be much better to reject the folly entirely.

But what is this thing which Mr. Burke calls monarchy? Will he explain it? All men can understand what representation is; and that it must necessarily include a variety of knowledge and talents. But what security is there for the same qualities on the part of monarchy? or, when the monarchy is a child, where then is the wisdom? What does it know about government? Who then is the monarch, or where is the monarchy? If it is to be performed by regency, it proves to be a farce. A regency is a mock species of republic, and the whole of monarchy deserves no better description. It is a thing as various as imagination can paint. It has none of the stable character that government ought to possess. Every succession is a revolution, and every regency a counter-revolution. The whole of it is a scene of perpetual court cabal and intrigue, of which Mr. Burke is himself an instance. To render monarchy consistent with government, the next in succession should not be born a child, but a man at once, and that man a Solomon. It is ridiculous that nations are to wait and government be interrupted till boys grow to be men.

Whether I have too little sense to see, or too much to be imposed upon; whether I have too much or too little pride, or of anything else, I leave out of the question; but certain it is, that what is called monarchy, always appears to me a silly, contemptible thing. I compare it to something kept behind a curtain, about which there is a great deal of bustle and fuss, and a wonderful air of seeming solemnity; but when, by any accident, the curtain happens to be open—and the company see what it is, they burst into laughter.

In the representative system of government, nothing of this can happen. Like the nation itself, it possesses a perpetual stamina, as well of body as of mind, and presents itself on the open theatre of the world in a fair and manly manner. Whatever are its excellences or defects, they are visible to all. It exists not by fraud and mystery; it deals not in cant and sophistry; but inspires a language that, passing from heart to heart, is felt and understood.

We must shut our eyes against reason, we must basely degrade our understanding, not to see the folly of what is called monarchy. Nature is orderly in all her works; but this is a mode of government that counteracts nature. It turns the progress of the human faculties upside down. It subjects age to be governed by children, and wisdom by folly.

On the contrary, the representative system is always parallel with the order and immutable laws of nature, and meets the reason of man in every part. For example:

In the American Federal Government, more power is delegated to the President of the United States than to any other individual member of Congress. He cannot, therefore, be elected to this office under the age of thirty-five years. By this time the judgment of man becomes more matured, and he has lived long enough to be acquainted with men and things, and the country with him.— But on the monarchial plan (exclusive of the numerous chances there are against every man born into the world, of drawing a prize in the lottery of human faculties), the next in succession, whatever he may be, is put at the head of a nation, and of a government, at the age of eighteen years. Does this appear like an action of wisdom? Is it consistent with the proper dignity and the manly character of a nation? Where is the propriety of calling such a lad the father of the people?—In all other cases, a person is a minor until the age of twenty-one years. Before this period, he is not trusted with the management of an acre of land, or with the heritable property of a flock of sheep, or an herd of swine; but, wonderful to tell! he may, at the age of eighteen years, be trusted with a nation.

That monarchy is all a bubble, a mere court artifice to procure money, is evident (at least to me) in every character in which it can be viewed. It would be impossible, on the rational system of representative government, to make out a bill of expenses to such an enormous amount as this deception admits. Government is not of itself a very chargeable institution. The whole expense of the federal government of America, founded, as I have already said, on the system of representation, and extending over a country nearly ten times as large as England, is but six hundred thousand dollars, or one hundred and thirty-five thousand pounds sterling.

I presume that no man in his sober senses will compare the character of any of the kings of Europe with that of General Washington. Yet, in France, and also in England, the expense of the civil list only, for the support of one man, is eight times greater than the whole expense of the federal government in America. To assign a reason for this, appears almost impossible. The generality of people in America, especially the poor, are more able to pay taxes, than the generality of people either in France or England.

But the case is, that the representative system diffuses such a body of knowledge throughout a nation, on the subject of government, as to explode ignorance and preclude imposition. The craft of courts cannot be acted on that ground. There is no place for mystery; nowhere for it to begin. Those who are not in the representation, know as much of the nature of business as those who are. An affectation of mysterious importance would there be scouted. Nations can have no secrets; and the secrets of courts, like those of individuals, are always their defects.

In the representative system, the reason for everything must publicly appear. Every man is a proprietor in government, and considers it a necessary part of his business to understand. It concerns his interest, because it affects his property. He examines the cost, and compares it with the advantages; and above all, he does not adopt the slavish custom of following what in other governments are called Leaders.

It can only be by blinding the understanding of man, and making him believe that government is some wonderful mysterious thing, that excessive revenues are obtained. Monarchy is well calculated to ensure this end. It is the popery of government; a thing kept up to amuse the ignorant, and quiet them into taxes.

The government of a free country, properly speaking, is not in the persons, but in the laws. The enacting of those requires no great expense; and when they are administered, the whole of civil government is performed—the rest is all court contrivance.

CHAPTER IV. OF CONSTITUTIONS

That men mean distinct and separate things when they speak of constitutions and of governments, is evident; or why are those terms distinctly and separately used? A constitution is not the act of a government, but of a people constituting a government; and government without a constitution, is power without a right.

All power exercised over a nation, must have some beginning. It must either be delegated or assumed. There are no other sources. All delegated power is trust, and all assumed power is usurpation. Time does not alter the nature and quality of either.

In viewing this subject, the case and circumstances of America present themselves as in the beginning of a world; and our enquiry into the origin of government is shortened, by referring to the facts that have arisen in our own day. We have no occasion to roam for information into the obscure field of antiquity, nor hazard ourselves upon conjecture. We are brought at once to the point of seeing government begin, as if we had lived in the beginning of time. The real volume, not of history, but of facts, is directly before us, unmutilated by contrivance, or the errors of tradition.

I will here concisely state the commencement of the American constitutions; by which the difference between constitutions and governments will sufficiently appear.

It may not appear improper to remind the reader that the United States of America consist of thirteen separate states, each of which established a government for itself, after the declaration of independence, done the 4th of July, 1776. Each state acted independently of the rest, in forming its governments; but the same general principle pervades the whole. When the several state governments were formed, they proceeded to form the federal government, that acts over the whole in all matters which concern the interest of the whole, or which relate to the intercourse of the several states with each other, or with foreign nations. I will begin with giving an instance from one of the state governments (that of Pennsylvania) and then proceed to the federal government.

The state of Pennsylvania, though nearly of the same extent of territory as England, was then divided into only twelve counties. Each of those counties had elected a committee at the commencement of the dispute with the English government; and as the city of Philadelphia, which also had its committee, was the most central for intelligence, it became the center of communication to the several country committees. When it became necessary to proceed to the formation of a government, the committee of Philadelphia proposed a conference of all the committees, to be held in that city, and which met the latter end of July, 1776.

Though these committees had been duly elected by the people, they were not elected expressly for the purpose, nor invested with the authority of forming a constitution; and as they could not, consistently with the American idea of rights, assume such a power, they could only confer upon the matter, and put it into a train of operation. The conferees, therefore, did no more than state the case, and recommend to the several counties to elect six representatives for each county, to meet in convention at Philadelphia, with powers to form a constitution, and propose it for public consideration.

This convention, of which Benjamin Franklin was president, having met and deliberated, and agreed upon a constitution, they next ordered it to be published, not as a thing established, but for the consideration of the whole people, their approbation or rejection, and then adjourned to a stated time. When the time of adjournment was expired, the convention re-assembled; and as the general opinion of the people in approbation of it was then known, the constitution was signed, sealed, and proclaimed on the authority of the people and the original instrument deposited as a public record. The convention then appointed a day for the general election of the representatives who were to compose the government, and the time it should commence; and having done this they dissolved, and returned to their several homes and occupations.

In this constitution were laid down, first, a declaration of rights; then followed the form which the government should have, and the powers it should possess—the authority of the courts of judicature, and of juries—the manner in which elections should be conducted, and the proportion of representatives to the number of electors—the time which each succeeding assembly should continue, which was one year—the mode of levying, and of accounting for the expenditure, of public money—of appointing public officers, etc., etc., etc.

No article of this constitution could be altered or infringed at the discretion of the government that was to ensue. It was to that government a law. But as it would have been unwise to preclude the benefit of experience, and in order also to prevent the accumulation of errors, if any should be found, and to preserve an unison of government with the circumstances of the state at all times, the constitution provided that, at the expiration of every seven years, a convention should be elected, for the express purpose of revising the constitution, and making alterations, additions, or abolitions therein, if any such should be found necessary.

Here we see a regular process—a government issuing out of a constitution, formed by the people in their original character; and that constitution serving, not only as an authority, but as a law of control to the government. It was the political bible of the state. Scarcely a family was without it. Every member of the government had a copy; and nothing was more common, when any debate arose on the principle of a bill, or on the extent of any species of authority, than for the members to take the printed constitution out of their pocket, and read the chapter with which such matter in debate was connected.

Having thus given an instance from one of the states, I will show the proceedings by which the federal constitution of the United States arose and was formed.

Congress, at its two first meetings, in September 1774, and May 1775, was nothing more than a deputation from the legislatures of the several provinces, afterwards states; and had no other authority than what arose from common consent, and the necessity of its acting as a public body. In everything which related to the internal affairs of America, congress went no further than to issue recommendations to the several provincial assemblies, who at discretion adopted them or not. Nothing on the part of congress was compulsive; yet, in this situation, it was more faithfully and affectionately obeyed than was any government in Europe. This instance, like that of the national assembly in France, sufficiently shows, that the strength of government does not consist in any thing itself, but in the attachment of a nation, and the interest which a people feel in supporting it. When this is lost, government is but a child in power; and though, like the old government in France, it may harass individuals for a while, it but facilitates its own fall.

After the declaration of independence, it became consistent with the principle on which representative government is founded, that the authority of congress should be defined and established. Whether that authority should be more or less than congress then discretionarily exercised was not the question. It was merely the rectitude of the measure.

For this purpose, the act, called the act of confederation (which was a sort of imperfect federal constitution), was proposed, and, after long deliberation, was concluded in the year 1781. It was not the act of congress, because it is repugnant to the principles of representative government that a body should give power to itself. Congress first informed the several states, of the powers which it conceived were necessary to be invested in the union, to enable it to perform the duties and services required from it; and the states severally agreed with each other, and concentrated in congress those powers.

It may not be improper to observe that in both those instances (the one of Pennsylvania, and the other of the United States), there is no such thing as the idea of a compact between the people on one side, and the government on the other. The compact was that of the people with each other, to produce and constitute a government. To suppose that any government can be a party in a compact with the whole people, is to suppose it to have existence before it can have a right to exist. The only instance in which a compact can take place between the people and those who exercise the government, is, that the people shall pay them, while they choose to employ them.

Government is not a trade which any man, or any body of men, has a right to set up and exercise for his own emolument, but is altogether a trust, in right of those by whom that trust is delegated, and by whom it is always resumeable. It has of itself no rights; they are altogether duties.

Having thus given two instances of the original formation of a constitution, I will show the manner in which both have been changed since their first establishment.

The powers vested in the governments of the several states, by the state constitutions, were found, upon experience, to be too great; and those vested in the federal government, by the act of confederation, too little. The defect was not in the principle, but in the distribution of power.

Numerous publications, in pamphlets and in the newspapers, appeared, on the propriety and necessity of new modelling the federal government. After some time of public discussion, carried on through the channel of the press, and in conversations, the state of Virginia, experiencing some inconvenience with respect to commerce, proposed holding a continental conference; in consequence of which, a deputation from five or six state assemblies met at Annapolis, in Maryland, in 1786. This meeting, not conceiving itself sufficiently authorised to go into the business of a reform, did no more than state their general opinions of the propriety of the measure, and recommend that a convention of all the states should be held the year following.

The convention met at Philadelphia in May, 1787, of which General Washington was elected president. He was not at that time connected with any of the state governments, or with congress. He delivered up his commission when the war ended, and since then had lived a private citizen.

The convention went deeply into all the subjects; and having, after a variety of debate and investigation, agreed among themselves upon the several parts of a federal constitution, the next question was, the manner of giving it authority and practice.

For this purpose they did not, like a cabal of courtiers, send for a Dutch Stadtholder, or a German Elector; but they referred the whole matter to the sense and interest of the country.

They first directed that the proposed constitution should be published. Secondly, that each state should elect a convention, expressly for the purpose of taking it into consideration, and of ratifying or rejecting it; and that as soon as the approbation and ratification of any nine states should be given, that those states shall proceed to the election of their proportion of members to the new federal government; and that the operation of it should then begin, and the former federal government cease.

The several states proceeded accordingly to elect their conventions. Some of those conventions ratified the constitution by very large majorities, and two or three unanimously. In others there were much debate and division of opinion. In the Massachusetts convention, which met at Boston, the majority was not above nineteen or twenty, in about three hundred members; but such is the nature of representative government, that it quietly decides all matters by majority. After the debate in the Massachusetts convention was closed, and the vote taken, the objecting members rose and declared, "That though they had argued and voted against it, because certain parts appeared to them in a different light to what they appeared to other members; yet, as the vote had decided in favour of the constitution as proposed, they should give it the same practical support as if they had for it."

As soon as nine states had concurred (and the rest followed in the order their conventions were elected), the old fabric of the federal government was taken down, and the new one erected, of which General Washington is president.—In this place I cannot help remarking, that the character and services of this gentleman are sufficient to put all those men called kings to shame. While they are receiving from the sweat and labours of mankind, a prodigality of pay, to which neither their abilities nor their services can entitle them, he is rendering every service in his power, and refusing every pecuniary reward. He accepted no pay as commander-in-chief; he accepts none as president of the United States.

After the new federal constitution was established, the state of Pennsylvania, conceiving that some parts of its own constitution required to be altered, elected a convention for that purpose. The proposed alterations were published, and the people concurring therein, they were established.

In forming those constitutions, or in altering them, little or no inconvenience took place. The ordinary course of things was not interrupted, and the advantages have been much. It is always the interest of a far greater number of people in a nation to have things right, than to let them remain wrong; and when public matters are open to debate, and the public judgment free, it will not decide wrong, unless it decides too hastily.

In the two instances of changing the constitutions, the governments then in being were not actors either way. Government has no right to make itself a party in any debate respecting the principles or modes of forming, or of changing, constitutions. It is not for the benefit of those who exercise the powers of government that constitutions, and the governments issuing from them, are established. In all those matters the right of judging and acting are in those who pay, and not in those who receive.

A constitution is the property of a nation, and not of those who exercise the government. All the constitutions of America are declared to be established on the authority of the people. In France, the word nation is used instead of the people; but in both cases, a constitution is a thing antecedent to the government, and always distinct there from.

In England it is not difficult to perceive that everything has a constitution, except the nation. Every society and association that is established, first agreed upon a number of original articles, digested into form, which are its constitution. It then appointed its officers, whose powers and authorities are described in that constitution, and the government of that society then commenced. Those officers, by whatever name they are called, have no authority to add to, alter, or abridge the original articles. It is only to the constituting power that this right belongs.

From the want of understanding the difference between a constitution and a government, Dr. Johnson, and all writers of his description, have always bewildered themselves. They could not but perceive, that there must necessarily be a controlling power existing somewhere, and they placed this power in the discretion of the persons exercising the government, instead of placing it in a constitution formed by the nation. When it is in a constitution, it has the nation for its support, and the natural and the political controlling powers are together. The laws which are enacted by governments, control men only as individuals, but the nation, through its constitution, controls the whole government, and has a natural ability to do so. The final controlling power, therefore, and the original constituting power, are one and the same power.

Dr. Johnson could not have advanced such a position in any country where there was a constitution; and he is himself an evidence that no such thing as a constitution exists in England. But it may be put as a question, not improper to be investigated, that if a constitution does not exist, how came the idea of its existence so generally established?

In order to decide this question, it is necessary to consider a constitution in both its cases:—First, as creating a government and giving it powers. Secondly, as regulating and restraining the powers so given.

If we begin with William of Normandy, we find that the government of England was originally a tyranny, founded on an invasion and conquest of the country. This being admitted, it will then appear, that the exertion of the nation, at different periods, to abate that tyranny, and render it less intolerable, has been credited for a constitution.

Magna Charta, as it was called (it is now like an almanack of the same date), was no more than compelling the government to renounce a part of its assumptions. It did not create and give powers to government in a manner a constitution does; but was, as far as it went, of the nature of a re-conquest, and not a constitution; for could the nation have totally expelled the usurpation, as France has done its despotism, it would then have had a constitution to form.

The history of the Edwards and the Henries, and up to the commencement of the Stuarts, exhibits as many instances of tyranny as could be acted within the limits to which the nation had restricted it. The Stuarts endeavoured to pass those limits, and their fate is well known. In all those instances we see nothing of a constitution, but only of restrictions on assumed power.

After this, another William, descended from the same stock, and claiming from the same origin, gained possession; and of the two evils, James and William, the nation preferred what it thought the least; since, from circumstances, it must take one. The act, called the Bill of Rights, comes here into view. What is it, but a bargain, which the parts of the government made with each other to divide powers, profits, and privileges? You shall have so much, and I will have the rest; and with respect to the nation, it said, for your share, You shall have the right of petitioning. This being the case, the bill of rights is more properly a bill of wrongs, and of insult. As to what is called the convention parliament, it was a thing that made itself, and then made the authority by which it acted. A few persons got together, and called themselves by that name. Several of them had never been elected, and none of them for the purpose.

From the time of William a species of government arose, issuing out of this coalition bill of rights; and more so, since the corruption introduced at the Hanover succession by the agency of Walpole; that can be described by no other name than a despotic legislation. Though the parts may embarrass each other, the whole has no bounds; and the only right it acknowledges out of itself, is the right of petitioning. Where then is the constitution either that gives or restrains power?

It is not because a part of the government is elective, that makes it less a despotism, if the persons so elected possess afterwards, as a parliament, unlimited powers. Election, in this case, becomes separated from representation, and the candidates are candidates for despotism.

I cannot believe that any nation, reasoning on its own rights, would have thought of calling these things a constitution, if the cry of constitution had not been set up by the government. It has got into circulation like the words bore and quoz [quiz], by being chalked up in the speeches of parliament, as those words were on window shutters and doorposts; but whatever the constitution may be in other respects, it has undoubtedly been the most productive machine of taxation that was ever invented. The taxes in France, under the new constitution, are not quite thirteen shillings per head,*18 and the taxes in England, under what is called its present constitution, are forty-eight shillings and sixpence per head—men, women, and children—amounting to nearly seventeen millions sterling, besides the expense of collecting, which is upwards of a million more.

In a country like England, where the whole of the civil Government is executed by the people of every town and county, by means of parish officers, magistrates, quarterly sessions, juries, and assize; without any trouble to what is called the government or any other expense to the revenue than the salary of the judges, it is astonishing how such a mass of taxes can be employed. Not even the internal defence of the country is paid out of the revenue. On all occasions, whether real or contrived, recourse is continually had to new loans and new taxes. No wonder, then, that a machine of government so advantageous to the advocates of a court, should be so triumphantly extolled! No wonder, that St. James's or St. Stephen's should echo with the continual cry of constitution; no wonder, that the French revolution should be reprobated, and the res-publica treated with reproach! The red book of England, like the red book of France, will explain the reason.*19

I will now, by way of relaxation, turn a thought or two to Mr. Burke. I ask his pardon for neglecting him so long.

"America," says he (in his speech on the Canada Constitution bill), "never dreamed of such absurd doctrine as the Rights of Man."

Mr. Burke is such a bold presumer, and advances his assertions and his premises with such a deficiency of judgment, that, without troubling ourselves about principles of philosophy or politics, the mere logical conclusions they produce, are ridiculous. For instance,

If governments, as Mr. Burke asserts, are not founded on the Rights of Man, and are founded on any rights at all, they consequently must be founded on the right of something that is not man. What then is that something?

Generally speaking, we know of no other creatures that inhabit the earth than man and beast; and in all cases, where only two things offer themselves, and one must be admitted, a negation proved on any one, amounts to an affirmative on the other; and therefore, Mr. Burke, by proving against the Rights of Man, proves in behalf of the beast; and consequently, proves that government is a beast; and as difficult things sometimes explain each other, we now see the origin of keeping wild beasts in the Tower; for they certainly can be of no other use than to show the origin of the government. They are in the place of a constitution. O John Bull, what honours thou hast lost by not being a wild beast. Thou mightest, on Mr. Burke's system, have been in the Tower for life.

If Mr. Burke's arguments have not weight enough to keep one serious, the fault is less mine than his; and as I am willing to make an apology to the reader for the liberty I have taken, I hope Mr. Burke will also make his for giving the cause.

Having thus paid Mr. Burke the compliment of remembering him, I return to the subject.

From the want of a constitution in England to restrain and regulate the wild impulse of power, many of the laws are irrational and tyrannical, and the administration of them vague and problematical.

The attention of the government of England (for I rather choose to call it by this name than the English government) appears, since its political connection with Germany, to have been so completely engrossed and absorbed by foreign affairs, and the means of raising taxes, that it seems to exist for no other purposes. Domestic concerns are neglected; and with respect to regular law, there is scarcely such a thing.

Almost every case must now be determined by some precedent, be that precedent good or bad, or whether it properly applies or not; and the practice is become so general as to suggest a suspicion, that it proceeds from a deeper policy than at first sight appears.

Since the revolution of America, and more so since that of France, this preaching up the doctrines of precedents, drawn from times and circumstances antecedent to those events, has been the studied practice of the English government. The generality of those precedents are founded on principles and opinions, the reverse of what they ought; and the greater distance of time they are drawn from, the more they are to be suspected. But by associating those precedents with a superstitious reverence for ancient things, as monks show relics and call them holy, the generality of mankind are deceived into the design. Governments now act as if they were afraid to awaken a single reflection in man. They are softly leading him to the sepulchre of precedents, to deaden his faculties and call attention from the scene of revolutions. They feel that he is arriving at knowledge faster than they wish, and their policy of precedents is the barometer of their fears. This political popery, like the ecclesiastical popery of old, has had its day, and is hastening to its exit. The ragged relic and the antiquated precedent, the monk and the monarch, will moulder together.

Government by precedent, without any regard to the principle of the precedent, is one of the vilest systems that can be set up. In numerous instances, the precedent ought to operate as a warning, and not as an example, and requires to be shunned instead of imitated; but instead of this, precedents are taken in the lump, and put at once for constitution and for law.

Either the doctrine of precedents is policy to keep a man in a state of ignorance, or it is a practical confession that wisdom degenerates in governments as governments increase in age, and can only hobble along by the stilts and crutches of precedents. How is it that the same persons who would proudly be thought wiser than their predecessors, appear at the same time only as the ghosts of departed wisdom? How strangely is antiquity treated! To some purposes it is spoken of as the times of darkness and ignorance, and to answer others, it is put for the light of the world.

If the doctrine of precedents is to be followed, the expenses of government need not continue the same. Why pay men extravagantly, who have but little to do? If everything that can happen is already in precedent, legislation is at an end, and precedent, like a dictionary, determines every case. Either, therefore, government has arrived at its dotage, and requires to be renovated, or all the occasions for exercising its wisdom have occurred.

We now see all over Europe, and particularly in England, the curious phenomenon of a nation looking one way, and the government the other—the one forward and the other backward. If governments are to go on by precedent, while nations go on by improvement, they must at last come to a final separation; and the sooner, and the more civilly they determine this point, the better.*[20]

Having thus spoken of constitutions generally, as things distinct from actual governments, let us proceed to consider the parts of which a constitution is composed.

Opinions differ more on this subject than with respect to the whole. That a nation ought to have a constitution, as a rule for the conduct of its government, is a simple question in which all men, not directly courtiers, will agree. It is only on the component parts that questions and opinions multiply.

But this difficulty, like every other, will diminish when put into a train of being rightly understood.

The first thing is, that a nation has a right to establish a constitution.

Whether it exercises this right in the most judicious manner at first is quite another case. It exercises it agreeably to the judgment it possesses; and by continuing to do so, all errors will at last be exploded.

When this right is established in a nation, there is no fear that it will be employed to its own injury. A nation can have no interest in being wrong.

Though all the constitutions of America are on one general principle, yet no two of them are exactly alike in their component parts, or in the distribution of the powers which they give to the actual governments. Some are more, and others less complex.

In forming a constitution, it is first necessary to consider what are the ends for which government is necessary? Secondly, what are the best means, and the least expensive, for accomplishing those ends?

Government is nothing more than a national association; and the object of this association is the good of all, as well individually as collectively. Every man wishes to pursue his occupation, and to enjoy the fruits of his labours and the produce of his property in peace and safety, and with the least possible expense. When these things are accomplished, all the objects for which government ought to be established are answered.

It has been customary to consider government under three distinct general heads. The legislative, the executive, and the judicial.

But if we permit our judgment to act unincumbered by the habit of multiplied terms, we can perceive no more than two divisions of power, of which civil government is composed, namely, that of legislating or enacting laws, and that of executing or administering them. Everything, therefore, appertaining to civil government, classes itself under one or other of these two divisions.

So far as regards the execution of the laws, that which is called the judicial power, is strictly and properly the executive power of every country. It is that power to which every individual has appeal, and which causes the laws to be executed; neither have we any other clear idea with respect to the official execution of the laws. In England, and also in America and France, this power begins with the magistrate, and proceeds up through all the courts of judicature.

I leave to courtiers to explain what is meant by calling monarchy the executive power. It is merely a name in which acts of government are done; and any other, or none at all, would answer the same purpose. Laws have neither more nor less authority on this account. It must be from the justness of their principles, and the interest which a nation feels therein, that they derive support; if they require any other than this, it is a sign that something in the system of government is imperfect. Laws difficult to be executed cannot be generally good.

With respect to the organization of the legislative power, different modes have been adopted in different countries. In America it is generally composed of two houses. In France it consists but of one, but in both countries, it is wholly by representation.

The case is, that mankind (from the long tyranny of assumed power) have had so few opportunities of making the necessary trials on modes and principles of government, in order to discover the best, that government is but now beginning to be known, and experience is yet wanting to determine many particulars.

The objections against two houses are, first, that there is an inconsistency in any part of a whole legislature, coming to a final determination by vote on any matter, whilst that matter, with respect to that whole, is yet only in a train of deliberation, and consequently open to new illustrations.

Secondly, That by taking the vote on each, as a separate body, it always admits of the possibility, and is often the case in practice, that the minority governs the majority, and that, in some instances, to a degree of great inconsistency.

Thirdly, That two houses arbitrarily checking or controlling each other is inconsistent; because it cannot be proved on the principles of just representation, that either should be wiser or better than the other. They may check in the wrong as well as in the right therefore to give the power where we cannot give the wisdom to use it, nor be assured of its being rightly used, renders the hazard at least equal to the precaution.*21

The objection against a single house is, that it is always in a condition of committing itself too soon.—But it should at the same time be remembered, that when there is a constitution which defines the power, and establishes the principles within which a legislature shall act, there is already a more effectual check provided, and more powerfully operating, than any other check can be. For example,

Were a Bill to be brought into any of the American legislatures similar to that which was passed into an act by the English parliament, at the commencement of George the First, to extend the duration of the assemblies to a longer period than they now sit, the check is in the constitution, which in effect says, Thus far shalt thou go and no further.

But in order to remove the objection against a single house (that of acting with too quick an impulse), and at the same time to avoid the inconsistencies, in some cases absurdities, arising from two houses, the following method has been proposed as an improvement upon both.

First, To have but one representation.

Secondly, To divide that representation, by lot, into two or three parts.

Thirdly, That every proposed bill shall be first debated in those parts by succession, that they may become the hearers of each other, but without taking any vote. After which the whole representation to assemble for a general debate and determination by vote.

To this proposed improvement has been added another, for the purpose of keeping the representation in the state of constant renovation; which is, that one-third of the representation of each county, shall go out at the expiration of one year, and the number be replaced by new elections. Another third at the expiration of the second year replaced in like manner, and every third year to be a general election.*22

But in whatever manner the separate parts of a constitution may be arranged, there is one general principle that distinguishes freedom from slavery, which is, that all hereditary government over a people is to them a species of slavery, and representative government is freedom.

Considering government in the only light in which it should be considered, that of a National Association, it ought to be so constructed as not to be disordered by any accident happening among the parts; and, therefore, no extraordinary power, capable of producing such an effect, should be lodged in the hands of any individual. The death, sickness, absence or defection, of any one individual in a government, ought to be a matter of no more consequence, with respect to the nation, than if the same circumstance had taken place in a member of the English Parliament, or the French National Assembly.

Scarcely anything presents a more degrading character of national greatness, than its being thrown into confusion, by anything happening to or acted by any individual; and the ridiculousness of the scene is often increased by the natural insignificance of the person by whom it is occasioned. Were a government so constructed, that it could not go on unless a goose or a gander were present in the senate, the difficulties would be just as great and as real, on the flight or sickness of the goose, or the gander, as if it were called a King. We laugh at individuals for the silly difficulties they make to themselves, without perceiving that the greatest of all ridiculous things are acted in governments.*23

All the constitutions of America are on a plan that excludes the childish embarrassments which occur in monarchical countries. No suspension of government can there take place for a moment, from any circumstances whatever. The system of representation provides for everything, and is the only system in which nations and governments can always appear in their proper character.

As extraordinary power ought not to be lodged in the hands of any individual, so ought there to be no appropriations of public money to any person, beyond what his services in a state may be worth. It signifies not whether a man be called a president, a king, an emperor, a senator, or by any other name which propriety or folly may devise or arrogance assume; it is only a certain service he can perform in the state; and the service of any such individual in the routine of office, whether such office be called monarchical, presidential, senatorial, or by any other name or title, can never exceed the value of ten thousand pounds a year. All the great services that are done in the world are performed by volunteer characters, who accept nothing for them; but the routine of office is always regulated to such a general standard of abilities as to be within the compass of numbers in every country to perform, and therefore cannot merit very extraordinary recompense. Government, says Swift, is a Plain thing, and fitted to the capacity of many heads.

It is inhuman to talk of a million sterling a year, paid out of the public taxes of any country, for the support of any individual, whilst thousands who are forced to contribute thereto, are pining with want, and struggling with misery. Government does not consist in a contrast between prisons and palaces, between poverty and pomp; it is not instituted to rob the needy of his mite, and increase the wretchedness of the wretched.—But on this part of the subject I shall speak hereafter, and confine myself at present to political observations.

When extraordinary power and extraordinary pay are allotted to any individual in a government, he becomes the center, round which every kind of corruption generates and forms. Give to any man a million a year, and add thereto the power of creating and disposing of places, at the expense of a country, and the liberties of that country are no longer secure. What is called the splendour of a throne is no other than the corruption of the state. It is made up of a band of parasites, living in luxurious indolence, out of the public taxes.

When once such a vicious system is established it becomes the guard and protection of all inferior abuses. The man who is in the receipt of a million a year is the last person to promote a spirit of reform, lest, in the event, it should reach to himself. It is always his interest to defend inferior abuses, as so many outworks to protect the citadel; and on this species of political fortification, all the parts have such a common dependence that it is never to be expected they will attack each other.*24

Monarchy would not have continued so many ages in the world, had it not been for the abuses it protects. It is the master-fraud, which shelters all others. By admitting a participation of the spoil, it makes itself friends; and when it ceases to do this it will cease to be the idol of courtiers.

As the principle on which constitutions are now formed rejects all hereditary pretensions to government, it also rejects all that catalogue of assumptions known by the name of prerogatives.

If there is any government where prerogatives might with apparent safety be entrusted to any individual, it is in the federal government of America. The president of the United States of America is elected only for four years. He is not only responsible in the general sense of the word, but a particular mode is laid down in the constitution for trying him. He cannot be elected under thirty-five years of age; and he must be a native of the country.

In a comparison of these cases with the Government of England, the difference when applied to the latter amounts to an absurdity. In England the person who exercises prerogative is often a foreigner; always half a foreigner, and always married to a foreigner. He is never in full natural or political connection with the country, is not responsible for anything, and becomes of age at eighteen years; yet such a person is permitted to form foreign alliances, without even the knowledge of the nation, and to make war and peace without its consent.

But this is not all. Though such a person cannot dispose of the government in the manner of a testator, he dictates the marriage connections, which, in effect, accomplish a great part of the same end. He cannot directly bequeath half the government to

Prussia, but he can form a marriage partnership that will produce almost the same thing. Under such circumstances, it is happy for England that she is not situated on the Continent, or she might, like Holland, fall under the dictatorship of Prussia. Holland, by marriage, is as effectually governed by Prussia, as if the old tyranny of bequeathing the government had been the means.

The presidency in America (or, as it is sometimes called, the executive) is the only office from which a foreigner is excluded, and in England it is the only one to which he is admitted. A foreigner cannot be a member of Parliament, but he may be what is called a king. If there is any reason for excluding foreigners, it ought to be from those offices where mischief can most be acted, and where, by uniting every bias of interest and attachment, the trust is best secured. But as nations proceed in the great business of forming constitutions, they will examine with more precision into the nature and business of that department which is called the executive. What the legislative and judicial departments are every one can see; but with respect to what, in Europe, is called the executive, as distinct from those two, it is either a political superfluity or a chaos of unknown things.

Some kind of official department, to which reports shall be made from the different parts of a nation, or from abroad, to be laid before the national representatives, is all that is necessary; but there is no consistency in calling this the executive; neither can it be considered in any other light than as inferior to the legislative. The sovereign authority in any country is the power of making laws, and everything else is an official department.

Next to the arrangement of the principles and the organization of the several parts of a constitution, is the provision to be made for the support of the persons to whom the nation shall confide the administration of the constitutional powers.

A nation can have no right to the time and services of any person at his own expense, whom it may choose to employ or entrust in any department whatever; neither can any reason be given for making provision for the support of any one part of a government and not for the other.

But admitting that the honour of being entrusted with any part of a government is to be considered a sufficient reward, it ought to be so to every person alike. If the members of the legislature of any country are to serve at their own expense that which is called the executive, whether monarchical or by any other name, ought to serve in like manner. It is inconsistent to pay the one, and accept the service of the other gratis.

In America, every department in the government is decently provided for; but no one is extravagantly paid. Every member of Congress, and of the Assemblies, is allowed a sufficiency for his expenses. Whereas in England, a most prodigal provision is made for the support of one part of the Government, and none for the other, the consequence of which is that the one is furnished with the means of corruption and the other is put into the condition of being corrupted. Less than a fourth part of such expense, applied as it is in America, would remedy a great part of the corruption.

Another reform in the American constitution is the exploding all oaths of personality. The oath of allegiance in America is to the nation only. The putting any individual as a figure for a nation is improper. The happiness of a nation is the superior object, and therefore the intention of an oath of allegiance ought not to be obscured by being figuratively taken, to, or in the name of, any person. The oath, called the civic oath, in France, viz., "the nation, the law, and the king," is improper. If taken at all, it ought to be as in America, to the nation only. The law may or may not be good; but, in this place, it can have no other meaning, than as being conducive to the happiness of a nation, and therefore is included in it. The remainder of the oath is improper, on the ground, that all personal oaths ought to be abolished. They are the remains of tyranny on one part and slavery on the other; and the name of the Creator ought not to be introduced to witness the degradation of his creation; or if taken, as is already mentioned, as figurative of the nation, it is in this place redundant. But whatever apology may be made for oaths at the first establishment of a government, they ought not to be permitted afterwards. If a government requires the support of oaths, it is a sign that it is not worth supporting, and ought not to be supported. Make government what it ought to be, and it will support itself.

To conclude this part of the subject:—One of the greatest improvements that have been made for the perpetual security and progress of constitutional liberty, is the provision which the new constitutions make for occasionally revising, altering, and amending them.

The principle upon which Mr. Burke formed his political creed, that of "binding and controlling posterity to the end of time, and of renouncing and abdicating the rights of all posterity, for ever," is now become too detestable to be made a subject of debate; and therefore, I pass it over with no other notice than exposing it.

Government is but now beginning to be known. Hitherto it has been the mere exercise of power, which forbade all effectual enquiry into rights, and grounded itself wholly on possession. While the enemy of liberty was its judge, the progress of its principles must have been small indeed.

The constitutions of America, and also that of France, have either affixed a period for their revision, or laid down the mode by which improvement shall be made. It is perhaps impossible to establish anything that combines principles with opinions and practice, which the progress of circumstances, through a length of years, will not in some measure derange, or render inconsistent; and, therefore, to prevent inconveniences accumulating, till they discourage reformations or provoke revolutions, it is best to provide the means of regulating them as they occur. The Rights of Man are the rights of all generations of men, and cannot be monopolised by any. That which is worth following, will be followed for the sake of its worth, and it is in this that its security lies, and not in any conditions with which it may be encumbered. When a man leaves property to his heirs, he does not connect it with an obligation that they shall accept it. Why, then, should we do otherwise with respect to constitutions? The best constitution that could now be devised, consistent with the condition of the present moment, may be far short of that excellence which a few years may afford. There is a morning of reason rising upon man on the subject of government, that has not appeared before. As the barbarism of the present old governments expires, the moral conditions of nations with respect to each other will be changed. Man will not be brought up with the savage idea of considering his species as his enemy, because the accident of birth gave the individuals existence in countries distinguished by different names; and as constitutions have always some relation to external as well as to domestic circumstances, the means of benefitting by every change, foreign or domestic, should be a part of every constitution. We already see an alteration in the national disposition of England and France towards each other, which, when we look back to only a few years, is itself a Revolution. Who could have foreseen, or who could have believed, that a French National Assembly would ever have been a popular toast in England, or that a friendly alliance of the two nations should become the wish of either? It shows that man, were he not corrupted by governments, is naturally the friend of man, and that human nature is not of itself vicious. That spirit of jealousy and ferocity, which the governments of the two countries inspired, and which they rendered subservient to the purpose of taxation, is now yielding to the dictates of reason, interest, and humanity. The trade of courts is beginning to be understood, and the affectation of mystery, with all the artificial sorcery by which they imposed upon mankind, is on the decline. It has received its death-wound; and though it may linger, it will expire. Government ought to be as much open to improvement as anything which appertains to man, instead of which it has been monopolised from age to age, by the most ignorant and vicious of the human race. Need we any other proof of their wretched management, than the excess of debts and taxes with which every nation groans, and the quarrels into which they have precipitated the world? Just emerging from such a barbarous condition, it is too soon to determine to what extent of improvement government may yet be carried. For what we can foresee, all Europe may form but one great Republic, and man be free of the whole.

CHAPTER V. WAYS AND MEANS OF IMPROVING THE CONDITION OF EUROPE

INTERSPERSED WITH MISCELLANEOUS OBSERVATIONS

In contemplating a subject that embraces with equatorial magnitude the whole region of humanity it is impossible to confine the pursuit in one single direction. It takes ground on every character and condition that appertains to man, and blends the individual, the nation, and the world. From a small spark, kindled in America, a flame has arisen not to be extinguished. Without consuming, like the Ultima Ratio Regum, it winds its progress from nation to nation, and conquers by a silent operation. Man finds himself changed, he scarcely perceives how. He acquires a knowledge of his rights by attending justly to his interest, and discovers in the event that the strength and powers of despotism consist wholly in the fear of resisting it, and that, in order "to be free, it is sufficient that he wills it."

Having in all the preceding parts of this work endeavoured to establish a system of principles as a basis on which governments ought to be erected, I shall proceed in this, to the ways and means of rendering them into practice. But in order to introduce this part of the subject with more propriety, and stronger effect, some preliminary observations, deducible from, or connected with, those principles, are necessary.

Whatever the form or constitution of government may be, it ought to have no other object than the general happiness. When, instead of this, it operates to create and increase wretchedness in any of the parts of society, it is on a wrong system, and reformation is necessary. Customary language has classed the condition of man under the two descriptions of civilised and uncivilised life. To the one it has ascribed felicity and affluence; to the other hardship and want. But, however our imagination may be impressed by painting and comparison, it is nevertheless true, that a great portion of mankind, in what are called civilised countries, are in a state of poverty and wretchedness, far below the condition of an Indian. I speak not of one country, but of all. It is so in England, it is so all over Europe. Let us enquire into the cause.

It lies not in any natural defect in the principles of civilisation, but in preventing those principles having a universal operation; the consequence of which is, a perpetual system of war and expense, that drains the country, and defeats the general felicity of which civilisation is capable. All the European governments (France now excepted) are constructed not on the principle of universal civilisation, but on the reverse of it. So far as those governments relate to each other, they are in the same condition as we conceive of savage uncivilised life; they put themselves beyond the law as well of God as of man, and are, with respect to principle and reciprocal conduct, like so many individuals in a state of nature. The inhabitants of every country, under the civilisation of laws, easily civilise together, but governments being yet in an uncivilised state, and almost continually at war, they pervert the abundance which civilised life produces to carry on the uncivilised part to a greater extent. By thus engrafting the barbarism of government upon the internal civilisation of a country, it draws from the latter, and more especially from the poor, a great portion of those earnings, which should be applied to their own subsistence and comfort. Apart from all reflections of morality and philosophy, it is a melancholy fact that more than one-fourth of the labour of mankind is annually consumed by this barbarous system. What has served to continue this evil, is the pecuniary advantage which all the governments of Europe have found in keeping up this state of uncivilisation. It affords to them pretences for power, and revenue, for which there would be neither occasion nor apology, if the circle of civilisation were rendered complete. Civil government alone, or the government of laws, is not productive of pretences for many taxes; it operates at home, directly under the eye of the country, and precludes the possibility of much imposition. But when the scene is laid in the uncivilised contention of governments, the field of pretences is enlarged, and the country, being no longer a judge, is open to every imposition, which governments please to act. Not a thirtieth, scarcely a fortieth, part of the taxes which are raised in England are either occasioned by, or applied to, the purpose of civil government. It is not difficult to see, that the whole which the actual government does in this respect, is to enact laws, and that the country administers and executes them, at its own expense, by means of magistrates, juries, sessions, and assize, over and above the taxes which it pays. In this view of the case, we have two distinct characters of government; the one the civil government, or the government of laws, which operates at home, the other the court or cabinet government, which operates abroad, on the rude plan of uncivilised life; the one attended with little charge, the other with boundless extravagance; and so distinct are the two, that if the latter were to sink, as it were, by a sudden opening of the earth, and totally disappear, the former would not be deranged. It would still proceed, because it is the common interest of the nation that it should, and all the means are in practice. Revolutions, then, have for their object a change in the moral condition of governments, and with this change the burthen of public taxes will lessen, and civilisation will be left to the enjoyment of that abundance, of which it is now deprived. In contemplating the whole of this subject, I extend my views into the department of commerce. In all my publications, where the matter would admit, I have been an advocate for commerce, because I am a friend to its effects. It is a pacific system, operating to cordialise mankind, by rendering nations, as well as individuals, useful to each other. As to the mere theoretical reformation, I have never preached it up. The most effectual process is that of improving the condition of man by means of his interest; and it is on this ground that I take my stand. If commerce were permitted to act to the universal extent it is capable, it would extirpate the system of war, and produce a revolution in the uncivilised state of governments. The invention of commerce has arisen since those governments began, and is the greatest approach towards universal civilisation that has yet been made by any means not immediately flowing from moral principles. Whatever has a tendency to promote the civil intercourse of nations by an exchange of benefits, is a subject as worthy of philosophy as of politics. Commerce is no other than the traffic of two individuals, multiplied on a scale of numbers; and by the same rule that nature intended for the intercourse of two, she intended that of all. For this purpose she has distributed the materials of manufactures and commerce, in various and distant parts of a nation and of the world; and as they cannot be procured by war so cheaply or so commodiously as by commerce, she has rendered the latter the means of extirpating the former. As the two are nearly the opposite of each other, consequently, the uncivilised state of the European governments is injurious to commerce. Every kind of destruction or embarrassment serves to lessen the quantity, and it matters but little in what part of the commercial world the reduction begins. Like blood, it cannot be taken from any of the parts, without being taken from the whole mass in circulation, and all partake of the loss. When the ability in any nation to buy is destroyed, it equally involves the seller. Could the government of England destroy the commerce of all other nations, she would most effectually ruin her own. It is possible that a nation may be the carrier for the world, but she cannot be the merchant. She cannot be the seller and buyer of her own merchandise. The ability to buy must reside out of herself; and, therefore, the prosperity of any commercial nation is regulated by the prosperity of the rest. If they are poor she cannot be rich, and her condition, be what it may, is an index of the height of the commercial tide in other nations. That the principles of commerce, and its universal operation may be understood, without understanding the practice, is a position that reason will not deny; and it is on this ground only that I argue the subject. It is one thing in the counting-house, in the world it is another. With respect to its operation it must necessarily be contemplated as a reciprocal thing; that only one-half its powers resides within the nation, and that the whole is as effectually destroyed by the destroying the half that resides without, as if the destruction had been committed on that which is within; for neither can act without the other. When in the last, as well as in former wars, the commerce of England sunk, it was because the quantity was lessened everywhere; and it now rises, because commerce is in a rising state in every nation. If England, at this day, imports and exports more than at any former period, the nations with which she trades must necessarily do the same; her imports are their exports, and vice versa. There can be no such thing as a nation flourishing alone in commerce: she can only participate; and the destruction of it in any part must necessarily affect all. When, therefore, governments are at war, the attack is made upon a common stock of commerce, and the consequence is the same as if each had attacked his own. The present increase of commerce is not to be attributed to ministers, or to any political contrivances, but to its own natural operation in consequence of peace. The regular markets had been destroyed, the channels of trade broken up, the high road of the seas infested with robbers of every nation, and the attention of the world called to other objects. Those interruptions have ceased, and peace has restored the deranged condition of things to their proper order.*25 It is worth remarking that every nation reckons the balance of trade in its own favour; and therefore something must be irregular in the common ideas upon this subject. The fact, however, is true, according to what is called a balance; and it is from this cause that commerce is universally supported. Every nation feels the advantage, or it would abandon the practice: but the deception lies in the mode of making up the accounts, and in attributing what are called profits to a wrong cause. Mr. Pitt has sometimes amused himself, by showing what he called a balance of trade from the custom-house books. This mode of calculating not only affords no rule that is true, but one that is false. In the first place, Every cargo that departs from the custom-house appears on the books as an export; and, according to the custom-house balance, the losses at sea, and by foreign failures, are all reckoned on the side of profit because they appear as exports.

Secondly, Because the importation by the smuggling trade does not appear on the custom-house books, to arrange against the exports.

No balance, therefore, as applying to superior advantages, can be drawn from these documents; and if we examine the natural operation of commerce, the idea is fallacious; and if true, would soon be injurious. The great support of commerce consists in the balance being a level of benefits among all nations.

Two merchants of different nations trading together, will both become rich, and each makes the balance in his own favour; consequently, they do not get rich of each other; and it is the same with respect to the nations in which they reside. The case must be, that each nation must get rich out of its own means, and increases that riches by something which it procures from another in exchange.

If a merchant in England sends an article of English manufacture abroad which costs him a shilling at home, and imports something which sells for two, he makes a balance of one shilling in his favour; but this is not gained out of the foreign nation or the foreign merchant, for he also does the same by the articles he receives, and neither has the advantage upon the other. The original value of the two articles in their proper countries was but two shillings; but by changing their places, they acquire a new idea of value, equal to double what they had first, and that increased value is equally divided.

There is no otherwise a balance on foreign than on domestic commerce. The merchants of London and Newcastle trade on the same principles, as if they resided in different nations, and make their balances in the same manner: yet London does not get rich out of Newcastle, any more than Newcastle out of London: but coals, the merchandize of Newcastle, have an additional value at London, and London merchandize has the same at Newcastle.

Though the principle of all commerce is the same, the domestic, in a national view, is the part the most beneficial; because the whole of the advantages, an both sides, rests within the nation; whereas, in foreign commerce, it is only a participation of one-half.

The most unprofitable of all commerce is that connected with foreign dominion. To a few individuals it may be beneficial, merely because it is commerce; but to the nation it is a loss. The expense of maintaining dominion more than absorbs the profits of any trade. It does not increase the general quantity in the world, but operates to lessen it; and as a greater mass would be afloat by relinquishing dominion, the participation without the expense would be more valuable than a greater quantity with it.

But it is impossible to engross commerce by dominion; and therefore it is still more fallacious. It cannot exist in confined channels, and necessarily breaks out by regular or irregular means, that defeat the attempt: and to succeed would be still worse. France, since the Revolution, has been more indifferent as to foreign possessions, and other nations will become the same when they investigate the subject with respect to commerce.

To the expense of dominion is to be added that of navies, and when the amounts of the two are subtracted from the profits of commerce, it will appear, that what is called the balance of trade, even admitting it to exist, is not enjoyed by the nation, but absorbed by the Government.

The idea of having navies for the protection of commerce is delusive. It is putting means of destruction for the means of protection. Commerce needs no other protection than the reciprocal interest which every nation feels in supporting it—it is common stock—it exists by a balance of advantages to all; and the only interruption it meets, is from the present uncivilised state of governments, and which it is its common interest to reform.*[26]

Quitting this subject, I now proceed to other matters.—As it is necessary to include England in the prospect of a general reformation, it is proper to inquire into the defects of its government. It is only by each nation reforming its own, that the whole can be improved, and the full benefit of reformation enjoyed. Only partial advantages can flow from partial reforms.

France and England are the only two countries in Europe where a reformation in government could have successfully begun. The one secure by the ocean, and the other by the immensity of its internal strength, could defy the malignancy of foreign despotism. But it is with revolutions as with commerce, the advantages increase by their becoming general, and double to either what each would receive alone.

As a new system is now opening to the view of the world, the European courts are plotting to counteract it. Alliances, contrary to all former systems, are agitating, and a common interest of courts is forming against the common interest of man. This combination draws a line that runs throughout Europe, and presents a cause so entirely new as to exclude all calculations from former circumstances. While despotism warred with despotism, man had no interest in the contest; but in a cause that unites the soldier with the citizen, and nation with nation, the despotism of courts, though it feels the danger and meditates revenge, is afraid to strike.

No question has arisen within the records of history that pressed with the importance of the present. It is not whether this or that party shall be in or not, or Whig or Tory, high or low shall prevail; but whether man shall inherit his rights, and universal civilisation take place? Whether the fruits of his labours shall be enjoyed by himself or consumed by the profligacy of governments? Whether robbery shall be banished from courts, and wretchedness from countries?

When, in countries that are called civilised, we see age going to the workhouse and youth to the gallows, something must be wrong in the system of government. It would seem, by the exterior appearance of such countries, that all was happiness; but there lies hidden from the eye of common observation, a mass of wretchedness, that has scarcely any other chance, than to expire in poverty or infamy. Its entrance into life is marked with the presage of its fate; and until this is remedied, it is in vain to punish.

Civil government does not exist in executions; but in making such provision for the instruction of youth and the support of age, as to exclude, as much as possible, profligacy from the one and despair from the other. Instead of this, the resources of a country are lavished upon kings, upon courts, upon hirelings, impostors and prostitutes; and even the poor themselves, with all their wants upon them, are compelled to support the fraud that oppresses them.

Why is it that scarcely any are executed but the poor? The fact is a proof, among other things, of a wretchedness in their condition. Bred up without morals, and cast upon the world without a prospect, they are the exposed sacrifice of vice and legal barbarity. The millions that are superfluously wasted upon governments are more than sufficient to reform those evils, and to benefit the condition of every man in a nation, not included within the purlieus of a court. This I hope to make appear in the progress of this work.

It is the nature of compassion to associate with misfortune. In taking up this subject I seek no recompense—I fear no consequence. Fortified with that proud integrity, that disdains to triumph or to yield, I will advocate the Rights of Man.

It is to my advantage that I have served an apprenticeship to life. I know the value of moral instruction, and I have seen the danger of the contrary.

At an early period—little more than sixteen years of age, raw and adventurous, and heated with the false heroism of a master*[27] who had served in a man-of-war—I began the carver of my own fortune, and entered on board the Terrible Privateer, Captain Death. From this adventure I was happily prevented by the affectionate and moral remonstrance of a good father, who, from his own habits of life, being of the Quaker profession, must begin to look upon me as lost. But the impression, much as it effected at the time, began to wear away, and I entered afterwards in the King of Prussia Privateer, Captain Mendez, and went with her to sea. Yet, from such a beginning, and with all the inconvenience of early life against me, I am proud to say, that with a perseverance undismayed by difficulties, a disinterestedness that compelled respect, I have not only contributed to raise a new empire in the world, founded on a new system of government, but I have arrived at an eminence in political literature, the most difficult of all lines to succeed and excel in, which aristocracy with all its aids has not been able to reach or to rival.*[28]

Knowing my own heart and feeling myself as I now do, superior to all the skirmish of party, the inveteracy of interested or mistaken opponents, I answer not to falsehood or abuse, but proceed to the defects of the English Government.

I begin with charters and corporations.

It is a perversion of terms to say that a charter gives rights. It operates by a contrary effect—that of taking rights away. Rights are inherently in all the inhabitants; but charters, by annulling those rights, in the majority, leave the right, by exclusion, in the hands of a few. If charters were constructed so as to express in direct terms, "that every inhabitant, who is not a member of a corporation, shall not exercise the right of voting," such charters would, in the face, be charters not of rights, but of exclusion. The effect is the same under the form they now stand; and the only persons on whom they operate are the persons whom they exclude. Those whose rights are guaranteed, by not being taken away, exercise no other rights than as members of the community they are entitled to without a charter; and, therefore, all charters have no other than an indirect negative operation. They do not give rights to A, but they make a difference in favour of A by taking away the right of B, and consequently are instruments of injustice.

But charters and corporations have a more extensive evil effect than what relates merely to elections. They are sources of endless contentions in the places where they exist, and they lessen the common rights of national society. A native of England, under the operation of these charters and corporations, cannot be said to be an Englishman in the full sense of the word. He is not free of the nation, in the same manner that a Frenchman is free of France, and an American of America. His rights are circumscribed to the town, and, in some cases, to the parish of his birth; and all other parts, though in his native land, are to him as a foreign country. To acquire a residence in these, he must undergo a local naturalisation by purchase, or he is forbidden or expelled the place. This species of feudality is kept up to aggrandise the corporations at the ruin of towns; and the effect is visible.

The generality of corporation towns are in a state of solitary decay, and prevented from further ruin only by some circumstance in their situation, such as a navigable river, or a plentiful surrounding country. As population is one of the chief sources of wealth (for without it land itself has no value), everything which operates to prevent it must lessen the value of property; and as corporations have not only this tendency, but directly this effect, they cannot but be injurious. If any policy were to be followed, instead of that of general freedom, to every person to settle where he chose (as in France or America) it would be more consistent to give encouragement to new comers than to preclude their admission by exacting premiums from them.*29

The persons most immediately interested in the abolition of corporations are the inhabitants of the towns where corporations are established. The instances of Manchester, Birmingham, and Sheffield show, by contrast, the injuries which those Gothic institutions are to property and commerce. A few examples may be found, such as that of London, whose natural and commercial advantage, owing to its situation on the Thames, is capable of bearing up against the political evils of a corporation; but in almost all other cases the fatality is too visible to be doubted or denied.

Though the whole nation is not so directly affected by the depression of property in corporation towns as the inhabitants themselves, it partakes of the consequence. By lessening the value of property, the quantity of national commerce is curtailed. Every man is a customer in proportion to his ability; and as all parts of a nation trade with each other, whatever affects any of the parts must necessarily communicate to the whole.

As one of the Houses of the English Parliament is, in a great measure, made up of elections from these corporations; and as it is unnatural that a pure stream should flow from a foul fountain, its vices are but a continuation of the vices of its origin. A man of moral honour and good political principles cannot submit to the mean drudgery and disgraceful arts, by which such elections are carried. To be a successful candidate, he must be destitute of the qualities that constitute a just legislator; and being thus disciplined to corruption by the mode of entering into Parliament, it is not to be expected that the representative should be better than the man.

Mr. Burke, in speaking of the English representation, has advanced as bold a challenge as ever was given in the days of chivalry. "Our representation," says he, "has been found perfectly adequate to all the purposes for which a representation of the people can be desired or devised." "I defy," continues he, "the enemies of our constitution to show the contrary."—This declaration from a man who has been in constant opposition to all the measures of parliament the whole of his political life, a year or two excepted, is most extraordinary; and, comparing him with himself, admits of no other alternative, than that he acted against his judgment as a member, or has declared contrary to it as an author.

But it is not in the representation only that the defects lie, and therefore I proceed in the next place to the aristocracy.

What is called the House of Peers, is constituted on a ground very similar to that, against which there is no law in other cases. It amounts to a combination of persons in one common interest. No better reason can be given, why a house of legislation should be composed entirely of men whose occupation consists in letting landed property, than why it should be composed of those who hire, or of brewers, or bakers, or any other separate class of men. Mr. Burke calls this house "the great ground and pillar of security to the landed interest." Let us examine this idea.

What pillar of security does the landed interest require more than any other interest in the state, or what right has it to a distinct and separate representation from the general interest of a nation? The only use to be made of this power (and which it always has made), is to ward off taxes from itself, and throw the burthen upon those articles of consumption by which itself would be least affected.

That this has been the consequence (and will always be the consequence) of constructing governments on combinations, is evident with respect to England, from the history of its taxes.

Notwithstanding taxes have increased and multiplied upon every article of common consumption, the land-tax, which more particularly affects this "pillar," has diminished. In 1778 the amount of the land-tax was L1,950,000, which is half-a-million less than it produced almost a hundred years ago,*30 notwithstanding the rentals are in many instances doubled since that period.

Before the coming of the Hanoverians, the taxes were divided in nearly equal proportions between the land and articles of consumption, the land bearing rather the largest share: but since that era nearly thirteen millions annually of new taxes have been thrown upon consumption. The consequence of which has been a constant increase in the number and wretchedness of the poor, and in the amount of the poor-rates. Yet here again the burthen does not fall in equal proportions on the aristocracy with the rest of the community. Their residences, whether in town or country, are not mixed with the habitations of the poor. They live apart from distress, and the expense of relieving it. It is in manufacturing towns and labouring villages that those burthens press the heaviest; in many of which it is one class of poor supporting another.

Several of the most heavy and productive taxes are so contrived, as to give an exemption to this pillar, thus standing in its own defence. The tax upon beer brewed for sale does not affect the aristocracy, who brew their own beer free from this duty. It falls only on those who have not conveniency or ability to brew, and who must purchase it in small quantities. But what will mankind think of the justice of taxation, when they know that this tax alone, from which the aristocracy are from circumstances exempt, is nearly equal to the whole of the land-tax, being in the year 1788, and it is not less now, L1,666,152, and with its proportion of the taxes on malt and hops, it exceeds it.—That a single article, thus partially consumed, and that chiefly by the working part, should be subject to a tax, equal to that on the whole rental of a nation, is, perhaps, a fact not to be paralleled in the histories of revenues.

This is one of the circumstances resulting from a house of legislation, composed on the ground of a combination of common interest; for whatever their separate politics as to parties may be, in this they are united. Whether a combination acts to raise the price of any article for sale, or rate of wages; or whether it acts to throw taxes from itself upon another class of the community, the principle and the effect are the same; and if the one be illegal, it will be difficult to show that the other ought to exist.

It is no use to say that taxes are first proposed in the House of Commons; for as the other house has always a negative, it can always defend itself; and it would be ridiculous to suppose that its acquiescence in the measures to be proposed were not understood before hand. Besides which, it has obtained so much influence by borough-traffic, and so many of its relations and connections are distributed on both sides the commons, as to give it, besides an absolute negative in one house, a preponderancy in the other, in all matters of common concern.

It is difficult to discover what is meant by the landed interest, if it does not mean a combination of aristocratical landholders, opposing their own pecuniary interest to that of the farmer, and every branch of trade, commerce, and manufacture. In all other respects it is the only interest that needs no partial protection. It enjoys the general protection of the world. Every individual, high or low, is interested in the fruits of the earth; men, women, and children, of all ages and degrees, will turn out to assist the farmer, rather than a harvest should not be got in; and they will not act thus by any other property. It is the only one for which the common prayer of mankind is put up, and the only one that can never fail from the want of means. It is the interest, not of the policy, but of the existence of man, and when it ceases, he must cease to be.

No other interest in a nation stands on the same united support. Commerce, manufactures, arts, sciences, and everything else, compared with this, are supported but in parts. Their prosperity or their decay has not the same universal influence. When the valleys laugh and sing, it is not the farmer only, but all creation that rejoice. It is a prosperity that excludes all envy; and this cannot be said of anything else.

Why then, does Mr. Burke talk of his house of peers as the pillar of the landed interest? Were that pillar to sink into the earth, the same landed property would continue, and the same ploughing, sowing, and reaping would go on. The aristocracy are not the farmers who work the land, and raise the produce, but are the mere consumers of the rent; and when compared with the active world are the drones, a seraglio of males, who neither collect the honey nor form the hive, but exist only for lazy enjoyment.

Mr. Burke, in his first essay, called aristocracy "the Corinthian capital of polished society." Towards completing the figure, he has now added the pillar; but still the base is wanting; and whenever a nation choose to act a Samson, not blind, but bold, down will go the temple of Dagon, the Lords and the Philistines.

If a house of legislation is to be composed of men of one class, for the purpose of protecting a distinct interest, all the other interests should have the same. The inequality, as well as the burthen of taxation, arises from admitting it in one case, and not in all. Had there been a house of farmers, there had been no game laws; or a house of merchants and manufacturers, the taxes had neither been so unequal nor so excessive. It is from the power of taxation being in the hands of those who can throw so great a part of it from their own shoulders, that it has raged without a check.

Men of small or moderate estates are more injured by the taxes being thrown on articles of consumption, than they are eased by warding it from landed property, for the following reasons:

First, They consume more of the productive taxable articles, in proportion to their property, than those of large estates.

Secondly, Their residence is chiefly in towns, and their property in houses; and the increase of the poor-rates, occasioned by taxes on consumption, is in much greater proportion than the land-tax has been favoured. In Birmingham, the poor-rates are not less than seven shillings in the pound. From this, as is already observed, the aristocracy are in a great measure exempt.

These are but a part of the mischiefs flowing from the wretched scheme of an house of peers.

As a combination, it can always throw a considerable portion of taxes from itself; and as an hereditary house, accountable to nobody, it resembles a rotten borough, whose consent is to be courted by interest. There are but few of its members, who are not in some mode or other participators, or disposers of the public money. One turns a candle-holder, or a lord in waiting; another a lord of the bed-chamber, a groom of the stole, or any insignificant nominal office to which a salary is annexed, paid out of the public taxes, and which avoids the direct appearance of corruption. Such situations are derogatory to the character of man; and where they can be submitted to, honour cannot reside.

To all these are to be added the numerous dependants, the long list of younger branches and distant relations, who are to be provided for at the public expense: in short, were an estimation to be made of the charge of aristocracy to a nation, it will be found nearly equal to that of supporting the poor. The Duke of Richmond alone (and there are cases similar to his) takes away as much for himself as would maintain two thousand poor and aged persons. Is it, then, any wonder, that under such a system of government, taxes and rates have multiplied to their present extent?

In stating these matters, I speak an open and disinterested language, dictated by no passion but that of humanity. To me, who have not only refused offers, because I thought them improper, but have declined rewards I might with reputation have accepted, it is no wonder that meanness and imposition appear disgustful. Independence is my happiness, and I view things as they are, without regard to place or person; my country is the world, and my religion is to do good.

Mr. Burke, in speaking of the aristocratical law of primogeniture, says, "it is the standing law of our landed inheritance; and which, without question, has a tendency, and I think," continues he, "a happy tendency, to preserve a character of weight and consequence."

Mr. Burke may call this law what he pleases, but humanity and impartial reflection will denounce it as a law of brutal injustice. Were we not accustomed to the daily practice, and did we only hear of it as the law of some distant part of the world, we should conclude that the legislators of such countries had not arrived at a state of civilisation.

As to its preserving a character of weight and consequence, the case appears to me directly the reverse. It is an attaint upon character; a sort of privateering on family property. It may have weight among dependent tenants, but it gives none on a scale of national, and much less of universal character. Speaking for myself, my parents were not able to give me a shilling, beyond what they gave me in education; and to do this they distressed themselves: yet, I possess more of what is called consequence, in the world, than any one in Mr. Burke's catalogue of aristocrats.

Having thus glanced at some of the defects of the two houses of parliament, I proceed to what is called the crown, upon which I shall be very concise.

It signifies a nominal office of a million sterling a year, the business of which consists in receiving the money. Whether the person be wise or foolish, sane or insane, a native or a foreigner, matters not. Every ministry acts upon the same idea that Mr. Burke writes, namely, that the people must be hood-winked, and held in superstitious ignorance by some bugbear or other; and what is called the crown answers this purpose, and therefore it answers all the purposes to be expected from it. This is more than can be said of the other two branches.

The hazard to which this office is exposed in all countries, is not from anything that can happen to the man, but from what may happen to the nation—the danger of its coming to its senses.

It has been customary to call the crown the executive power, and the custom is continued, though the reason has ceased.

It was called the executive, because the person whom it signified used, formerly, to act in the character of a judge, in administering or executing the laws. The tribunals were then a part of the court. The power, therefore, which is now called the judicial, is what was called the executive and, consequently, one or other of the terms is redundant, and one of the offices useless. When we speak of the crown now, it means nothing; it signifies neither a judge nor a general: besides which it is the laws that govern, and not the man. The old terms are kept up, to give an appearance of consequence to empty forms; and the only effect they have is that of increasing expenses.

Before I proceed to the means of rendering governments more conducive to the general happiness of mankind, than they are at present, it will not be improper to take a review of the progress of taxation in England.

It is a general idea, that when taxes are once laid on, they are never taken off. However true this may have been of late, it was not always so. Either, therefore, the people of former times were more watchful over government than those of the present, or government was administered with less extravagance.

It is now seven hundred years since the Norman conquest, and the establishment of what is called the crown. Taking this portion of time in seven separate periods of one hundred years each, the amount of the annual taxes, at each period, will be as follows:

Annual taxes levied by William the Conqueror,

beginning in the year 1066   L400,000

Annual taxes at 100 years from the conquest (1166)   200,000

Annual taxes at 200 years from the conquest (1266)   150,000

Annual taxes at 300 years from the conquest (1366)   130,000

Annual taxes at 400 years from the conquest (1466)   100,000

These statements and those which follow, are taken from Sir John Sinclair's History of the Revenue; by which it appears, that taxes continued decreasing for four hundred years, at the expiration of which time they were reduced three-fourths, viz., from four hundred thousand pounds to one hundred thousand. The people of England of the present day, have a traditionary and historical idea of the bravery of their ancestors; but whatever their virtues or their vices might have been, they certainly were a people who would not be imposed upon, and who kept governments in awe as to taxation, if not as to principle. Though they were not able to expel the monarchical usurpation, they restricted it to a republican economy of taxes.

Let us now review the remaining three hundred years:

Annual amount of taxes at:

500 years from the conquest (1566)   500,000

600 years from the conquest (1666)   1,800,000

the present time (1791)   17,000,000

The difference between the first four hundred years and the last three, is so astonishing, as to warrant an opinion, that the national character of the English has changed. It would have been impossible to have dragooned the former English, into the excess of taxation that now exists; and when it is considered that the pay of the army, the navy, and of all the revenue officers, is the same now as it was about a hundred years ago, when the taxes were not above a tenth part of what they are at present, it appears impossible to account for the enormous increase and expenditure on any other ground, than extravagance, corruption, and intrigue.*[31]

With the Revolution of 1688, and more so since the Hanover succession, came the destructive system of continental intrigues, and the rage for foreign wars and foreign dominion; systems of such secure mystery that the expenses admit of no accounts; a single line stands for millions. To what excess taxation might have extended had not the French revolution contributed to break up the system, and put an end to pretences, is impossible to say. Viewed, as that revolution ought to be, as the fortunate means of lessening the load of taxes of both countries, it is of as much importance to England as to France; and, if properly improved to all the advantages of which it is capable, and to which it leads, deserves as much celebration in one country as the other.

In pursuing this subject, I shall begin with the matter that first presents itself, that of lessening the burthen of taxes; and shall then add such matter and propositions, respecting the three countries of England, France, and America, as the present prospect of things appears to justify: I mean, an alliance of the three, for the purposes that will be mentioned in their proper place.

What has happened may happen again. By the statement before shown of the progress of taxation, it is seen that taxes have been lessened to a fourth part of what they had formerly been. Though the present circumstances do not admit of the same reduction, yet they admit of such a beginning, as may accomplish that end in less time than in the former case.

The amount of taxes for the year ending at Michaelmas 1788, was as follows:

Land-tax	L 1,950,000
Customs	3,789,274
Excise (including old and new malt)	6,751,727
Stamps	1,278,214
Miscellaneous taxes and incidents	1,803,755

L15,572,755

Since the year 1788, upwards of one million new taxes have been laid on, besides the produce of the lotteries; and as the taxes have in general been more productive since than before, the amount may be taken, in round numbers, at L17,000,000. (The expense of collection and the drawbacks, which together amount to nearly two millions, are paid out of the gross amount; and the above is the net sum paid into the exchequer). This sum of seventeen millions is applied to two different purposes; the one to pay the interest of the National Debt, the other to the current expenses of each year. About nine millions are appropriated to the former; and the remainder, being nearly eight millions, to the latter. As to the million, said to be applied to the reduction of the debt, it is so much like paying with one hand and taking out with the other, as not to merit much notice. It happened, fortunately for France, that she possessed national domains for paying off her debt, and thereby lessening her taxes; but as this is not the case with England, her reduction of taxes can only take place by reducing the current expenses, which may now be done to the amount of four or five millions annually, as will hereafter appear. When this is accomplished it will more than counter-balance the enormous charge of the American war; and the saving will be from the same source from whence the evil arose. As to the national debt, however heavy the interest may be in taxes, yet, as it serves to keep alive a capital useful to commerce, it balances by its effects a considerable part of its own weight; and as the quantity of gold and silver is, by some means or other, short of its proper proportion, being not more than twenty millions, whereas it should be sixty (foreign intrigue, foreign wars, foreign dominions, will in a great measure account for the deficiency), it would, besides the injustice, be bad policy to extinguish a capital that serves to supply that defect. But with respect to the current expense, whatever is saved therefrom is gain. The excess may serve to keep corruption alive, but it has no re-action on credit and commerce, like the interest of the debt.

It is now very probable that the English Government (I do not mean the nation) is unfriendly to the French Revolution. Whatever serves to expose the intrigue and lessen the influence of courts, by lessening taxation, will be unwelcome to those who feed upon the spoil. Whilst the clamour of French intrigue, arbitrary power, popery, and wooden shoes could be kept up, the nation was easily allured and alarmed into taxes. Those days are now past: deception, it is to be hoped, has reaped its last harvest, and better times are in prospect for both countries, and for the world.

Taking it for granted that an alliance may be formed between England, France, and America for the purposes hereafter to be mentioned, the national expenses of France and England may consequently be lessened. The same fleets and armies will no longer be necessary to either, and the reduction can be made ship for ship on each side. But to accomplish these objects the governments must necessarily be fitted to a common and correspondent principle. Confidence can never take place while an hostile disposition remains in either, or where mystery and secrecy on one side is opposed to candour and openness on the other.

These matters admitted, the national expenses might be put back, for the sake of a precedent, to what they were at some period when France and England were not enemies. This, consequently, must be prior to the Hanover succession, and also to the Revolution of 1688.*32 The first instance that presents itself, antecedent to those dates, is in the very wasteful and profligate times of Charles the Second; at which time England and France acted as allies. If I have chosen a period of great extravagance, it will serve to show modern extravagance in a still worse light; especially as the pay of the navy, the army, and the revenue officers has not increased since that time.

The peace establishment was then as follows (see Sir John Sinclair's History of the Revenue):

Navy	L 300,000
Army	212,000
Ordnance	40,000
Civil List	462,115

L1,014,115

The parliament, however, settled the whole annual peace establishment at $1,200,000.*33 If we go back to the time of Elizabeth the amount of all the taxes was but half a million, yet the nation sees nothing during that period that reproaches it with want of consequence.

All circumstances, then, taken together, arising from the French revolution, from the approaching harmony and reciprocal interest of the two nations, the abolition of the court intrigue on both sides, and the progress of knowledge in the science of government, the annual expenditure might be put back to one million and a half, viz.:

Navy	L 500,000
Army	500,000

Expenses of Government   500,000

L1,500,000

Even this sum is six times greater than the expenses of government are in America, yet the civil internal government in England (I mean that administered by means of quarter sessions, juries and assize, and which, in fact, is nearly the whole, and performed by the nation), is less expense upon the revenue, than the same species and portion of government is in America.

It is time that nations should be rational, and not be governed like animals, for the pleasure of their riders. To read the history of kings, a man would be almost inclined to suppose that government consisted in stag-hunting, and that every nation paid a million a-year to a huntsman. Man ought to have pride, or shame enough to blush at being thus imposed upon, and when he feels his proper character he will. Upon all subjects of this nature, there is often passing in the mind, a train of ideas he has not yet accustomed himself to encourage and communicate. Restrained by something that puts on the character of prudence, he acts the hypocrite upon himself as well as to others. It is, however, curious to observe how soon this spell can be dissolved. A single expression, boldly conceived and uttered, will sometimes put a whole company into their proper feelings: and whole nations are acted on in the same manner.

As to the offices of which any civil government may be composed, it matters but little by what names they are described. In the routine of business, as before observed, whether a man be styled a president, a king, an emperor, a senator, or anything else, it is impossible that any service he can perform, can merit from a nation more than ten thousand pounds a year; and as no man should be paid beyond his services, so every man of a proper heart will not accept more. Public money ought to be touched with the most scrupulous consciousness of honour. It is not the produce of riches only, but of the hard earnings of labour and poverty. It is drawn even from the bitterness of want and misery. Not a beggar passes, or perishes in the streets, whose mite is not in that mass.

Were it possible that the Congress of America could be so lost to their duty, and to the interest of their constituents, as to offer General Washington, as president of America, a million a year, he would not, and he could not, accept it. His sense of honour is of another kind. It has cost England almost seventy millions sterling, to maintain a family imported from abroad, of very inferior capacity to thousands in the nation; and scarcely a year has passed that has not produced some new mercenary application. Even the physicians' bills have been sent to the public to be paid. No wonder that jails are crowded, and taxes and poor-rates increased. Under such systems, nothing is to be looked for but what has already happened; and as to reformation, whenever it come, it must be from the nation, and not from the government.

To show that the sum of five hundred thousand pounds is more than sufficient to defray all the expenses of the government, exclusive of navies and armies, the following estimate is added, for any country, of the same extent as England.

In the first place, three hundred representatives fairly elected, are sufficient for all the purposes to which legislation can apply, and preferable to a larger number. They may be divided into two or three houses, or meet in one, as in France, or in any manner a constitution shall direct.

As representation is always considered, in free countries, as the most honourable of all stations, the allowance made to it is merely to defray the expense which the representatives incur by that service, and not to it as an office.

```
If an allowance, at the rate of five hundred pounds per
annum, be made to every representative, deducting for
non-attendance, the expense, if the whole number
attended for six months, each year, would be         L 75,00

The official departments cannot reasonably exceed the
following number, with the salaries annexed:

Three offices at ten thousand pounds each            L 30,000
Ten ditto, at five thousand pounds each                50,000
Twenty ditto, at two thousand pounds each              40,000
Forty ditto, at one thousand pounds each               40,000
Two hundred ditto, at five hundred pounds each        100,000
Three hundred ditto, at two hundred pounds each        60,000
Five hundred ditto, at one hundred pounds each         50,000
Seven hundred ditto, at seventy-five pounds each       52,500
                                                     ————
L497,500
```

If a nation choose, it can deduct four per cent. from all offices, and make one of twenty thousand per annum.

All revenue officers are paid out of the monies they collect, and therefore, are not in this estimation.

The foregoing is not offered as an exact detail of offices, but to show the number of rate of salaries which five hundred thousand pounds will support; and it will, on experience, be found impracticable to find business sufficient to justify even this expense. As to the manner in which office business is now performed, the Chiefs, in several offices, such as the post-office, and certain offices in the exchequer, etc., do little more than sign their names three or four times a year; and the whole duty is performed by under-clerks.

Taking, therefore, one million and a half as a sufficient peace establishment for all the honest purposes of government, which is three hundred thousand pounds more than the peace establishment in the profligate and prodigal times of Charles the Second (notwithstanding, as has been already observed, the pay and salaries of the army, navy, and revenue officers, continue the same as at that period), there will remain a surplus of upwards of six millions out of the present current expenses. The question then will be, how to dispose of this surplus.

Whoever has observed the manner in which trade and taxes twist themselves together, must be sensible of the impossibility of separating them suddenly.

First. Because the articles now on hand are already charged with the duty, and the reduction cannot take place on the present stock.

Secondly. Because, on all those articles on which the duty is charged in the gross, such as per barrel, hogshead, hundred weight, or ton, the abolition of the duty does not admit of being divided down so as fully to relieve the consumer, who purchases by the pint, or the pound. The last duty laid on strong beer and ale was three shillings per barrel, which, if taken off, would lessen the purchase only half a farthing per pint, and consequently, would not reach to practical relief.

This being the condition of a great part of the taxes, it will be necessary to look for such others as are free from this embarrassment and where the relief will be direct and visible, and capable of immediate operation.

In the first place, then, the poor-rates are a direct tax which every house-keeper feels, and who knows also, to a farthing, the sum which he pays. The national amount of the whole of the poor-rates is not positively known, but can be procured. Sir John Sinclair, in his History of the Revenue has stated it at L2,100,587. A considerable part of which is expended in litigations, in which the poor, instead of being relieved, are tormented. The expense, however, is the same to the parish from whatever cause it arises.

In Birmingham, the amount of poor-rates is fourteen thousand pounds a year. This, though a large sum, is moderate, compared with the population. Birmingham is said to contain seventy thousand souls, and on a proportion of seventy thousand to fourteen thousand pounds poor-rates, the national amount of poor-rates, taking the population of England as seven millions, would be but one million four hundred thousand pounds. It is, therefore, most probable, that the population of Birmingham is over-rated. Fourteen thousand pounds is the proportion upon fifty thousand souls, taking two millions of poor-rates, as the national amount.

Be it, however, what it may, it is no other than the consequence of excessive burthen of taxes, for, at the time when the taxes were very low, the poor were able to maintain themselves; and there were no poor-rates.*[34] In the present state of things a labouring man, with a wife or two or three children, does not pay less than between seven and eight pounds a year in taxes. He is not sensible of this, because it is disguised to him in the articles which he buys, and he thinks only of their dearness; but as the taxes take from him, at least, a fourth part of his yearly earnings, he is consequently disabled from providing for a family, especially, if himself, or any of them, are afflicted with sickness.

The first step, therefore, of practical relief, would be to abolish the poor-rates entirely, and in lieu thereof, to make a remission of taxes to the poor of double the amount of the present poor-rates, viz., four millions annually out of the surplus taxes. By this measure, the poor would be benefited two millions, and the house-keepers two millions. This alone would be equal to a reduction of one hundred and twenty millions of the National Debt, and consequently equal to the whole expense of the American War.

It will then remain to be considered, which is the most effectual mode of distributing this remission of four millions.

It is easily seen, that the poor are generally composed of large families of children, and old people past their labour. If these two classes are provided for, the remedy will so far reach to the full extent of the case, that what remains will be incidental, and, in a great measure, fall within the compass of benefit clubs, which, though of humble invention, merit to be ranked among the best of modern institutions.

Admitting England to contain seven millions of souls; if one-fifth thereof are of that class of poor which need support, the number will be one million four hundred thousand. Of this number, one hundred and forty thousand will be aged poor, as will be hereafter shown, and for which a distinct provision will be proposed.

There will then remain one million two hundred and sixty thousand which, at five souls to each family, amount to two hundred and fifty-two thousand families, rendered poor from the expense of children and the weight of taxes.

The number of children under fourteen years of age, in each of those families, will be found to be about five to every two families; some having two, and others three; some one, and others four: some none, and others five; but it rarely happens that more than five are under fourteen years of age, and after this age they are capable of service or of being apprenticed.

Allowing five children (under fourteen years) to every two families,

The number of children will be 630,000

The number of parents, were they all living, would be 504,000

It is certain, that if the children are provided for, the parents are relieved of consequence, because it is from the expense of bringing up children that their poverty arises.

Having thus ascertained the greatest number that can be supposed to need support on account of young families, I proceed to the mode of relief or distribution, which is,

To pay as a remission of taxes to every poor family, out of the surplus taxes, and in room of poor-rates, four pounds a year for every child under fourteen years of age; enjoining the parents of such children to send them to school, to learn reading, writing, and common arithmetic; the ministers of every parish, of every denomination to certify jointly to an office, for that purpose, that this duty is performed. The amount of this expense will be,

For six hundred and thirty thousand children

at four pounds per annum each   L2,520,000

By adopting this method, not only the poverty of the parents will be relieved, but ignorance will be banished from the rising generation, and the number of poor will hereafter become less, because their abilities, by the aid of education, will be greater. Many a youth, with good natural genius, who is apprenticed to a mechanical trade, such as a carpenter, joiner, millwright, shipwright, blacksmith, etc., is prevented getting forward the whole of his life from the want of a little common education when a boy.

I now proceed to the case of the aged.

I divide age into two classes. First, the approach of age, beginning at fifty. Secondly, old age commencing at sixty.

At fifty, though the mental faculties of man are in full vigour, and his judgment better than at any preceding date, the bodily powers for laborious life are on the decline. He cannot bear the same quantity of fatigue as at an earlier period. He begins to earn less, and is less capable of enduring wind and weather; and in those more retired employments where much sight is required, he fails apace, and sees himself, like an old horse, beginning to be turned adrift.

At sixty his labour ought to be over, at least from direct necessity. It is painful to see old age working itself to death, in what are called civilised countries, for daily bread.

To form some judgment of the number of those above fifty years of age, I have several times counted the persons I met in the streets of London, men, women, and children, and have generally found that the average is about one in sixteen or seventeen. If it be said that aged persons do not come much into the streets, so neither do infants; and a great proportion of grown children are in schools and in work-shops as apprentices. Taking, then, sixteen for a divisor, the whole number of persons in England of fifty years and upwards, of both sexes, rich and poor, will be four hundred and twenty thousand.

The persons to be provided for out of this gross number will be husbandmen, common labourers, journeymen of every trade and their wives, sailors, and disbanded soldiers, worn out servants of both sexes, and poor widows.

There will be also a considerable number of middling tradesmen, who having lived decently in the former part of life, begin, as age approaches, to lose their business, and at last fall to decay.

Besides these there will be constantly thrown off from the revolutions of that wheel which no man can stop nor regulate, a number from every class of life connected with commerce and adventure.

To provide for all those accidents, and whatever else may befall, I take the number of persons who, at one time or other of their lives, after fifty years of age, may feel it necessary or comfortable to be better supported, than they can support themselves, and that not as a matter of grace and favour, but of right, at one-third of the whole number, which is one hundred and forty thousand, as stated in a previous page, and for whom a distinct provision was proposed to be made. If there be more, society, notwithstanding the show and pomposity of government, is in a deplorable condition in England.

Of this one hundred and forty thousand, I take one half, seventy thousand, to be of the age of fifty and under sixty, and the other half to be sixty years and upwards. Having thus ascertained the probable proportion of the number of aged persons, I proceed to the mode of rendering their condition comfortable, which is:

To pay to every such person of the age of fifty years, and until he shall arrive at the age of sixty, the sum of six pounds per annum out of the surplus taxes, and ten pounds per annum during life after the age of sixty. The expense of which will be,

Seventy thousand persons, at L6 per annum   L 420,000

Seventy thousand persons, at L10 per annum   700,000

———-

L1,120,000

This support, as already remarked, is not of the nature of a charity but of a right. Every person in England, male and female, pays on an average in taxes two pounds eight shillings and sixpence per annum from the day of his (or her) birth; and, if the expense of collection be added, he pays two pounds eleven shillings and sixpence; consequently, at the end of fifty years he has paid one hundred and twenty-eight pounds fifteen shillings; and at sixty one hundred and fifty-four pounds ten shillings. Converting, therefore, his (or her) individual tax in a tontine, the money he shall receive after fifty years is but little more than the legal interest of the net money he has paid; the rest is made up from those whose circumstances do not require them to draw such support, and the capital in both cases defrays the expenses of government. It is on this ground that I have extended the probable claims to one-third of the number of aged persons in the nation.—Is it, then, better that the lives of one hundred and forty thousand aged persons be rendered comfortable, or that a million a year of public money be expended on any one individual, and him often of the most worthless or insignificant character? Let reason and justice, let honour and humanity, let even hypocrisy, sycophancy and Mr. Burke, let George, let Louis, Leopold, Frederic, Catherine, Cornwallis, or Tippoo Saib, answer the question.*35

The sum thus remitted to the poor will be,

```
To two hundred and fifty-two thousand poor families,
containing six hundred and thirty thousand children   L2,520,000
To one hundred and forty thousand aged persons         1,120,000
                                                      ─────────
L3,640,000
```

There will then remain three hundred and sixty thousand pounds out of the four millions, part of which may be applied as follows:—

After all the above cases are provided for there will still be a number of families who, though not properly of the class of poor, yet find it difficult to give education to their children; and such children, under such a case, would be in a worse condition than if their parents were actually poor. A nation under a well-regulated government should permit none to remain uninstructed. It is monarchical and aristocratical government only that requires ignorance for its support.

Suppose, then, four hundred thousand children to be in this condition, which is a greater number than ought to be supposed after the provisions already made, the method will be:

To allow for each of those children ten shillings a year for the expense of schooling for six years each, which will give them six months schooling each year, and half a crown a year for paper and spelling books.

The expense of this will be annually L250,000.*36

There will then remain one hundred and ten thousand pounds.

Notwithstanding the great modes of relief which the best instituted and best principled government may devise, there will be a number of smaller cases, which it is good policy as well as beneficence in a nation to consider.

Were twenty shillings to be given immediately on the birth of a child, to every woman who should make the demand, and none will make it whose circumstances do not require it, it might relieve a great deal of instant distress.

There are about two hundred thousand births yearly in England; and if claimed by one fourth,

```
The amount would be        L50,000
```

And twenty shillings to every new-married couple who should claim in like manner. This would not exceed the sum of L20,000.

Also twenty thousand pounds to be appropriated to defray the funeral expenses of persons, who, travelling for work, may die at a distance from their friends. By relieving parishes from this charge, the sick stranger will be better treated.

I shall finish this part of the subject with a plan adapted to the particular condition of a metropolis, such as London.

Cases are continually occurring in a metropolis, different from those which occur in the country, and for which a different, or rather an additional, mode of relief is necessary. In the country, even in large towns, people have a knowledge of each other, and distress never rises to that extreme height it sometimes does in a metropolis. There is no such thing in the country as persons, in the literal sense of the word, starved to death, or dying with cold from the want of a lodging. Yet such cases, and others equally as miserable, happen in London.

Many a youth comes up to London full of expectations, and with little or no money, and unless he get immediate employment he is already half undone; and boys bred up in London without any means of a livelihood, and as it often happens of dissolute parents, are in a still worse condition; and servants long out of place are not much better off. In short, a world of little cases is continually arising, which busy or affluent life knows not of, to open the first door to distress. Hunger is not among the postponable wants, and a day, even a few hours, in such a condition is often the crisis of a life of ruin.

These circumstances which are the general cause of the little thefts and pilferings that lead to greater, may be prevented. There yet remain twenty thousand pounds out of the four millions of surplus taxes, which with another fund hereafter to be mentioned, amounting to about twenty thousand pounds more, cannot be better applied than to this purpose. The plan will then be:

First, To erect two or more buildings, or take some already erected, capable of containing at least six thousand persons, and to have in each of these places as many kinds of employment as can be contrived, so that every person who shall come may find something which he or she can do.

Secondly, To receive all who shall come, without enquiring who or what they are. The only condition to be, that for so much, or so many hours' work, each person shall receive so many meals of wholesome food, and a warm lodging, at least as good as a barrack. That a certain portion of what each person's work shall be worth shall be reserved, and given to him or her, on their going away; and that each person shall stay as long or as short a time, or come as often as he choose, on these conditions.

If each person stayed three months, it would assist by rotation twenty-four thousand persons annually, though the real number, at all times, would be but six thousand. By establishing an asylum of this kind, such persons to whom temporary distresses occur, would have an opportunity to recruit themselves, and be enabled to look out for better employment.

Allowing that their labour paid but one half the expense of supporting them, after reserving a portion of their earnings for themselves, the sum of forty thousand pounds additional would defray all other charges for even a greater number than six thousand.

The fund very properly convertible to this purpose, in addition to the twenty thousand pounds, remaining of the former fund, will be the produce of the tax upon coals, so iniquitously and wantonly applied to the support of the Duke of Richmond. It is horrid that any man, more especially at the price coals now are, should live on the distresses of a community; and any government permitting such an abuse, deserves to be dismissed. This fund is said to be about twenty thousand pounds per annum.

I shall now conclude this plan with enumerating the several particulars, and then proceed to other matters.

The enumeration is as follows:—

First, Abolition of two millions poor-rates.

Secondly, Provision for two hundred and fifty thousand poor families.

Thirdly, Education for one million and thirty thousand children.

Fourthly, Comfortable provision for one hundred and forty thousand aged persons.

Fifthly, Donation of twenty shillings each for fifty thousand births.

Sixthly, Donation of twenty shillings each for twenty thousand marriages.

Seventhly, Allowance of twenty thousand pounds for the funeral expenses of persons travelling for work, and dying at a distance from their friends.

Eighthly, Employment, at all times, for the casual poor in the cities of London and Westminster.

By the operation of this plan, the poor laws, those instruments of civil torture, will be superseded, and the wasteful expense of litigation prevented. The hearts of the humane will not be shocked by ragged and hungry children, and persons of seventy and eighty years of age, begging for bread. The dying poor will not be dragged from place to place to breathe their last, as a reprisal of parish upon parish. Widows will have a maintenance for their children, and not be carted away, on the death of their husbands, like culprits and criminals; and children will no longer be considered as increasing the distresses of their parents. The haunts of the wretched will be known, because it will be to their advantage; and the number of petty crimes, the offspring of distress and poverty, will be lessened. The poor, as well as the rich, will then be interested in the support of government, and the cause and apprehension of riots and tumults will cease.—Ye who sit in ease, and solace yourselves in plenty, and such there are in Turkey and Russia, as well as in England, and who say to yourselves, "Are we not well off?" have ye thought of these things? When ye do, ye will cease to speak and feel for yourselves alone.

The plan is easy in practice. It does not embarrass trade by a sudden interruption in the order of taxes, but effects the relief by changing the application of them; and the money necessary for the purpose can be drawn from the excise collections, which are made eight times a year in every market town in England.

Having now arranged and concluded this subject, I proceed to the next.

Taking the present current expenses at seven millions and an half, which is the least amount they are now at, there will remain (after the sum of one million and an half be taken for the new current expenses and four millions for the before-mentioned service) the sum of two millions; part of which to be applied as follows:

Though fleets and armies, by an alliance with France, will, in a great measure, become useless, yet the persons who have devoted themselves to those services, and have thereby unfitted themselves for other lines of life, are not to be sufferers by the means that make others happy. They are a different description of men from those who form or hang about a court.

A part of the army will remain, at least for some years, and also of the navy, for which a provision is already made in the former part of this plan of one million, which is almost half a million more than the peace establishment of the army and navy in the prodigal times of Charles the Second.

Suppose, then, fifteen thousand soldiers to be disbanded, and that an allowance be made to each of three shillings a week during life, clear of all deductions, to be paid in the same manner as the Chelsea College pensioners are paid, and for them to return to their trades and their friends; and also that an addition of fifteen thousand sixpences per week be made to the pay of the soldiers who shall remain; the annual expenses will be:

```
To the pay of fifteen thousand disbanded soldiers
at three shillings per week                              L117,000
Additional pay to the remaining soldiers                   19,500
Suppose that the pay to the officers of the
disbanded corps be the same amount as sum allowed
to the men                                                117,000
                                                          ―――――
                                                                    L253,500

To prevent bulky estimations, admit the same sum
to the disbanded navy as to the army,
and the same increase of pay                              253,500
                                                          ―――――
```

```
    Total           L507,000
```

Every year some part of this sum of half a million (I omit the odd seven thousand pounds for the purpose of keeping the account unembarrassed) will fall in, and the whole of it in time, as it is on the ground of life annuities, except the increased pay of twenty-nine thousand pounds. As it falls in, part of the taxes may be taken off; and as, for instance, when thirty thousand pounds fall in, the duty on hops may be wholly taken off; and as other parts fall in, the duties on candles and soap may be lessened, till at last they will totally cease. There now remains at least one million and a half of surplus taxes.

The tax on houses and windows is one of those direct taxes, which, like the poor-rates, is not confounded with trade; and, when taken off, the relief will be instantly felt. This tax falls heavy on the middle class of people. The amount of this tax, by the returns of 1788, was:

```
Houses and windows:              L         s.       d.
  By the act of 1766          385,459     11        7
  By the act be 1779          130,739     14        5 1/2
  ─────────────
  Total            516,199     6        0 1/2
```

If this tax be struck off, there will then remain about one million of surplus taxes; and as it is always proper to keep a sum in reserve, for incidental matters, it may be best not to extend reductions further in the first instance, but to consider what may be accomplished by other modes of reform.

Among the taxes most heavily felt is the commutation tax. I shall therefore offer a plan for its abolition, by substituting another in its place, which will effect three objects at once: 1, that of removing the burthen to where it can best be borne; 2, restoring justice among families by a distribution of property; 3, extirpating the overgrown influence arising from the unnatural law of primogeniture, which is one of the principal sources of corruption at elections. The amount of commutation tax by the returns of 1788, was L771,657.

When taxes are proposed, the country is amused by the plausible language of taxing luxuries. One thing is called a luxury at one time, and something else at another; but the real luxury does not consist in the article, but in the means of procuring it, and this is always kept out of sight.

I know not why any plant or herb of the field should be a greater luxury in one country than another; but an overgrown estate in either is a luxury at all times, and, as such, is the proper object of taxation. It is, therefore, right to take those kind tax-making gentlemen up on their own word, and argue on the principle themselves have laid down, that of taxing luxuries. If they or their champion, Mr. Burke, who, I fear, is growing out of date, like the man in armour, can prove that an estate of twenty, thirty, or forty thousand pounds a year is not a luxury, I will give up the argument.

Admitting that any annual sum, say, for instance, one thousand pounds, is necessary or sufficient for the support of a family, consequently the second thousand is of the nature of a luxury, the third still more so, and by proceeding on, we shall at last arrive at a sum that may not improperly be called a prohibitable luxury. It would be impolitic to set bounds to property acquired by industry, and therefore it is right to place the prohibition beyond the probable acquisition to which industry can extend; but there ought to be a limit to property or the accumulation of it by bequest. It should pass in some other line. The richest in every nation have poor relations, and those often very near in consanguinity.

The following table of progressive taxation is constructed on the above principles, and as a substitute for the commutation tax. It will reach the point of prohibition by a regular operation, and thereby supersede the aristocratical law of primogeniture.

```
TABLE I
A tax on all estates of the clear yearly value of L50,
after deducting the land tax, and up

To L500                        0s    3d per pound
From L500 to L1,000            0     6
On the second     thousand     0     9
On the third         "         1     0
On the fourth        "         1     6
On the fifth         "         2     0
On the sixth         "         3     0
On the seventh       "         4     0
On the eighth        "         5     0
On the ninth         "         6s    0d per pound
On the tenth         "         7     0
On the eleventh      "         8     0
On the twelfth       "         9     0
On the thirteenth    "        10     0
On the fourteenth    "        11     0
On the fifteenth     "        12     0
On the sixteenth     "        13     0
On the seventeenth   "        14     0
On the eighteenth    "        15     0
```

```
On the nineteenth       "    16   0
On the twentieth        "    17   0
On the twenty-first     "    18   0
On the twenty-second    "    19   0
On the twenty-third     "    20   0
```

The foregoing table shows the progression per pound on every progressive thousand. The following table shows the amount of the tax on every thousand separately, and in the last column the total amount of all the separate sums collected.

```
TABLE II
An estate of:
L 50 per annum       at 3d per pound pays    L0   12   6
100    "     "            "         "         1    5   0
200    "     "            "         "         2   10   0
300    "     "            "         "         3   15   0
400    "     "            "         "         5    0   0
500    "     "            "         "         7    5   0
```

After L500, the tax of 6d. per pound takes place on the second L500; consequently an estate of L1,000 per annum pays L2l, 15s., and so on.

```
Total amount
For the 1st L500 at   0s  3d per pound   L7    5s
2nd      "        0   6                  14   10   L21   15s
2nd 1000 at       0   9                  37   11    59    5
3rd      "        1   0                  50    0   109    5
(Total amount)
4th 1000 at       1s  6d per pound   L75   0s   L184   5s
5th      "        2   0              100   0    284    5
6th      "        3   0              150   0    434    5
7th      "        4   0              200   0    634    5
8th      "        5   0              250   0    880    5
9th      "        6   0              300   0   1100    5
10th     "        7   0              350   0   1530    5
11th     "        8   0              400   0   1930    5
12th     "        9   0              450   0   2380    5
13th     "       10   0              500   0   2880    5
14th     "       11   0              550   0   3430    5
15th     "       12   0              600   0   4030    5
16th     "       13   0              650   0   4680    5
17th     "       14   0              700   0   5380    5
18th     "       15   0              750   0   6130    5
19th     "       16   0              800   0   6930    5
20th     "       17   0              850   0   7780    5
21st     "       18   0              900   0   8680    5
(Total amount)
22nd 1000 at     19s  0d per pound   L950  0s   L9630   5s
23rd     "       20   0             1000   0   10630    5
```

At the twenty-third thousand the tax becomes 20s. in the pound, and consequently every thousand beyond that sum can produce no profit but by dividing the estate. Yet formidable as this tax appears, it will not, I believe, produce so much as the commutation tax; should it produce more, it ought to be lowered to that amount upon estates under two or three thousand a year.

On small and middling estates it is lighter (as it is intended to be) than the commutation tax. It is not till after seven or eight thousand a year that it begins to be heavy. The object is not so much the produce of the tax as the justice of the measure. The aristocracy has screened itself too much, and this serves to restore a part of the lost equilibrium.

As an instance of its screening itself, it is only necessary to look back to the first establishment of the excise laws, at what is called the Restoration, or the coming of Charles the Second. The aristocratical interest then in power, commuted the feudal services itself was under, by laying a tax on beer brewed for sale; that is, they compounded with Charles for an exemption from those services for themselves and their heirs, by a tax to be paid by other people. The aristocracy do not purchase beer brewed for sale, but brew their own beer free of the duty, and if any commutation at that time were necessary, it ought to have been at the expense of those for whom the exemptions from those services were intended;*[37] instead of which, it was thrown on an entirely different class of men.

But the chief object of this progressive tax (besides the justice of rendering taxes more equal than they are) is, as already stated, to extirpate the overgrown influence arising from the unnatural law of primogeniture, and which is one of the principal sources of corruption at elections.

It would be attended with no good consequences to enquire how such vast estates as thirty, forty, or fifty thousand a year could commence, and that at a time when commerce and manufactures were not in a state to admit of such acquisitions. Let it be sufficient to remedy the evil by putting them in a condition of descending again to the community by the quiet means of apportioning them among all the heirs and heiresses of those families. This will be the more necessary, because hitherto the aristocracy have quartered their younger children and connections upon the public in useless posts, places and offices, which when abolished will leave them destitute, unless the law of primogeniture be also abolished or superseded.

A progressive tax will, in a great measure, effect this object, and that as a matter of interest to the parties most immediately concerned, as will be seen by the following table; which shows the net produce upon every estate, after subtracting the tax. By this it will appear that after an estate exceeds thirteen or fourteen thousand a year, the remainder produces but little profit to the holder, and consequently, Will pass either to the younger children, or to other kindred.

TABLE III

Showing the net produce of every estate from one thousand

to twenty-three thousand pounds a year

No of thousand per annum	Total tax subtracted	Net produce
L1000	L21	L979
2000	59	1941
3000	109	2891
4000	184	3816
5000	284	4716
6000	434	5566
7000	634	6366
8000	880	7120
9000	1100	7900
10,000	1530	8470
11,000	1930	9070
12,000	2380	9620
13,000	2880	10,120
(No of thousand per annum)	(Total tax subtracted)	(Net produce)
14,000	3430	10,570
15,000	4030	10,970
16,000	4680	11,320
17,000	5380	11,620
18,000	6130	11,870
19,000	6930	12,170
20,000	7780	12,220

21,000	8680	12,320
22,000	9630	12,370
23,000	10,630	12,370

N.B. The odd shillings are dropped in this table.

According to this table, an estate cannot produce more than L12,370 clear of the land tax and the progressive tax, and therefore the dividing such estates will follow as a matter of family interest. An estate of L23,000 a year, divided into five estates of four thousand each and one of three, will be charged only L1,129 which is but five per cent., but if held by one possessor, will be charged L10,630.

Although an enquiry into the origin of those estates be unnecessary, the continuation of them in their present state is another subject. It is a matter of national concern. As hereditary estates, the law has created the evil, and it ought also to provide the remedy. Primogeniture ought to be abolished, not only because it is unnatural and unjust, but because the country suffers by its operation. By cutting off (as before observed) the younger children from their proper portion of inheritance, the public is loaded with the expense of maintaining them; and the freedom of elections violated by the overbearing influence which this unjust monopoly of family property produces. Nor is this all. It occasions a waste of national property. A considerable part of the land of the country is rendered unproductive, by the great extent of parks and chases which this law serves to keep up, and this at a time when the annual production of grain is not equal to the national consumption.*38—In short, the evils of the aristocratical system are so great and numerous, so inconsistent with every thing that is just, wise, natural, and beneficent, that when they are considered, there ought not to be a doubt that many, who are now classed under that description, will wish to see such a system abolished.

What pleasure can they derive from contemplating the exposed condition, and almost certain beggary of their younger offspring? Every aristocratical family has an appendage of family beggars hanging round it, which in a few ages, or a few generations, are shook off, and console themselves with telling their tale in almshouses, workhouses, and prisons. This is the natural consequence of aristocracy. The peer and the beggar are often of the same family. One extreme produces the other: to make one rich many must be made poor; neither can the system be supported by other means.

There are two classes of people to whom the laws of England are particularly hostile, and those the most helpless; younger children, and the poor. Of the former I have just spoken; of the latter I shall mention one instance out of the many that might be produced, and with which I shall close this subject.

Several laws are in existence for regulating and limiting work-men's wages. Why not leave them as free to make their own bargains, as the law-makers are to let their farms and houses? Personal labour is all the property they have. Why is that little, and the little freedom they enjoy, to be infringed? But the injustice will appear stronger, if we consider the operation and effect of such laws. When wages are fixed by what is called a law, the legal wages remain stationary, while every thing else is in progression; and as those who make that law still continue to lay on new taxes by other laws, they increase the expense of living by one law, and take away the means by another.

But if these gentlemen law-makers and tax-makers thought it right to limit the poor pittance which personal labour can produce, and on which a whole family is to be supported, they certainly must feel themselves happily indulged in a limitation on their own part, of not less than twelve thousand a-year, and that of property they never acquired (nor probably any of their ancestors), and of which they have made never acquire so ill a use.

Having now finished this subject, I shall bring the several particulars into one view, and then proceed to other matters.

The first eight articles, mentioned earlier, are;

1. Abolition of two millions poor-rates.

2. Provision for two hundred and fifty-two thousand poor families, at the rate of four pounds per head for each child under fourteen years of age; which, with the addition of two hundred and fifty thousand pounds, provides also education for one million and thirty thousand children.

3. Annuity of six pounds (per annum) each for all poor persons, decayed tradesmen, and others (supposed seventy thousand) of the age of fifty years, and until sixty.

4. Annuity of ten pounds each for life for all poor persons, decayed tradesmen, and others (supposed seventy thousand) of the age of sixty years.

5. Donation of twenty shillings each for fifty thousand births.

6. Donation of twenty shillings each for twenty thousand marriages.

7. Allowance of twenty thousand pounds for the funeral expenses of persons travelling for work, and dying at a distance from their friends.

8. Employment at all times for the casual poor in the cities of London and Westminster.

Second Enumeration

9. Abolition of the tax on houses and windows.

10. Allowance of three shillings per week for life to fifteen thousand disbanded soldiers, and a proportionate allowance to the officers of the disbanded corps.

11. Increase of pay to the remaining soldiers of L19,500 annually.

12. The same allowance to the disbanded navy, and the same increase of pay, as to the army.

13. Abolition of the commutation tax.

14. Plan of a progressive tax, operating to extirpate the unjust and unnatural law of primogeniture, and the vicious influence of the aristocratical system.*39

There yet remains, as already stated, one million of surplus taxes. Some part of this will be required for circumstances that do not immediately present themselves, and such part as shall not be wanted, will admit of a further reduction of taxes equal to that amount.

Among the claims that justice requires to be made, the condition of the inferior revenue-officers will merit attention. It is a reproach to any government to waste such an immensity of revenue in sinecures and nominal and unnecessary places and officers, and not allow even a decent livelihood to those on whom the labour falls. The salary of the inferior officers of the revenue has stood at the petty pittance of less than fifty pounds a year for upwards of one hundred years. It ought to be seventy. About one hundred and twenty thousand pounds applied to this purpose, will put all those salaries in a decent condition.

This was proposed to be done almost twenty years ago, but the treasury-board then in being, startled at it, as it might lead to similar expectations from the army and navy; and the event was, that the King, or somebody for him, applied to parliament to have his own salary raised an hundred thousand pounds a year, which being done, every thing else was laid aside.

With respect to another class of men, the inferior clergy, I forbear to enlarge on their condition; but all partialities and prejudices for, or against, different modes and forms of religion aside, common justice will determine, whether there ought to be an income of twenty or thirty pounds a year to one man, and of ten thousand to another. I speak on this subject with the more freedom, because I am known not to be a Presbyterian; and therefore the cant cry of court sycophants, about church and meeting, kept up to amuse and bewilder the nation, cannot be raised against me.

Ye simple men on both sides the question, do you not see through this courtly craft? If ye can be kept disputing and wrangling about church and meeting, ye just answer the purpose of every courtier, who lives the while on the spoils of the taxes, and laughs at your credulity. Every religion is good that teaches man to be good; and I know of none that instructs him to be bad.

All the before-mentioned calculations suppose only sixteen millions and an half of taxes paid into the exchequer, after the expense of collection and drawbacks at the custom-house and excise-office are deducted; whereas the sum paid into the exchequer is very nearly, if not quite, seventeen millions. The taxes raised in Scotland and Ireland are expended in those countries, and therefore their savings will come out of their own taxes; but if any part be paid into the English exchequer, it might be remitted. This will not make one hundred thousand pounds a year difference.

There now remains only the national debt to be considered. In the year 1789, the interest, exclusive of the tontine, was L9,150,138. How much the capital has been reduced since that time the minister best knows. But after paying the interest, abolishing the tax on houses and windows, the commutation tax, and the poor-rates; and making all the provisions for the poor, for the education of children, the support of the aged, the disbanded part of the army and navy, and increasing the pay of the remainder, there will be a surplus of one million.

The present scheme of paying off the national debt appears to me, speaking as an indifferent person, to be an ill-concerted, if not a fallacious job. The burthen of the national debt consists not in its being so many millions, or so many hundred millions, but in the quantity of taxes collected every year to pay the interest. If this quantity continues the same, the burthen of the national debt is the same to all intents and purposes, be the capital more or less. The only knowledge which the public can have of the reduction of the debt, must be through the reduction of taxes for paying the interest. The debt, therefore, is not reduced one farthing to the public by all the millions that have been paid; and it would require more money now to purchase up the capital, than when the scheme began.

Digressing for a moment at this point, to which I shall return again, I look back to the appointment of Mr. Pitt, as minister.

I was then in America. The war was over; and though resentment had ceased, memory was still alive.

When the news of the coalition arrived, though it was a matter of no concern to I felt it as a man. It had something in it which shocked, by publicly sporting with decency, if not with principle. It was impudence in Lord North; it was a want of firmness in Mr. Fox.

Mr. Pitt was, at that time, what may be called a maiden character in politics. So far from being hackneyed, he appeared not to be initiated into the first mysteries of court intrigue. Everything was in his favour. Resentment against the coalition served as friendship to him, and his ignorance of vice was credited for virtue. With the return of peace, commerce and prosperity would rise of itself; yet even this increase was thrown to his account.

When he came to the helm, the storm was over, and he had nothing to interrupt his course. It required even ingenuity to be wrong, and he succeeded. A little time showed him the same sort of man as his predecessors had been. Instead of profiting by those errors which had accumulated a burthen of taxes unparalleled in the world, he sought, I might almost say, he advertised for enemies, and provoked means to increase taxation. Aiming at something, he knew not what, he ransacked Europe and India for adventures, and abandoning the fair pretensions he began with, he became the knight-errant of modern times.

It is unpleasant to see character throw itself away. It is more so to see one's-self deceived. Mr. Pitt had merited nothing, but he promised much. He gave symptoms of a mind superior to the meanness and corruption of courts. His apparent candour encouraged expectations; and the public confidence, stunned, wearied, and confounded by a chaos of parties, revived and attached itself to him. But mistaking, as he has done, the disgust of the nation against the coalition, for merit in himself, he has rushed into measures which a man less supported would not have presumed to act.

All this seems to show that change of ministers amounts to nothing. One goes out, another comes in, and still the same measures, vices, and extravagance are pursued. It signifies not who is minister. The defect lies in the system. The foundation and the superstructure of the government is bad. Prop it as you please, it continually sinks into court government, and ever will.

I return, as I promised, to the subject of the national debt, that offspring of the Dutch-Anglo revolution, and its handmaid the Hanover succession.

But it is now too late to enquire how it began. Those to whom it is due have advanced the money; and whether it was well or ill spent, or pocketed, is not their crime. It is, however, easy to see, that as the nation proceeds in contemplating the nature and principles of government, and to understand taxes, and make comparisons between those of America, France, and England, it will be next to impossible to keep it in the same torpid state it has hitherto been. Some reform must, from the necessity of the case, soon begin. It is not whether these principles press with little or much force in the present moment. They are out. They are abroad in the world, and no force can stop them. Like a secret told, they are beyond recall; and he must be blind indeed that does not see that a change is already beginning.

Nine millions of dead taxes is a serious thing; and this not only for bad, but in a great measure for foreign government. By putting the power of making war into the hands of the foreigners who came for what they could get, little else was to be expected than what has happened.

Reasons are already advanced in this work, showing that whatever the reforms in the taxes may be, they ought to be made in the current expenses of government, and not in the part applied to the interest of the national debt. By remitting the taxes of the poor, they will be totally relieved, and all discontent will be taken away; and by striking off such of the taxes as are already mentioned, the nation will more than recover the whole expense of the mad American war.

There will then remain only the national debt as a subject of discontent; and in order to remove, or rather to prevent this, it would be good policy in the stockholders themselves to consider it as property, subject like all other property, to bear some portion of the taxes. It would give to it both popularity and security, and as a great part of its present inconvenience is balanced by the capital which it keeps alive, a measure of this kind would so far add to that balance as to silence objections.

This may be done by such gradual means as to accomplish all that is necessary with the greatest ease and convenience.

Instead of taxing the capital, the best method would be to tax the interest by some progressive ratio, and to lessen the public taxes in the same proportion as the interest diminished.

Suppose the interest was taxed one halfpenny in the pound the first year, a penny more the second, and to proceed by a certain ratio to be determined upon, always less than any other tax upon property. Such a tax would be subtracted from the interest at the time of payment, without any expense of collection.

One halfpenny in the pound would lessen the interest and consequently the taxes, twenty thousand pounds. The tax on wagons amounts to this sum, and this tax might be taken off the first year. The second year the tax on female servants, or some other of the like amount might also be taken off, and by proceeding in this manner, always applying the tax raised from the property of the debt toward its extinction, and not carry it to the current services, it would liberate itself.

The stockholders, notwithstanding this tax, would pay less taxes than they do now. What they would save by the extinction of the poor-rates, and the tax on houses and windows, and the commutation tax, would be considerably greater than what this tax, slow, but certain in its operation, amounts to.

It appears to me to be prudence to look out for measures that may apply under any circumstances that may approach. There is, at this moment, a crisis in the affairs of Europe that requires it. Preparation now is wisdom. If taxation be once let loose, it will be difficult to re-instate it; neither would the relief be so effectual, as if it proceeded by some certain and gradual reduction.

The fraud, hypocrisy, and imposition of governments, are now beginning to be too well understood to promise them any long career. The farce of monarchy and aristocracy, in all countries, is following that of chivalry, and Mr. Burke is dressing aristocracy, in all countries, is following that of chivalry, and Mr. Burke is dressing for the funeral. Let it then pass quietly to the tomb of all other follies, and the mourners be comforted.

The time is not very distant when England will laugh at itself for sending to Holland, Hanover, Zell, or Brunswick for men, at the expense of a million a year, who understood neither her laws, her language, nor her interest, and whose capacities would scarcely have fitted them for the office of a parish constable. If government could be trusted to such hands, it must be some easy and simple thing indeed, and materials fit for all the purposes may be found in every town and village in England.

When it shall be said in any country in the world, my poor are happy; neither ignorance nor distress is to be found among them; my jails are empty of prisoners, my streets of beggars; the aged are not in want, the taxes are not oppressive; the rational world is my friend, because I am the friend of its happiness: when these things can be said, then may that country boast its constitution and its government.

Within the space of a few years we have seen two revolutions, those of America and France. In the former, the contest was long, and the conflict severe; in the latter, the nation acted with such a consolidated impulse, that having no foreign enemy to contend with, the revolution was complete in power the moment it appeared. From both those instances it is evident, that the greatest forces that can be brought into the field of revolutions, are reason and common interest. Where these can have the opportunity of acting, opposition dies with fear, or crumbles away by conviction. It is a great standing which they have now universally obtained; and we may hereafter hope to see revolutions, or changes in governments, produced with the same quiet operation by which any measure, determinable by reason and discussion, is accomplished.

When a nation changes its opinion and habits of thinking, it is no longer to be governed as before; but it would not only be wrong, but bad policy, to attempt by force what ought to be accomplished by reason. Rebellion consists in forcibly opposing the general will of a nation, whether by a party or by a government. There ought, therefore, to be in every nation a method of occasionally ascertaining the state of public opinion with respect to government. On this point the old government of France was superior to the present government of England, because, on extraordinary occasions, recourse could be had what was then called the States General. But in England there are no such occasional bodies; and as to those who are now called Representatives, a great part of them are mere machines of the court, placemen, and dependants.

I presume, that though all the people of England pay taxes, not an hundredth part of them are electors, and the members of one of the houses of parliament represent nobody but themselves. There is, therefore, no power but the voluntary will of the people that has a right to act in any matter respecting a general reform; and by the same right that two persons can confer on such a subject, a thousand may. The object, in all such preliminary proceedings, is to find out what the general sense of a nation is, and to be governed by it. If it prefer a bad or defective government to a reform or choose to pay ten times more taxes than there is any occasion for, it has a right so to do; and so long as the majority do not impose conditions on the minority, different from what they impose upon themselves, though there may be much error, there is no injustice. Neither will the error continue long. Reason and discussion will soon bring things right, however wrong they may begin. By such a process no tumult is to be apprehended. The poor, in all countries, are naturally both peaceable and grateful in all reforms in which their interest and happiness is included. It is only by neglecting and rejecting them that they become tumultuous.

The objects that now press on the public attention are, the French revolution, and the prospect of a general revolution in governments. Of all nations in Europe there is none so much interested in the French revolution as England. Enemies for ages, and that at a vast expense, and without any national object, the opportunity now presents itself of amicably closing the scene, and joining their efforts to reform the rest of Europe. By doing this they will not only prevent the further effusion of blood, and increase of taxes, but be in a condition of getting rid of a considerable part of their present burthens, as has been already stated. Long experience however has shown, that reforms of this kind are not those which old governments wish to promote, and therefore it is to nations, and not to such governments, that these matters present themselves.

In the preceding part of this work, I have spoken of an alliance between England, France, and America, for purposes that were to be afterwards mentioned. Though I have no direct authority on the part of America, I have good reason to conclude, that she is disposed to enter into a consideration of such a measure, provided, that the governments with which she might ally, acted as national governments, and not as courts enveloped in intrigue and mystery. That France as a nation, and a national government, would prefer an alliance with England, is a matter of certainty. Nations, like individuals, who have long been enemies, without knowing each other, or knowing why, become the better friends when they discover the errors and impositions under which they had acted.

Admitting, therefore, the probability of such a connection, I will state some matters by which such an alliance, together with that of Holland, might render service, not only to the parties immediately concerned, but to all Europe.

It is, I think, certain, that if the fleets of England, France, and Holland were confederated, they could propose, with effect, a limitation to, and a general dismantling of, all the navies in Europe, to a certain proportion to be agreed upon.

First, That no new ship of war shall be built by any power in Europe, themselves included.

Second, That all the navies now in existence shall be put back, suppose to one-tenth of their present force. This will save to France and England, at least two millions sterling annually to each, and their relative force be in the same proportion as it is now. If men will permit themselves to think, as rational beings ought to think, nothing can appear more ridiculous and absurd, exclusive of all moral reflections, than to be at the expense of building navies, filling them with men, and then hauling them into the ocean, to try which can sink each other fastest. Peace, which costs nothing, is attended with infinitely more advantage, than any victory with all its expense. But this, though it best answers the purpose of nations, does not that of court governments, whose habited policy is pretence for taxation, places, and offices.

It is, I think, also certain, that the above confederated powers, together with that of the United States of America, can propose with effect, to Spain, the independence of South America, and the opening those countries of immense extent and wealth to the general commerce of the world, as North America now is.

With how much more glory, and advantage to itself, does a nation act, when it exerts its powers to rescue the world from bondage, and to create itself friends, than when it employs those powers to increase ruin, desolation, and misery. The horrid scene that is now acting by the English government in the East-Indies, is fit only to be told of Goths and Vandals, who, destitute of principle, robbed and tortured the world they were incapable of enjoying.

The opening of South America would produce an immense field of commerce, and a ready money market for manufactures, which the eastern world does not. The East is already a country full of manufactures, the importation of which is not only an injury to the manufactures of England, but a drain upon its specie. The balance against England by this trade is regularly upwards of half a million annually sent out in the East-India ships in silver; and this is the reason, together with German intrigue, and German subsidies, that there is so little silver in England.

But any war is harvest to such governments, however ruinous it may be to a nation. It serves to keep up deceitful expectations which prevent people from looking into the defects and abuses of government. It is the lo here! and the lo there! that amuses and cheats the multitude.

Never did so great an opportunity offer itself to England, and to all Europe, as is produced by the two Revolutions of America and France. By the former, freedom has a national champion in the western world; and by the latter, in Europe. When another nation shall join France, despotism and bad government will scarcely dare to appear. To use a trite expression, the iron is becoming hot all over Europe. The insulted German and the enslaved Spaniard, the Russ and the Pole, are beginning to think. The present age will hereafter merit to be called the Age of Reason, and the present generation will appear to the future as the Adam of a new world.

When all the governments of Europe shall be established on the representative system, nations will become acquainted, and the animosities and prejudices fomented by the intrigue and artifice of courts, will cease. The oppressed soldier will become a freeman; and the tortured sailor, no longer dragged through the streets like a felon, will pursue his mercantile voyage in safety. It would be better that nations should wi continue the pay of their soldiers during their lives, and give them their discharge and restore them to freedom and their friends, and cease recruiting, than retain such multitudes at the same expense, in a condition useless to society and to themselves. As soldiers have hitherto been treated in most countries, they might be said to be without a friend. Shunned by the citizen on an apprehension of their being enemies to liberty, and too often insulted by those who commanded them, their condition was a double oppression. But where genuine principles of liberty pervade a people, every thing is restored to order; and the soldier civilly treated, returns the civility.

In contemplating revolutions, it is easy to perceive that they may arise from two distinct causes; the one, to avoid or get rid of some great calamity; the other, to obtain some great and positive good; and the two may be distinguished by the names of active and passive revolutions. In those which proceed from the former cause, the temper becomes incensed and soured; and the redress, obtained by danger, is too often sullied by revenge. But in those which proceed from the latter, the heart, rather animated than agitated, enters serenely upon the subject. Reason and discussion, persuasion and conviction, become the weapons in the contest, and it is only when those are attempted to be suppressed that recourse is had to violence. When men unite in agreeing that a thing is good, could it be obtained, such for instance as relief from a burden of taxes and the extinction of corruption, the object is more than half accomplished. What they approve as the end, they will promote in the means.

Will any man say, in the present excess of taxation, falling so heavily on the poor, that a remission of five pounds annually of taxes to one hundred and four thousand poor families is not a good thing? Will he say that a remission of seven pounds annually to one hundred thousand other poor families—of eight pounds annually to another hundred thousand poor families, and of ten pounds annually to fifty thousand poor and widowed families, are not good things? And, to proceed a step further in this climax, will he say that to provide against the misfortunes to which all human life is subject, by securing six pounds annually for all poor, distressed, and reduced persons of the age of fifty and until sixty, and of ten pounds annually after sixty, is not a good thing?

Will he say that an abolition of two millions of poor-rates to the house-keepers, and of the whole of the house and window-light tax and of the commutation tax is not a good thing? Or will he say that to abolish corruption is a bad thing?

If, therefore, the good to be obtained be worthy of a passive, rational, and costless revolution, it would be bad policy to prefer waiting for a calamity that should force a violent one. I have no idea, considering the reforms which are now passing and spreading throughout Europe, that England will permit herself to be the last; and where the occasion and the opportunity quietly offer, it is better than to wait for a turbulent necessity. It may be considered as an honour to the animal faculties of man to obtain redress by courage and danger, but it is far greater honour to the rational faculties to accomplish the same object by reason, accommodation, and general consent.*40

As reforms, or revolutions, call them which you please, extend themselves among nations, those nations will form connections and conventions, and when a few are thus confederated, the progress will be rapid, till despotism and corrupt government be totally expelled, at least out of two quarters of the world, Europe and America. The Algerine piracy may then be commanded to cease, for it is only by the malicious policy of old governments, against each other, that it exists.

Throughout this work, various and numerous as the subjects are, which I have taken up and investigated, there is only a single paragraph upon religion, viz. "that every religion is good that teaches man to be good."

I have carefully avoided to enlarge upon the subject, because I am inclined to believe that what is called the present ministry, wish to see contentions about religion kept up, to prevent the nation turning its attention to subjects of government. It is as if they were to say, "Look that way, or any way, but this."

But as religion is very improperly made a political machine, and the reality of it is thereby destroyed, I will conclude this work with stating in what light religion appears to me.

If we suppose a large family of children, who, on any particular day, or particular circumstance, made it a custom to present to their parents some token of their affection and gratitude, each of them would make a different offering, and most probably in a different manner. Some would pay their congratulations in themes of verse and prose, by some little devices, as their genius dictated, or according to what they thought would please; and, perhaps, the least of all, not able to do any of those things, would ramble into the garden, or the field, and gather what it thought the prettiest flower it could find, though, perhaps, it might be but a simple weed. The parent would be more gratified by such a variety, than if the whole of them had acted on a concerted plan, and each had made exactly the same offering. This would have the cold appearance of contrivance, or the harsh one of control. But of all unwelcome things, nothing could more afflict the parent than to know, that the whole of them had afterwards gotten together by the ears, boys and girls, fighting, scratching, reviling, and abusing each other about which was the best or the worst present.

Why may we not suppose, that the great Father of all is pleased with variety of devotion; and that the greatest offence we can act, is that by which we seek to torment and render each other miserable? For my own part, I am fully satisfied that what I am now doing, with an endeavour to conciliate mankind, to render their condition happy, to unite nations that have hitherto been enemies, and to extirpate the horrid practice of war, and break the chains of slavery and oppression is acceptable in his sight, and being the best service I can perform, I act it cheerfully.

I do not believe that any two men, on what are called doctrinal points, think alike who think at all. It is only those who have not thought that appear to agree. It is in this case as with what is called the British constitution. It has been taken for granted to be good, and encomiums have supplied the place of proof. But when the nation comes to examine into its principles and the abuses it admits, it will be found to have more defects than I have pointed out in this work and the former.

As to what are called national religions, we may, with as much propriety, talk of national Gods. It is either political craft or the remains of the Pagan system, when every nation had its separate and particular deity. Among all the writers of the English church clergy, who have treated on the general subject of religion, the present Bishop of Llandaff has not been excelled, and it is with much pleasure that I take this opportunity of expressing this token of respect.

I have now gone through the whole of the subject, at least, as far as it appears to me at present. It has been my intention for the five years I have been in Europe, to offer an address to the people of England on the subject of government, if the opportunity presented itself before I returned to America. Mr. Burke has thrown it in my way, and I thank him. On a certain occasion, three years ago, I pressed him to propose a national convention, to be fairly elected, for the purpose of taking the state of the nation into consideration; but I found, that however strongly the parliamentary current was then setting against the party he acted with, their policy was to keep every thing within that field of corruption, and trust to accidents. Long experience had shown that parliaments would follow any change of ministers, and on this they rested their hopes and their expectations.

Formerly, when divisions arose respecting governments, recourse was had to the sword, and a civil war ensued. That savage custom is exploded by the new system, and reference is had to national conventions. Discussion and the general will arbitrates the question, and to this, private opinion yields with a good grace, and order is preserved uninterrupted.

Some gentlemen have affected to call the principles upon which this work and the former part of Rights of Man are founded, "a new-fangled doctrine." The question is not whether those principles are new or old, but whether they are right or wrong. Suppose the former, I will show their effect by a figure easily understood.

It is now towards the middle of February. Were I to take a turn into the country, the trees would present a leafless, wintery appearance. As people are apt to pluck twigs as they walk along, I perhaps might do the same, and by chance might observe, that a single bud on that twig had begun to swell. I should reason very unnaturally, or rather not reason at all, to suppose this was the only bud in England which had this appearance. Instead of deciding thus, I should instantly conclude, that the same appearance was beginning, or about to begin, every where; and though the vegetable sleep will continue longer on some trees and plants than on others, and though some of them may not blossom for two or three years, all will be in leaf in the summer, except those which are rotten. What pace the political summer may keep with the natural, no human foresight can determine. It is, however, not difficult to perceive that the spring is begun.—Thus wishing, as I sincerely do, freedom and happiness to all nations, I close the Second Part.

APPENDIX

As the publication of this work has been delayed beyond the time intended, I think it not improper, all circumstances considered, to state the causes that have occasioned delay.

The reader will probably observe, that some parts in the plan contained in this work for reducing the taxes, and certain parts in Mr. Pitt's speech at the opening of the present session, Tuesday, January 31, are so much alike as to induce a belief, that either the author had taken the hint from Mr. Pitt, or Mr. Pitt from the author.—I will first point out the parts that are similar, and then state such circumstances as I am acquainted with, leaving the reader to make his own conclusion.

Considering it as almost an unprecedented case, that taxes should be proposed to be taken off, it is equally extraordinary that such a measure should occur to two persons at the same time; and still more so (considering the vast variety and multiplicity of taxes) that they should hit on the same specific taxes. Mr. Pitt has mentioned, in his speech, the tax on Carts and Wagons—that on Female Servantsthe lowering the tax on Candles and the taking off the tax of three shillings on Houses having under seven windows.

Every one of those specific taxes are a part of the plan contained in this work, and proposed also to be taken off. Mr. Pitt's plan, it is true, goes no further than to a reduction of three hundred and twenty thousand pounds; and the reduction proposed in this work, to nearly six millions. I have made my calculations on only sixteen millions and an half of revenue, still asserting that it was "very nearly, if not quite, seventeen millions." Mr. Pitt states it at 16,690,000. I know enough of the matter to say, that he has not overstated it. Having thus given the particulars, which correspond in this work and his speech, I will state a chain of circumstances that may lead to some explanation.

The first hint for lessening the taxes, and that as a consequence flowing from the French revolution, is to be found in the Address and Declaration of the Gentlemen who met at the Thatched-House Tavern, August 20, 1791. Among many other particulars stated in that Address, is the following, put as an interrogation to the government opposers of the French Revolution. "Are they sorry that the pretence for new oppressive taxes, and the occasion for continuing many old taxes will be at an end?"

It is well known that the persons who chiefly frequent the Thatched-House Tavern, are men of court connections, and so much did they take this Address and Declaration respecting the French Revolution, and the reduction of taxes in disgust, that the Landlord was under the necessity of informing the Gentlemen, who composed the meeting of the 20th of August, and who proposed holding another meeting, that he could not receive them.*41

What was only hinted in the Address and Declaration respecting taxes and principles of government, will be found reduced to a regular system in this work. But as Mr. Pitt's speech contains some of the same things respecting taxes, I now come to give the circumstances before alluded to.

The case is: This work was intended to be published just before the meeting of Parliament, and for that purpose a considerable part of the copy was put into the printer's hands in September, and all the remaining copy, which contains the part to which Mr. Pitt's speech is similar, was given to him full six weeks before the meeting of Parliament, and he was informed of the time at which it was to appear. He had composed nearly the whole about a fortnight before the time of Parliament meeting, and had given me a proof of the next sheet. It was then in sufficient forwardness to be out at the time proposed, as two other sheets were ready for striking off. I had before told him, that if he thought he should be straitened for time, I could get part of the work done at another press, which he desired me not to do. In this manner the work stood on the Tuesday fortnight preceding the meeting of Parliament, when all at once, without any previous intimation, though I had been with him the evening before, he sent me, by one of his workmen, all the remaining copy, declining to go on with the work on any consideration.

To account for this extraordinary conduct I was totally at a loss, as he stopped at the part where the arguments on systems and principles of government closed, and where the plan for the reduction of taxes, the education of children, and the support of the poor and the aged begins; and still more especially, as he had, at the time of his beginning to print, and before he had seen the whole copy, offered a thousand pounds for the copy-right, together with the future copy-right of the former part of the Rights of Man. I told the person who brought me this offer that I should not accept it, and wished it not to be renewed, giving him as my reason, that though I believed the printer to be an honest man, I would never put it in the power of any printer or publisher to suppress or alter a work of mine, by making him master of the copy, or give to him the right of selling it to any minister, or to any other person, or to treat as a mere matter of traffic, that which I intended should operate as a principle.

His refusal to complete the work (which he could not purchase) obliged me to seek for another printer, and this of consequence would throw the publication back till after the meeting of Parliament, otherways it would have appeared that Mr. Pitt had only taken up a part of the plan which I had more fully stated.

Whether that gentleman, or any other, had seen the work, or any part of it, is more than I have authority to say. But the manner in which the work was returned, and the particular time at which this was done, and that after the offers he had made, are suspicious circumstances. I know what the opinion of booksellers and publishers is upon such a case, but as to my own opinion, I choose to make no declaration. There are many ways by which proof sheets may be procured by other persons before a work publicly appears; to which I shall add a certain circumstance, which is,

A ministerial bookseller in Piccadilly who has been employed, as common report says, by a clerk of one of the boards closely connected with the ministry (the board of trade and plantation, of which Hawkesbury is president) to publish what he calls my Life, (I wish his own life and those of the cabinet were as good), used to have his books printed at the same printing-office that I employed; but when the former part of Rights of Man came out, he took his work away in dudgeon; and about a week or ten days before the printer returned my copy, he came to make him an offer of his work again, which was accepted. This would consequently give him admission into the printing-office where the sheets of this work were then lying; and as booksellers and printers are free with each other, he would have the opportunity of seeing what was going on.—Be the case, however, as it may, Mr. Pitt's plan, little and diminutive as it is, would have made a very awkward appearance, had this work appeared at the time the printer had engaged to finish it.

I have now stated the particulars which occasioned the delay, from the proposal to purchase, to the refusal to print. If all the Gentlemen are innocent, it is very unfortunate for them that such a variety of suspicious circumstances should, without any design, arrange themselves together.

Having now finished this part, I will conclude with stating another circumstance.

About a fortnight or three weeks before the meeting of Parliament, a small addition, amounting to about twelve shillings and sixpence a year, was made to the pay of the soldiers, or rather their pay was docked so much less. Some Gentlemen who knew, in part, that this work would contain a plan of reforms respecting the oppressed condition of soldiers, wished me to add a note to the work, signifying that the part upon that subject had been in the printer's hands some weeks before that addition of pay was proposed. I declined doing this, lest it should be interpreted into an air of vanity, or an endeavour to excite suspicion (for which perhaps there might be no grounds) that some of the government gentlemen had, by some means or other, made out what this work would contain: and had not the printing been interrupted so as to occasion a delay beyond the time fixed for publication, nothing contained in this appendix would have appeared.

Thomas Paine

THE AUTHOR'S NOTES FOR PART ONE AND PART TWO

[Footnote 1: The main and uniform maxim of the judges is, the greater the truth the greater the libel.]

[Footnote 2: Since writing the above, two other places occur in Mr. Burke's pamphlet in which the name of the Bastille is mentioned, but in the same manner. In the one he introduces it in a sort of obscure question, and asks: "Will any ministers who now serve such a king, with but a decent appearance of respect, cordially obey the orders of those whom but the other day, in his name, they had committed to the Bastille?" In the other the taking it is mentioned as implying criminality in the French guards, who assisted in demolishing it. "They have not," says he, "forgot the taking the king's castles at Paris." This is Mr. Burke, who pretends to write on constitutional freedom.]

[Footnote 3: I am warranted in asserting this, as I had it personally from M. de la Fayette, with whom I lived in habits of friendship for fourteen years.]

[Footnote 4: An account of the expedition to Versailles may be seen in No. 13 of the Revolution de Paris containing the events from the 3rd to the 10th of October, 1789.]

[Footnote 5: It is a practice in some parts of the country, when two travellers have but one horse, which, like the national purse, will not carry double, that the one mounts and rides two or three miles ahead, and then ties the horse to a gate and walks on. When the second traveller arrives he takes the horse, rides on, and passes his companion a mile or two, and ties again, and so on--Ride and tie.]

[Footnote 6: The word he used was renvoye, dismissed or sent away.]

[Footnote 7: When in any country we see extraordinary circumstances taking place, they naturally lead any man who has a talent for observation and investigation, to enquire into the causes. The manufacturers of Manchester, Birmingham, and Sheffield, are the principal manufacturers in England. From whence did this arise? A little observation will explain the case. The principal, and the generality of the inhabitants of those places, are not of what is called in England, the church established by law: and they, or their fathers, (for it is within but a few years) withdrew from the persecution of the chartered towns, where test-laws more particularly operate, and established a sort of asylum for themselves in those places. It was the only asylum that then offered, for the rest of Europe was worse.--But the case is now changing. France and America bid all comers welcome, and initiate them into all the rights of citizenship. Policy and interest, therefore, will, but perhaps too late, dictate in England, what reason and justice could not. Those manufacturers are withdrawing, and arising in other places. There is now erecting in Passey, three miles from Paris, a large cotton manufactory, and several are already erected in America. Soon after the rejecting the Bill for repealing the test-law, one of the richest manufacturers in England said in my hearing, "England, Sir, is not a country for a dissenter to live in,--we must go to France." These are truths, and it is doing justice to both parties to tell them. It is chiefly the dissenters that have carried English manufactures to the height they are now at, and the same men have it in their power to carry them away; and though those manufactures would afterwards continue in those places, the foreign market will be lost. There frequently appear in the London Gazette, extracts from certain acts to prevent machines and persons, as far as they can extend to persons, from going out of the country. It appears from these that the ill effects of the test-laws and church-establishment begin to be much suspected; but the remedy of force can never supply the remedy of reason. In the progress of less than a century, all the unrepresented part of England, of all denominations, which is at least an hundred times the most numerous, may begin to feel the necessity of a constitution, and then all those matters will come regularly before them.]

[Footnote 8: When the English Minister, Mr. Pitt, mentions the French finances again in the English Parliament, it would be well that he noticed this as an example.]

[Footnote 9: Mr. Burke, (and I must take the liberty of telling him that he is very unacquainted with French affairs), speaking upon this subject, says, "The first thing that struck me in calling the States-General, was a great departure from the ancient course";--and he soon after says, "From the moment I read the list, I saw distinctly, and very nearly as it has happened, all that was to follow."--Mr. Burke certainly did not see an that was to follow. I endeavoured to impress him, as well before

as after the States-General met, that there would be a revolution; but
was not able to make him see it, neither would he believe it. How then
he could distinctly see all the parts, when the whole was out of sight,
is beyond my comprehension. And with respect to the "departure from the
ancient course," besides the natural weakness of the remark, it shows
that he is unacquainted with circumstances. The departure was necessary,
from the experience had upon it, that the ancient course was a bad one.
The States-General of 1614 were called at the commencement of the civil
war in the minority of Louis XIII.; but by the class of arranging them
by orders, they increased the confusion they were called to compose. The
author of L'Intrigue du Cabinet, (Intrigue of the Cabinet), who
wrote before any revolution was thought of in France, speaking of the
States-General of 1614, says, "They held the public in suspense five
months; and by the questions agitated therein, and the heat with which
they were put, it appears that the great (les grands) thought more to
satisfy their particular passions, than to procure the goods of the
nation; and the whole time passed away in altercations, ceremonies and
parade."--L'Intrigue du Cabinet, vol. i. p. 329.]

[Footnote 10: There is a single idea, which, if it strikes rightly upon the mind,
either in a legal or a religious sense, will prevent any man or any body
of men, or any government, from going wrong on the subject of religion;
which is, that before any human institutions of government were known in
the world, there existed, if I may so express it, a compact between
God and man, from the beginning of time: and that as the relation and
condition which man in his individual person stands in towards his Maker
cannot be changed by any human laws or human authority, that religious
devotion, which is a part of this compact, cannot so much as be made a
subject of human laws; and that all laws must conform themselves to this
prior existing compact, and not assume to make the compact conform to
the laws, which, besides being human, are subsequent thereto. The first
act of man, when he looked around and saw himself a creature which he
did not make, and a world furnished for his reception, must have been
devotion; and devotion must ever continue sacred to every individual
man, as it appears, right to him; and governments do mischief by
interfering.]

[Footnote 11: See this work, Part I starting at line number 254.--N.B. Since the
taking of the Bastille, the occurrences have been published: but the
matters recorded in this narrative, are prior to that period; and some
of them, as may be easily seen, can be but very little known.]

[Footnote 12: See "Estimate of the Comparative Strength of Great Britain," by G.
Chalmers.]

[Footnote 13: See "Administration of the Finances of France," vol. iii, by M.
Neckar.]

[Footnote 14: "Administration of the Finances of France," vol. iii.]

[Footnote 15: Whether the English commerce does not bring in money, or whether the government sends it out after it is brought in, is a matter which the parties concerned can best explain; but that the deficiency exists, is not in the power of either to disprove. While Dr. Price, Mr. Eden, (now Auckland), Mr. Chalmers, and others, were debating whether the quantity of money in England was greater or less than at the Revolution, the circumstance was not adverted to, that since the Revolution, there cannot have been less than four hundred millions sterling imported into Europe; and therefore the quantity in England ought at least to have been four times greater than it was at the Revolution, to be on a proportion with Europe. What England is now doing by paper, is what she would have been able to do by solid money, if gold and silver had come into the nation in the proportion it ought, or had not been sent out; and she is endeavouring to restore by paper, the balance she has lost by money. It is certain, that the gold and silver which arrive annually in the register-ships to Spain and Portugal, do not remain in those countries. Taking the value half in gold and half in silver, it is about four hundred tons annually; and from the number of ships and galloons employed in the trade of bringing those metals from South-America to Portugal and Spain, the quantity sufficiently proves itself, without referring to the registers.

In the situation England now is, it is impossible she can increase in money. High taxes not only lessen the property of the individuals, but they lessen also the money capital of the nation, by inducing smuggling, which can only be carried on by gold and silver. By the politics which the British Government have carried on with the Inland Powers of Germany and the Continent, it has made an enemy of all the Maritime Powers, and is therefore obliged to keep up a large navy; but though the navy is built in England, the naval stores must be purchased from abroad, and that from countries where the greatest part must be paid for in gold and silver. Some fallacious rumours have been set afloat in England to induce a belief in money, and, among others, that of the French refugees bringing great quantities. The idea is ridiculous. The general part of the money in France is silver; and it would take upwards of twenty of the largest broad wheel wagons, with ten horses each, to remove one million sterling of silver. Is it then to be supposed, that a few people fleeing on horse-back or in post-chaises, in a secret manner, and having the French Custom-House to pass, and the sea to cross, could bring even a sufficiency for their own expenses?

When millions of money are spoken of, it should be recollected, that such sums can only accumulate in a country by slow degrees, and a long procession of time. The most frugal system that England could now adopt, would not recover in a century the balance she has lost in money since the commencement of the Hanover succession. She is seventy millions behind France, and she must be in some considerable proportion behind every country in Europe, because the returns of the English mint do not

show an increase of money, while the registers of Lisbon and Cadiz
show an European increase of between three and four hundred millions
sterling.]

[Footnote 16: That part of America which is generally called New-England,
including New-Hampshire, Massachusetts, Rhode-Island, and Connecticut,
is peopled chiefly by English descendants. In the state of New-York
about half are Dutch, the rest English, Scotch, and Irish. In
New-Jersey, a mixture of English and Dutch, with some Scotch and Irish.
In Pennsylvania about one third are English, another Germans, and
the remainder Scotch and Irish, with some Swedes. The States to the
southward have a greater proportion of English than the middle States,
but in all of them there is a mixture; and besides those enumerated,
there are a considerable number of French, and some few of all the
European nations, lying on the coast. The most numerous religious
denomination are the Presbyterians; but no one sect is established above
another, and all men are equally citizens.]

[Footnote 17: For a character of aristocracy, the reader is referred to Rights of
Man, Part I., starting at line number 1457.]

[Footnote 18: The whole amount of the assessed taxes of France, for the present
year, is three hundred millions of francs, which is twelve millions
and a half sterling; and the incidental taxes are estimated at three
millions, making in the whole fifteen millions and a half; which among
twenty-four millions of people, is not quite thirteen shillings per
head. France has lessened her taxes since the revolution, nearly nine
millions sterling annually. Before the revolution, the city of Paris
paid a duty of upwards of thirty per cent. on all articles brought into
the city. This tax was collected at the city gates. It was taken off on
the first of last May, and the gates taken down.]

[Footnote 19: What was called the livre rouge, or the red book, in France, was not
exactly similar to the Court Calendar in England; but it sufficiently
showed how a great part of the taxes was lavished.]

[Footnote 20: In England the improvements in agriculture, useful arts,
manufactures, and commerce, have been made in opposition to the genius
of its government, which is that of following precedents. It is from
the enterprise and industry of the individuals, and their numerous
associations, in which, tritely speaking, government is neither pillow
nor bolster, that these improvements have proceeded. No man thought
about government, or who was in, or who was out, when he was planning
or executing those things; and all he had to hope, with respect to
government, was, that it would let him alone. Three or four very silly
ministerial newspapers are continually offending against the spirit of
national improvement, by ascribing it to a minister. They may with as
much truth ascribe this book to a minister.]

[Footnote 21: With respect to the two houses, of which the English parliament is composed, they appear to be effectually influenced into one, and, as a legislature, to have no temper of its own. The minister, whoever he at any time may be, touches it as with an opium wand, and it sleeps obedience.

But if we look at the distinct abilities of the two houses, the difference will appear so great, as to show the inconsistency of placing power where there can be no certainty of the judgment to use it. Wretched as the state of representation is in England, it is manhood compared with what is called the house of Lords; and so little is this nick-named house regarded, that the people scarcely enquire at any time what it is doing. It appears also to be most under influence, and the furthest removed from the general interest of the nation. In the debate on engaging in the Russian and Turkish war, the majority in the house of peers in favor of it was upwards of ninety, when in the other house, which was more than double its numbers, the majority was sixty-three.]

The proceedings on Mr. Fox's bill, respecting the rights of juries, merits also to be noticed. The persons called the peers were not the objects of that bill. They are already in possession of more privileges than that bill gave to others. They are their own jury, and if any one of that house were prosecuted for a libel, he would not suffer, even upon conviction, for the first offense. Such inequality in laws ought not to exist in any country. The French constitution says, that the law is the same to every individual, whether to Protect or to punish. All are equal in its sight.]

[Footnote 22: As to the state of representation in England, it is too absurd to be reasoned upon. Almost all the represented parts are decreasing in population, and the unrepresented parts are increasing. A general convention of the nation is necessary to take the whole form of government into consideration.]

[Footnote 23: It is related that in the canton of Berne, in Switzerland, it has been customary, from time immemorial, to keep a bear at the public expense, and the people had been taught to believe that if they had not a bear they should all be undone. It happened some years ago that the bear, then in being, was taken sick, and died too suddenly to have his place immediately supplied with another. During this interregnum the people discovered that the corn grew, and the vintage flourished, and the sun and moon continued to rise and set, and everything went on the same as before, and taking courage from these circumstances, they resolved not to keep any more bears; for, said they, "a bear is a very voracious expensive animal, and we were obliged to pull out his claws, lest he should hurt the citizens." The story of the bear of Berne was related in some of the French newspapers, at the time of the flight of Louis Xvi., and the application of it to monarchy could not be mistaken in France; but it seems that the aristocracy of Berne applied it to themselves, and have since prohibited the reading of French newspapers.]

[Footnote 24: It is scarcely possible to touch on any subject, that will not suggest an allusion to some corruption in governments. The simile of "fortifications," unfortunately involves with it a circumstance, which is directly in point with the matter above alluded to.]

Among the numerous instances of abuse which have been acted or protected by governments, ancient or modern, there is not a greater than that of quartering a man and his heirs upon the public, to be maintained at its expense.

Humanity dictates a provision for the poor; but by what right, moral or political, does any government assume to say, that the person called the Duke of Richmond, shall be maintained by the public? Yet, if common report is true, not a beggar in London can purchase his wretched pittance of coal, without paying towards the civil list of the Duke of Richmond. Were the whole produce of this imposition but a shilling a year, the iniquitous principle would be still the same; but when it amounts, as it is said to do, to no less than twenty thousand pounds per annum, the enormity is too serious to be permitted to remain. This is one of the effects of monarchy and aristocracy.

In stating this case I am led by no personal dislike. Though I think it mean in any man to live upon the public, the vice originates in the government; and so general is it become, that whether the parties are in the ministry or in the opposition, it makes no difference: they are sure of the guarantee of each other.]

[Footnote 25: In America the increase of commerce is greater in proportion than in England. It is, at this time, at least one half more than at any period prior to the revolution. The greatest number of vessels cleared out of the port of Philadelphia, before the commencement of the war, was between eight and nine hundred. In the year 1788, the number was upwards of twelve hundred. As the State of Pennsylvania is estimated at an eighth part of the United States in population, the whole number of vessels must now be nearly ten thousand.]

[Footnote 26: When I saw Mr. Pitt's mode of estimating the balance of trade, in one of his parliamentary speeches, he appeared to me to know nothing of the nature and interest of commerce; and no man has more wantonly tortured it than himself. During a period of peace it has been havocked with the calamities of war. Three times has it been thrown into stagnation, and the vessels unmanned by impressing, within less than four years of peace.]

[Footnote 27: Rev. William Knowle, master of the grammar school of Thetford, in Norfolk.]

[Footnote 28: Politics and self-interest have been so uniformly connected that the world, from being so often deceived, has a right to be suspicious of public characters, but with regard to myself I am perfectly easy on this head. I did not, at my first setting out in public life, nearly seventeen years ago, turn my thoughts to subjects of government from motives of interest, and my conduct from that moment to this proves the fact. I saw an opportunity in which I thought I could do some good, and I followed exactly what my heart dictated. I neither read books, nor studied other people's opinion. I thought for myself. The case was this:--

During the suspension of the old governments in America, both prior to and at the breaking out of hostilities, I was struck with the order and decorum with which everything was conducted, and impressed with the idea that a little more than what society naturally performed was all the government that was necessary, and that monarchy and aristocracy were frauds and impositions upon mankind. On these principles I published the pamphlet Common Sense. The success it met with was beyond anything since the invention of printing. I gave the copyright to every state in the Union, and the demand ran to not less than one hundred thousand copies. I continued the subject in the same manner, under the title of The Crisis, till the complete establishment of the Revolution.

After the declaration of independence Congress unanimously, and unknown to me, appointed me Secretary in the Foreign Department. This was agreeable to me, because it gave me the opportunity of seeing into the abilities of foreign courts, and their manner of doing business. But a misunderstanding arising between Congress and me, respecting one of their commissioners then in Europe, Mr. Silas Deane, I resigned the office, and declined at the same time the pecuniary offers made by the Ministers of France and Spain, M. Gerald and Don Juan Mirralles.]
I had by this time so completely gained the ear and confidence of America, and my own independence was become so visible, as to give me a range in political writing beyond, perhaps, what any man ever possessed in any country, and, what is more extraordinary, I held it undiminished to the end of the war, and enjoy it in the same manner to the present moment. As my object was not myself, I set out with the determination, and happily with the disposition, of not being moved by praise or censure, friendship or calumny, nor of being drawn from my purpose by any personal altercation, and the man who cannot do this is not fit for a public character.

When the war ended I went from Philadelphia to Borden-Town, on the east bank of the Delaware, where I have a small place. Congress was at this time at Prince-Town, fifteen miles distant, and General Washington had taken his headquarters at Rocky Hill, within the neighbourhood of Congress, for the purpose of resigning up his commission (the object for which he accepted it being accomplished), and of retiring to private life. While he was on this business he wrote me the letter which I here subjoin:

"Rocky-Hill, Sept. 10, 1783.

"I have learned since I have been at this place that you are at Borden-Town. Whether for the sake of retirement or economy I know not. Be it for either, for both, or whatever it may, if you will come to this place, and partake with me, I shall be exceedingly happy to see you at it.

"Your presence may remind Congress of your past services to this country, and if it is in my power to impress them, command my best exertions with freedom, as they will be rendered cheerfully by one who entertains a lively sense of the importance of your works, and who, with much pleasure, subscribes himself, Your sincere friend,

G. Washington."

During the war, in the latter end of the year 1780, I formed to myself a design of coming over to England, and communicated it to General Greene, who was then in Philadelphia on his route to the southward, General Washington being then at too great a distance to communicate with immediately. I was strongly impressed with the idea that if I could get over to England without being known, and only remain in safety till I could get out a publication, that I could open the eyes of the country with respect to the madness and stupidity of its Government. I saw that the parties in Parliament had pitted themselves as far as they could go, and could make no new impressions on each other. General Greene entered fully into my views, but the affair of Arnold and Andre happening just after, he changed his mind, under strong apprehensions for my safety, wrote very pressingly to me from Annapolis, in Maryland, to give up the design, which, with some reluctance, I did. Soon after this I accompanied Colonel Lawrens, son of Mr. Lawrens, who was then in the Tower, to France on business from Congress. We landed at L'orient, and while I remained there, he being gone forward, a circumstance occurred that renewed my former design. An English packet from Falmouth to New York, with the Government dispatches on board, was brought into L'orient. That a packet should be taken is no extraordinary thing, but that the dispatches should be taken with it will scarcely be credited, as they are always slung at the cabin window in a bag loaded with cannon-ball, and ready to be sunk at a moment. The fact, however, is as I have stated it, for the dispatches came into my hands, and I read them. The capture, as I was informed, succeeded by the following stratagem:--The captain of the "Madame" privateer, who spoke English, on coming up with the packet, passed himself for the captain of an English frigate, and invited the captain of the packet on board, which, when done, he sent some of his own hands back, and he secured the mail. But be the circumstance of the capture what it may, I speak with certainty as to the Government dispatches. They were sent up to Paris to Count

Vergennes, and when Colonel Lawrens and myself returned to America we took the originals to Congress.

By these dispatches I saw into the stupidity of the English Cabinet far more than I otherwise could have done, and I renewed my former design. But Colonel Lawrens was so unwilling to return alone, more especially as, among other matters, we had a charge of upwards of two hundred thousand pounds sterling in money, that I gave in to his wishes, and finally gave up my plan. But I am now certain that if I could have executed it that it would not have been altogether unsuccessful.]

[Footnote 29: It is difficult to account for the origin of charter and corporation towns, unless we suppose them to have arisen out of, or been connected with, some species of garrison service. The times in which they began justify this idea. The generality of those towns have been garrisons, and the corporations were charged with the care of the gates of the towns, when no military garrison was present. Their refusing or granting admission to strangers, which has produced the custom of giving, selling, and buying freedom, has more of the nature of garrison authority than civil government. Soldiers are free of all corporations throughout the nation, by the same propriety that every soldier is free of every garrison, and no other persons are. He can follow any employment, with the permission of his officers, in any corporation towns throughout the nation.]

[Footnote 30: See Sir John Sinclair's History of the Revenue. The land-tax in 1646 was L2,473,499.]

[Footnote 31: Several of the court newspapers have of late made frequent mention of Wat Tyler. That his memory should be traduced by court sycophants and an those who live on the spoil of a public is not to be wondered at. He was, however, the means of checking the rage and injustice of taxation in his time, and the nation owed much to his valour. The history is concisely this:--In the time of Richard Ii. a poll tax was levied of one shilling per head upon every person in the nation of whatever estate or condition, on poor as well as rich, above the age of fifteen years. If any favour was shown in the law it was to the rich rather than to the poor, as no person could be charged more than twenty shillings for himself, family and servants, though ever so numerous; while all other families, under the number of twenty were charged per head. Poll taxes had always been odious, but this being also oppressive and unjust, it excited as it naturally must, universal detestation among the poor and middle classes. The person known by the name of Wat Tyler, whose proper name was Walter, and a tiler by trade, lived at Deptford. The gatherer of the poll tax, on coming to his house, demanded tax for one of his daughters, whom Tyler declared was under the age of fifteen. The tax-gatherer insisted on satisfying himself, and began an indecent examination of the girl, which, enraging the father, he struck him with a hammer that brought him to the ground, and was the cause of his death. This circumstance served to bring the discontent to an issue. The inhabitants of the neighbourhood espoused the cause of Tyler, who in a few days was joined, according to some histories, by upwards of fifty thousand men, and chosen their chief. With this force he marched to London, to demand an abolition of the tax and a redress of other grievances. The Court, finding itself in a forlorn condition, and, unable to make resistance, agreed, with Richard at its head, to hold a conference with Tyler in Smithfield, making many fair professions, courtier-like, of its dispositions to redress the oppressions. While Richard and Tyler were in conversation on these matters, each being on horseback, Walworth, then Mayor of London, and one of the creatures of the Court, watched an opportunity, and like a cowardly assassin, stabbed Tyler with a dagger, and two or three others falling upon him, he was instantly sacrificed. Tyler appears to have been an intrepid disinterested man with respect to himself. All his proposals made to Richard were on a more just and public ground than those which had been made to John by the Barons, and notwithstanding the sycophancy of historians and men like Mr. Burke, who seek to gloss over a base action of the Court by traducing Tyler, his fame will outlive their falsehood. If the Barons merited a monument to be erected at Runnymede, Tyler merited one in Smithfield.]

[Footnote 32: I happened to be in England at the celebration of the centenary of the Revolution of 1688. The characters of William and Mary have always appeared to be detestable; the one seeking to destroy his uncle, and the other her father, to get possession of power themselves; yet, as the nation was disposed to think something of that event, I felt hurt at seeing it ascribe the whole reputation of it to a man who had undertaken it as a job and who, besides what he otherwise got, charged six hundred thousand pounds for the expense of the fleet that brought him from Holland. George the First acted the same close-fisted part as William had done, and bought the Duchy of Bremen with the money he got from England, two hundred and fifty thousand pounds over and above his pay as king, and having thus purchased it at the expense of England, added it to his Hanoverian dominions for his own private profit. In fact, every nation that does not govern itself is governed as a job. England has been the prey of jobs ever since the Revolution.]

[Footnote 33: Charles, like his predecessors and successors, finding that war was the harvest of governments, engaged in a war with the Dutch, the expense of which increased the annual expenditure to L1,800,000 as stated under the date of 1666; but the peace establishment was but L1,200,000.]

[Footnote 34: Poor-rates began about the time of Henry VIII., when the taxes began to increase, and they have increased as the taxes increased ever since.]

[Footnote 35: Reckoning the taxes by families, five to a family, each family pays on an average L12 7s. 6d. per annum. To this sum are to be added the poor-rates. Though all pay taxes in the articles they consume, all do

not pay poor-rates. About two millions are exempted: some as not being
house-keepers, others as not being able, and the poor themselves
who receive the relief. The average, therefore, of poor-rates on the
remaining number, is forty shillings for every family of five persons,
which make the whole average amount of taxes and rates L14 17s. 6d. For
six persons L17 17s. For seven persons L20 16s. 6d.
The average of taxes in America, under the new or representative system
of government, including the interest of the debt contracted in the
war, and taking the population at four millions of souls, which it now
amounts to, and it is daily increasing, is five shillings per head,
men, women, and children. The difference, therefore, between the two
governments is as under:

```
          England        America
          L    s.  d.    L    s.  d.
For a family of five persons    14   17   6    1    5   0
For a family of six persons     17   17   0    1   10   0
For a family of seven persons   20   16   6    1   15   0
```

[Footnote 36: Public schools do not answer the general purpose of the poor.
They are chiefly in corporation towns from which the country towns and
villages are excluded, or, if admitted, the distance occasions a great
loss of time. Education, to be useful to the poor, should be on the
spot, and the best method, I believe, to accomplish this is to enable
the parents to pay the expenses themselves. There are always persons of
both sexes to be found in every village, especially when growing into
years, capable of such an undertaking. Twenty children at ten shillings
each (and that not more than six months each year) would be as much as
some livings amount to in the remotest parts of England, and there are
often distressed clergymen's widows to whom such an income would be
acceptable. Whatever is given on this account to children answers two
purposes. To them it is education--to those who educate them it is a
livelihood.]

[Footnote 37: The tax on beer brewed for sale, from which the aristocracy are
exempt, is almost one million more than the present commutation tax,
being by the returns of 1788, L1,666,152--and, consequently, they ought
to take on themselves the amount of the commutation tax, as they are
already exempted from one which is almost a million greater.]

[Footnote 38: See the Reports on the Corn Trade.]

[Footnote 39: When enquiries are made into the condition of the poor, various
degrees of distress will most probably be found, to render a different
arrangement preferable to that which is already proposed. Widows with
families will be in greater want than where there are husbands living.
There is also a difference in the expense of living in different
counties: and more so in fuel.

```
Suppose then fifty thousand extraordinary cases, at
the rate of ten pounds per family per annum          L500,000
100,000 families, at L8 per family per annum          800,000
100,000 families, at L7 per family per annum          700,000
104,000 families, at L5 per family per annum          520,000

And instead of ten shillings per head for the education
of other children, to allow fifty shillings per family
for that purpose to fifty thousand families          250,000
                                                     ───────
L2,770,000
140,000 aged persons as before                     1,120,000
                                                     ───────
                            L3,890,000
```

This arrangement amounts to the same sum as stated in this work, Part II, line number 1068, including the L250,000 for education; but it provides (including the aged people) for four hundred and four thousand families, which is almost one third of an the families in England.]

[Footnote 40: I know it is the opinion of many of the most enlightened characters in France (there always will be those who see further into events than others), not only among the general mass of citizens, but of many of the principal members of the former National Assembly, that the monarchical plan will not continue many years in that country. They have found out, that as wisdom cannot be made hereditary, power ought not; and that, for a man to merit a million sterling a year from a nation, he ought to have a mind capable of comprehending from an atom to a universe, which, if he had, he would be above receiving the pay. But they wished not to appear to lead the nation faster than its own reason and interest dictated. In all the conversations where I have been present upon this subject, the idea always was, that when such a time, from the general opinion of the nation, shall arrive, that the honourable and liberal method would be, to make a handsome present in fee simple to the person, whoever he may be, that shall then be in the monarchical office, and for him to retire to the enjoyment of private life, possessing his share of general rights and privileges, and to be no more accountable to the public for his time and his conduct than any other citizen.]

[Footnote 41: The gentleman who signed the address and declaration as chairman of the meeting, Mr. Horne Tooke, being generally supposed to be the person who drew it up, and having spoken much in commendation of it, has been jocularly accused of praising his own work. To free him from this embarrassment, and to save him the repeated trouble of mentioning the author, as he has not failed to do, I make no hesitation in saying, that as the opportunity of benefiting by the French Revolution easily occurred to me, I drew up the publication in question, and showed it to him and some other gentlemen, who, fully approving it, held a meeting for the purpose of making it public, and subscribed to the amount of fifty guineas to defray the expense of advertising. I believe there are at this time, in England, a greater number of men acting on disinterested principles, and determined to look into the nature and practices of government themselves, and not blindly trust, as has hitherto been the case, either to government generally, or to parliaments, or to parliamentary opposition, than at any former period. Had this been done a century ago, corruption and taxation had not arrived to the height they are now at.]

2 – COMMON SENSE;

addressed to the
INHABITANTS of AMERICA,

On the following interesting

SUBJECTS

1. Of the Origin and Design of Government in general, with concise Remarks on the English Constitution.
2. Of Monarchy and Hereditary Succession
3. Thoughts on the present State of American Affairs
4. Of the present Ability of America, with some miscellaneous Reflections

Man knows no Master save creating HEAVEN
Or those whom choice and common good ordain.
THOMSON.

PHILADELPHIA
Printed and sold by W. & T. Bradford, February 14, 1776.

MDCCLXXVI

Common Sense

INTRODUCTION.

PERHAPS the sentiments contained in the following pages, are not *yet* sufficiently fashionable to procure them general favor; a long habit of not thinking a thing *wrong*, gives it a superficial appearance of being *right*, and raises at first a formidable outcry in defense of custom. But the tumult soon subsides. Time makes more converts than reason.

As a long and violent abuse of power, is generally the Means of calling the right of it in question (and in Matters too which might never have been thought of, had not the Sufferers been aggravated into the inquiry) and as the King of England hath undertaken in his *own Right*, to support the Parliament in what he calls *Theirs*, and as the good people of this country are grievously oppressed by the combination, they have an undoubted privilege to inquire into the pretensions of both, and equally to reject the usurpation of either.

In the following sheets, the author hath studiously avoided every thing which is personal among ourselves. Compliments as well as censure to individuals make no part thereof. The wise, and the worthy, need not the triumph of a pamphlet; and those whose sentiments are injudicious, or unfriendly, will cease of themselves unless too much pains are bestowed upon their conversion.

The cause of America is in a great measure the cause of all mankind. Many circumstances hath, and will arise, which are not local, but universal, and through which the principles of all Lovers of Mankind are affected, and in the Event of which, their Affections are interested. The laying a Country desolate with Fire and Sword, declaring War against the natural rights of all Mankind, and extirpating the Defenders thereof from the Face of the Earth, is the Concern of every Man to whom Nature hath given the Power of feeling; of which Class, regardless of Party Censure, is the

AUTHOR

P.S. The Publication of this new Edition hath been delayed, with a View of taking notice (had it been necessary) of any Attempt to refute the Doctrine of Independance: As no Answer hath yet appeared, it is now presumed that none will, the Time needful for getting such a Performance ready for the Public being considerably past.

Who the Author of this Production is, is wholly unnecessary to the Public, as the Object for Attention is the *Doctrine itself*, not the *Man*. Yet it may not be unnecessary to say, That he is unconnected with any Party, and under no sort of Influence public or private, but the influence of reason and principle.

Philadelphia, February 14, 1776

OF THE ORIGIN AND DESIGN OF GOVERNMENT IN GENERAL, WITH CONCISE REMARKS ON THE ENGLISH CONSTITUTION.

SOME writers have so confounded society with government, as to leave little or no distinction between them; whereas they are not only different, but have different origins. Society is produced by our wants, and government by our wickedness; the former promotes our happiness *positively* by uniting our affections, the latter *negatively* by restraining our vices. The one encourages intercourse, the other creates distinctions. The first a patron, the last a punisher.

Society in every state is a blessing, but government even in its best state is but a necessary evil; in its worst state an intolerable one; for when we suffer, or are exposed to the same miseries *by a government*, which we might expect in a country *without government*, our calamity is heightened by reflecting that we furnish the means by which we suffer. Government, like dress, is the badge of lost innocence; the palaces of kings are built on the ruins of the bowers of paradise. For were the impulses of conscience clear, uniform, and irresistibly obeyed, man would need no other lawgiver; but that not being the case, he finds it necessary to surrender up a part of his property to furnish means for the protection of the rest; and this he is induced to do by the same prudence which in every other case advises him out of two evils to choose the least. *Wherefore*, security being the true design and end of government, it unanswerably follows that whatever *form* thereof appears most likely to ensure it to us, with the least expence and greatest benefit, is preferable to all others.

In order to gain a clear and just idea of the design and end of government, let us suppose a small number of persons settled in some sequestered part of the earth, unconnected with the rest, they will then represent the first peopling of any country, or of the world. In this state of natural liberty, society will be their first thought. A thousand motives will excite them thereto, the strength of one man is so unequal to his wants, and his mind so unfitted for perpetual solitude, that he is soon obliged to seek assistance and relief of another, who in his turn requires the same. Four or five united would be able to raise a tolerable dwelling in the midst of a wilderness, but *one* man might labour out of the common period of life without accomplishing any thing; when he had felled his timber he could not remove it, nor erect it after it was removed; hunger in the mean time would urge him from his work, and every different want call him a different way. Disease, nay even misfortune would be death, for though neither might be mortal, yet either would disable him from living, and reduce him to a state in which he might rather be said to perish than to die.

Thus necessity, like a gravitating power, would soon form our newly arrived emigrants into society, the reciprocal blessings of which, would supersede, and render the obligations of law and government unnecessary while they remained perfectly just to each other; but as nothing but heaven is impregnable to vice, it will unavoidably happen, that in proportion as they surmount the first difficulties of emigration, which bound them together in a common cause, they will begin to relax in their duty and attachment to each other; and this remissness, will point out the necessity, of establishing some form of government to supply the defect of moral virtue.

Some convenient tree will afford them a State-House, under the branches of which, the whole colony may assemble to deliberate on public matters. It is more than probable that their first laws will have the title only of REGULATIONS, and be enforced by no other penalty than public disesteem. In this first parliament every man, by natural right, will have a seat.

But as the colony increases, the public concerns will increase likewise, and the distance at which the members may be separated, will render it too inconvenient for all of them to meet on every occasion as at first, when their number was small, their habitations near, and the public concerns few and trifling. This will point out the convenience of their consenting to leave the legislative part to be managed by a select number chosen from the whole body, who are supposed to have the same concerns at stake which those who appointed them, and who will act in the same manner as the whole body would act were they present. If the colony continue increasing, it will become necessary to augment the number of the representatives, and that the interest of every part of the colony may be attended to, it will be found best to divide the whole into convenient parts, each part sending its proper number; and that the *elected* might never form to themselves an interest separate from the *electors*, prudence will point out the propriety of having elections often; because as the *elected* might by that means return and mix again with the general body of the *electors* in a few months, their fidelity to the public will be secured by the prudent reflexion of not making a rod for themselves. And as this frequent interchange will establish a common interest with every part of the community, they will mutually and naturally support each other, and on this (not on the unmeaning name of king) depends the *strength of government, and the happiness of the governed.*

Here then is the origin and rise of government; namely, a mode rendered necessary by the inability of moral virtue to govern the world; here too is the design and end of government, viz. freedom and security. And however our eyes may be dazzled with show, or our ears deceived by sound; however prejudice may warp our wills, or interest darken our understanding, the simple voice of nature and of reason will say, it is right.

I draw my idea of the form of government from a principle in nature, which no art can overturn, viz. that the more simple any thing is, the less liable it is to be disordered; and the easier repaired when disordered; and with this maxim in view, I offer a few remarks on the so much boasted constitution of England. That it was noble for the dark and slavish times in which it was erected, is granted. When the world was over run with tyranny the least remove therefrom was a glorious rescue. But that it is imperfect, subject to convulsions, and incapable of producing what it seems to promise, is easily demonstrated.

Absolute governments (tho' the disgrace of human nature) have this advantage with them, that they are simple; if the people suffer, they know the head from which their suffering springs, know likewise the remedy, and are not bewildered by a variety of causes and cures. But the constitution of England is so exceedingly complex, that the nation may suffer for years together without being able to discover in which part the fault lies, some will say in one and some in another, and every political physician will advise a different medicine.

I know it is difficult to get over local or long standing prejudices, yet if we will suffer ourselves to examine the component parts of the English constitution, we shall find them to be the base remains of two ancient tyrannies, compounded with some new republican materials.

First. —The remains of monarchical tyranny in the person of the king.

Secondly. —The remains of aristocratical tyranny in the persons of the peers.

Thirdly. —The new republican materials, in the persons of the commons, on whose virtue depends the freedom of England.

The two first, by being hereditary, are independent of the people; wherefore in a *constitutional sense* they contribute nothing towards the freedom of the state.

To say that the constitution of England is a *union* of three powers reciprocally *checking* each other, is farcical, either the words have no meaning, or they are flat contradictions.

To say that the commons is a check upon the king, presupposes two things:

First. —That the king is not to be trusted without being looked after, or in other words, that a thirst for absolute power is the natural disease of monarchy.

Secondly. —That the commons, by being appointed for that purpose, are either wiser or more worthy of confidence than the crown.

But as the same constitution which gives the commons a power to check the king by withholding the supplies, gives afterwards the king a power to check the commons, by empowering him to reject their other bills; it again supposes that the king is wiser than those whom it has already supposed to be wiser than him. A mere absurdity!

There is something exceedingly ridiculous in the composition of monarchy; it first excludes a man from the means of information, yet empowers him to act in cases where the highest judgment is required. The state of a king shuts him from the world, yet the business of a king requires him to know it thoroughly; wherefore the different parts, by unnaturally opposing and destroying each other, prove the whole character to be absurd and useless.

Some writers have explained the English constitution thus; the king, say they, is one, the people another; the peers are an house in behalf of the king; the commons in behalf of the people; but this hath all the distinctions of a house divided against itself; and though the expressions be pleasantly arranged, yet when examined they appear idle and ambiguous; and it will always happen, that the nicest construction that words are capable of, when applied to the description of some thing which either cannot exist, or is too incomprehensible to be within the compass of description, will be words of sound only, and though they may amuse the ear, they cannot inform the mind, for this explanation includes a previous question, viz. *How came the king by a power which the people are afraid to trust, and always obliged to check?* Such a power could not be the gift of a wise people, neither can any power, *which needs checking*, be from God; yet the provision, which the constitution makes, supposes such a power to exist.

But the provision is unequal to the task; the means either cannot or will not accomplish the end, and the whole affair is a felo de se; for as the greater weight will always carry up the less, and as all the wheels of a machine are put in motion by one, it only remains to know which power in the constitution has the most weight, for that will govern; and though the others, or a part of them, may clog, or, as the phrase is, check the rapidity of its motion, yet so long as they cannot stop it, their endeavors will be ineffectual; the first moving power will at last have its way, and what it wants in speed is supplied by time.

That the crown is this overbearing part in the English constitution needs not be mentioned, and that it derives its whole consequence merely from being the giver of places and pensions is self-evident, wherefore, though we have been wise enough to shut and lock a door against absolute monarchy, we at the same time have been foolish enough to put the crown in possession of the key.

The prejudice of Englishmen, in favour of their own government by king, lords and commons, arises as much or more from national pride than reason. Individuals are undoubtedly safer in England than in some other countries, but the *will* of the king is as much the *law* of the land in Britain as in France, with this difference, that instead of proceeding directly from his mouth, it is handed to the people under the more formidable shape of an act of parliament. For the fate of Charles the first, hath only made kings more subtle—not more just.

Wherefore, laying aside all national pride and prejudice in favour of modes and forms, the plain truth is, that *it is wholly owing to the constitution of the people, and not to the constitution of the government* that the crown is not as oppressive in England as in Turkey.

An inquiry into the *constitutional errors* in the English form of government is at this time highly necessary, for as we are never in a proper condition of doing justice to others, while we continue under the influence of some leading partiality, so neither are we capable of doing it to ourselves while we remain fettered by any obstinate prejudice. And as a man, who is attached to a prostitute, is unfitted to choose or judge of a wife, so any prepossession in favour of a rotten constitution of government will disable us from discerning a good one.

OF MONARCHY AND HEREDITARY SUCCESSION.

MANKIND being originally equals in the order of creation, the equality could only be destroyed by some subsequent circumstance; the distinctions of rich, and poor, may in a great measure be accounted for, and that without having recourse to the harsh ill sounding names of oppression and avarice. Oppression is often the *consequence*, but seldom or never the *means* of riches; and though avarice will preserve a man from being necessitously poor, it generally makes him too timorous to be wealthy.

But there is another and greater distinction for which no truly natural or religious reason can be assigned, and that is, the distinction of men into KINGS and SUBJECTS. Male and female are the distinctions of nature, good and bad the distinctions of heaven; but how a race of men came into the world so exalted above the rest, and distinguished like some new species, is worth enquiring into, and whether they are the means of happiness or of misery to mankind.

In the early ages of the world, according to the scripture chronology, there were no kings; the consequence of which was there were no wars; it is the pride of kings which throw mankind into confusion. Holland without a king hath enjoyed more peace for this last century than any of the monarchial governments in Europe. Antiquity favors the same remark; for the quiet and rural lives of the first patriarchs hath a happy something in them, which vanishes away when we come to the history of Jewish royalty.

Government by kings was first introduced into the world by the Heathens, from whom the children of Israel copied the custom. It was the most prosperous invention the Devil ever set on foot for the promotion of idolatry. The Heathens paid divine honors to their deceased kings, and the christian world hath improved on the plan by doing the same to their living ones. How impious is the title of sacred majesty applied to a worm, who in the midst of his splendor is crumbling into dust!

As the exalting one man so greatly above the rest cannot be justified on the equal rights of nature, so neither can it be defended on the authority of scripture; for the will of the Almighty, as declared by Gideon and the prophet Samuel, expressly disapproves of government by kings. All anti-monarchical parts of scripture have been very smoothly glossed over in monarchical governments, but they undoubtedly merit the attention of countries which have their governments yet to form. "*Render unto Cæsar the things which are Cæsar's*" is the scripture doctrine of courts, yet it is no support of monarchical government, for the Jews at that time were without a king, and in a state of vassalage to the Romans.

Near three thousand years passed away from the Mosaic account of the creation, till the Jews under a national delusion requested a king. Till then their form of government (except in extraordinary cases, where the Almighty interposed) was a kind of republic administred by a judge and the elders of the tribes. Kings they had none, and it was held sinful to acknowledge any being under that title but the Lord of Hosts. And when a man seriously reflects on the idolatrous homage which is paid to the persons of Kings, he need not wonder, that the Almighty ever jealous of his honor, should disapprove of a form of government which so impiously invades the prerogative of heaven.

Monarchy is ranked in scripture as one of the sins of the Jews, for which a curse in reserve is denounced against them. The history of that transaction is worth attending to.

The children of Israel being oppressed by the Midianites, Gideon marched against them with a small army, and victory, thro' the divine interposition, decided in his favour. The Jews elate with success, and attributing it to the generalship of Gideon, proposed making him a king, saying, *Rule thou over us, thou and thy son and thy son's son*. Here was temptation in its fullest extent; not a kingdom only, but an hereditary one, but Gideon in the piety of his soul replied, *I will not rule over you, neither shall my son rule over you*. THE LORD SHALL RULE OVER YOU. Words need not be more explicit; Gideon doth not *decline* the honor, but denieth their right to give it; neither doth he compliment them with invented declarations of his thanks, but in the positive stile of a prophet charges them with disaffection to their proper Sovereign, the King of heaven.

About one hundred and thirty years after this, they fell again into the same error. The hankering which the Jews had for the idolatrous customs of the Heathens, is something exceedingly unaccountable; but so it was, that laying hold of the misconduct of Samuel's two sons, who were entrusted with some secular concerns, they came in an abrupt and clamorous manner to Samuel, saying, Behold thou art old, and thy sons walk not in thy ways, now make us a king to judge us like all other nations. And here we cannot but observe that their motives were bad, viz. that they might be like unto other nations, i.e. the Heathens, whereas their true glory laid in being as much unlike them as possible. But the thing displeased Samuel when they said, Give us a king to judge us; and Samuel prayed unto the Lord, and the Lord said unto Samuel, Hearken unto the voice of the people in all that they say unto thee, for they have not rejected thee, but they have rejected me, THAT I SHOULD NOT REIGN OVER THEM. According to all the works which they have done since the day that I brought them up out of Egypt, even unto this day; wherewith they have forsaken me and served other Gods; so do they also unto thee. Now therefore hearken unto their voice, howbeit, protest solemnly unto them and shew them the manner of the king that shall reign over them, i.e. not of any particular king, but the general manner of the kings of the earth, whom Israel was so eagerly copying after. And notwithstanding the great distance of time and difference of manners, the character is still in fashion. And Samuel told all the words of the Lord unto the people, that asked of him a king. And he said, This shall be the manner of the king that shall reign over you; he will take your sons and appoint them for himself, for his chariots, and to be his horsemen, and some shall run before his chariots (this description agrees with the present mode of impressing men) and he will appoint him captains over thousands and captains over fifties, and will set them to ear his ground and to reap his harvest, and to make his instruments of war, and instruments of his chariots; and he will take your daughters to be confectionaries, and to be cooks and to be bakers (this describes the expence and luxury as well as the oppression of kings) and he will take your fields and your olive yards, even the best of them, and give them to his servants; and he will take the tenth of your feed, and of your vineyards, and give them to his officers and to his servants (by which we see that bribery, corruption and favoritism are the standing vices of kings) and he will take the tenth of your men servants, and your maid servants, and your goodliest young men and your asses, and put them to his work; and he will take the tenth of your sheep, and ye shall be his servants, and ye shall cry out in that day because of your king which ye shall have chosen, AND THE LORD WILL NOT HEAR YOU IN THAT DAY. This accounts for the continuation of monarchy; neither do the characters of the few good kings which have lived since, either sanctify the title, or blot out the sinfulness of the origin; the high encomium given of David takes no notice of him officially as a king, but only as a man after God's own heart. Nevertheless the People refused to obey the voice of Samuel, and they said, Nay, but we will have a king over us, that we may be like all the nations, and that our king may judge us, and go out before us, and fight our battles. Samuel continued to reason with them, but to no purpose; he set before them their ingratitude, but all would not avail; and seeing them fully bent on their folly, he cried out, I will call unto the Lord, and he shall send thunder and rain (which then was a punishment, being in the time of wheat harvest) that ye may perceive and see that your wickedness is great which ye have done in the sight of the Lord, IN ASKING YOU A KING. So Samuel called unto the Lord, and the Lord sent thunder and rain that day, and all the people greatly feared the Lord and Samuel. And all the people said unto Samuel, Pray for thy servants unto the Lord thy God that we die not, for WE HAVE ADDED UNTO OUR SINS THIS EVIL, TO ASK A KING. These portions of scripture are direct and positive. They admit of no equivocal construction. That the Almighty hath here entered his protest against monarchical government is true, or the scripture is false. And a man hath good reason to believe that there is as much of king-craft, as priest-craft, in withholding the scripture from the public in Popish countries. For monarchy in every instance is the Popery of government.

To the evil of monarchy we have added that of hereditary succession; and as the first is a degradation and lessening of ourselves, so the second, claimed as a matter of right, is an insult and an imposition on posterity. For all men being originally equals, no *one* by *birth* could have a right to set up his own family in perpetual preference to all others for ever, and though himself might deserve *some* decent degree of honors of his cotemporaries, yet his descendants might be far too unworthy to inherit them. One of the strongest *natural* proofs of the folly of hereditary right in kings, is, that nature disapproves it, otherwise she would not so frequently turn it into ridicule by giving mankind an *ass for a lion.*

Secondly, as no man at first could possess any other public honors than were bestowed upon him, so the givers of those honors could have no power to give away the right of posterity, and though they might say "We choose you for *our* head," they could not, without manifest injustice to their children, say "that your children and your children's children shall reign over *ours* for ever." Because such an unwise, unjust, unnatural compact might (perhaps) in the next succession put them under the government of a rogue or a fool. Most wise men, in their private sentiments, have ever treated hereditary right with contempt; yet it is one of those evils, which when once established is not easily removed; many submit from fear, others from superstition, and the more powerful part shares with the king the plunder of the rest.

This is supposing the present race of kings in the world to have had an honorable origin; whereas it is more than probable, that could we take off the dark covering of antiquity, and trace them to their first rise, that we should find the first of them nothing better than the principal ruffian of some restless gang, whose savage manners or pre-eminence in subtilty obtained him the title of chief among plunderers; and who by increasing in power, and extending his depredations, over-awed the quiet and defenceless to purchase their safety by frequent contributions. Yet his electors could have no idea of giving hereditary right to his descendants, because such a perpetual exclusion of themselves was incompatible with the free and unrestrained principles they professed to live by. Wherefore, hereditary succession in the early ages of monarchy could not take place as a matter of claim, but as something casual or complimental; but as few or no records were extant in those days, and traditional history stuffed with fables, it was very easy, after the lapse of a few generations, to trump up some superstitious tale, conveniently timed, Mahomet like, to cram hereditary right down the throats of the vulgar. Perhaps the disorders which threatened, or seemed to threaten, on the decease of a leader and the choice of a new one (for elections among ruffians could not be very orderly) induced many at first to favor hereditary pretensions; by which means it happened, as it hath happened since, that what at first was submitted to as a convenience, was afterwards claimed as a right.

England, since the conquest, hath known some few good monarchs, but groaned beneath a much larger number of bad ones; yet no man in his senses can say that their claim under William the Conqueror is a very honorable one. A French bastard landing with an armed banditti, and establishing himself king of England against the consent of the natives, is in plain terms a very paltry rascally original.—It certainly hath no divinity in it. However, it is needless to spend much time in exposing the folly of hereditary right; if there are any so weak as to believe it, let them promiscuously worship the ass and lion, and welcome. I shall neither copy their humility, nor disturb their devotion.

Yet I should be glad to ask how they suppose kings came at first? The question admits but of three answers, viz. either by lot, by election, or by usurpation. If the first king was taken by lot, it establishes a precedent for the next, which excludes hereditary succession. Saul was by lot, yet the succession was not hereditary, neither does it appear from that transaction there was any intention it ever should. If the first king of any country was by election, that likewise establishes a precedent for the next; for to say, that the *right* of all future generations is taken away, by the act of the first electors, in their choice not only of a king, but of a family of kings for ever, hath no parrallel in or out of scripture but the doctrine of original sin, which supposes the free will of all men lost in Adam; and from such comparison, and it will admit of no other, hereditary succession can derive no glory. For as in Adam all sinned, and as in the first electors all men obeyed; as in the one all mankind were subjected to Satan, and in the other to Sovereignty; as our innocence was lost in the first, and our authority in the last; and as both disable us from reassuming some former state and privilege, it unanswerably follows that original sin and hereditary succession are parellels. Dishonorable rank! Inglorious connexion! Yet the most subtile sophist cannot produce a juster simile.

As to usurpation, no man will be so hardy as to defend it; and that William the Conqueror was an usurper is a fact not to be contradicted. The plain truth is, that the antiquity of English monarchy will not bear looking into.

But it is not so much the absurdity as the evil of hereditary succession which concerns mankind. Did it ensure a race of good and wise men it would have the seal of divine authority, but as it opens a door to the *foolish*, the *wicked*, and the *improper*, it hath in it the nature of oppression. Men who look upon themselves born to reign, and others to obey, soon grow insolent; selected from the rest of mankind their minds are early poisoned by importance; and the world they act in differs so materially from the world at large, that they have but little opportunity of knowing its true interests, and when they succeed to the government are frequently the most ignorant and unfit of any throughout the dominions.

Another evil which attends hereditary succession is, that the throne is subject to be possessed by a minor at any age; all which time the regency, acting under the cover of a king, have every opportunity and inducement to betray their trust. The same national misfortune happens, when a king worn out with age and infirmity, enters the last stage of human weakness. In both these cases the public becomes a prey to every miscreant, who can tamper successfully with the follies either of age or infancy.

The most plausible plea, which hath ever been offered in favour of hereditary succession, is, that it preserves a nation from civil wars; and were this true, it would be weighty; whereas, it is the most barefaced falsity ever imposed upon mankind. The whole history of England disowns the fact. Thirty kings and two minors have reigned in that distracted kingdom since the conquest, in which time there have been (including the Revolution) no less than eight civil wars and nineteen rebellions. Wherefore instead of making for peace, it makes against it, and destroys the very foundation it seems to stand on.

The contest for monarchy and succession, between the houses of York and Lancaster, laid England in a scene of blood for many years. Twelve pitched battles, besides skirmishes and sieges, were fought between Henry and Edward. Twice was Henry prisoner to Edward, who in his turn was prisoner to Henry. And so uncertain is the fate of war and the temper of a nation, when nothing but personal matters are the ground of a quarrel, that Henry was taken in triumph from a prison to a palace, and Edward obliged to fly from a palace to a foreign land; yet, as sudden transitions of temper are seldom lasting, Henry in his turn was driven from the throne, and Edward recalled to succeed him. The parliament always following the strongest side.

This contest began in the reign of Henry the Sixth, and was not entirely extinguished till Henry the Seventh, in whom the families were united. Including a period of 67 years, viz. from 1422 to 1489.

In short, monarchy and succession have laid (not this or that kingdom only) but the world in blood and ashes. 'Tis a form of government which the word of God bears testimony against, and blood will attend it.

If we inquire into the business of a king, we shall find that in some countries they have none; and after sauntering away their lives without pleasure to themselves or advantage to the nation, withdraw from the scene, and leave their successors to tread the same idle round. In absolute monarchies the whole weight of business, civil and military, lies on the king; the children of Israel in their request for a king, urged this plea "that he may judge us, and go out before us and fight our battles." But in countries where he is neither a judge nor a general, as in England, a man would be puzzled to know what *is* his business.

The nearer any government approaches to a republic the less business there is for a king. It is somewhat difficult to find a proper name for the government of England. Sir William Meredith calls it a republic; but in its present state it is unworthy of the name, because the corrupt influence of the crown, by having all the places in its disposal, hath so effectually swallowed up the power, and eaten out the virtue of the house of commons (the republican part in the constitution) that the government of England is nearly as monarchical as that of France or Spain. Men fall out with names without understanding them. For it is the republican and not the monarchical part of the constitution of England which Englishmen glory in, viz. the liberty of choosing a house of commons from out of their own body—and it is easy to see that when republican virtue fails, slavery ensues. Why is the constitution of England sickly, but because monarchy hath poisoned the republic, the crown hath engrossed the commons?

In England a king hath little more to do than to make war and give away places; which in plain terms, is to impoverish the nation and set it together by the ears. A pretty business indeed for a man to be allowed eight hundred thousand sterling a year for, and worshipped into the bargain! Of more worth is one honest man to society and in the sight of God, than all the crowned ruffians that ever lived.

THOUGHTS ON THE PRESENT STATE OF AMERICAN AFFAIRS.

IN the following pages I offer nothing more than simple facts, plain arguments, and common sense; and have no other preliminaries to settle with the reader, than that he will divest himself of prejudice and prepossession, and suffer his reason and his feelings to determine for themselves; that he will put *on*, or rather that he will not put *off*, the true character of a man, and generously enlarge his views beyond the present day.

Volumes have been written on the subject of the struggle between England and America. Men of all ranks have embarked in the controversy, from different motives, and with various designs; but all have been ineffectual, and the period of debate is closed. Arms, as the last resource, decide the contest; the appeal was the choice of the king, and the continent hath accepted the challenge.

It hath been reported of the late Mr. Pelham (who tho' an able minister was not without his faults) that on his being attacked in the house of commons, on the score, that his measures were only of a temporary kind, replied "*they will last my time.*" Should a thought so fatal and unmanly possess the colonies in the present contest, the name of ancestors will be remembered by future generations with detestation.

The sun never shined on a cause of greater worth. 'Tis not the affair of a city, a country, a province, or a kingdom, but of a continent—of at least one eighth part of the habitable globe. 'Tis not the concern of a day, a year, or an age; posterity are virtually involved in the contest, and will be more or less affected, even to the end of time, by the proceedings now. Now is the seed time of continental union, faith and honor. The least fracture now will be like a name engraved with the point of a pin on the tender rind of a young oak; the wound will enlarge with the tree, and posterity read it in full grown characters.

By referring the matter from argument to arms, a new æra for politics is struck; a new method of thinking hath arisen. All plans, proposals, &c. prior to the nineteenth of April, *i.e.* to the commencement of hostilities, are like the almanacks of the last year; which, though proper then, are superseded and useless now. Whatever was advanced by the advocates on either side of the question then, terminated in one and the same point, viz. a union with Great-Britain; the only difference between the parties was the method of effecting it; the one proposing force, the other friendship; but it hath so far happened that the first hath failed, and the second hath withdrawn her influence.

As much hath been said of the advantages of reconciliation, which, like an agreeable dream, hath passed away and left us as we were, it is but right, that we should examine the contrary side of the argument, and inquire into some of the many material injuries which these colonies sustain, and always will sustain, by being connected with, and dependant on Great-Britain. To examine that connexion and dependance, on the principles of nature and common sense, to see what we have to trust to, if separated, and what we are to expect, if dependant.

I have heard it asserted by some, that as America hath flourished under her former connexion with Great-Britain, that the same connexion is necessary towards her future happiness, and will always have the same effect. Nothing can be more fallacious than this kind of argument. We may as well assert that because a child has thrived upon milk, that it is never to have meat, or that the first twenty years of our lives is to become a precedent for the next twenty. But even this is admitting more than is true, for I answer roundly, that America would have flourished as much, and probably much more, had no European power had any thing to do with her. The commerce, by which she hath enriched herself are the necessaries of life, and will always have a market while eating is the custom of Europe.

But she has protected us, say some. That she has engrossed us is true, and defended the continent at our expence as well as her own is admitted, and she would have defended Turkey from the same motive, viz. the sake of trade and dominion.

Alas, we have been long led away by ancient prejudices, and made large sacrifices to superstition. We have boasted the protection of Great-Britain, without considering, that her motive was *interest* not *attachment*; that she did not protect us from *our enemies* on *our account*, but from *her enemies* on *her own account*, from those who had no quarrel with us on any *other account*, and who will always be our enemies on the *same account*. Let Britain wave her pretensions to the continent, or the continent throw off the dependance, and we should be at peace with France and Spain were they at war with Britain. The miseries of Hanover last war ought to warn us against connexions.

It has lately been asserted in parliament, that the colonies have no relation to each other but through the parent country, *i.e.* that Pennsylvania and the Jerseys, and so on for the rest, are sister colonies by the way of England; this is certainly a very roundabout way of proving relationship, but it is the nearest and only true way of proving enemyship, if I may so call it. France and Spain never were, nor perhaps ever will be our enemies as *Americans*, but as our being the *subjects of Great-Britain*.

But Britain is the parent country, say some. Then the more shame upon her conduct. Even brutes do not devour their young, nor savages make war upon their families; wherefore the assertion, if true, turns to her reproach; but it happens not to be true, or only partly so, and the phrase *parent* or *mother country* hath been jesuitically adopted by the king and his parasites, with a low papistical design of gaining an unfair bias on the credulous weakness of our minds. Europe, and not England, is the parent country of America. This new world hath been the asylum for the persecuted lovers of civil and religious liberty from *every part* of Europe. Hither have they fled, not from the tender embraces of the mother, but from the cruelty of the monster; and it is so far true of England, that the same tyranny which drove the first emigrants from home, pursues their descendants still.

In this extensive quarter of the globe, we forget the narrow limits of three hundred and sixty miles (the extent of England) and carry our friendship on a larger scale; we claim brotherhood with every European christian, and triumph in the generosity of the sentiment.

It is pleasant to observe by what regular gradations we surmount the force of local prejudice, as we enlarge our acquaintance with the world. A man born in any town in England divided into parishes, will naturally associate most with his fellow parishioners (because their interests in many cases will be common) and distinguish him by the name of *neighbour*; if he meet him but a few miles from home, he drops the narrow idea of a street, and salutes him by the name of *townsman*; if he travel out of the county, and meet him in any other, he forgets the minor divisions of street and town, and calls him *countryman, i.e. countyman*; but if in their foreign excursions they should associate in France or any other part of *Europe*, their local remembrance would be enlarged into that of *Englishmen*. And by a just parity of reasoning, all Europeans meeting in America, or any other quarter of the globe, are *countrymen*; for England, Holland, Germany, or Sweden, when compared with the whole, stand in the same places on the larger scale, which the divisions of street, town, and county do on the smaller ones; distinctions too limited for continental minds. Not one third of the inhabitants, even of this province, are of English descent. Wherefore I reprobate the phrase of parent or mother country applied to England only, as being false, selfish, narrow and ungenerous.

But admitting, that we were all of English descent, what does it amount to? Nothing. Britain, being now an open enemy, extinguishes every other name and title: And to say that reconciliation is our duty, is truly farcical. The first king of England, of the present line (William the Conqueror) was a Frenchman, and half the Peers of England are descendants from the same country; therefore, by the same method of reasoning, England ought to be governed by France.

Much hath been said of the united strength of Britain and the colonies, that in conjunction they might bid defiance to the world. But this is mere presumption; the fate of war is uncertain, neither do the expressions mean any thing; for this continent would never suffer itself to be drained of inhabitants, to support the British arms in either Asia, Africa, or Europe.

Besides what have we to do with setting the world at defiance? Our plan is commerce, and that, well attended to, will secure us the peace and friendship of all Europe; because, it is the interest of all Europe to have America a *free port*. Her trade will always be a protection, and her barrenness of gold and silver secure her from invaders.

I challenge the warmest advocate for reconciliation, to shew, a single advantage that this continent can reap, by being connected with Great Britain. I repeat the challenge, not a single advantage is derived. Our corn will fetch its price in any market in Europe, and our imported goods must be paid for buy them where we will.

But the injuries and disadvantages we sustain by that connection, are without number; and our duty to mankind at large, as well as to ourselves, instruct us to renounce the alliance: Because, any submission to, or dependance on Great-Britain, tends directly to involve this continent in European wars and quarrels; and sets us at variance with nations, who would otherwise seek our friendship, and against whom, we have neither anger nor complaint. As Europe is our market for trade, we ought to form no partial connection with any part of it. It is the true interest of America to steer clear of European contentions, which she never can do, while by her dependence on Britain, she is made the make-weight in the scale of British politics.

Europe is too thickly planted with kingdoms to be long at peace, and whenever a war breaks out between England and any foreign power, the trade of America goes to ruin, *because of her connection with Britain*. The next war may not turn out like the last, and should it not, the advocates for reconciliation now will be wishing for separation then, because, neutrality in that case, would be a safer convoy than a man of war. Every thing that is right or natural pleads for separation. The blood of the slain, the weeping voice of nature cries, 'TIS TIME TO PART. Even the distance at which the Almighty hath placed England and America, is a strong and natural proof, that the authority of the one, over the other, was never the design of Heaven. The time likewise at which the continent was discovered, adds weight to the argument, and the manner in which it was peopled encreases the force of it. The reformation was preceded by the discovery of America, as if the Almighty graciously meant to open a sanctuary to the persecuted in future years, when home should afford neither friendship nor safety.

The authority of Great-Britain over this continent, is a form of government, which sooner or later must have an end: And a serious mind can draw no true pleasure by looking forward, under the painful and positive conviction, that what he calls "the present constitution" is merely temporary. As parents, we can have no joy, knowing that *this government* is not sufficiently lasting to ensure any thing which we may bequeath to posterity: And by a plain method of argument, as we are running the next generation into debt, we ought to do the work of it, otherwise we use them meanly and pitifully. In order to discover the line of our duty rightly, we should take our children in our hand, and fix our station a few years farther into life; that eminence will present a prospect, which a few present fears and prejudices conceal from our sight.

Though I would carefully avoid giving unnecessary offence, yet I am inclined to believe, that all those who espouse the doctrine of reconciliation, may be included within the following descriptions. Interested men, who are not to be trusted; weak men, who *cannot* see; prejudiced men, who *will not* see; and a certain set of moderate men, who think better of the European world than it deserves; and this last class, by an ill-judged deliberation, will be the cause of more calamities to this continent, than all the other three.

It is the good fortune of many to live distant from the scene of sorrow; the evil is not sufficient brought to *their* doors to make *them* feel the precariousness with which all American property is possessed. But let our imaginations transport us for a few moments to Boston, that seat of wretchedness will teach us wisdom, and instruct us for ever to renounce a power in whom we can have no trust. The inhabitants of that unfortunate city, who but a few months ago were in ease and affluence, have now, no other alternative than to stay and starve, or turn out to beg. Endangered by the fire of their friends if they continue within the city, and plundered by the soldiery if they leave it. In their present condition they are prisoners without the hope of redemption, and in a general attack for their relief, they would be exposed to the fury of both armies.

Men of passive tempers look somewhat lightly over the offences of Britain, and, still hoping for the best, are apt to call out, "*Come, come, we shall be friends again, for all this.*" But examine the passions and feelings of mankind, Bring the doctrine of reconciliation to the touchstone of nature, and then tell me, whether you can hereafter love, honour, and faithfully serve the power that hath carried fire and sword into your land? If you cannot do all these, then are you only deceiving yourselves, and by your delay bringing ruin upon posterity. Your future connection with Britain, whom you can neither love nor honour, will be forced and unnatural, and being formed only on the plan of present convenience, will in a little time fall into a relapse more wretched than the first. But if you say, you can still pass the violations over, then I ask, Hath your house been burnt? Hath your property been destroyed before your face? Are your wife and children destitute of a bed to lie on, or bread to live on? Have you lost a parent or a child by their hands, and yourself the ruined and wretched survivor? If you have not, then are you not a judge of those who have. But if you have, and still can shake hands with the murderers, then are you unworthy of the name of husband, father, friend, or lover, and whatever may be your rank or title in life, you have the heart of a coward, and the spirit of a sycophant.

This is not inflaming or exaggerating matters, but trying them by those feelings and affections which nature justifies, and without which, we should be incapable of discharging the social duties of life, or enjoying the felicities of it. I mean not to exhibit horror for the purpose of provoking revenge, but to awaken us from fatal and unmanly slumbers, that we may pursue determinately some fixed object. It is not in the power of Britain or of Europe to conquer America, if she do not conquer herself by *delay* and *timidity*. The present winter is worth an age if rightly employed, but if lost or neglected, the whole continent will partake of the misfortune; and there is no punishment which that man will not deserve, be he who, or what, or where he will, that may be the means of sacrificing a season so precious and useful.

It is repugnant to reason, to the universal order of things to all examples from former ages, to suppose, that this continent can longer remain subject to any external power. The most sanguine in Britain does not think so. The utmost stretch of human wisdom cannot, at this time, compass a plan short of separation, which can promise the continent even a year's security. Reconciliation is *now* a fallacious dream. Nature hath deserted the connexion, and Art cannot supply her place. For, as Milton wisely expresses, "never can true reconcilement grow where wounds of deadly hate have pierced so deep."

Every quiet method for peace hath been ineffectual. Our prayers have been rejected with disdain; and only tended to convince us, that nothing flatters vanity, or confirms obstinacy in Kings more than repeated petitioning—and nothing hath contributed more than that very measure to make the Kings of Europe absolute: Witness Denmark and Sweden. Wherefore, since nothing but blows will do, for God's sake, let us come to a final separation, and not leave the next generation to be cutting throats, under the violated unmeaning names of parent and child.

To say, they will never attempt it again is idle and visionary, we thought so at the repeal of the stamp-act, yet a year or two undeceived us; as well may we suppose that nations, which have been once defeated, will never renew the quarrel.

As to government matters, it is not in the power of Britain to do this continent justice: The business of it will soon be too weighty, and intricate, to be managed with any tolerable degree of convenience, by a power, so distant from us, and so very ignorant of us; for if they cannot conquer us, they cannot govern us. To be always running three or four thousand miles with a tale or a petition, waiting four or five months for an answer, which when obtained requires five or six more to explain it in, will in a few years be looked upon as folly and childishness—There was a time when it was proper, and there is a proper time for it to cease.

Small islands not capable of protecting themselves, are the proper objects for kingdoms to take under their care; but there is something very absurd, in supposing a continent to be perpetually governed by an island. In no instance hath nature made the satellite larger than its primary planet, and as England and America, with respect to each other, reverses the common order of nature, it is evident they belong to different systems: England to Europe, America to itself.

I am not induced by motives of pride, party, or resentment to espouse the doctrine of separation and independance; I am clearly, positively, and conscientiously persuaded that it is the true interest of this continent to be so; that every thing short of *that* is mere patchwork, that it can afford no lasting felicity,—that it is leaving the sword to our children, and shrinking back at a time, when, a little more, a little farther, would have rendered this continent the glory of the earth.

As Britain hath not manifested the least inclination towards a compromise, we may be assured that no terms can be obtained worthy the acceptance of the continent, or any ways equal to the expence of blood and treasure we have been already put to.

The object, contended for, ought always to bear some just proportion to the expence. The removal of North, or the whole detestable junto, is a matter unworthy the millions we have expended. A temporary stoppage of trade, was an inconvenience, which would have sufficiently ballanced the repeal of all the acts complained of, had such repeals been obtained; but if the whole continent must take up arms, if every man must be a soldier, it is scarcely worth our while to fight against a contemptible ministry only. Dearly, dearly, do we pay for the repeal of the acts, if that is all we fight for; for in a just estimation, it is as great a folly to pay a Bunker-hill price for law, as for land. As I have always considered the independancy of this continent, as an event, which sooner or later must arrive, so from the late rapid progress of the continent to maturity, the event could not be far off. Wherefore, on the breaking out of hostilities, it was not worth the while to have disputed a matter, which time would have finally redressed, unless we meant to be in earnest; otherwise, it is like wasting an estate on a suit at law, to regulate the trespasses of a tenant, whose lease is just expiring. No man was a warmer wisher for reconciliation than myself, before the fatal nineteenth of April 1775, but the moment the event of that day was made known, I rejected the hardened, sullen tempered Pharaoh of England for ever; and disdain the wretch, that with the pretended title of FATHER OF HIS PEOPLE can unfeelingly hear of their slaughter, and composedly sleep with their blood upon his soul.

But admitting that matters were now made up, what would be the event? I answer, the ruin of the continent. And that for several reasons.

First. The powers of governing still remaining in the hands of the king, he will have a negative over the whole legislation of this continent. And as he hath shewn himself such an inveterate enemy to liberty, and discovered such a thirst for arbitrary power; is he, or is he not, a proper man to say to these colonies, "*You shall make no laws but what I please.*" And is there any inhabitant in America so ignorant, as not to know, that according to what is called the *present constitution*, that this continent can make no laws but what the king gives leave to; and is there any man so unwise, as not to see, that (considering what has happened) he will suffer no law to be made here, but such as suit *his* purpose. We may be as effectually enslaved by the want of laws in America, as by submitting to laws made for us in England. After matters are made up (as it is called) can there be any doubt, but the whole power of the crown will be exerted, to keep this continent as low and humble as possible? Instead of going forward we shall go backward, or be perpetually quarrelling or ridiculously petitioning.—We are already greater than the king wishes us to be, and will he not hereafter endeavour to make us less? To bring the matter to one point. Is the power who is jealous of our prosperity, a proper power to govern us? Whoever says *No* to this question is an *independant*, for independancy means no more, than, whether we shall make our own laws, or whether the king, the greatest enemy this continent hath, or can have, shall tell us "*there shall be no laws but such as I like.*"

But the king you will say has a negative in England; the people there can make no laws without his consent. In point of right and good order, there is something very ridiculous, that a youth of twenty-one (which hath often happened) shall say to several millions of people, older and wiser than himself, I forbid this or that act of yours to be law. But in this place I decline this sort of reply, though I will never cease to expose the absurdity of it, and only answer, that England being the King's residence, and America not so, makes quite another case. The king's negative *here* is ten times more dangerous and fatal than it can be in England, for *there* he will scarcely refuse his consent to a bill for putting England into as strong a state of defence as possible, and in America he would never suffer such a bill to be passed.

America is only a secondary object in the system of British politics, England consults the good of *this* country, no farther than it answers her *own* purpose. Wherefore, her own interest leads her to suppress the growth of *ours* in every case which doth not promote her advantage, or in the least interferes with it. A pretty state we should soon be in under such a second-hand government, considering what has happened! Men do not change from enemies to friends by the alteration of a name: And in order to shew that reconciliation *now* is a dangerous doctrine, I affirm, *that it would be policy in the king at this time, to repeal the acts for the sake of reinstating himself in the government of the provinces;* in order, that HE MAY ACCOMPLISH BY CRAFT AND SUBTILTY, IN THE LONG RUN, WHAT HE CANNOT DO BY FORCE AND VIOLENCE IN THE SHORT ONE. Reconciliation and ruin are nearly related.

Secondly. That as even the best terms, which we can expect to obtain, can amount to no more than a temporary expedient, or a kind of government by guardianship, which can last no longer than till the colonies come of age, so the general face and state of things, in the interim, will be unsettled and unpromising. Emigrants of property will not choose to come to a country whose form of government hangs but by a thread, and who is every day tottering on the brink of commotion and disturbance; and numbers of the present inhabitants would lay hold of the interval, to dispense of their effects, and quit the continent.

But the most powerful of all arguments, is, that nothing but independance, i.e. a continental form of government, can keep the peace of the continent and preserve it inviolate from civil wars. I dread the event of a reconciliation with Britain now, as it is more than probable, that it will be followed by a revolt somewhere or other, the consequences of which may be far more fatal than all the malice of Britain.

Thousands are already ruined by British barbarity; (thousands more will probably suffer the same fate) Those men have other feelings than us who have nothing suffered. All they *now* possess is liberty, what they before enjoyed is sacrificed to its service, and having nothing more to lose, they disdain submission. Besides, the general temper of the colonies, towards a British government, will be like that of a youth, who is nearly out of his time; they will care very little about her. And a government which cannot preserve the peace, is no government at all, and in that case we pay our money for nothing; and pray what is it that Britain can do, whose power will be wholly on paper, should a civil tumult break out the very day after reconciliation? I have heard some men say, many of whom I believe spoke without thinking, that they dreaded an independance, fearing that it would produce civil wars. It is but seldom that our first thoughts are truly correct, and that is the case here; for there are ten times more to dread from a patched up connexion than from independance. I make the sufferers case my own, and I protest, that were I driven from house and home, my property destroyed, and my circumstances ruined, that as man, sensible of injuries, I could never relish the doctrine of reconciliation, or consider myself bound thereby.

The colonies have manifested such a spirit of good order and obedience to continental government, as is sufficient to make every reasonable person easy and happy on that head. No man can assign the least pretence for his fears, on any other grounds, than such as are truly childish and ridiculous, viz. that one colony will be striving for superiority over another.

Where there are no distinctions there can be no superiority, perfect equality affords no temptation. The republics of Europe are all (and we may say always) in peace. Holland and Swisserland are without wars, foreign or domestic: Monarchical governments, it is true, are never long at rest; the crown itself is a temptation to enterprizing ruffians at *home*; and that degree of pride and insolence ever attendant on regal authority, swells into a rupture with foreign powers, in instances, where a republican government, by being formed on more natural principles, would negociate the mistake.

If there is any true cause of fear respecting independance, it is because no plan is yet laid down. Men do not see their way out—Wherefore, as an opening into that business, I offer the following hints; at the same time modestly affirming, that I have no other opinion of them myself, than that they may be the means of giving rise to something better. Could the straggling thoughts of individuals be collected, they would frequently form materials for wise and able men to improve into useful matter.

Let the assemblies be annual, with a President only. The representation more equal. Their business wholly domestic, and subject to the authority of a Continental Congress.

Let each colony be divided into six, eight, or ten, convenient districts, each district to send a proper number of delegates to Congress, so that each colony send at least thirty. The whole number in Congress will be at least 390. Each Congress to sit and to choose a president by the following method. When the delegates are met, let a colony be taken from the whole thirteen colonies by lot, after which, let the whole Congress choose (by ballot) a president from out of the delegates of *that* province. In the next

Congress, let a colony be taken by lot from twelve only, omitting that colony from which the president was taken in the former Congress, and so proceeding on till the whole thirteen shall have had their proper rotation. And in order that nothing may pass into a law but what is satisfactorily just, not less than three fifths of the Congress to be called a majority.—He that will promote discord, under a government so equally formed as this, would have joined Lucifer in his revolt.

But as there is a peculiar delicacy, from whom, or in what manner, this business must first arise, and as it seems most agreeable and consistent that it should come from some intermediate body between the governed and the governors, that is, between the Congress and the people, let a CONTINENTAL CONFERENCE be held, in the following manner, and for the following purpose.

A committee of twenty-six members of Congress, viz. two for each colony. Two members from each House of Assembly, or Provincial Convention; and five representatives of the people at large, to be chosen in the capital city or town of each province, for, and in behalf of the whole province, by as many qualified voters as shall think proper to attend from all parts of the province for that purpose; or, if more convenient, the representatives may be chosen in two or three of the most populous parts thereof. In this conference, thus assembled, will be united, the two grand principles of business, *knowledge* and *power*. The members of Congress, Assemblies, or Conventions, by having had experience in national concerns, will be able and useful counsellors, and the whole, being impowered by the people, will have a truly legal authority.

The conferring members being met, let their business be to frame a CONTINENTAL CHARTER, or Charter of the United Colonies; (answering to what is called the Magna Charta of England) fixing the number and manner of choosing members of Congress, members of Assembly, with their date of sitting, and drawing the line of business and jurisdiction between them: (Always remembering, that our strength is continental, not provincial:) Securing freedom and property to all men, and above all things, the free exercise of religion, according to the dictates of conscience; with such other matter as is necessary for a charter to contain. Immediately after which, the said Conference to dissolve, and the bodies which shall be chosen comfortable to the said charter, to be the legislators and governors of this continent for the time being: Whose peace and happiness, may God preserve, Amen.

Should any body of men be hereafter delegated for this or some similar purpose, I offer them the following extracts from that wise observer on governments *Dragonetti*. "The science" says he "of the politician consists in fixing the true point of happiness and freedom. Those men would deserve the gratitude of ages, who should discover a mode of government that contained the greatest sum of individual happiness, with the least national expense.

Dragonetti on virtue and rewards."

But where says some is the King of America? I'll tell you Friend, he reigns above, and doth not make havoc of mankind like the Royal Brute of Britain. Yet that we may not appear to be defective even in earthly honors, let a day be solemnly set apart for proclaiming the charter; let it be brought forth placed on the divine law, the word of God; let a crown be placed thereon, by which the world may know, that so far as we approve of monarchy, that in America THE LAW IS KING. For as in absolute governments the King is law, so in free countries the law *ought* to be King; and there ought to be no other. But lest any ill use should afterwards arise, let the crown at the conclusion of the ceremony be demolished, and scattered among the people whose right it is.

A government of our own is our natural right: And when a man seriously reflects on the precariousness of human affairs, he will become convinced, that it is infinitely wiser and safer, to form a constitution of our own in a cool deliberate manner, while we have it in our power, than to trust such an interesting event to time and chance. If we omit it now, some Massanello ⊠ may hereafter arise, who laying hold of popular disquietudes, may collect together the desperate and the discontented, and by assuming to themselves the powers of government, may sweep away the liberties of the continent like a deluge. Should the government of America return again into the hands of Britain, the tottering situation of things, will be a temptation for some desperate adventurer to try his fortune; and in such a case, what relief can Britain give? Ere she could hear the news, the fatal business might be done; and ourselves suffering like the wretched Britons under the oppression of the Conqueror. Ye that oppose independance now, ye know not what ye do; ye are opening a door to eternal tyranny, by keeping vacant the seat of government. There are thousands, and tens of thousands, who would think it glorious to expel from the continent, that barbarous and hellish power, which hath stirred up the Indians and Negroes to destroy us, the cruelty hath a double guilt, it is dealing brutally by us, and treacherously by them.

✠ Thomas Anello, otherwise Massanello, a fisherman of Naples, who after spiriting up his countrymen in the public market place, against the oppressions of the Spaniards, to whom the place was then subject, prompted them to revolt, and in the space of a day became king.

To talk of friendship with those in whom our reason forbids us to have faith, and our affections wounded through a thousand pores instruct us to detest, is madness and folly. Every day wears out the little remains of kindred between us and them, and can there be any reason to hope, that as the relationship expires, the affection will increase, or that we shall agree better, when we have ten times more and greater concerns to quarrel over than ever?

Ye that tell us of harmony and reconciliation, can ye restore to us the time that is past? Can ye give to prostitution its former innocence? Neither can ye reconcile Britain and America. The last cord now is broken, the people of England are presenting addresses against us. There are injuries which nature cannot forgive; she would cease to be nature if she did. As well can the lover forgive the ravisher of his mistress, as the continent forgive the murders of Britain. The Almighty hath implanted in us these unextinguishable feelings for good and wise purposes. They are the guardians of his image in our hearts. They distinguish us from the herd of common animals. The social compact would dissolve, and justice be extirpated the earth, or have only a casual existence were we callous to the touches of affection. The robber, and the murderer, would often escape unpunished, did not the injuries which our tempers sustain, provoke us into justice.

O ye that love mankind! Ye that dare oppose, not only the tyranny, but the tyrant, stand forth! Every spot of the old world is overrun with oppression. Freedom hath been hunted round the globe. Asia, and Africa, have long expelled her—Europe regards her like a stranger, and England hath given her warning to depart. O! receive the fugitive, and prepare in time an asylum for mankind.

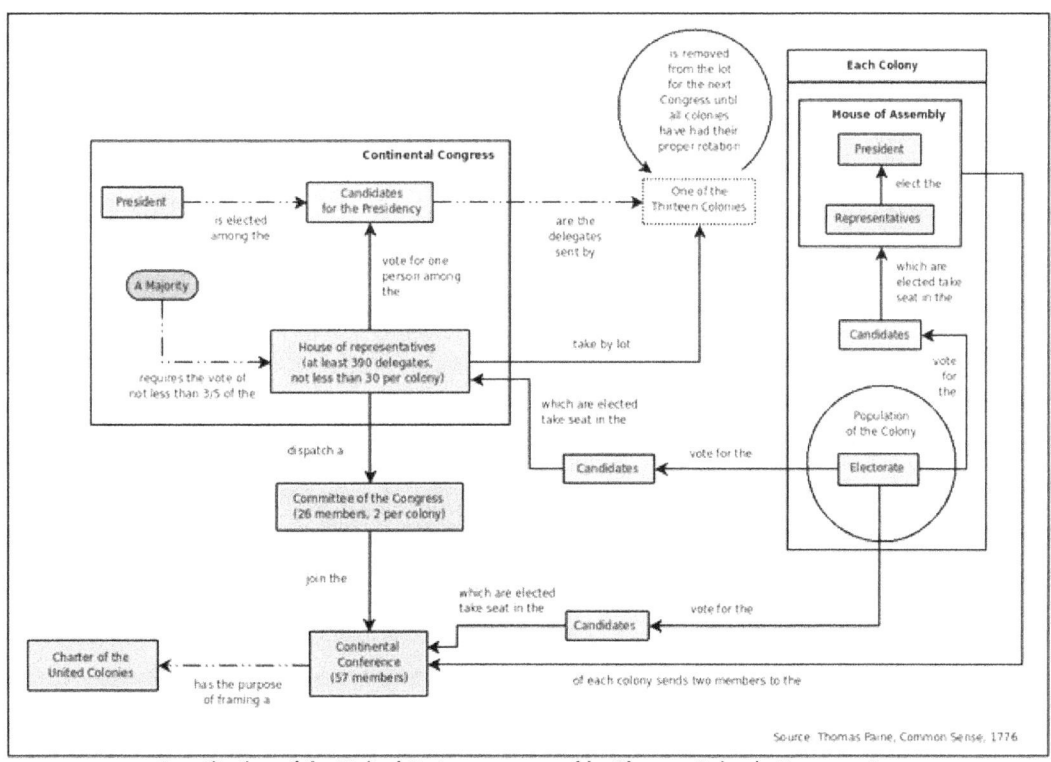

Constitution of the United States as proposed by Thomas Paine in Common Sense

OF THE PRESENT ABILITY OF AMERICA, WITH SOME MISCELLANEOUS REFLEXIONS.

I HAVE never met with a man, either in England or America, who hath not confessed his opinion, that a separation between the countries, would take place one time or other: And there is no instance, in which we have shewn less judgment, than in endeavouring to describe, what we call, the ripeness or fitness of the Continent for independance.

As all men allow the measure, and vary only in their opinion of the time, let us, in order to remove mistakes, take a general survey of things, and endeavour, if possible, to find out the *very* time. But we need not go far, the inquiry ceases at once, for, the *time hath found us.* The general concurrence, the glorious union of all things prove the fact.

It is not in numbers, but in unity, that our great strength lies; yet our present numbers are sufficient to repel the force of all the world. The Continent hath, at this time, the largest body of armed and disciplined men of any power under Heaven; and is just arrived at that pitch of strength, in which no single colony is able to support itself, and the whole, when united, can accomplish the matter, and either more, or, less than this, might be fatal in its effects. Our land force is already sufficient, and as to naval affairs, we cannot be insensible, that Britain would never suffer an American man of war to be built, while the continent remained in her hands. Wherefore, we should be no forwarder an hundred years hence in that branch, than we are now; but the truth is, we should be less so, because the timber of the country is every day diminishing, and that, which will remain at last, will be far off and difficult to procure.

Were the continent crowded with inhabitants, her sufferings under the present circumstances would be intolerable. The more sea port towns we had, the more should we have both to defend and to lose. Our present numbers are so happily proportioned to our wants, that no man need be idle. The diminution of trade affords an army, and the necessities of an army create a new trade.

Debts we have none; and whatever we may contract on this account will serve as a glorious memento of our virtue. Can we but leave posterity with a settled form of government, an independant constitution of its own, the purchase at any price will be cheap. But to expend millions for the sake of getting a few vile acts repealed, and routing the present ministry only, is unworthy the charge, and is using posterity with the utmost cruelty; because it is leaving them the great work to do, and a debt upon their backs, from which they derive no advantage. Such a thought is unworthy a man of honor, and is the true characteristic of a narrow heart and a pedling politician.

The debt we may contract doth not deserve our regard if the work be but accomplished. No nation ought to be without a debt. A national debt is a national bond; and when it bears no interest, is in no case a grievance. Britain is oppressed with a debt of upwards of one hundred and forty millions sterling, for which she pays upwards of four millions interest. And as a compensation for her debt, she has a large navy; America is without a debt, and without a navy; yet for the twentieth part of the English national debt, could have a navy as large again. The navy of England is not worth, at this time, more than three millions and an half sterling.

The first and second editions of this pamphlet were published without the following calculations, which are now given as a proof that the above estimation of the navy is just. *See Entic's naval history, intro.* page 56.

The charge of building a ship of each rate, and furnishing her with masts, yards, sails and rigging, together with a proportion of eight months boatswain's and carpenter's sea-stores, as calculated by Mr. Burchett, Secretary to the navy.

	£ [pounds sterling]
For a ship of 100 guns =	35,553
90 =	29,886
80 =	23,638
70 =	17,785
60 =	14,197
50 =	10,606

40	=	7,558
30	=	5,846
20	=	3,710

And from hence it is easy to sum up the value, or cost rather, of the whole British navy, which in the year 1757, when it was at its greatest glory consisted of the following ships and guns:

Ships.	Guns.	Cost of one.	Cost of all.
		Cost in £ [pounds sterling]	
6	100	35,553	213,318
12	90	29,886	358,632
12	80	23,638	283,656
43	70	17,785	764,755
35	60	14,197	496,895
40	50	10,606	424,240
45	40	7,558	340,110
58	20	3,710	215,180
85	Sloops, bombs and fireships, one with another, at	2,000	170,000

Cost	3,266,786
Remains for Guns	233,214
	3,500,000

No country on the globe is so happily situated, or so internally capable of raising a fleet as America. Tar, timber, iron, and cordage are her natural produce. We need go abroad for nothing. Whereas the Dutch, who make large profits by hiring out their ships of war to the Spaniards and Portuguese, are obliged to import most of the materials they use. We ought to view the building a fleet as an article of commerce, it being the natural manufactory of this country. It is the best money we can lay out. A navy when finished is worth more than it cost. And is that nice point in national policy, in which commerce and protection are united. Let us build; if we want them not, we can sell; and by that means replace our paper currency with ready gold and silver.

In point of manning a fleet, people in general run into great errors; it is not necessary that one fourth part should be sailors. The Terrible privateer, Captain Death, stood the hottest engagement of any ship last war, yet had not twenty sailors on board, though her complement of men was upwards of two hundred. A few able and social sailors will soon instruct a sufficient number of active landmen in the common work of a ship. Wherefore, we never can be more capable to begin on maritime matters than now, while our timber is standing, our fisheries blocked up, and our sailors and shipwrights out of employ. Men of war, of seventy and eighty guns were built forty years ago in New-England, and why not the same now? Ship-building is America's greatest pride, and in which, she will in time excel the whole world. The great empires of the east are mostly inland, and consequently excluded from the possibility of rivalling her. Africa is in a state of barbarism; and no power in Europe, hath either such an extent of coast, or such an internal supply of materials. Where nature hath given the one, she has withheld the other; to America only hath she been liberal of both. The vast empire of Russia is almost shut out from the sea; wherefore, her boundless forests, her tar, iron, and cordage are only articles of commerce.

In point of safety, ought we to be without a fleet? We are not the little people now, which we were sixty years ago; at that time we might have trusted our property in the streets, or fields rather; and slept securely without locks or bolts to our doors or windows. The case now is altered, and our methods of defence, ought to improve with our increase of property. A common pirate, twelve months ago, might have come up the Delaware, and laid the city of Philadelphia under instant contribution, for what sum he pleased; and the same might have happened to other places. Nay, any daring fellow, in a brig of fourteen or sixteen guns, might have robbed the whole Continent, and carried off half a million of money. These are circumstances which demand our attention, and point out the necessity of naval protection.

Some, perhaps, will say, that after we have made it up with Britain, she will protect us. Can we be so unwise as to mean, that she shall keep a navy in our harbours for that purpose? Common sense will tell us, that the power which hath endeavoured to subdue us, is of all others, the most improper to defend us. Conquest may be effected under the pretence of friendship; and ourselves, after a long and brave resistance, be at last cheated into slavery. And if her ships are not to be admitted into our harbours, I would ask, how is she to protect us? A navy three or four thousand miles off can be of little use, and on sudden emergencies, none at all. Wherefore, if we must hereafter protect ourselves, why not do it for ourselves? Why do it for another?

The English list of ships of war, is long and formidable, but not a tenth part of them are at any one time fit for service, numbers of them not in being; yet their names are pompously continued in the list, if only a plank be left of the ship: and not a fifth part, of such as are fit for service, can be spared on any one station at one time. The East and West Indies, Mediterranean, Africa, and other parts over which Britain extends her claim, make large demands upon her navy. From a mixture of prejudice and inattention, we have contracted a false notion respecting the navy of England, and have talked as if we should have the whole of it to encounter at once, and for that reason, supposed, that we must have one as large; which not being instantly practicable, have been made use of by a set of disguised Tories to discourage our beginning thereon. Nothing can be farther from truth than this; for if America had only a twentieth part of the naval force of Britain, she would be by far an over match for her; because, as we neither have, nor claim any foreign dominion, our whole force would be employed on our own coast, where we should, in the long run, have two to one the advantage of those who had three or four thousand miles to sail over, before they could attack us, and the same distance to return in order to refit and recruit. And although Britain by her fleet, hath a check over our trade to Europe, we have as large a one over her trade to the West-Indies, which, by laying in the neighbourhood of the Continent, is entirely at its mercy.

Some method might be fallen on to keep up a naval force in time of peace, if we should not judge it necessary to support a constant navy. If premiums were to be given to merchants, to build and employ in their service ships mounted with twenty, thirty, forty or fifty guns, (the premiums to be in proportion to the loss of bulk to the merchants) fifty or sixty of those ships, with a few guardships on constant duty, would keep up a sufficient navy, and that without burdening ourselves with the evil so loudly complained of in England, of suffering their fleet, in time of peace to lie rotting in the docks. To unite the sinews of commerce and defense is sound policy; for when our strength and our riches play into each other's hand, we need fear no external enemy.

In almost every article of defense we abound. Hemp flourishes even to rankness, so that we need not want cordage. Our iron is superior to that of other countries. Our small arms equal to any in the world. Cannon we can cast at pleasure. Saltpetre and gunpowder we are every day producing. Our knowledge is hourly improving. Resolution is our inherent character, and courage hath never yet forsaken us. Wherefore, what is it that we want? Why is it that we hesitate? From Britain we can expect nothing but ruin. If she is once admitted to the government of America again, this Continent will not be worth living in. Jealousies will be always arising; insurrections will be constantly happening; and who will go forth to quell them? Who will venture his life to reduce his own countrymen to a foreign obedience? The difference between Pennsylvania and Connecticut, respecting some unlocated lands, shews the insignificance of a British government, and fully proves, that nothing but Continental authority can regulate Continental matters.

Another reason why the present time is preferable to all others, is, that the fewer our numbers are, the more land there is yet unoccupied, which instead of being lavished by the king on his worthless dependants, may be hereafter applied, not only to the discharge of the present debt, but to the constant support of government. No nation under heaven hath such an advantage as this.

The infant state of the Colonies, as it is called, so far from being against, is an argument in favour of independence. We are sufficiently numerous, and were we more so, we might be less united. It is a matter worthy of observation, that the more a country is peopled, the smaller their armies are. In military numbers, the ancients far exceeded the moderns: and the reason is evident. For trade being the consequence of population, men become too much absorbed thereby to attend to anything else. Commerce diminishes the spirit, both of patriotism and military defence. And history sufficiently informs us, that the bravest achievements were always accomplished in the non-age of a nation. With the increase of commerce, England hath lost its spirit. The city of London, notwithstanding its numbers, submits to continued insults with the patience of a coward. The more men have to lose, the less willing are they to venture. The rich are in general slaves to fear, and submit to courtly power with the trembling duplicity of a Spaniel.

Youth is the seed time of good habits, as well in nations as in individuals. It might be difficult, if not impossible, to form the Continent into one government half a century hence. The vast variety of interests, occasioned by an increase of trade and population, would create confusion. Colony would be against colony. Each being able might scorn each other's assistance: and while the proud and foolish gloried in their little distinctions, the wise would lament, that the union had not been formed before. Wherefore, the *present time* is the *true time* for establishing it. The intimacy which is contracted in infancy, and the friendship which is formed in misfortune, are, of all others, the most lasting and unalterable. Our present union is marked with both these characters: we are young and we have been distressed; but our concord hath withstood our troubles, and fixes a memorable area for posterity to glory in.

The present time, likewise, is that peculiar time, which never happens to a nation but once, viz. the time of forming itself into a government. Most nations have let slip the opportunity, and by that means have been compelled to receive laws from their conquerors, instead of making laws for themselves. First, they had a king, and then a form of government; whereas, the articles or charter of government, should be formed first, and men delegated to execute them afterward: but from the errors of other nations, let us learn wisdom, and lay hold of the present opportunity—*To begin government at the right end.*

When William the Conqueror subdued England, he gave them law at the point of the sword; and until we consent, that the seat of government, in America, be legally and authoritatively occupied, we shall be in danger of having it filled by some fortunate ruffian, who may treat us in the same manner, and then, where will be our freedom? where our property?

As to religion, I hold it to be the indispensable duty of all government, to protect all conscientious professors thereof, and I know of no other business which government hath to do therewith. Let a man throw aside that narrowness of soul, that selfishness of principle, which the niggards of all professions are so unwilling to part with, and he will be at once delivered of his fears on that head. Suspicion is the companion of mean souls, and the bane of all good society. For myself, I fully and conscientiously believe, that it is the will of the Almighty, that there should be diversity of religious opinions among us: It affords a larger field for our Christian kindness. Were we all of one way of thinking, our religious dispositions would want matter for probation; and on this liberal principle, I look on the various denominations among us, to be like children of the same family, differing only, in what is called, their Christian names.

In page forty, I threw out a few thoughts on the propriety of a Continental Charter, (for I only presume to offer hints, not plans) and in this place, I take the liberty of re-mentioning the subject, by observing, that a charter is to be understood as a bond of solemn obligation, which the whole enters into, to support the right of every separate part, whether of religion, personal freedom, or property. A firm bargain and a right reckoning make long friends.

In a former page I likewise mentioned the necessity of a large and equal representation; and there is no political matter which more deserves our attention. A small number of electors, or a small number of representatives, are equally dangerous. But if the number of the representatives be not only small, but unequal, the danger is increased. As an instance of this, I mention the following; when the Associators petition was before the House of Assembly of Pennsylvania; twenty-eight members only were present, all the Bucks county members, being eight, voted against it, and had seven of the Chester members done the same, this whole province had been governed by two counties only, and this danger it is always exposed to. The unwarrantable stretch likewise, which that house made in their last sitting, to gain an undue authority over the delegates of that province, ought to warn the people at large, how they trust power out of their own hands. A set of instructions for the Delegates were put together, which in point of sense and business would have dishonoured a schoolboy, and after being approved by a *few*, a *very few* without doors, were carried into the House, and there passed *in behalf of the whole colony*; whereas, did the whole colony know, with what ill-will that House hath entered on some necessary public measures, they would not hesitate a moment to think them unworthy of such a trust.

Immediate necessity makes many things convenient, which if continued would grow into oppressions. Expedience and right are different things. When the calamities of America required a consultation, there was no method so ready, or at that time so proper, as to appoint persons from the several Houses of Assembly for that purpose; and the wisdom with which they have proceeded hath preserved this continent from ruin. But as it is more than probable that we shall never be without a CONGRESS, every well wisher to good order, must own, that the mode for choosing members of that body, deserves consideration. And I put it as a question to those, who make a study of mankind, whether *representation and election* is not too great a power for one and the same body of men to possess? When we are planning for posterity, we ought to remember, that virtue is not hereditary.

It is from our enemies that we often gain excellent maxims, and are frequently surprised into reason by their mistakes. Mr. Cornwall (one of the Lords of the Treasury) treated the petition of the New-York Assembly with contempt, because *that* House, he said, consisted but of twenty-six members, which trifling number, he argued, could not with decency be put for the whole. We thank him for his involuntary honesty. ◼

◼ Those who would fully understand of what great consequence a large and equal representation is to a state, should read Burgh's political disquisitions.

To Conclude, however strange it may appear to some, or however unwilling they may be to think so, matters not, but many strong and striking reasons may be given, to shew, that nothing can settle our affairs so expeditiously as an open and determined declaration for independence. Some of which are,

First.—It is the custom of nations, when any two are at war, for some other powers, not engaged in the quarrel, to step in as mediators, and bring about the preliminaries of a peace: but while America calls herself the Subject of Great-Britain, no power, however well disposed she may be, can offer her mediation. Wherefore, in our present state we may quarrel on for ever.

Secondly.—It is unreasonable to suppose, that France or Spain will give us any kind of assistance, if we mean only, to make use of that assistance for the purpose of repairing the breach, and strengthening the connection between Britain and America; because, those powers would be sufferers by the consequences.

Thirdly.—While we profess ourselves the subjects of Britain, we must, in the eye of foreign nations, be considered as rebels. The precedent is somewhat dangerous to *their peace*, for men to be in arms under the name of subjects; we, on the spot, can solve the paradox: but to unite resistance and subjection, requires an idea much too refined for common understanding.

Fourthly.—Were a manifesto to be published, and despatched to foreign courts, setting forth the miseries we have endured, and the peaceable methods we have ineffectually used for redress; declaring, at the same time, that not being able, any longer, to live happily or safely under the cruel disposition of the British court, we had been driven to the necessity of breaking off all connections with her; at the same time, assuring all such courts of our peaceable disposition towards them, and of our desire of entering into trade with them: Such a memorial would produce more good effects to this Continent, than if a ship were freighted with petitions to Britain.

Under our present denomination of British subjects, we can neither be received nor heard abroad: The custom of all courts is against us, and will be so, until, by an independance, we take rank with other nations.

These proceedings may at first appear strange and difficult; but, like all other steps which we have already passed over, will in a little time become familiar and agreeable; and, until an independance is declared, the Continent will feel itself like a man who continues putting off some unpleasant business from day to day, yet knows it must be done, hates to set about it, wishes it over, and is continually haunted with the thoughts of its necessity.

APPENDIX.

Since the publication of the first edition of this pamphlet, or rather, on the same day on which it came out, the King's Speech made its appearance in this city. Had the spirit of prophecy directed the birth of this production, it could not have brought it forth, at a more seasonable juncture, or a more necessary time. The bloody mindedness of the one, shew the necessity of pursuing the doctrine of the other. Men read by way of revenge. And the Speech, instead of terrifying, prepared a way for the manly principles of Independance.

Ceremony, and even, silence, from whatever motive they may arise, have a hurtful tendency, when they give the least degree of countenance to base and wicked performances; wherefore, if this maxim be admitted, it naturally follows, that the King's Speech, as being a piece of finished villainy, deserved, and still deserves, a general execration both by the Congress and the people. Yet, as the domestic tranquillity of a nation, depends greatly, on the *chastity* of what may properly be called NATIONAL MANNERS, it is often better, to pass some things over in silent disdain, than to make use of such new methods of dislike, as might introduce the least innovation, on that guardian of our peace and safety. And, perhaps, it is chiefly owing to this prudent delicacy, that the King's Speech, hath not, before now, suffered a public execution. The Speech if it may be called one, is nothing better than a wilful audacious libel against the truth, the common good, and the existence of mankind; and is a formal and pompous method of offering up human sacrifices to the pride of tyrants. But this general massacre of mankind, is one of the privileges, and the certain consequence of Kings; for as nature knows them *not*, they know *not her*, and although they are beings of our *own* creating, they know not *us*, and are become the gods of their creators. The Speech hath one good quality, which is, that it is not calculated to deceive, neither can we, even if we would, be deceived by it. Brutality and tyranny appear on the face of it. It leaves us at no loss: And every line convinces, even in the moment of reading, that He, who hunts the woods for prey, the naked and untutored Indian, is less a Savage than the King of Britain.

Sir John Dalrymple, the putative father of a whining jesuitical piece, fallaciously called, "*The Address of the people of* England *to the inhabitants of* America," hath, perhaps, from a vain supposition, that the people *here* were to be frightened at the pomp and description of a king, given, (though very unwisely on his part) the real character of the present one: "But" says this writer, "if you are inclined to pay compliments to an administration, which we do not complain of," (meaning the Marquis of Rockingham's at the repeal of the Stamp Act) "it is very unfair in you to withhold them from that prince, *by whose* NOD ALONE *they were permitted to do any thing.*" This is toryism with a witness! Here is idolatry even without a mask: And he who can calmly hear, and digest such doctrine, hath forfeited his claim to rationality—an apostate from the order of manhood; and ought to be considered—as one, who hath not only given up the proper dignity of man, but sunk himself beneath the rank of animals, and contemptibly crawls through the world like a worm.

However, it matters very little now, what the king of England either says or does; he hath wickedly broken through every moral and human obligation, trampled nature and conscience beneath his feet; and by a steady and constitutional spirit of insolence and cruelty, procured for himself an universal hatred. It is *now* the interest of America to provide for herself. She hath already a large and young family, whom it is more her duty to take care of, than to be granting away her property, to support a power who is become a reproach to the names of men and christians—Ye, whose office it is to watch over the morals of a nation, of whatsoever sect or denomination ye are of, as well as ye, who are more immediately the guardians of the public liberty, if ye wish to preserve your native country uncontaminated by European corruption, ye must in secret wish a separation—But leaving the moral part to private reflection, I shall chiefly confine my farther remarks to the following heads.

First. That it is the interest of America to be separated from Britain.

Secondly. Which is the easiest and most practicable plan, RECONCILIATION or INDEPENDANCE? with some occasional remarks.

In support of the first, I could, if I judged it proper, produce the opinion of some of the ablest and most experienced men on this continent; and whose sentiments, on that head, are not yet publicly known. It is in reality a self-evident position: For no nation in a state of foreign dependance, limited in its commerce, and cramped and fettered in its legislative powers, can ever arrive at any material eminence. America doth not yet know what opulence is; and although the progress which she hath made stands unparalleled in the history of other nations, it is but childhood, compared with what she would be capable of arriving at, had she, as she ought to have, the legislative powers in her own hands. England is, at this time, proudly coveting what would do her no good, were she to accomplish it; and the Continent hesitating on a matter, which will be her final ruin if neglected. It is the commerce and not the conquest of America, by which England is to be benefited, and that would in a great measure continue, were the countries as independant of each other as France and Spain; because in many articles, neither can go to a better market. But it is the independance of this country of Britain or any other, which is now the main and only object worthy of contention, and which, like all other truths discovered by necessity, will appear clearer and stronger every day.

First. Because it will come to that one time or other.

Secondly. Because, the longer it is delayed the harder it will be to accomplish.

I have frequently amused myself both in public and private companies, with silently remarking, the specious errors of those who speak without reflecting. And among the many which I have heard, the following seems the most general, viz. that had this rupture happened forty or fifty years hence, instead of *now*, the Continent would have been more able to have shaken off the dependance. To which I reply, that our military ability, *at this time*, arises from the experience gained in the last war, and which in forty or fifty years time, would have been totally extinct. The Continent, would not, by that time, have had a General, or even a military officer left; and we, or those who may succeed us, would have been as ignorant of martial matters as the ancient Indians: And this single position, closely attended to, will unanswerably prove, that the present time is preferable to all others. The argument turns thus—at the conclusion of the last war, we had experience, but wanted numbers; and forty or fifty years hence, we should have numbers, without experience; wherefore, the proper point of time, must be some particular point between the two extremes, in which a sufficiency of the former remains, and a proper increase of the latter is obtained: And that point of time is the present time.

The reader will pardon this digression, as it does not properly come under the head I first set out with, and to which I again return by the following position, viz.

Should affairs be patched up with Britain, and she to remain the governing and sovereign power of America, (which, as matters are now circumstanced, is giving up the point intirely) we shall deprive ourselves of the very means of sinking the debt we have, or may contract. The value of the back lands which some of the provinces are clandestinely deprived of, by the unjust extention of the limits of Canada, valued only at five pounds sterling per hundred acres, amount to upwards of twenty-five millions, Pennsylvania currency; and the quit-rents at one penny sterling per acre, to two millions yearly.

It is by the sale of those lands that the debt may be sunk, without burthen to any, and the quit-rent reserved thereon, will always lessen, and in time, will wholly support the yearly expence of government. It matters not how long the debt is in paying, so that the lands when sold be applied to the discharge of it, and for the execution of which, the Congress for the time being, will be the continental trustees.

I proceed now to the second head, viz. Which is the easiest and most practicable plan, RECONCILIATION or INDEPENDANCE; with some occasional remarks.

He who takes nature for his guide is not easily beaten out of his argument, and on that ground, I answer generally—That INDEPENDENCE *being a* SINGLE SIMPLE LINE, *contained within ourselves; and reconciliation, a matter exceedingly perplexed and complicated, and in which, a treacherous capricious court is to interfere, gives the answer without a doubt.*

The present state of America is truly alarming to every man who is capable of reflexion. Without law, without government, without any other mode of power than what is founded on, and granted by courtesy. Held together by an unexampled concurrence of sentiment, which, is nevertheless subject to change, and which every secret enemy is endeavouring to dissolve. Our present condition, is, Legislation without law; wisdom without a plan; constitution without a name; and, what is strangely astonishing, perfect Independance contending for dependance. The instance is without a precedent; the case never existed before; and who can tell what may be the event? The property of no man is secure in the present unbraced system of things. The mind of the multitude is left at random, and seeing no fixed object before them, they pursue such as fancy or opinion starts. Nothing is criminal; there is no such thing as treason; wherefore, every one thinks himself at liberty to act as he pleases. The Tories dared not have assembled offensively, had they known that their lives, by that act, were forfeited to the laws of the state. A line of distinction should be drawn, between, English soldiers taken in battle, and inhabitants of America taken in arms. The first are prisoners, but the latter traitors. The one forfeits his liberty, the other his head.

Notwithstanding our wisdom, there is a visible feebleness in some of our proceedings which gives encouragement to dissensions. The Continental Belt is too loosely buckled. And if something is not done in time, it will be too late to do any thing, and we shall fall into a state, in which, neither *Reconciliation* nor *Independance* will be practicable. The king and his worthless adherents are got at their old game of dividing the Continent, and there are not wanting among us, Printers, who will be busy in spreading specious falsehoods. The artful and hypocritical letter which appeared a few months ago in two of the New-York papers, and likewise in two others, is an evidence that there are men who want either judgment or honesty.

It is easy getting into holes and corners and talking of reconciliation: But do such men seriously consider, how difficult the task is, and how dangerous it may prove, should the Continent divide thereon. Do they take within their view, all the various orders of men whose situation and circumstances, as well as their own, are to be considered therein. Do they put themselves in the place of the sufferer whose *all* is *already* gone, and of the soldier, who hath quitted *all* for the defence of his country. If their ill judged moderation be suited to their own private situations *only*, regardless of others, the event will convince them, that "they are reckoning without their Host."

Put us, say some, on the footing we were on in sixty-three: To which I answer, the request is not *now* in the power of Britain to comply with, neither will she propose it; but if it were, and even should be granted, I ask, as a reasonable question, By what means is such a corrupt and faithless court to be kept to its engagements? Another parliament, nay, even the present, may hereafter repeal the obligation, on the pretence, of its being violently obtained, or unwisely granted; and in that case, Where is our redress?—No going to law with nations; cannon are the barristers of Crowns; and the sword, not of justice, but of war, decides the suit. To be on the footing of sixty-three, it is not sufficient, that the laws only be put on the same state, but, that our circumstances, likewise, be put on the same state; Our burnt and destroyed towns repaired or built up, our private losses made good, our public debts (contracted for defence) discharged; otherwise, we shall be millions worse than we were at that enviable period. Such a request, had it been complied with a year ago, would have won the heart and soul of the Continent—but now it is too late, "The Rubicon is passed."

Besides, the taking up arms, merely to enforce the repeal of a pecuniary law, seems as unwarrantable by the divine law, and as repugnant to human feelings, as the taking up arms to enforce obedience thereto. The object, on either side, doth not justify the means; for the lives of men are too valuable to be cast away on such trifles. It is the violence which is done and threatened to our persons; the destruction of our property by an armed force; the invasion of our country by fire and sword, which conscientiously qualifies the use of arms: And the instant, in which such a mode of defence became necessary, all subjection to Britain ought to have ceased; and the independancy of America, should have been considered, as dating its æra from, and published by, *the first musket that was fired against her*. This line is a line of consistency; neither drawn by caprice, nor extended by ambition; but produced by a chain of events, of which the colonies were not the authors.

I shall conclude these remarks, with the following timely and well intended hints. We ought to reflect, that there are three different ways, by which an independancy may hereafter be effected; and that *one* of those *three*, will one day or other, be the fate of America, viz. By the legal voice of the people in Congress; by a military power; or by a mob: It may not always happen that our soldiers are citizens, and the multitude a body of reasonable men; virtue, as I have already remarked, is not hereditary, neither is it perpetual. Should an independancy be brought about by the first of those means, we have every opportunity and every encouragement before us, to form the noblest purest constitution on the face of the earth. We have it in our power to begin the world over again. A situation, similar to the present, hath not happened since the days of Noah until now. The birthday of a new world is at hand, and a race of men, perhaps as numerous as all Europe contains, are to receive their portion of freedom from the event of a few months. The Reflexion is awful—and in this point of view, How trifling, how ridiculous, do the little, paltry cavellings, of a few weak or interested men appear, when weighed against the business of a world.

Should we neglect the present favorable and inviting period, and an Independance be hereafter effected by any other means, we must charge the consequence to ourselves, or to those rather, whose narrow and prejudiced souls, are habitually opposing the measure, without either inquiring or reflecting. There are reasons to be given in support of Independance, which men should rather privately think of, than be publicly told of. We ought not now to be debating whether we shall be independant or not, but, anxious to accomplish it on a firm, secure, and honorable basis, and uneasy rather that it is not yet began upon. Every day convinces us of its necessity. Even the Tories (if such beings yet remain among us) should, of all men, be the most solicitous to promote it; for, as the appointment of committees at first, protected them from popular rage, so, a wise and well established form of government, will be the only certain means of continuing it securely to them. *Wherefore*, if they have not virtue enough to be Whigs, they ought to have prudence enough to wish for Independence.

In short, Independance is the only Bond that can tye and keep us together. We shall then see our object, and our ears will be legally shut against the schemes of an intriguing, as well, as a cruel enemy. We shall then too, be on a proper footing, to treat with Britain; for there is reason to conclude, that the pride of that court, will be less hurt by treating with the American states for terms of peace, than with those, whom she denominates, "rebellious subjects," for terms of accommodation. It is our delaying it that encourages her to hope for conquest, and our backwardness tends only to prolong the war. As we have, without any good effect therefrom, withheld our trade to obtain a redress of our grievances, let us *now* try the alternative, by *independantly* redressing them ourselves, and then offering to open the trade. The mercantile and reasonable part in England, will be still with us; because, peace *with* trade, is preferable to war *without* it. And if this offer be not accepted, other courts may be applied to.

On these grounds I rest the matter. And as no offer hath yet been made to refute the doctrine contained in the former editions of this pamphlet, it is a negative proof, that either the doctrine cannot be refuted, or, that the party in favour of it are too numerous to be opposed. WHEREFORE, instead of gazing at each other with suspicious or doubtful curiosity; let each of us, hold out to his neighbour the hearty hand of friendship, and unite in drawing a line, which, like an act of oblivion shall bury in forgetfulness every former dissension. Let the names of Whig and Tory be extinct; and let none other be heard among us, than those of *a good citizen, an open and resolute friend, and a virtuous supporter of the* RIGHTS *of* MANKIND *and of the* FREE AND INDEPENDANT STATES OF AMERICA.

To the Representatives of the Religious Society of the People called Quakers, or to so many of them as were concerned in publishing the late piece, entitled "The Ancient Testimony and Principles of the People called Quakers renewed, with Respect to the King and Government, and touching the Commotions now prevailing in these and other parts of America addressed to the People in General."

The Writer of this, is one of those few, who never dishonours religion either by ridiculing, or cavilling at any denomination whatsoever. To God, and not to man, are all men accountable on the score of religion. Wherefore, this epistle is not so properly addressed to you as a religious, but as a political body, dabbling in matters, which the professed Quietude of your Principles instruct you not to meddle with.

As you have, without a proper authority for so doing, put yourselves in the place of the whole body of the Quakers, so, the writer of this, in order to be on an equal rank with yourselves, is under the necessity, of putting himself in the place of all those, who, approve the very writings and principles, against which your testimony is directed: And he hath chosen this singular situation, in order, that you might discover in him that presumption of character which you cannot see in yourselves. For neither he nor you can have any claim or title to *Political Representation*.

When men have departed from the right way, it is no wonder that they stumble and fall. And it is evident from the manner in which ye have managed your testimony, that politics, (as a religious body of men) is not your proper Walk; for however well adapted it might appear to you, it is, nevertheless, a jumble of good and bad put unwisely together, and the conclusion drawn therefrom, both unnatural and unjust.

The two first pages, (and the whole doth not make four) we give you credit for, and expect the same civility from you, because the love and desire of peace is not confined to Quakerism, it is the natural, as well the religious wish of all denominations of men. And on this ground, as men labouring to establish an Independant Constitution of our own, do we exceed all others in our hope, end, and aim. *Our plan is peace for ever.* We are tired of contention with Britain, and can see no real end to it but in a final separation. We act consistently, because for the sake of introducing an endless and uninterrupted peace, do we bear the evils and burthens of the present day. We are endeavoring, and will steadily continue to endeavour, to separate and dissolve a connexion which hath already filled our land with blood; and which, while the name of it remains, will be the fatal cause of future mischiefs to both countries.

We fight neither for revenge nor conquest; neither from pride nor passion; we are not insulting the world with our fleets and armies, nor ravaging the globe for plunder. Beneath the shade of our own vines are we attacked; in our own houses, and on our own lands, is the violence committed against us. We view our enemies in the character of Highwaymen and Housebreakers, and having no defence for ourselves in the civil law, are obliged to punish them by the military one, and apply the sword, in the very case, where you have before now, applied the halter—Perhaps we feel for the ruined and insulted sufferers in all and every part of the continent, with a degree of tenderness which hath not yet made its way into some of your bosoms. But be ye sure that ye mistake not the cause and ground of your Testimony. Call not coldness of soul, religion; nor put the *Bigot* in the place of the *Christian*.

O ye partial ministers of your own acknowledged principles. If the bearing arms be sinful, the first going to war must be more so, by all the difference between wilful attack and unavoidable defence. Wherefore, if ye really preach from conscience, and mean not to make a political hobby-horse of your religion, convince the world thereof, by proclaiming your doctrine to our enemies, *for they likewise bear* ARMS. Give us proof of your sincerity by publishing it at St. James's, to the commanders in chief at Boston, to the Admirals and Captains who are piratically ravaging our coasts, and to all the murdering miscreants who are acting in authority under HIM whom ye profess to serve. Had ye the honest soul of *Barclay* ✕ ye would preach repentance to *your* king; Ye would tell the Royal Wretch his sins, and warn him of eternal ruin. Ye would not spend your partial invectives against the injured and the insulted only, but, like faithful ministers, would cry aloud and *spare none*. Say not that ye are persecuted, neither endeavour to make us the authors of that reproach, which, ye are bringing upon yourselves; for we testify unto all men, that we do not complain against you because ye are *Quakers*, but because ye pretend to *be* and are NOT Quakers.

✕ "Thou hast tasted of prosperity and adversity; thou knowest what it is to be banished thy native country, to be over-ruled as well as to rule, and set upon the throne; and being *oppressed* thou hast reason to know how *hateful* the *oppressor* is both to God and man: If after all these warnings and advertisements, thou dost not turn unto the Lord with all thy heart, but forget him who remembered thee in thy distress, and give up thyself to follow lust and vanity, surely great will be thy condemnation.—Against which snare, as well as the temptation of those who may or do feed thee, and prompt thee to evil, the most excellent and prevalent remedy will be, to apply thyself to that light of Christ which shineth in thy conscience, and which neither can, nor will flatter thee, nor suffer thee to be at ease in thy sins."

—Barclay's address to Charles II.

Alas! it seems by the particular tendency of some part of your testimony, and other parts of your conduct, as if, all sin was reduced to, and comprehended in, *the act of bearing arms*, and that by the *people* only. Ye appear to us, to have mistaken party for conscience; because, the general tenor of your actions wants uniformity: And it is exceedingly difficult to us to give credit to many of your pretended scruples; because, we see them made by the same men, who, in the very instant that they are exclaiming against the mammon of this world, are nevertheless, hunting after it with a step as steady as Time, and an appetite as keen as Death.

The quotation which ye have made from Proverbs, in the third page of your testimony, that, "when a man's ways please the Lord, he maketh even his enemies to be at peace with him"; is very unwisely chosen on your part; because, it amounts to a proof, that the king's ways (whom ye are desirous of supporting) do *not* please the Lord, otherwise, his reign would be in peace.

I now proceed to the latter part of your testimony, and that, for which all the foregoing seems only an introduction, viz.

"It hath ever been our judgment and principle, since we were called to profess the light of Christ Jesus, manifested in our consciences unto this day, that the setting up and putting down kings and governments, is God's peculiar prerogative; for causes best known to himself: And that it is not our business to have any hand or contrivance therein; nor to be busy bodies above our station, much less to plot and contrive the ruin, or overturn of any of them, but to pray for the king, and safety of our nation, and good of all men: That we may live a peaceable and quiet life, in all godliness and honesty; *under the government which God is pleased to set over us.*"—If these are *really* your principles why do ye not abide by them? Why do ye not leave that, which ye call God's Work, to be managed by himself? These very principles instruct you to wait with patience and humility, for the event of all public measures, and to receive *that event* as the divine will towards you. *Wherefore*, what occasion is there for your *political testimony* if you fully believe what it contains: And the very publishing it proves, that either, ye do not believe what ye profess, or have not virtue enough to practise what ye believe.

The principles of Quakerism have a direct tendency to make a man the quiet and inoffensive subject of any, and every government *which is set over him*. And if the setting up and putting down of kings and governments is God's peculiar prerogative, he most certainly will not be robbed thereof by us; wherefore, the principle itself leads you to approve of every thing, which ever happened, or may happen to kings as being his work. OLIVER CROMWELL thanks you. CHARLES, then, died not by the hands of man; and should the present Proud Imitator of him, come to the same untimely end, the writers and publishers of the Testimony, are bound, by the doctrine it contains, to applaud the fact. Kings are not taken away by miracles, neither are changes in governments brought about by any other means than such as are common and human; and such as we are now using. Even the dispersion of the Jews, though foretold by our Saviour, was effected by arms. Wherefore, as ye refuse to be the means on one side, ye ought not to be meddlers on the other; but to wait the issue in silence; and unless ye can produce divine authority, to prove, that the Almighty who hath created and placed this *new* world, at the greatest distance it could possibly stand, east and west, from every part of the old, doth, nevertheless, disapprove of its being independant of the corrupt and abandoned court of Britain, unless I say, ye can shew this, how can ye on the ground of your principles, justify the exciting and stirring up the people "firmly to unite in the *abhorrence* of all such *writings*, and *measures*, as evidence a desire and design to break off the *happy* connexion we have hitherto enjoyed, with the kingdom of Great-Britain, and our just and necessary subordination to the king, and those who are lawfully placed in authority under him." What a slap of the face is here! the men, who in the very paragraph before, have quietly and passively resigned up the ordering, altering, and disposal of kings and governments, into the hands of God, are now, recalling their principles, and putting in for a share of the business. Is it possible, that the conclusion, which is here justly quoted, can any ways follow from the doctrine laid down? The inconsistency is too glaring not to be seen; the absurdity too great not to be laughed at; and such as could only have been made by those, whose understandings were darkened by the narrow and crabby spirit of a despairing political party; for ye are not to be considered as the whole body of the Quakers but only as a factional and fractional part thereof.

Here ends the examination of your testimony; (which I call upon no man to abhor, as ye have done, but only to read and judge of fairly;) to which I subjoin the following remark; "That the setting up and putting down of kings," most certainly mean, the making him a king, who is yet not so, and the making him no king who is already one. And pray what hath this to do in the present case? We neither mean to *set up* nor to *put down*, neither to *make* nor to *unmake*, but to have nothing to *do* with them. Wherefore, your testimony in whatever light it is viewed serves only to dishonor your judgement, and for many other reasons had better have been let alone than published.

First, Because it tends to the decrease and reproach of all religion whatever, and is of the utmost danger to society, to make it a party in political disputes.

Secondly, Because it exhibits a body of men, numbers of whom disavow the publishing political testimonies, as being concerned therein and approvers thereof.

Thirdly, Because it hath a tendency to undo that continental harmony and friendship which yourselves by your late liberal and charitable donations hath lent a hand to establish; and the preservation of which, is of the utmost consequence to us all.

And here without anger or resentment I bid you farewell. Sincerely wishing, that as men and christians, ye may always fully and uninterruptedly enjoy every civil and religious right; and be, in your turn, the means of securing it to others; but that the example which ye have unwisely set, of mingling religion with politics, *may be disavowed and reprobated by every inhabitant of* AMERICA.

F I N I S.

HISTORICAL CONTEXT

Paine has a claim to the title The Father of the American Revolution, which rests on his pamphlets, especially Common Sense, which crystallized sentiment for independence in 1776. It was published in Philadelphia on January 10, 1776, and signed anonymously "by an Englishman". It became an immediate success, quickly spreading 100,000 copies in three months to the two million residents of the 13 colonies. During the course of the American Revolution, a total of about 500,000 copies were sold, including unauthorized editions. Paine's original title for the pamphlet was Plain Truth, but Paine's friend, pro-independence advocate Benjamin Rush, suggested Common Sense instead.

The pamphlet came into circulation in January 1776, after the Revolution had started. It was passed around and often read aloud in taverns, contributing significantly to spreading the idea of republicanism, bolstering enthusiasm for separation from Britain, and encouraging recruitment for the Continental Army. Paine provided a new and convincing argument for independence by advocating a complete break with history. Common Sense is oriented to the future in a way that compels the reader to make an immediate choice. It offers a solution for Americans disgusted with and alarmed at the threat of tyranny.

Paine's attack on monarchy in Common Sense is essentially an attack on George III. Whereas colonial resentments were originally directed primarily against the king's ministers and Parliament, Paine laid the responsibility firmly at the king's door. Common Sense was the most widely read pamphlet of the American Revolution. It was a clarion call for unity against the corrupt British court, so as to realize America's providential role in providing an asylum for liberty. Written in a direct and lively style, it denounced the decaying despotisms of Europe and pilloried hereditary monarchy as an absurdity. At a time when many still hoped for reconciliation with Britain, Common Sense demonstrated to many the inevitability of separation.

Paine was not on the whole expressing original ideas in Common Sense, but rather employing rhetoric as a means to arouse resentment of the Crown. To achieve these ends, he pioneered a style of political writing suited to the democratic society he envisioned, with Common Sense serving as a primary example. Part of Paine's work was to render complex ideas intelligible to average readers of the day, with clear, concise writing unlike the formal, learned style favored by many of Paine's contemporaries. Scholars have put forward various explanations to account for its success, including the historic moment, Paine's easy-to-understand style, his democratic ethos, and his use of psychology and ideology.

Common Sense was immensely popular in disseminating to a very wide audience ideas that were already in common use among the elite who comprised Congress and the leadership cadre of the emerging nation, who rarely cited Paine's arguments in their public calls for independence.The pamphlet probably had little direct influence on the Continental Congress' decision to issue a Declaration of Independence, since that body was more concerned with how declaring independence would affect the war effort. One distinctive idea in Common Sense is Paine's beliefs regarding the peaceful nature of republics; his views were an early and strong conception of what scholars would come to call the democratic peace theory.

Loyalists vigorously attacked Common Sense; one attack, titled Plain Truth (1776), by Marylander James Chalmers, said Paine was a political quack and warned that without monarchy, the government would "degenerate into democracy". Even some American revolutionaries objected to Common Sense; late in life John Adams called it a "crapulous mass". Adams disagreed with the type of radical democracy promoted by Paine (that men who did not own property should still be allowed to vote and hold public office) and published Thoughts on Government in 1776 to advocate a more conservative approach to republicanism.

Sophia Rosenfeld argues that Paine was highly innovative in his use of the commonplace notion of "common sense". He synthesized various philosophical and political uses of the term in a way that permanently impacted American political thought. He used two ideas from Scottish Common Sense Realism: that ordinary people can indeed make sound judgments on major political issues, and that there exists a body of popular wisdom that is readily apparent to anyone. Paine also used a notion of "common sense" favored by philosophes in the Continental Enlightenment. They held that common sense could refute the claims of traditional institutions. Thus, Paine used "common sense" as a weapon to delegitimize the monarchy and overturn prevailing conventional wisdom. Rosenfeld concludes that the phenomenal appeal of his pamphlet resulted from his synthesis of popular and elite elements in the independence movement.

According to historian Robert Middlekauff, Common Sense became immensely popular mainly because Paine appealed to widespread convictions. Monarchy, he said, was preposterous and it had a heathenish origin. It was an institution of the devil. Paine pointed to the Old Testament, where almost all kings had seduced the Israelites to worship idols instead of God. Paine also denounced aristocracy, which together with monarchy were "two ancient tyrannies." They violated the laws of nature, human reason, and the "universal order of things," which began with God. That was, Middlekauff says, exactly what most Americans wanted to hear. He calls the Revolutionary generation "the children of the twice-born". because in their childhood they had experienced the Great Awakening, which, for the first time, had tied Americans together, transcending denominational and ethnic boundaries and giving them a sense of patriotism.

ON COMMON SENSE

"No writer has exceeded Paine in ease and familiarity of style, in perspicuity of expression, happiness of elucidation, and in simple and unassuming language."
Thomas Jefferson
"A pamphlet called 'Commonsense' makes a great noise. One of the vilest things that ever was published to the world. Full of false representations, lies, calumny, and treason, whose principles are to subvert all Kingly Governments and erect an Independent Republic."
Nicholas Cresswell
"I dreaded the effect so popular a pamphlet might have among the people, and determined to do all in my Power to counteract the effect of it."
John Adams
"Its effects were sudden and extensive upon the American mind. It was read by public men."
Dr. Benjamin Rush
"Have you read the pamphlet Common Sense? I never saw such a masterful performance.... In short, I own myself convinced, by the arguments, of the necessity of separation."
General Charles Lee

3.1 – THE AGE OF REASON

(1796)

EDITOR'S INTRODUCTION
WITH SOME RESULTS OF RECENT RESEARCHES

IN the opening year, 1793, when revolutionary France had beheaded its king, the wrath turned next upon the King of kings, by whose grace every tyrant claimed to reign. But eventualities had brought among them a great English and American heart—Thomas Paine. He had pleaded for Louis Caper—"Kill the king but spare the man." Now he pleaded,—"Disbelieve in the King of kings, but do not confuse with that idol the Father of Mankind!"

In Paine's Preface to the Second Part of "The Age of Reason" he describes himself as writing the First Part near the close of the year 1793. "I had not finished it more than six hours, in the state it has since appeared, before a guard came about three in the morning, with an order signed by the two Committees of Public Safety and Surety General, for putting me in arrestation." This was on the morning of December 28. But it is necessary to weigh the words just quoted—"in the state it has since appeared." For on August 5, 1794, Francois Lanthenas, in an appeal for Paine's liberation, wrote as follows: "I deliver to Merlin de Thionville a copy of the last work of T. Payne [The Age of Reason], formerly our colleague, and in custody since the decree excluding foreigners from the national representation. This book was written by the author in the beginning of the year '93 (old style). I undertook its translation before the revolution against priests, and it was published in French about the same time. Couthon, to whom I sent it, seemed offended with me for having translated this work."

Under the frown of Couthon, one of the most atrocious colleagues of Robespierre, this early publication seems to have been so effectually suppressed that no copy bearing that date, 1793, can be found in France or elsewhere. In Paine's letter to Samuel Adams, printed in the present volume, he says that he had it translated into French, to stay the progress of atheism, and that he endangered his life "by opposing atheism." The time indicated by Lanthenas as that in which he submitted the work to Couthon would appear to be the latter part of March, 1793, the fury against the priesthood having reached its climax in the decrees against them of March 19 and 26. If the moral deformity of Couthon, even greater than that of his body, be remembered, and the readiness with which death was inflicted for the most theoretical opinion not approved by the "Mountain," it will appear probable that the offence given Couthon by Paine's book involved danger to him and his translator. On May 31, when the Girondins were accused, the name of Lanthenas was included, and he barely escaped; and on the same day Danton persuaded Paine not to appear in the Convention, as his life might be in danger. Whether this was because of the "Age of Reason," with its fling at the "Goddess Nature" or not, the statements of author and translator are harmonized by the fact that Paine prepared the manuscript, with considerable additions and changes, for publication in English, as he has stated in the Preface to Part II.

A comparison of the French and English versions, sentence by sentence, proved to me that the translation sent by Lanthenas to Merlin de Thionville in 1794 is the same as that he sent to Couthon in 1793. This discovery was the means of recovering several interesting sentences of the original work. I have given as footnotes translations of such clauses and phrases of the French work as appeared to be important. Those familiar with the translations of Lanthenas need not be reminded that he was too much of a literalist to depart from the manuscript before him, and indeed he did not even venture to alter it in an instance (presently considered) where it was obviously needed. Nor would Lanthenas have omitted any of the paragraphs lacking in his translation. This original work was divided into seventeen chapters, and these I have restored, translating their headings into English. The "Age of Reason" is thus for the first time given to the world with nearly its original completeness.

It should be remembered that Paine could not have read the proof of his "Age of Reason" (Part I.) which went through the press while he was in prison. To this must be ascribed the permanence of some sentences as abbreviated in the haste he has described. A notable instance is the dropping out of his estimate of Jesus the words rendered by Lanthenas "trop peu imite, trop oublie, trop meconnu." The addition of these words to Paine's tribute makes it the more notable that almost the only recognition of the human character and life of Jesus by any theological writer of that generation came from one long branded as an infidel.

To the inability of the prisoner to give his work any revision must be attributed the preservation in it of the singular error already alluded to, as one that Lanthenas, but for his extreme fidelity, would have corrected. This is Paine's repeated mention of six planets, and enumeration of them, twelve years after the discovery of Uranus. Paine was a devoted student of astronomy, and it cannot for a moment be supposed that he had not participated in the universal welcome of Herschel's discovery. The omission of any allusion to it convinces me that the astronomical episode was printed from a manuscript written before 1781, when Uranus was discovered. Unfamiliar with French in 1793, Paine might not have discovered the erratum in Lanthenas' translation, and, having no time for copying, he would naturally use as much as possible of the same manuscript in preparing his work for English readers. But he had no opportunity of revision, and there remains an erratum which, if my conjecture be correct, casts a significant light on the paragraphs in which he alludes to the preparation of the work. He states that soon after his publication of "Common Sense" (1776), he "saw the exceeding probability that a revolution in the system of government would be followed by a revolution in the system of religion," and that "man would return to the pure, unmixed, and unadulterated belief of one God and no more." He tells Samuel Adams that it had long been his intention to publish his thoughts upon religion, and he had made a similar remark to John Adams in 1776. Like the Quakers among whom he was reared Paine could then readily use the phrase "word of God" for anything in the Bible which approved itself to his "inner light," and as he had drawn from the first Book of Samuel a divine condemnation of monarchy, John Adams, a Unitarian, asked him if he believed in the inspiration of the Old Testament. Paine replied that he did not, and at a later period meant to publish his views on the subject. There is little doubt that he wrote from time to time on religious points, during the American war, without publishing his thoughts, just as he worked on the problem of steam navigation, in which he had invented a practicable method (ten years before John Fitch made his discovery) without publishing it. At any rate it appears to me certain that the part of "The Age of Reason" connected with Paine's favorite science, astronomy, was written before 1781, when Uranus was discovered.

Paine's theism, however invested with biblical and Christian phraseology, was a birthright. It appears clear from several allusions in "The Age of Reason" to the Quakers that in his early life, or before the middle of the eighteenth century, the people so called were substantially Deists. An interesting confirmation of Paine's statements concerning them appears as I write in an account sent by Count Leo Tolstoi to the London 'Times' of the Russian sect called Dukhobortsy (The Times, October 23, 1895). This sect sprang up in the last century, and the narrative says:

"The first seeds of the teaching called afterwards 'Dukhoborcheskaya' were sown by a foreigner, a Quaker, who came to Russia. The fundamental idea of his Quaker teaching was that in the soul of man dwells God himself, and that He himself guides man by His inner word. God lives in nature physically and in man's soul spiritually. To Christ, as to an historical personage, the Dukhobortsy do not ascribe great importance... Christ was God's son, but only in the sense in which we call, ourselves 'sons of God.' The purpose of Christ's sufferings was no other than to show us an example of suffering for truth. The Quakers who, in 1818, visited the Dukhobortsy, could not agree with them upon these religious subjects; and when they heard from them their opinion about Jesus Christ (that he was a man), exclaimed 'Darkness!' From the Old and New Testaments,' they say, 'we take only what is useful,' mostly the moral teaching.... The moral ideas of the Dukhobortsy are the following:—All men are, by nature, equal; external distinctions, whatsoever they may be, are worth nothing. This idea of men's equality the Dukhoborts have directed further, against the State authority.... Amongst themselves they hold subordination, and much more, a monarchical Government, to be contrary to their ideas."

Here is an early Hicksite Quakerism carried to Russia long before the birth of Elias Hicks, who recovered it from Paine, to whom the American Quakers refused burial among them. Although Paine arraigned the union of Church and State, his ideal Republic was religious; it was based on a conception of equality based on the divine son-ship of every man. This faith underlay equally his burden against claims to divine partiality by a "Chosen People," a Priesthood, a Monarch "by the grace of God," or an Aristocracy. Paine's "Reason" is only an expansion of the Quaker's "inner light"; and the greater impression, as compared with previous republican and deistic writings made by his "Rights of Man" and "Age of Reason" (really volumes of one work), is partly explained by the apostolic fervor which made him a spiritual, successor of George Fox.

Paine's mind was by no means skeptical, it was eminently instructive. That he should have waited until his fifty-seventh year before publishing his religious convictions was due to a desire to work out some positive and practicable system to take the place of that which he believed was crumbling. The English engineer Hall, who assisted Paine in making the model of his iron bridge, wrote to his friends in England, in 1786: "My employer has Common Sense enough to disbelieve most of the common systematic theories of Divinity, but does not seem to establish any for himself." But five years later Paine was able to lay the corner-stone of his temple: "With respect to religion itself, without regard to names, and as directing itself from the universal family of mankind to the 'Divine object of all adoration, it is man bringing to his Maker the fruits of his heart; and though those fruits may differ from each other like the fruits of the earth, the grateful tribute of every one, is accepted." ("Rights of Man." See my edition of Paine's Writings, ii., p. 326.) Here we have a reappearance of George Fox confuting the doctor in America who "denied the light and Spirit of God to be in every one; and affirmed that it was not in the Indians. Whereupon I called an Indian to us, and asked him 'whether or not, when he lied, or did wrong to anyone, there was not something in him that reproved him for it?' He said, 'There was such a thing in him that did so reprove him; and he was ashamed when he had done wrong, or spoken wrong.' So we shamed the doctor before the governor and the people." (Journal of George Fox, September 1672.)

Paine, who coined the phrase "Religion of Humanity" (The Crisis, vii., 1778), did but logically defend it in "The Age of Reason," by denying a special revelation to any particular tribe, or divine authority in any particular creed of church; and the centenary of this much-abused publication has been celebrated by a great conservative champion of Church and State, Mr. Balfour, who, in his "Foundations of Belief," affirms that "inspiration" cannot be denied to the great Oriental teachers, unless grapes may be gathered from thorns.

The centenary of the complete publication of "The Age of Reason," (October 25, 1795), was also celebrated at the Church Congress, Norwich, on October 10, 1895, when Professor Bonney, F.R.S., Canon of Manchester, read a paper in which he said: "I cannot deny that the increase of scientific knowledge has deprived parts of the earlier books of the Bible of the historical value which was generally attributed to them by our forefathers. The story of Creation in the Book of Genesis, unless we play fast and loose either with words or with science, cannot be brought into harmony with what we have learnt from geology. Its ethnological statements are imperfect, if not sometimes inaccurate. The stories of the Fall, of the Flood, and of the Tower of Babel, are incredible in their present form. Some historical element may underlie many of the traditions in the first eleven chapters in that book, but this we cannot hope to recover." Canon Bonney proceeded to say of the New Testament also, that "the Gospels are not so far as we know, strictly contemporaneous records, so we must admit the possibility of variations and even inaccuracies in details being introduced by oral tradition." The Canon thinks the interval too short for these importations to be serious, but that any question of this kind is left open proves the Age of Reason fully upon us. Reason alone can determine how many texts are as spurious as the three heavenly witnesses (i John v. 7), and like it "serious" enough to have cost good men their lives, and persecutors their charities. When men interpolate, it is because they believe their interpolation seriously needed. It will be seen by a note in Part II. of the work, that Paine calls attention to an interpolation introduced into the first American edition without indication of its being an editorial footnote. This footnote was: "The book of Luke was carried by a majority of one only. Vide Moshelm's Ecc. History." Dr. Priestley, then in America, answered Paine's work, and in quoting less than a page from the "Age of Reason" he made three alterations,—one of which changed "church mythologists" into "Christian mythologists,"—and also raised the editorial footnote into the text, omitting the reference to Mosheim. Having done this, Priestley writes: "As to the gospel of Luke being carried by a majority of one only, it is a legend, if not of Mr. Paine's own invention, of no better authority whatever." And so on with further castigation of the author for what he never wrote, and which he himself (Priestley) was the unconscious means of introducing into the text within the year of Paine's publication.

If this could be done, unintentionally by a conscientious and exact man, and one not unfriendly to Paine, if such a writer as Priestley could make four mistakes in citing half a page, it will appear not very wonderful when I state that in a modern popular edition of "The Age of Reason," including both parts, I have noted about five hundred deviations from the original. These were mainly the accumulated efforts of friendly editors to improve Paine's grammar or spelling; some were misprints, or developed out of such; and some resulted from the sale in London of a copy of Part Second surreptitiously made from the manuscript. These facts add significance to Paine's footnote (itself altered in some editions!), in which he says: "If this has happened within such a short space of time, notwithstanding the aid of printing, which prevents the alteration of copies individually; what may not have happened in a much greater length of time, when there was no printing, and when any man who could write, could make a written copy, and call it an original, by Matthew, Mark, Luke, or John."

Nothing appears to me more striking, as an illustration of the far-reaching effects of traditional prejudice, than the errors into which some of our ablest contemporary scholars have fallen by reason of their not having studied Paine. Professor Huxley, for instance, speaking of the freethinkers of the eighteenth century, admires the acuteness, common sense, wit, and the broad humanity of the best of them, but says "there is rarely much to be said for their work as an example of the adequate treatment of a grave and difficult investigation," and that they shared with their adversaries "to the full the fatal weakness of a priori philosophizing." [NOTE: Science and Christian Tradition, p. 18 (Lon. ed., 1894).] Professor Huxley does not name Paine, evidently because he knows nothing about him. Yet Paine represents the turning-point of the historical freethinking movement; he renounced the 'a priori' method, refused to pronounce anything impossible outside pure mathematics, rested everything on evidence, and really founded the Huxleyan school. He plagiarized by anticipation many things from the rationalistic leaders of our time, from Strauss and Baur (being the first to expatiate on "Christian Mythology"), from Renan (being the first to attempt recovery of the human Jesus), and notably from Huxley, who has repeated Paine's arguments on the untrustworthiness of the biblical manuscripts and canon, on the inconsistencies of the narratives of Christ's resurrection, and various other points. None can be more loyal to the memory of Huxley than the present writer, and it is even because of my sense of his grand leadership that he is here mentioned as a typical instance of the extent to which the very elect of free-thought may be unconsciously victimized by the phantasm with which they are contending. He says that Butler overthrew freethinkers of the eighteenth century type, but Paine was of the nineteenth century type; and it was precisely because of his critical method that he excited more animosity than his deistical predecessors. He compelled the apologists to defend the biblical narratives in detail, and thus implicitly acknowledge the tribunal of reason and knowledge to which they were summoned. The ultimate answer by police was a confession of judgment. A hundred years ago England was suppressing Paine's works, and many an honest Englishman has gone to prison for printing and circulating his "Age of Reason." The same views are now freely expressed; they are heard in the seats of learning, and even in the Church Congress; but the suppression of Paine, begun by bigotry and ignorance, is continued in the long indifference of the representatives of our Age of Reason to their pioneer and founder. It is a grievous loss to them and to their cause. It is impossible to understand the religious history of England, and of America, without studying the phases of their evolution represented in the writings of Thomas Paine, in the controversies that grew out of them with such practical accompaniments as the foundation of the Theophilanthropist Church in Paris and New York, and of the great rationalist wing of Quakerism in America.

Whatever may be the case with scholars in our time, those of Paine's time took the "Age of Reason" very seriously indeed. Beginning with the learned Dr. Richard Watson, Bishop of Llandaff, a large number of learned men replied to Paine's work, and it became a signal for the commencement of those concessions, on the part of theology, which have continued to our time; and indeed the so-called "Broad Church" is to some extent an outcome of "The Age of Reason." It would too much enlarge this Introduction to cite here the replies made to Paine (thirty-six are catalogued in the British Museum), but it may be remarked that they were notably free, as a rule, from the personalities that raged in the pulpits. I must venture to quote one passage from his very learned antagonist, the Rev. Gilbert Wakefield, B.A., "late Fellow of Jesus College, Cambridge." Wakefield, who had resided in London during all the Paine panic, and was well acquainted with the slanders uttered against the author of "Rights of Man," indirectly brands them in answering Paine's argument that the original and traditional unbelief of the Jews, among whom the alleged miracles were wrought, is an important evidence against them. The learned divine writes:

"But the subject before us admits of further illustration from the example of Mr. Paine himself. In this country, where his opposition to the corruptions of government has raised him so many adversaries, and such a swarm of unprincipled hirelings have exerted themselves in blackening his character and in misrepresenting all the transactions and incidents of his life, will it not be a most difficult, nay an impossible task, for posterity, after a lapse of 1700 years, if such a wreck of modern literature as that of the ancient, should intervene, to identify the real circumstances, moral and civil, of the man? And will a true historian, such as the Evangelists, be credited at that future period against such a predominant incredulity, without large and mighty accessions of collateral attestation? And how transcendently extraordinary, I had almost said miraculous, will it be estimated by candid and reasonable minds, that a writer whose object was a melioration of condition to the common people, and their deliverance from oppression, poverty, wretchedness, to the numberless blessings of upright and equal government, should be reviled, persecuted, and burned in effigy, with every circumstance of insult and execration, by these very objects of his benevolent intentions, in every corner of the kingdom?" After the execution of Louis XVI., for whose life Paine pleaded so earnestly,—while in England he was denounced as an accomplice in the deed,—he devoted himself to the preparation of a Constitution, and also to gathering up his religious compositions and adding to them. This manuscript I suppose to have been prepared in what was variously known as White's Hotel or Philadelphia House, in Paris, No. 7 Passage des Petits Peres. This compilation of early and fresh manuscripts (if my theory be correct) was labelled, "The Age of Reason," and given for translation to Francois Lanthenas in March 1793. It is entered, in Qudrard (La France Literaire) under the year 1793, but with the title "L'Age de la Raison" instead of that which it bore in 1794, "Le Siecle de la Raison." The latter, printed "Au Burceau de l'imprimerie, rue du Theatre-Francais, No. 4," is said to be by "Thomas Paine, Citoyen et cultivateur de l'Amerique septentrionale, secretaire du Congres du departement des affaires etrangeres pendant la guerre d'Amerique, et auteur des ouvrages intitules: LA SENS COMMUN et LES DROITS DE L'HOMME."

When the Revolution was advancing to increasing terrors, Paine, unwilling to participate in the decrees of a Convention whose sole legal function was to frame a Constitution, retired to an old mansion and garden in the Faubourg St. Denis, No. 63. Mr. J.G. Alger, whose researches in personal details connected with the Revolution are original and useful, recently showed me in the National Archives at Paris, some papers connected with the trial of Georgeit, Paine's landlord, by which it appears that the present No. 63 is not, as I had supposed, the house in which Paine resided. Mr. Alger accompanied me to the neighborhood, but we were not able to identify the house. The arrest of Georgeit is mentioned by Paine in his essay on "Forgetfulness" (Writings, iii., 319). When his trial came on one of the charges was that he had kept in his house "Paine and other Englishmen,"—Paine being then in prison,—but he (Georgeit) was acquitted of the paltry accusations brought against him by his Section, the "Faubourg du Nord." This Section took in the whole east side of the Faubourg St. Denis, whereas the present No. 63 is on the west side. After Georgeit (or Georger) had been arrested, Paine was left alone in the large mansion (said by Rickman to have been once the hotel of Madame de Pompadour), and it would appear, by his account, that it was after the execution (October 31, 1793) Of his friends the Girondins, and political comrades, that he felt his end at hand, and set about his last literary bequest to the world,— "The Age of Reason,"—in the state in which it has since appeared, as he is careful to say. There was every probability, during the months in which he wrote (November and December 1793) that he would be executed. His religious testament was prepared with the blade of the guillotine suspended over him,—a fact which did not deter pious mythologists from portraying his death-bed remorse for having written the book.

In editing Part I. of "The Age of Reason," I follow closely the first edition, which was printed by Barrois in Paris from the manuscript, no doubt under the superintendence of Joel Barlow, to whom Paine, on his way to the Luxembourg, had confided it. Barlow was an American ex-clergyman, a speculator on whose career French archives cast an unfavorable light, and one cannot be certain that no liberties were taken with Paine's proofs.

I may repeat here what I have stated in the outset of my editorial work on Paine that my rule is to correct obvious misprints, and also any punctuation which seems to render the sense less clear. And to that I will now add that in following Paine's quotations from the Bible I have adopted the Plan now generally used in place of his occasionally too extended writing out of book, chapter, and verse.

Paine was imprisoned in the Luxembourg on December 28, 1793, and released on November 4, 1794. His liberation was secured by his old friend, James Monroe (afterwards President), who had succeeded his (Paine's) relentless enemy, Gouverneur Morris, as American Minister in Paris. He was found by Monroe more dead than alive from semi-starvation, cold, and an abscess contracted in prison, and taken to the Minister's own residence. It was not supposed that he could survive, and he owed his life to the tender care of Mr. and Mrs. Monroe. It was while thus a prisoner in his room, with death still hovering over him, that Paine wrote Part Second of "The Age of Reason."

The work was published in London by H.D. Symonds on October 25, 1795, and claimed to be "from the Author's manuscript." It is marked as "Entered at Stationers Hall," and prefaced by an apologetic note of "The Bookseller to the Public," whose commonplaces about avoiding both prejudice and partiality, and considering "both sides," need not be quoted. While his volume was going through the press in Paris, Paine heard of the publication in London, which drew from him the following hurried note to a London publisher, no doubt Daniel Isaacs Eaton:

"SIR,—I have seen advertised in the London papers the second Edition [part] of the Age of Reason, printed, the advertisement says, from the Author's Manuscript, and entered at Stationers Hall. I have never sent any manuscript to any person. It is therefore a forgery to say it is printed from the author's manuscript; and I suppose is done to give the Publisher a pretence of Copy Right, which he has no title to.

"I send you a printed copy, which is the only one I have sent to London. I wish you to make a cheap edition of it. I know not by what means any copy has got over to London. If any person has made a manuscript copy I have no doubt but it is full of errors. I wish you would talk to Mr. ——- upon this subject as I wish to know by what means this trick has been played, and from whom the publisher has got possession of any copy.

"T. PAINE.

"PARIS, December 4, 1795"

Eaton's cheap edition appeared January 1, 1796, with the above letter on the reverse of the title. The blank in the note was probably "Symonds" in the original, and possibly that publisher was imposed upon. Eaton, already in trouble for printing one of Paine's political pamphlets, fled to America, and an edition of the "Age of Reason" was issued under a new title; no publisher appears; it is said to be "printed for, and sold by all the Booksellers in Great Britain and Ireland." It is also said to be "By Thomas Paine, author of several remarkable performances." I have never found any copy of this anonymous edition except the one in my possession. It is evidently the edition which was suppressed by the prosecution of Williams for selling a copy of it.

A comparison with Paine's revised edition reveals a good many clerical and verbal errors in Symonds, though few that affect the sense. The worst are in the preface, where, instead of "1793," the misleading date "1790" is given as the year at whose close Paine completed Part First,—an error that spread far and wide and was fastened on by his calumnious American "biographer,"

Cheetham, to prove his inconsistency. The editors have been fairly demoralized by, and have altered in different ways, the following sentence of the preface in Symonds: "The intolerant spirit of religious persecution had transferred itself into politics; the tribunals, styled Revolutionary, supplied the place of the Inquisition; and the Guillotine of the State outdid the Fire and Faggot of the Church." The rogue who copied this little knew the care with which Paine weighed words, and that he would never call persecution "religious," nor connect the guillotine with the "State," nor concede that with all its horrors it had outdone the history of fire and faggot. What Paine wrote was: "The intolerant spirit of church persecution had transferred itself into politics; the tribunals, styled Revolutionary, supplied the place of an Inquisition and the Guillotine, of the Stake."

An original letter of Paine, in the possession of Joseph Cowen, ex-M.P., which that gentleman permits me to bring to light, besides being one of general interest makes clear the circumstances of the original publication. Although the name of the correspondent does not appear on the letter, it was certainly written to Col. John Fellows of New York, who copyrighted Part I. of the "Age of Reason." He published the pamphlets of Joel Barlow, to whom Paine confided his manuscript on his way to prison. Fellows was afterwards Paine's intimate friend in New York, and it was chiefly due to him that some portions of the author's writings, left in manuscript to Madame Bonneville while she was a freethinker were rescued from her devout destructiveness after her return to Catholicism. The letter which Mr. Cowen sends me, is dated at Paris, January 20, 1797.

"SIR,—Your friend Mr. Caritat being on the point of his departure for America, I make it the opportunity of writing to you. I received two letters from you with some pamphlets a considerable time past, in which you inform me of your entering a copyright of the first part of the Age of Reason: when I return to America we will settle for that matter.

"As Doctor Franklin has been my intimate friend for thirty years past you will naturally see the reason of my continuing the connection with his grandson. I printed here (Paris) about fifteen thousand of the second part of the Age of Reason, which I sent to Mr. F[ranklin] Bache. I gave him notice of it in September 1795 and the copy-right by my own direction was entered by him. The books did not arrive till April following, but he had advertised it long before.

"I sent to him in August last a manuscript letter of about 70 pages, from me to Mr. Washington to be printed in a pamphlet. Mr. Barnes of Philadelphia carried the letter from me over to London to be forwarded to America. It went by the ship Hope, Cap: Harley, who since his return from America told me that he put it into the post office at New York for Bache. I have yet no certain account of its publication. I mention this that the letter may be enquired after, in case it has not been published or has not arrived to Mr. Bache. Barnes wrote to me, from London 29 August informing me that he was offered three hundred pounds sterling for the manuscript. The offer was refused because it was my intention it should not appear till it appeared in America, as that, and not England was the place for its operation.

"You ask me by your letter to Mr. Caritat for a list of my several works, in order to publish a collection of them. This is an undertaking I have always reserved for myself. It not only belongs to me of right, but nobody but myself can do it; and as every author is accountable (at least in reputation) for his works, he only is the person to do it. If he neglects it in his life-time the case is altered. It is my intention to return to America in the course of the present year. I shall then [do] it by subscription, with historical notes. As this work will employ many persons in different parts of the Union, I will confer with you upon the subject, and such part of it as will suit you to undertake, will be at your choice. I have sustained so much loss, by disinterestedness and inattention to money matters, and by accidents, that I am obliged to look closer to my affairs than I have done. The printer (an Englishman) whom I employed here to print the second part of 'the Age of Reason' made a manuscript copy of the work while he was printing it, which he sent to London and sold. It was by this means that an edition of it came out in London.

"We are waiting here for news from America of the state of the federal elections. You will have heard long before this reaches you that the French government has refused to receive Mr. Pinckney as minister. While Mr. Monroe was minister he had the opportunity of softening matters with this government, for he was in good credit with them tho' they were in high indignation at the infidelity of the Washington Administration. It is time that Mr. Washington retire, for he has played off so much prudent hypocrisy between France and England that neither government believes anything he says.

"Your friend, etc.,

"THOMAS PAINE."

It would appear that Symonds' stolen edition must have got ahead of that sent by Paine to Franklin Bache, for some of its errors continue in all modern American editions to the present day, as well as in those of England. For in England it was only the shilling edition—that revised by Paine—which was suppressed. Symonds, who ministered to the half-crown folk, and who was also publisher of replies to Paine, was left undisturbed about his pirated edition, and the new Society for the suppression of Vice and Immorality fastened on one Thomas Williams, who sold pious tracts but was also convicted (June 24, 1797) of having sold one copy of the "Age of Reason." Erskine, who had defended Paine at his trial for the "Rights of Man," conducted the prosecution of Williams. He gained the victory from a packed jury, but was not much elated by it, especially after a certain adventure on his way to Lincoln's Inn. He felt his coat clutched and beheld at his feet a woman bathed in tears. She led him into the small book-shop of Thomas Williams, not yet called up for judgment, and there he beheld his victim stitching tracts in a wretched little room, where there were three children, two suffering with Smallpox. He saw that it would be ruin and even a sort of murder to take away to prison the husband, who was not a freethinker, and lamented his publication of the book, and a meeting of the Society which had retained him was summoned. There was a full meeting, the Bishop of London (Porteus) in the chair. Erskine reminded them that Williams was yet to be brought up for sentence, described the scene he had witnessed, and Williams' penitence, and, as the book was now suppressed, asked permission to move for a nominal sentence. Mercy, he urged, was a part of the Christianity they were defending. Not one of the Society took his side,—not even "philanthropic" Wilberforce—and Erskine threw up his brief. This action of Erskine led the Judge to give Williams only a year in prison instead of the three he said had been intended.

While Williams was in prison the orthodox colporteurs were circulating Erskine's speech on Christianity, but also an anonymous sermon "On the Existence and Attributes of the Deity," all of which was from Paine's "Age of Reason," except a brief "Address to the Deity" appended. This picturesque anomaly was repeated in the circulation of Paine's "Discourse to the Theophilanthropists" (their and the author's names removed) under the title of "Atheism Refuted." Both of these pamphlets are now before me, and beside them a London tract of one page just sent for my spiritual benefit. This is headed "A Word of Caution." It begins by mentioning the "pernicious doctrines of Paine," the first being "that there is No GOD" (sic,) then proceeds to adduce evidences of divine existence taken from Paine's works. It should be added that this one dingy page is the only "survival" of the ancient Paine effigy in the tract form which I have been able to find in recent years, and to this no Society or Publisher's name is attached.

The imprisonment of Williams was the beginning of a thirty years' war for religious liberty in England, in the course of which occurred many notable events, such as Eaton receiving homage in his pillory at Choring Cross, and the whole Carlile family imprisoned,—its head imprisoned more than nine years for publishing the "Age of Reason." This last victory of persecution was suicidal. Gentlemen of wealth, not adherents of Paine, helped in setting Carlile up in business in Fleet Street, where free-thinking publications have since been sold without interruption. But though Liberty triumphed in one sense, the "Age of Reason." remained to some extent suppressed among those whose attention it especially merited. Its original prosecution by a Society for the Suppression of Vice (a device to, relieve the Crown) amounted to a libel upon a morally clean book, restricting its perusal in families; and the fact that the shilling book sold by and among humble people was alone prosecuted, diffused among the educated an equally false notion that the "Age of Reason" was vulgar and illiterate. The theologians, as we have seen, estimated more justly the ability of their antagonist, the collaborator of Franklin, Rittenhouse, and Clymer, on whom the University of Pennsylvania had conferred the degree of Master of Arts,—but the gentry confused Paine with the class described by Burke as "the swinish multitude." Skepticism, or its free utterance, was temporarily driven out of polite circles by its complication with the out-lawed vindicator of the "Rights of Man." But that long combat has now passed away. Time has reduced the "Age of Reason" from a flag of popular radicalism to a comparatively conservative treatise, so far as its negations are concerned. An old friend tells me that in his youth he heard a sermon in which the preacher declared that "Tom Paine was so wicked that he could not be buried; his bones were thrown into a box which was bandied about the world till it came to a button-manufacturer; and now Paine is travelling round the world in the form of buttons!" This variant of the Wandering Jew myth may now be regarded as unconscious homage to the author whose metaphorical bones may be recognized in buttons now fashionable, and some even found useful in holding clerical vestments together.

But the careful reader will find in Paine's "Age of Reason" something beyond negations, and in conclusion I will especially call attention to the new departure in Theism indicated in a passage corresponding to a famous aphorism of Kant, indicated by a note in Part II. The discovery already mentioned, that Part I. was written at least fourteen years before Part II., led me to compare the two; and it is plain that while the earlier work is an amplification of Newtonian Deism, based on the phenomena of planetary motion, the work of 1795 bases belief in God on "the universal display of himself in the works of the creation and by that repugnance we feel in ourselves to bad actions, and disposition to do good ones." This exaltation of the moral nature of man to be the foundation of theistic religion, though now familiar, was a hundred years ago a new affirmation; it has led on a conception of deity subversive of last-century deism, it has steadily humanized religion, and its ultimate philosophical and ethical results have not yet been reached.

CHAPTER I - THE AUTHOR'S PROFESSION OF FAITH.

IT has been my intention, for several years past, to publish my thoughts upon religion; I am well aware of the difficulties that attend the subject, and from that consideration, had reserved it to a more advanced period of life. I intended it to be the last offering I should make to my fellow-citizens of all nations, and that at a time when the purity of the motive that induced me to it could not admit of a question, even by those who might disapprove the work.

The circumstance that has now taken place in France, of the total abolition of the whole national order of priesthood, and of everything appertaining to compulsive systems of religion, and compulsive articles of faith, has not only precipitated my intention, but rendered a work of this kind exceedingly necessary, lest, in the general wreck of superstition, of false systems of government, and false theology, we lose sight of morality, of humanity, and of the theology that is true.

As several of my colleagues, and others of my fellow-citizens of France, have given me the example of making their voluntary and individual profession of faith, I also will make mine; and I do this with all that sincerity and frankness with which the mind of man communicates with itself.

I believe in one God, and no more; and I hope for happiness beyond this life.

I believe the equality of man, and I believe that religious duties consist in doing justice, loving mercy, and endeavoring to make our fellow-creatures happy.

But, lest it should be supposed that I believe many other things in addition to these, I shall, in the progress of this work, declare the things I do not believe, and my reasons for not believing them.

I do not believe in the creed professed by the Jewish church, by the Roman church, by the Greek church, by the Turkish church, by the Protestant church, nor by any church that I know of. My own mind is my own church.

All national institutions of churches, whether Jewish, Christian, or Turkish, appear to me no other than human inventions set up to terrify and enslave mankind, and monopolize power and profit.

I do not mean by this declaration to condemn those who believe otherwise; they have the same right to their belief as I have to mine. But it is necessary to the happiness of man, that he be mentally faithful to himself. Infidelity does not consist in believing, or in disbelieving; it consists in professing to believe what he does not believe.

It is impossible to calculate the moral mischief, if I may so express it, that mental lying has produced in society. When a man has so far corrupted and prostituted the chastity of his mind, as to subscribe his professional belief to things he does not believe, he has prepared himself for the commission of every other crime. He takes up the trade of a priest for the sake of gain, and, in order to qualify himself for that trade, he begins with a perjury. Can we conceive anything more destructive to morality than this?

Soon after I had published the pamphlet COMMON SENSE, in America, I saw the exceeding probability that a revolution in the system of government would be followed by a revolution in the system of religion. The adulterous connection of church and state, wherever it had taken place, whether Jewish, Christian, or Turkish, had so effectually prohibited, by pains and penalties, every discussion upon established creeds, and upon first principles of religion, that until the system of government should be changed, those subjects could not be brought fairly and openly before the world; but that whenever this should be done, a revolution in the system of religion would follow. Human inventions and priest-craft would be detected; and man would return to the pure, unmixed, and unadulterated belief of one God, and no more.

CHAPTER II - OF MISSIONS AND REVELATIONS.

EVERY national church or religion has established itself by pretending some special mission from God, communicated to certain individuals. The Jews have their Moses; the Christians their Jesus Christ, their apostles and saints; and the Turks their Mahomet; as if the way to God was not open to every man alike.

Each of those churches shows certain books, which they call revelation, or the Word of God. The Jews say that their Word of God was given by God to Moses face to face; the Christians say, that their Word of God came by divine inspiration; and the Turks say, that their Word of God (the Koran) was brought by an angel from heaven. Each of those churches accuses the other of unbelief; and, for my own part, I disbelieve them all.

As it is necessary to affix right ideas to words, I will, before I proceed further into the subject, offer some observations on the word 'revelation.' Revelation when applied to religion, means something communicated immediately from God to man.

No one will deny or dispute the power of the Almighty to make such a communication if he pleases. But admitting, for the sake of a case, that something has been revealed to a certain person, and not revealed to any other person, it is revelation to that person only. When he tells it to a second person, a second to a third, a third to a fourth, and so on, it ceases to be a revelation to all those persons. It is revelation to the first person only, and hearsay to every other, and, consequently, they are not obliged to believe it.

It is a contradiction in terms and ideas to call anything a revelation that comes to us at second hand, either verbally or in writing. Revelation is necessarily limited to the first communication. After this, it is only an account of something which that person says was a revelation made to him; and though he may find himself obliged to believe it, it cannot be incumbent on me to believe it in the same manner, for it was not a revelation made to me, and I have only his word for it that it was made to him.

When Moses told the children of Israel that he received the two tables of the commandments from the hand of God, they were not obliged to believe him, because they had no other authority for it than his telling them so; and I have no other authority for it than some historian telling me so, the commandments carrying no internal evidence of divinity with them. They contain some good moral precepts such as any man qualified to be a lawgiver or a legislator could produce himself, without having recourse to supernatural intervention. [NOTE: It is, however, necessary to except the declamation which says that God 'visits the sins of the fathers upon the children'. This is contrary to every principle of moral justice.—Author.]

When I am told that the Koran was written in Heaven, and brought to Mahomet by an angel, the account comes to near the same kind of hearsay evidence and second hand authority as the former. I did not see the angel myself, and therefore I have a right not to believe it.

When also I am told that a woman, called the Virgin Mary, said, or gave out, that she was with child without any cohabitation with a man, and that her betrothed husband, Joseph, said that an angel told him so, I have a right to believe them or not: such a circumstance required a much stronger evidence than their bare word for it: but we have not even this; for neither Joseph nor Mary wrote any such matter themselves. It is only reported by others that they said so. It is hearsay upon hearsay, and I do not chose to rest my belief upon such evidence.

It is, however, not difficult to account for the credit that was given to the story of Jesus Christ being the Son of God. He was born when the heathen mythology had still some fashion and repute in the world, and that mythology had prepared the people for the belief of such a story. Almost all the extraordinary men that lived under the heathen mythology were reputed to be the sons of some of their gods. It was not a new thing at that time to believe a man to have been celestially begotten; the intercourse of gods with women was then a matter of familiar opinion. Their Jupiter, according to their accounts, had cohabited with hundreds; the story therefore had nothing in it either new, wonderful, or obscene; it was conformable to the opinions that then prevailed among the people called Gentiles, or mythologists, and it was those people only that believed it. The Jews, who had kept strictly to the belief of one God, and no more, and who had always rejected the heathen mythology, never credited the story.

It is curious to observe how the theory of what is called the Christian Church, sprung out of the tail of the heathen mythology. A direct incorporation took place in the first instance, by making the reputed founder to be celestially begotten. The trinity of gods that then followed was no other than a reduction of the former plurality, which was about twenty or thirty thousand. The statue of Mary succeeded the statue of Diana of Ephesus. The deification of heroes changed into the canonization of saints. The Mythologists had gods for everything; the Christian Mythologists had saints for everything. The church became as crowded with the one, as the pantheon had been with the other; and Rome was the place of both. The Christian theory is little else than the idolatry of the ancient mythologists, accommodated to the purposes of power and revenue; and it yet remains to reason and philosophy to abolish the amphibious fraud.

CHAPTER III – CONCERNING THE CHARACTER OF JESUS CHRIST, AND HIS HISTORY.

NOTHING that is here said can apply, even with the most distant disrespect, to the real character of Jesus Christ. He was a virtuous and an amiable man. The morality that he preached and practiced was of the most benevolent kind; and though similar systems of morality had been preached by Confucius, and by some of the Greek philosophers, many years before, by the Quakers since, and by many good men in all ages, it has not been exceeded by any.

Jesus Christ wrote no account of himself, of his birth, parentage, or anything else. Not a line of what is called the New Testament is of his writing. The history of him is altogether the work of other people; and as to the account given of his resurrection and ascension, it was the necessary counterpart to the story of his birth. His historians, having brought him into the world in a supernatural manner, were obliged to take him out again in the same manner, or the first part of the story must have fallen to the ground.

The wretched contrivance with which this latter part is told, exceeds everything that went before it. The first part, that of the miraculous conception, was not a thing that admitted of publicity; and therefore the tellers of this part of the story had this advantage, that though they might not be credited, they could not be detected. They could not be expected to prove it, because it was not one of those things that admitted of proof, and it was impossible that the person of whom it was told could prove it himself.

But the resurrection of a dead person from the grave, and his ascension through the air, is a thing very different, as to the evidence it admits of, to the invisible conception of a child in the womb. The resurrection and ascension, supposing them to have taken place, admitted of public and ocular demonstration, like that of the ascension of a balloon, or the sun at noon day, to all Jerusalem at least. A thing which everybody is required to believe, requires that the proof and evidence of it should be equal to all, and universal; and as the public visibility of this last related act was the only evidence that could give sanction to the former part, the whole of it falls to the ground, because that evidence never was given. Instead of this, a small number of persons, not more than eight or nine, are introduced as proxies for the whole world, to say they saw it, and all the rest of the world are called upon to believe it. But it appears that Thomas did not believe the resurrection; and, as they say, would not believe without having ocular and manual demonstration himself. So neither will I; and the reason is equally as good for me, and for every other person, as for Thomas.

It is in vain to attempt to palliate or disguise this matter. The story, so far as relates to the supernatural part, has every mark of fraud and imposition stamped upon the face of it. Who were the authors of it is as impossible for us now to know, as it is for us to be assured that the books in which the account is related were written by the persons whose names they bear. The best surviving evidence we now have respecting this affair is the Jews. They are regularly descended from the people who lived in the time this resurrection and ascension is said to have happened, and they say 'it is not true.' It has long appeared to me a strange inconsistency to cite the Jews as a proof of the truth of the story. It is just the same as if a man were to say, I will prove the truth of what I have told you, by producing the people who say it is false.

That such a person as Jesus Christ existed, and that he was crucified, which was the mode of execution at that day, are historical relations strictly within the limits of probability. He preached most excellent morality, and the equality of man; but he preached also against the corruptions and avarice of the Jewish priests, and this brought upon him the hatred and vengeance of the whole order of priest-hood. The accusation which those priests brought against him was that of sedition and conspiracy against the Roman government, to which the Jews were then subject and tributary; and it is not improbable that the Roman government might have some secret apprehension of the effects of his doctrine as well as the Jewish priests; neither is it improbable that Jesus Christ had in contemplation the delivery of the Jewish nation from the bondage of the Romans. Between the two, however, this virtuous reformer and revolutionist lost his life. [NOTE: The French work has here: "However this may be, for one or the other of these suppositions this virtuous reformer, this revolutionist, too little imitated, too much forgotten, too much misunderstood, lost his life."—Editor. (Conway)]

CHAPTER IV - OF THE BASES OF CHRISTIANITY.

IT is upon this plain narrative of facts, together with another case I am going to mention, that the Christian mythologists, calling themselves the Christian Church, have erected their fable, which for absurdity and extravagance is not exceeded by anything that is to be found in the mythology of the ancients.

The ancient mythologists tell us that the race of Giants made war against Jupiter, and that one of them threw a hundred rocks against him at one throw; that Jupiter defeated him with thunder, and confined him afterwards under Mount Etna; and that every time the Giant turns himself, Mount Etna belches fire. It is here easy to see that the circumstance of the mountain, that of its being a volcano, suggested the idea of the fable; and that the fable is made to fit and wind itself up with that circumstance.

The Christian mythologists tell that their Satan made war against the Almighty, who defeated him, and confined him afterwards, not under a mountain, but in a pit. It is here easy to see that the first fable suggested the idea of the second; for the fable of Jupiter and the Giants was told many hundred years before that of Satan.

Thus far the ancient and the Christian mythologists differ very little from each other. But the latter have contrived to carry the matter much farther. They have contrived to connect the fabulous part of the story of Jesus Christ with the fable originating from Mount Etna; and, in order to make all the parts of the story tie together, they have taken to their aid the traditions of the Jews; for the Christian mythology is made up partly from the ancient mythology, and partly from the Jewish traditions.

The Christian mythologists, after having confined Satan in a pit, were obliged to let him out again to bring on the sequel of the fable. He is then introduced into the garden of Eden in the shape of a snake, or a serpent, and in that shape he enters into familiar conversation with Eve, who is no ways surprised to hear a snake talk; and the issue of this tete-a-tate is, that he persuades her to eat an apple, and the eating of that apple damns all mankind.

After giving Satan this triumph over the whole creation, one would have supposed that the church mythologists would have been kind enough to send him back again to the pit, or, if they had not done this, that they would have put a mountain upon him, (for they say that their faith can remove a mountain) or have put him under a mountain, as the former mythologists had done, to prevent his getting again among the women, and doing more mischief. But instead of this, they leave him at large, without even obliging him to give his parole. The secret of which is, that they could not do without him; and after being at the trouble of making him, they bribed him to stay. They promised him ALL the Jews, ALL the Turks by anticipation, nine-tenths of the world beside, and Mahomet into the bargain. After this, who can doubt the bountifulness of the Christian Mythology?

Having thus made an insurrection and a battle in heaven, in which none of the combatants could be either killed or wounded—put Satan into the pit—let him out again—given him a triumph over the whole creation—damned all mankind by the eating of an apple, there Christian mythologists bring the two ends of their fable together. They represent this virtuous and amiable man, Jesus Christ, to be at once both God and man, and also the Son of God, celestially begotten, on purpose to be sacrificed, because they say that Eve in her longing [NOTE: The French work has: "yielding to an unrestrained appetite."—Editor.] had eaten an apple.

CHAPTER V - EXAMINATION IN DETAIL OF THE PRECEDING BASES.

PUTTING aside everything that might excite laughter by its absurdity, or detestation by its profaneness, and confining ourselves merely to an examination of the parts, it is impossible to conceive a story more derogatory to the Almighty, more inconsistent with his wisdom, more contradictory to his power, than this story is.

In order to make for it a foundation to rise upon, the inventors were under the necessity of giving to the being whom they call Satan a power equally as great, if not greater, than they attribute to the Almighty. They have not only given him the power of liberating himself from the pit, after what they call his fall, but they have made that power increase afterwards to infinity. Before this fall they represent him only as an angel of limited existence, as they represent the rest. After his fall, he becomes, by their account, omnipresent. He exists everywhere, and at the same time. He occupies the whole immensity of space.

Not content with this deification of Satan, they represent him as defeating by stratagem, in the shape of an animal of the creation, all the power and wisdom of the Almighty. They represent him as having compelled the Almighty to the direct necessity either of surrendering the whole of the creation to the government and sovereignty of this Satan, or of capitulating for its redemption by coming down upon earth, and exhibiting himself upon a cross in the shape of a man.

Had the inventors of this story told it the contrary way, that is, had they represented the Almighty as compelling Satan to exhibit himself on a cross in the shape of a snake, as a punishment for his new transgression, the story would have been less absurd, less contradictory. But, instead of this they make the transgressor triumph, and the Almighty fall.

That many good men have believed this strange fable, and lived very good lives under that belief (for credulity is not a crime) is what I have no doubt of. In the first place, they were educated to believe it, and they would have believed anything else in the same manner. There are also many who have been so enthusiastically enraptured by what they conceived to be the infinite love of God to man, in making a sacrifice of himself, that the vehemence of the idea has forbidden and deterred them from examining into the absurdity and profaneness of the story. The more unnatural anything is, the more is it capable of becoming the object of dismal admiration. [NOTE: The French work has "blind and" preceding dismal.—Editor.]

CHAPTER VI - OF THE TRUE THEOLOGY.

BUT if objects for gratitude and admiration are our desire, do they not present themselves every hour to our eyes? Do we not see a fair creation prepared to receive us the instant we are born—a world furnished to our hands, that cost us nothing? Is it we that light up the sun; that pour down the rain; and fill the earth with abundance? Whether we sleep or wake, the vast machinery of the universe still goes on. Are these things, and the blessings they indicate in future, nothing to, us? Can our gross feelings be excited by no other subjects than tragedy and suicide? Or is the gloomy pride of man become so intolerable, that nothing can flatter it but a sacrifice of the Creator?

I know that this bold investigation will alarm many, but it would be paying too great a compliment to their credulity to forbear it on that account. The times and the subject demand it to be done. The suspicion that the theory of what is called the Christian church is fabulous, is becoming very extensive in all countries; and it will be a consolation to men staggering under that suspicion, and doubting what to believe and what to disbelieve, to see the subject freely investigated. I therefore pass on to an examination of the books called the Old and the New Testament.

CHAPTER VII – EXAMINATION OF THE OLD TESTAMENT.

THESE books, beginning with Genesis and ending with Revelations, (which, by the bye, is a book of riddles that requires a revelation to explain it) are, we are told, the word of God. It is, therefore, proper for us to know who told us so, that we may know what credit to give to the report. The answer to this question is, that nobody can tell, except that we tell one another so. The case, however, historically appears to be as follows:

When the church mythologists established their system, they collected all the writings they could find, and managed them as they pleased. It is a matter altogether of uncertainty to us whether such of the writings as now appear under the name of the Old and the New Testament, are in the same state in which those collectors say they found them; or whether they added, altered, abridged, or dressed them up.

Be this as it may, they decided by vote which of the books out of the collection they had made, should be the WORD OF GOD, and which should not. They rejected several; they voted others to be doubtful, such as the books called the Apocrypha; and those books which had a majority of votes, were voted to be the word of God. Had they voted otherwise, all the people since calling themselves Christians had believed otherwise; for the belief of the one comes from the vote of the other. Who the people were that did all this, we know nothing of. They call themselves by the general name of the Church; and this is all we know of the matter.

As we have no other external evidence or authority for believing these books to be the word of God, than what I have mentioned, which is no evidence or authority at all, I come, in the next place, to examine the internal evidence contained in the books themselves.

In the former part of this essay, I have spoken of revelation. I now proceed further with that subject, for the purpose of applying it to the books in question.

Revelation is a communication of something, which the person, to whom that thing is revealed, did not know before. For if I have done a thing, or seen it done, it needs no revelation to tell me I have done it, or seen it, nor to enable me to tell it, or to write it.

Revelation, therefore, cannot be applied to anything done upon earth of which man is himself the actor or the witness; and consequently all the historical and anecdotal part of the Bible, which is almost the whole of it, is not within the meaning and compass of the word revelation, and, therefore, is not the word of God.

When Samson ran off with the gate-posts of Gaza, if he ever did so, (and whether he did or not is nothing to us,) or when he visited his Delilah, or caught his foxes, or did anything else, what has revelation to do with these things? If they were facts, he could tell them himself; or his secretary, if he kept one, could write them, if they were worth either telling or writing; and if they were fictions, revelation could not make them true; and whether true or not, we are neither the better nor the wiser for knowing them. When we contemplate the immensity of that Being, who directs and governs the incomprehensible WHOLE, of which the utmost ken of human sight can discover but a part, we ought to feel shame at calling such paltry stories the word of God.

As to the account of the creation, with which the book of Genesis opens, it has all the appearance of being a tradition which the Israelites had among them before they came into Egypt; and after their departure from that country, they put it at the head of their history, without telling, as it is most probable that they did not know, how they came by it. The manner in which the account opens, shows it to be traditionary. It begins abruptly. It is nobody that speaks. It is nobody that hears. It is addressed to nobody. It has neither first, second, nor third person. It has every criterion of being a tradition. It has no voucher. Moses does not take it upon himself by introducing it with the formality that he uses on other occasions, such as that of saying, "The Lords spake unto Moses, saying."

Why it has been called the Mosaic account of the creation, I am at a loss to conceive. Moses, I believe, was too good a judge of such subjects to put his name to that account. He had been educated among the Egyptians, who were a people as well skilled in science, and particularly in astronomy, as any people of their day; and the silence and caution that Moses observes, in not authenticating the account, is a good negative evidence that he neither told it nor believed it.—The case is, that every nation of people has been world-makers, and the Israelites had as much right to set up the trade of world-making as any of the rest; and as Moses was not an Israelite, he might not chose to contradict the tradition. The account, however, is harmless; and this is more than can be said for many other parts of the Bible.

Whenever we read the obscene stories, the voluptuous debaucheries, the cruel and torturous executions, the unrelenting vindictiveness, with which more than half the Bible [NOTE: It must be borne in mind that by the "Bible" Paine always means the Old Testament alone.—Editor.] is filled, it would be more consistent that we called it the word of a demon, than the Word of God. It is a history of wickedness, that has served to corrupt and brutalize mankind; and, for my own part, I sincerely detest it, as I detest everything that is cruel.

We scarcely meet with anything, a few phrases excepted, but what deserves either our abhorrence or our contempt, till we come to the miscellaneous parts of the Bible. In the anonymous publications, the Psalms, and the Book of Job, more particularly in the latter, we find a great deal of elevated sentiment reverentially expressed of the power and benignity of the Almighty; but they stand on no higher rank than many other compositions on similar subjects, as well before that time as since.

The Proverbs which are said to be Solomon's, though most probably a collection, (because they discover a knowledge of life, which his situation excluded him from knowing) are an instructive table of ethics. They are inferior in keenness to the proverbs of the Spaniards, and not more wise and oeconomical than those of the American Franklin.

All the remaining parts of the Bible, generally known by the name of the Prophets, are the works of the Jewish poets and itinerant preachers, who mixed poetry, anecdote, and devotion together—and those works still retain the air and style of poetry, though in translation. [NOTE: As there are many readers who do not see that a composition is poetry, unless it be in rhyme, it is for their information that I add this note.

Poetry consists principally in two things—imagery and composition. The composition of poetry differs from that of prose in the manner of mixing long and short syllables together. Take a long syllable out of a line of poetry, and put a short one in the room of it, or put a long syllable where a short one should be, and that line will lose its poetical harmony. It will have an effect upon the line like that of misplacing a note in a song.

The imagery in those books called the Prophets appertains altogether to poetry. It is fictitious, and often extravagant, and not admissible in any other kind of writing than poetry.

To show that these writings are composed in poetical numbers, I will take ten syllables, as they stand in the book, and make a line of the same number of syllables, (heroic measure) that shall rhyme with the last word. It will then be seen that the composition of those books is poetical measure. The instance I shall first produce is from Isaiah:—

> "Hear, O ye heavens, and give ear, O earth
> 'T is God himself that calls attention forth.

Another instance I shall quote is from the mournful Jeremiah, to which I shall add two other lines, for the purpose of carrying out the figure, and showing the intention of the poet.

> "O, that mine head were waters and mine eyes
> Were fountains flowing like the liquid skies;
> Then would I give the mighty flood release
> And weep a deluge for the human race."—Author.]

There is not, throughout the whole book called the Bible, any word that describes to us what we call a poet, nor any word that describes what we call poetry. The case is, that the word prophet, to which a later times have affixed a new idea, was the Bible word for poet, and the word 'propesying' meant the art of making poetry. It also meant the art of playing poetry to a tune upon any instrument of music.

We read of prophesying with pipes, tabrets, and horns—of prophesying with harps, with psalteries, with cymbals, and with every other instrument of music then in fashion. Were we now to speak of prophesying with a fiddle, or with a pipe and tabor, the expression would have no meaning, or would appear ridiculous, and to some people contemptuous, because we have changed the meaning of the word.

We are told of Saul being among the prophets, and also that he prophesied; but we are not told what they prophesied, nor what he prophesied. The case is, there was nothing to tell; for these prophets were a company of musicians and poets, and Saul joined in the concert, and this was called prophesying.

The account given of this affair in the book called Samuel, is, that Saul met a company of prophets; a whole company of them! coming down with a psaltery, a tabret, a pipe, and a harp, and that they prophesied, and that he prophesied with them. But it appears afterwards, that Saul prophesied badly, that is, he performed his part badly; for it is said that an "evil spirit from God [NOTE: As thos; men who call themselves divines and commentators are very fond of puzzling one another, I leave them to contest the meaning of the first part of the phrase, that of an evil spirit of God. I keep to my text. I keep to the meaning of the word prophesy.—Author.] came upon Saul, and he prophesied."

Now, were there no other passage in the book called the Bible, than this, to demonstrate to us that we have lost the original meaning of the word prophesy, and substituted another meaning in its place, this alone would be sufficient; for it is impossible to use and apply the word prophesy, in the place it is here used and applied, if we give to it the sense which later times have affixed to it. The manner in which it is here used strips it of all religious meaning, and shews that a man might then be a prophet, or he might Prophesy, as he may now be a poet or a musician, without any regard to the morality or the immorality of his character. The word was originally a term of science, promiscuously applied to poetry and to music, and not restricted to any subject upon which poetry and music might be exercised.

Deborah and Barak are called prophets, not because they predicted anything, but because they composed the poem or song that bears their name, in celebration of an act already done. David is ranked among the prophets, for he was a musician, and was also reputed to be (though perhaps very erroneously) the author of the Psalms. But Abraham, Isaac, and Jacob are not called prophets; it does not appear from any accounts we have, that they could either sing, play music, or make poetry.

We are told of the greater and the lesser prophets. They might as well tell us of the greater and the lesser God; for there cannot be degrees in prophesying consistently with its modern sense. But there are degrees in poetry, and there-fore the phrase is reconcilable to the case, when we understand by it the greater and the lesser poets.

It is altogether unnecessary, after this, to offer any observations upon what those men, styled prophets, have written. The axe goes at once to the root, by showing that the original meaning of the word has been mistaken, and consequently all the inferences that have been drawn from those books, the devotional respect that has been paid to them, and the laboured commentaries that have been written upon them, under that mistaken meaning, are not worth disputing about.—In many things, however, the writings of the Jewish poets deserve a better fate than that of being bound up, as they now are, with the trash that accompanies them, under the abused name of the Word of God.

If we permit ourselves to conceive right ideas of things, we must necessarily affix the idea, not only of unchangeableness, but of the utter impossibility of any change taking place, by any means or accident whatever, in that which we would honour with the name of the Word of God; and therefore the Word of God cannot exist in any written or human language.

The continually progressive change to which the meaning of words is subject, the want of an universal language which renders translation necessary, the errors to which translations are again subject, the mistakes of copyists and printers, together with the possibility of wilful alteration, are of themselves evidences that human language, whether in speech or in print, cannot be the vehicle of the Word of God.—The Word of God exists in something else.

Did the book called the Bible excel in purity of ideas and expression all the books now extant in the world, I would not take it for my rule of faith, as being the Word of God; because the possibility would nevertheless exist of my being imposed upon. But when I see throughout the greatest part of this book scarcely anything but a history of the grossest vices, and a collection of the most paltry and contemptible tales, I cannot dishonour my Creator by calling it by his name.

CHAPTER VIII - OF THE NEW TESTAMENT.

THUS much for the Bible; I now go on to the book called the New Testament. The new Testament! that is, the 'new' Will, as if there could be two wills of the Creator.

Had it been the object or the intention of Jesus Christ to establish a new religion, he would undoubtedly have written the system himself, or procured it to be written in his life time. But there is no publication extant authenticated with his name. All the books called the New Testament were written after his death. He was a Jew by birth and by profession; and he was the son of God in like manner that every other person is; for the Creator is the Father of All.

The first four books, called Matthew, Mark, Luke, and John, do not give a history of the life of Jesus Christ, but only detached anecdotes of him. It appears from these books, that the whole time of his being a preacher was not more than eighteen months; and it was only during this short time that those men became acquainted with him. They make mention of him at the age of twelve years, sitting, they say, among the Jewish doctors, asking and answering them questions. As this was several years before their acquaintance with him began, it is most probable they had this anecdote from his parents. From this time there is no account of him for about sixteen years. Where he lived, or how he employed himself during this interval, is not known. Most probably he was working at his father's trade, which was that of a carpenter. It does not appear that he had any school education, and the probability is, that he could not write, for his parents were extremely poor, as appears from their not being able to pay for a bed when he was born. [NOTE: One of the few errors traceable to Paine's not having a Bible at hand while writing Part I. There is no indication that the family was poor, but the reverse may in fact be inferred.—Editor.]

It is somewhat curious that the three persons whose names are the most universally recorded were of very obscure parentage. Moses was a foundling; Jesus Christ was born in a stable; and Mahomet was a mule driver. The first and the last of these men were founders of different systems of religion; but Jesus Christ founded no new system. He called men to the practice of moral virtues, and the belief of one God. The great trait in his character is philanthropy.

The manner in which he was apprehended shows that he was not much known, at that time; and it shows also that the meetings he then held with his followers were in secret; and that he had given over or suspended preaching publicly. Judas could no otherways betray him than by giving information where he was, and pointing him out to the officers that went to arrest him; and the reason for employing and paying Judas to do this could arise only from the causes already mentioned, that of his not being much known, and living concealed.

The idea of his concealment, not only agrees very ill with his reputed divinity, but associates with it something of pusillanimity; and his being betrayed, or in other words, his being apprehended, on the information of one of his followers, shows that he did not intend to be apprehended, and consequently that he did not intend to be crucified.

The Christian mythologists tell us that Christ died for the sins of the world, and that he came on Purpose to die. Would it not then have been the same if he had died of a fever or of the small pox, of old age, or of anything else?

The declaratory sentence which, they say, was passed upon Adam, in case he ate of the apple, was not, that thou shalt surely be crucified, but, thou shale surely die. The sentence was death, and not the manner of dying. Crucifixion, therefore, or any other particular manner of dying, made no part of the sentence that Adam was to suffer, and consequently, even upon their own tactic, it could make no part of the sentence that Christ was to suffer in the room of Adam. A fever would have done as well as a cross, if there was any occasion for either.

This sentence of death, which, they tell us, was thus passed upon Adam, must either have meant dying naturally, that is, ceasing to live, or have meant what these mythologists call damnation; and consequently, the act of dying on the part of Jesus Christ, must, according to their system, apply as a prevention to one or other of these two things happening to Adam and to us.

That it does not prevent our dying is evident, because we all die; and if their accounts of longevity be true, men die faster since the crucifixion than before: and with respect to the second explanation, (including with it the natural death of Jesus Christ as a substitute for the eternal death or damnation of all mankind,) it is impertinently representing the Creator as coming off, or revoking the sentence, by a pun or a quibble upon the word death. That manufacturer of, quibbles, St. Paul, if he wrote the books that bear his name, has helped this quibble on by making another quibble upon the word Adam. He makes there to be two Adams; the one who sins in fact, and suffers by proxy; the other who sins by proxy, and suffers in fact. A religion thus interlarded with quibble, subterfuge, and pun, has a tendency to instruct its professors in the practice of these arts. They acquire the habit without being aware of the cause.

If Jesus Christ was the being which those mythologists tell us he was, and that he came into this world to suffer, which is a word they sometimes use instead of 'to die,' the only real suffering he could have endured would have been 'to live.' His existence here was a state of exilement or transportation from heaven, and the way back to his original country was to die.—In fine, everything in this strange system is the reverse of what it pretends to be. It is the reverse of truth, and I become so tired of examining into its inconsistencies and absurdities, that I hasten to the conclusion of it, in order to proceed to something better.

How much, or what parts of the books called the New Testament, were written by the persons whose names they bear, is what we can know nothing of, neither are we certain in what language they were originally written. The matters they now contain may be classed under two heads: anecdote, and epistolary correspondence.

The four books already mentioned, Matthew, Mark, Luke, and John, are altogether anecdotal. They relate events after they had taken place. They tell what Jesus Christ did and said, and what others did and said to him; and in several instances they relate the same event differently. Revelation is necessarily out of the question with respect to those books; not only because of the disagreement of the writers, but because revelation cannot be applied to the relating of facts by the persons who saw them done, nor to the relating or recording of any discourse or conversation by those who heard it. The book called the Acts of the Apostles (an anonymous work) belongs also to the anecdotal part.

All the other parts of the New Testament, except the book of enigmas, called the Revelations, are a collection of letters under the name of epistles; and the forgery of letters has been such a common practice in the world, that the probability is at least equal, whether they are genuine or forged. One thing, however, is much less equivocal, which is, that out of the matters contained in those books, together with the assistance of some old stories, the church has set up a system of religion very contradictory to the character of the person whose name it bears. It has set up a religion of pomp and of revenue in pretended imitation of a person whose life was humility and poverty.

The invention of a purgatory, and of the releasing of souls therefrom, by prayers, bought of the church with money; the selling of pardons, dispensations, and indulgences, are revenue laws, without bearing that name or carrying that appearance. But the case nevertheless is, that those things derive their origin from the proxysm of the crucifixion, and the theory deduced therefrom, which was, that one person could stand in the place of another, and could perform meritorious services for him. The probability, therefore, is, that the whole theory or doctrine of what is called the redemption (which is said to have been accomplished by the act of one person in the room of another) was originally fabricated on purpose to bring forward and build all those secondary and pecuniary redemptions upon; and that the passages in the books upon which the idea of theory of redemption is built, have been manufactured and fabricated for that purpose. Why are we to give this church credit, when she tells us that those books are genuine in every part, any more than we give her credit for everything else she has told us; or for the miracles she says she has performed? That she could fabricate writings is certain, because she could write; and the composition of the writings in question, is of that kind that anybody might do it; and that she did fabricate them is not more inconsistent with probability, than that she should tell us, as she has done, that she could and did work miracles.

Since, then, no external evidence can, at this long distance of time, be produced to prove whether the church fabricated the doctrine called redemption or not, (for such evidence, whether for or against, would be subject to the same suspicion of being fabricated,) the case can only be referred to the internal evidence which the thing carries of itself; and this affords a very strong presumption of its being a fabrication. For the internal evidence is, that the theory or doctrine of redemption has for its basis an idea of pecuniary justice, and not that of moral justice.

If I owe a person money, and cannot pay him, and he threatens to put me in prison, another person can take the debt upon himself, and pay it for me. But if I have committed a crime, every circumstance of the case is changed. Moral justice cannot take the innocent for the guilty even if the innocent would offer itself. To suppose justice to do this, is to destroy the principle of its existence, which is the thing itself. It is then no longer justice. It is indiscriminate revenge.

This single reflection will show that the doctrine of redemption is founded on a mere pecuniary idea corresponding to that of a debt which another person might pay; and as this pecuniary idea corresponds again with the system of second redemptions, obtained through the means of money given to the church for pardons, the probability is that the same persons fabricated both the one and the other of those theories; and that, in truth, there is no such thing as redemption; that it is fabulous; and that man stands in the same relative condition with his Maker he ever did stand, since man existed; and that it is his greatest consolation to think so.

Let him believe this, and he will live more consistently and morally, than by any other system. It is by his being taught to contemplate himself as an out-law, as an out-cast, as a beggar, as a mumper, as one thrown as it were on a dunghill, at an immense distance from his Creator, and who must make his approaches by creeping, and cringing to intermediate beings, that he conceives either a contemptuous disregard for everything under the name of religion, or becomes indifferent, or turns what he calls devout. In the latter case, he consumes his life in grief, or the affectation of it. His prayers are reproaches. His humility is ingratitude. He calls himself a worm, and the fertile earth a dunghill; and all the blessings of life by the thankless name of vanities. He despises the choicest gift of God to man, the GIFT OF REASON; and having endeavoured to force upon himself the belief of a system against which reason revolts, he ungratefully calls it human reason, as if man could give reason to himself.

Yet, with all this strange appearance of humility, and this contempt for human reason, he ventures into the boldest presumptions. He finds fault with everything. His selfishness is never satisfied; his ingratitude is never at an end. He takes on himself to direct the Almighty what to do, even in the govemment of the universe. He prays dictatorially. When it is sunshine, he prays for rain, and when it is rain, he prays for sunshine. He follows the same idea in everything that he prays for; for what is the amount of all his prayers, but an attempt to make the Almighty change his mind, and act otherwise than he does? It is as if he were to say—thou knowest not so well as I.

CHAPTER IX - IN WHAT THE TRUE REVELATION CONSISTS.

BUT some perhaps will say—Are we to have no word of God—no revelation? I answer yes. There is a Word of God; there is a revelation.

THE WORD OF GOD IS THE CREATION WE BEHOLD: And it is in this word, which no human invention can counterfeit or alter, that God speaketh universally to man.

Human language is local and changeable, and is therefore incapable of being used as the means of unchangeable and universal information. The idea that God sent Jesus Christ to publish, as they say, the glad tidings to all nations, from one end of the earth unto the other, is consistent only with the ignorance of those who know nothing of the extent of the world, and who believed, as those world-saviours believed, and continued to believe for several centuries, (and that in contradiction to the discoveries of philosophers and the experience of navigators,) that the earth was flat like a trencher; and that a man might walk to the end of it.

But how was Jesus Christ to make anything known to all nations? He could speak but one language, which was Hebrew; and there are in the world several hundred languages. Scarcely any two nations speak the same language, or understand each other; and as to translations, every man who knows anything of languages, knows that it is impossible to translate from one language into another, not only without losing a great part of the original, but frequently of mistaking the sense; and besides all this, the art of printing was wholly unknown at the time Christ lived.

It is always necessary that the means that are to accomplish any end be equal to the accomplishment of that end, or the end cannot be accomplished. It is in this that the difference between finite and infinite power and wisdom discovers itself. Man frequently fails in accomplishing his end, from a natural inability of the power to the purpose; and frequently from the want of wisdom to apply power properly. But it is impossible for infinite power and wisdom to fail as man faileth. The means it useth are always equal to the end: but human language, more especially as there is not an universal language, is incapable of being used as an universal means of unchangeable and uniform information; and therefore it is not the means that God useth in manifesting himself universally to man.

It is only in the CREATION that all our ideas and conceptions of a word of God can unite. The Creation speaketh an universal language, independently of human speech or human language, multiplied and various as they be. It is an ever existing original, which every man can read. It cannot be forged; it cannot be counterfeited; it cannot be lost; it cannot be altered; it cannot be suppressed. It does not depend upon the will of man whether it shall be published or not; it publishes itself from one end of the earth to the other. It preaches to all nations and to all worlds; and this word of God reveals to man all that is necessary for man to know of God.

    Do we want to contemplate his power? We see it in the immensity of the creation. Do we want to contemplate his wisdom? We see it in the unchangeable order by which the incomprehensible Whole is governed. Do we want to contemplate his munificence? We see it in the abundance with which he fills the earth. Do we want to contemplate his mercy? We see it in his not withholding that abundance even from the unthankful. In fine, do we want to know what God is? Search not the book called the scripture, which any human hand might make, but the scripture called the Creation.

CHAPTER X - CONCERNING GOD, AND THE LIGHTS CAST ON HIS EXISTENCE AND ATTRIBUTES BY THE BIBLE.

THE only idea man can affix to the name of God, is that of a first cause, the cause of all things. And, incomprehensibly difficult as it is for a man to conceive what a first cause is, he arrives at the belief of it, from the tenfold greater difficulty of disbelieving it. It is difficult beyond description to conceive that space can have no end; but it is more difficult to conceive an end. It is difficult beyond the power of man to conceive an eternal duration of what we call time; but it is more impossible to conceive a time when there shall be no time.

In like manner of reasoning, everything we behold carries in itself the internal evidence that it did not make itself. Every man is an evidence to himself, that he did not make himself; neither could his father make himself, nor his grandfather, nor any of his race; neither could any tree, plant, or animal make itself; and it is the conviction arising from this evidence, that carries us on, as it were, by necessity, to the belief of a first cause eternally existing, of a nature totally different to any material existence we know of, and by the power of which all things exist; and this first cause, man calls God.

It is only by the exercise of reason, that man can discover God. Take away that reason, and he would be incapable of understanding anything; and in this case it would be just as consistent to read even the book called the Bible to a horse as to a man. How then is it that those people pretend to reject reason?

Almost the only parts in the book called the Bible, that convey to us any idea of God, are some chapters in Job, and the 19th Psalm; I recollect no other. Those parts are true deistical compositions; for they treat of the Deity through his works. They take the book of Creation as the word of God; they refer to no other book; and all the inferences they make are drawn from that volume.

I insert in this place the 19th Psalm, as paraphrased into English verse by Addison. I recollect not the prose, and where I write this I have not the opportunity of seeing it:

>The spacious firmament on high,
>With all the blue etherial sky,
>And spangled heavens, a shining frame,
>Their great original proclaim.
>The unwearied sun, from day to day,
>Does his Creator's power display,
>And publishes to every land
>The work of an Almighty hand.
>Soon as the evening shades prevail,
>The moon takes up the wondrous tale,
>And nightly to the list'ning earth
>Repeats the story of her birth;
>Whilst all the stars that round her burn,
>And all the planets, in their turn,
>Confirm the tidings as they roll,
>And spread the truth from pole to pole.
>What though in solemn silence all
>Move round this dark terrestrial ball
>What though no real voice, nor sound,
>Amidst their radiant orbs be found,
>In reason's ear they all rejoice,
>And utter forth a glorious voice,
>Forever singing as they shine,
>THE HAND THAT MADE US IS DIVINE.

What more does man want to know, than that the hand or power that made these things is divine, is omnipotent? Let him believe this, with the force it is impossible to repel if he permits his reason to act, and his rule of moral life will follow of course.

The allusions in Job have all of them the same tendency with this Psalm; that of deducing or proving a truth that would be otherwise unknown, from truths already known.

I recollect not enough of the passages in Job to insert them correctly; but there is one that occurs to me that is applicable to the subject I am speaking upon. "Canst thou by searching find out God; canst thou find out the Almighty to perfection?"

I know not how the printers have pointed this passage, for I keep no Bible; but it contains two distinct questions that admit of distinct answers.

First, Canst thou by searching find out God? Yes. Because, in the first place, I know I did not make myself, and yet I have existence; and by searching into the nature of other things, I find that no other thing could make itself; and yet millions of other things exist; therefore it is, that I know, by positive conclusion resulting from this search, that there is a power superior to all those things, and that power is God.

Secondly, Canst thou find out the Almighty to perfection? No. Not only because the power and wisdom He has manifested in the structure of the Creation that I behold is to me incomprehensible; but because even this manifestation, great as it is is probably but a small display of that immensity of power and wisdom, by which millions of other worlds, to me invisible by their distance, were created and continue to exist.

It is evident that both of these questions were put to the reason of the person to whom they are supposed to have been addressed; and it is only by admitting the first question to be answered affirmatively, that the second could follow. It would have been unnecessary, and even absurd, to have put a second question, more difficult than the first, if the first question had been answered negatively. The two questions have different objects; the first refers to the existence of God, the second to his attributes. Reason can discover the one, but it falls infinitely short in discovering the whole of the other.

I recollect not a single passage in all the writings ascribed to the men called apostles, that conveys any idea of what God is. Those writings are chiefly controversial; and the gloominess of the subject they dwell upon, that of a man dying in agony on a cross, is better suited to the gloomy genius of a monk in a cell, by whom it is not impossible they were written, than to any man breathing the open air of the Creation. The only passage that occurs to me, that has any reference to the works of God, by which only his power and wisdom can be known, is related to have been spoken by Jesus Christ, as a remedy against distrustful care. "Behold the lilies of the field, they toil not, neither do they spin." This, however, is far inferior to the allusions in Job and in the 19th Psalm; but it is similar in idea, and the modesty of the imagery is correspondent to the modesty of the man.

CHAPTER XI - OF THE THEOLOGY OF THE CHRISTIANS; AND THE TRUE THEOLOGY.

As to the Christian system of faith, it appears to me as a species of atheism; a sort of religious denial of God. It professes to believe in a man rather than in God. It is a compound made up chiefly of man-ism with but little deism, and is as near to atheism as twilight is to darkness. It introduces between man and his Maker an opaque body, which it calls a redeemer, as the moon introduces her opaque self between the earth and the sun, and it produces by this means a religious or an irreligious eclipse of light. It has put the whole orbit of reason into shade.

The effect of this obscurity has been that of turning everything upside down, and representing it in reverse; and among the revolutions it has thus magically produced, it has made a revolution in Theology.

That which is now called natural philosophy, embracing the whole circle of science, of which astronomy occupies the chief place, is the study of the works of God, and of the power and wisdom of God in his works, and is the true theology.

As to the theology that is now studied in its place, it is the study of human opinions and of human fancies concerning God. It is not the study of God himself in the works that he has made, but in the works or writings that man has made; and it is not among the least of the mischiefs that the Christian system has done to the world, that it has abandoned the original and beautiful system of theology, like a beautiful innocent, to distress and reproach, to make room for the hag of superstition.

The Book of Job and the 19th Psalm, which even the church admits to be more ancient than the chronological order in which they stand in the book called the Bible, are theological orations conformable to the original system of theology. The internal evidence of those orations proves to a demonstration that the study and contemplation of the works of creation, and of the power and wisdom of God revealed and manifested in those works, made a great part of the religious devotion of the times in which they were written; and it was this devotional study and contemplation that led to the discovery of the principles upon which what are now called Sciences are established; and it is to the discovery of these principles that almost all the Arts that contribute to the convenience of human life owe their existence. Every principal art has some science for its parent, though the person who mechanically performs the work does not always, and but very seldom, perceive the connection.

It is a fraud of the Christian system to call the sciences 'human inventions;' it is only the application of them that is human. Every science has for its basis a system of principles as fixed and unalterable as those by which the universe is regulated and governed. Man cannot make principles, he can only discover them.

For example: Every person who looks at an almanack sees an account when an eclipse will take place, and he sees also that it never fails to take place according to the account there given. This shows that man is acquainted with the laws by which the heavenly bodies move. But it would be something worse than ignorance, were any church on earth to say that those laws are an human invention.

It would also be ignorance, or something worse, to say that the scientific principles, by the aid of which man is enabled to calculate and foreknow when an eclipse will take place, are an human invention. Man cannot invent any thing that is eternal and immutable; and the scientific principles he employs for this purpose must, and are, of necessity, as eternal and immutable as the laws by which the heavenly bodies move, or they could not be used as they are to ascertain the time when, and the manner how, an eclipse will take place.

The scientific principles that man employs to obtain the foreknowledge of an eclipse, or of any thing else relating to the motion of the heavenly bodies, are contained chiefly in that part of science that is called trigonometry, or the properties of a triangle, which, when applied to the study of the heavenly bodies, is called astronomy; when applied to direct the course of a ship on the ocean, it is called navigation; when applied to the construction of figures drawn by a rule and compass, it is called geometry; when applied to the construction of plans of edifices, it is called architecture; when applied to the measurement of any portion of the surface of the earth, it is called land-surveying. In fine, it is the soul of science. It is an eternal truth: it contains the mathematical demonstration of which man speaks, and the extent of its uses are unknown.

It may be said, that man can make or draw a triangle, and therefore a triangle is an human invention.

But the triangle, when drawn, is no other than the image of the principle: it is a delineation to the eye, and from thence to the mind, of a principle that would otherwise be imperceptible. The triangle does not make the principle, any more than a candle taken into a room that was dark, makes the chairs and tables that before were invisible. All the properties of a triangle exist independently of the figure, and existed before any triangle was drawn or thought of by man. Man had no more to do in the formation of those properties or principles, than he had to do in making the laws by which the heavenly bodies move; and therefore the one must have the same divine origin as the other.

In the same manner as, it may be said, that man can make a triangle, so also, may it be said, he can make the mechanical instrument called a lever. But the principle by which the lever acts, is a thing distinct from the instrument, and would exist if the instrument did not; it attaches itself to the instrument after it is made; the instrument, therefore, can act no otherwise than it does act; neither can all the efforts of human invention make it act otherwise. That which, in all such cases, man calls the effect, is no other than the principle itself rendered perceptible to the senses.

Since, then, man cannot make principles, from whence did he gain a knowledge of them, so as to be able to apply them, not only to things on earth, but to ascertain the motion of bodies so immensely distant from him as all the heavenly bodies are? From whence, I ask, could he gain that knowledge, but from the study of the true theology?

It is the structure of the universe that has taught this knowledge to man. That structure is an ever-existing exhibition of every principle upon which every part of mathematical science is founded. The offspring of this science is mechanics; for mechanics is no other than the principles of science applied practically. The man who proportions the several parts of a mill uses the same scientific principles as if he had the power of constructing an universe, but as he cannot give to matter that invisible agency by which all the component parts of the immense machine of the universe have influence upon each other, and act in motional unison together, without any apparent contact, and to which man has given the name of attraction, gravitation, and repulsion, he supplies the place of that agency by the humble imitation of teeth and cogs. All the parts of man's microcosm must visibly touch. But could he gain a knowledge of that agency, so as to be able to apply it in practice, we might then say that another canonical book of the word of God had been discovered.

If man could alter the properties of the lever, so also could he alter the properties of the triangle: for a lever (taking that sort of lever which is called a steel-yard, for the sake of explanation) forms, when in motion, a triangle. The line it descends from, (one point of that line being in the fulcrum,) the line it descends to, and the chord of the arc, which the end of the lever describes in the air, are the three sides of a triangle. The other arm of the lever describes also a triangle; and the corresponding sides of those two triangles, calculated scientifically, or measured geometrically,—and also the sines, tangents, and secants generated from the angles, and geometrically measured,—have the same proportions to each other as the different weights have that will balance each other on the lever, leaving the weight of the lever out of the case.

It may also be said, that man can make a wheel and axis; that he can put wheels of different magnitudes together, and produce a mill. Still the case comes back to the same point, which is, that he did not make the principle that gives the wheels those powers. This principle is as unalterable as in the former cases, or rather it is the same principle under a different appearance to the eye.

The power that two wheels of different magnitudes have upon each other is in the same proportion as if the semi-diameter of the two wheels were joined together and made into that kind of lever I have described, suspended at the part where the semi-diameters join; for the two wheels, scientifically considered, are no other than the two circles generated by the motion of the compound lever.

It is from the study of the true theology that all our knowledge of science is derived; and it is from that knowledge that all the arts have originated.

The Almighty lecturer, by displaying the principles of science in the structure of the universe, has invited man to study and to imitation. It is as if he had said to the inhabitants of this globe that we call ours, "I have made an earth for man to dwell upon, and I have rendered the starry heavens visible, to teach him science and the arts. He can now provide for his own comfort, AND LEARN FROM MY MUNIFICENCE TO ALL, TO BE KIND TO EACH OTHER."

Of what use is it, unless it be to teach man something, that his eye is endowed with the power of beholding, to an incomprehensible distance, an immensity of worlds revolving in the ocean of space? Or of what use is it that this immensity of worlds is visible to man? What has man to do with the Pleiades, with Orion, with Sirius, with the star he calls the north star, with the moving orbs he has named Saturn, Jupiter, Mars, Venus, and Mercury, if no uses are to follow from their being visible? A less power of vision would have been sufficient for man, if the immensity he now possesses were given only to waste itself, as it were, on an immense desert of space glittering with shows.

It is only by contemplating what he calls the starry heavens, as the book and school of science, that he discovers any use in their being visible to him, or any advantage resulting from his immensity of vision. But when he contemplates the subject in this light, he sees an additional motive for saying, that nothing was made in vain; for in vain would be this power of vision if it taught man nothing.

CHAPTER XII - THE EFFECTS OF CHRISTIANISM ON EDUCATION; PROPOSED

REFORMS.

As the Christian system of faith has made a revolution in theology, so also has it made a revolution in the state of learning. That which is now called learning, was not learning originally. Learning does not consist, as the schools now make it consist, in the knowledge of languages, but in the knowledge of things to which language gives names.

The Greeks were a learned people, but learning with them did not consist in speaking Greek, any more than in a Roman's speaking Latin, or a Frenchman's speaking French, or an Englishman's speaking English. From what we know of the Greeks, it does not appear that they knew or studied any language but their own, and this was one cause of their becoming so learned; it afforded them more time to apply themselves to better studies. The schools of the Greeks were schools of science and philosophy, and not of languages; and it is in the knowledge of the things that science and philosophy teach that learning consists.

Almost all the scientific learning that now exists, came to us from the Greeks, or the people who spoke the Greek language. It therefore became necessary to the people of other nations, who spoke a different language, that some among them should learn the Greek language, in order that the learning the Greeks had might be made known in those nations, by translating the Greek books of science and philosophy into the mother tongue of each nation.

The study, therefore, of the Greek language (and in the same manner for the Latin) was no other than the drudgery business of a linguist; and the language thus obtained, was no other than the means, or as it were the tools, employed to obtain the learning the Greeks had. It made no part of the learning itself; and was so distinct from it as to make it exceedingly probable that the persons who had studied Greek sufficiently to translate those works, such for instance as Euclid's Elements, did not understand any of the learning the works contained.

As there is now nothing new to be learned from the dead languages, all the useful books being already translated, the languages are become useless, and the time expended in teaching and in learning them is wasted. So far as the study of languages may contribute to the progress and communication of knowledge (for it has nothing to do with the creation of knowledge) it is only in the living languages that new knowledge is to be found; and certain it is, that, in general, a youth will learn more of a living language in one year, than of a dead language in seven; and it is but seldom that the teacher knows much of it himself. The difficulty of learning the dead languages does not arise from any superior abstruseness in the languages themselves, but in their being dead, and the pronunciation entirely lost. It would be the same thing with any other language when it becomes dead. The best Greek linguist that now exists does not understand Greek so well as a Grecian plowman did, or a Grecian milkmaid; and the same for the Latin, compared with a plowman or a milkmaid of the Romans; and with respect to pronunciation and idiom, not so well as the cows that she milked. It would therefore be advantageous to the state of learning to abolish the study of the dead languages, and to make learning consist, as it originally did, in scientific knowledge.

The apology that is sometimes made for continuing to teach the dead languages is, that they are taught at a time when a child is not capable of exerting any other mental faculty than that of memory. But this is altogether erroneous. The human mind has a natural disposition to scientific knowledge, and to the things connected with it. The first and favourite amusement of a child, even before it begins to play, is that of imitating the works of man. It builds houses with cards or sticks; it navigates the little ocean of a bowl of water with a paper boat; or dams the stream of a gutter, and contrives something which it calls a mill; and it interests itself in the fate of its works with a care that resembles affection. It afterwards goes to school, where its genius is killed by the barren study of a dead language, and the philosopher is lost in the linguist.

But the apology that is now made for continuing to teach the dead languages, could not be the cause at first of cutting down learning to the narrow and humble sphere of linguistry; the cause therefore must be sought for elsewhere. In all researches of this kind, the best evidence that can be produced, is the internal evidence the thing carries with itself, and the evidence of circumstances that unites with it; both of which, in this case, are not difficult to be discovered.

Putting then aside, as matter of distinct consideration, the outrage offered to the moral justice of God, by supposing him to make the innocent suffer for the guilty, and also the loose morality and low contrivance of supposing him to change himself into the shape of a man, in order to make an excuse to himself for not executing his supposed sentence upon Adam; putting, I say, those things aside as matter of distinct consideration, it is certain that what is called the christian system of faith, including in it the whimsical account of the creation—the strange story of Eve, the snake, and the apple—the amphibious idea of a man-god—the corporeal idea of the death of a god—the mythological idea of a family of gods, and the christian system of arithmetic, that three are one, and one is three, are all irreconcilable, not only to the divine gift of reason, that God has given to man, but to the knowledge that man gains of the power and wisdom of God by the aid of the sciences, and by studying the structure of the universe that God has made.

The setters up, therefore, and the advocates of the Christian system of faith, could not but foresee that the continually progressive knowledge that man would gain by the aid of science, of the power and wisdom of God, manifested in the structure of the universe, and in all the works of creation, would militate against, and call into question, the truth of their system of faith; and therefore it became necessary to their purpose to cut learning down to a size less dangerous to their project, and this they effected by restricting the idea of learning to the dead study of dead languages.

They not only rejected the study of science out of the christian schools, but they persecuted it; and it is only within about the last two centuries that the study has been revived. So late as 1610, Galileo, a Florentine, discovered and introduced the use of telescopes, and by applying them to observe the motions and appearances of the heavenly bodies, afforded additional means for ascertaining the true structure of the universe. Instead of being esteemed for these discoveries, he was sentenced to renounce them, or the opinions resulting from them, as a damnable heresy. And prior to that time Virgilius was condemned to be burned for asserting the antipodes, or in other words, that the earth was a globe, and habitable in every part where there was land; yet the truth of this is now too well known even to be told. [NOTE: I cannot discover the source of this statement concerning the ancient author whose Irish name Feirghill was Latinized into Virgilius. The British Museum possesses a copy of the work (Decalogiunt) which was the pretext of the charge of heresy made by Boniface, Archbishop of Mayence, against Virgilius, Abbot—bishop of Salzburg, These were leaders of the rival "British" and "Roman parties, and the British champion made a countercharge against Boniface of irreligious practices." Boniface had to express a "regret," but none the less pursued his rival. The Pope, Zachary II., decided that if his alleged "doctrine, against God and his soul, that beneath the earth there is another world, other men, or sun and moon," should be acknowledged by Virgilius, he should be excommunicated by a Council and condemned with canonical sanctions. Whatever may have been the fate involved by condemnation with "canonicis sanctionibus," in the middle of the eighth century, it did not fall on Virgilius. His accuser, Boniface, was martyred, 755, and it is probable that Virgilius harmonied his Antipodes with orthodoxy. The gravamen of the heresy seems to have been the suggestion that there were men not of the progeny of Adam. Virgilius was made Bishop of Salzburg in 768. He bore until his death, 789, the curious title, "Geometer and Solitary," or "lone wayfarer" (Solivagus). A suspicion of heresy clung to his memory until 1233, when he was raised by Gregory IX, to sainthood beside his accuser, St. Boniface.—Editor. (Conway)]

If the belief of errors not morally bad did no mischief, it would make no part of the moral duty of man to oppose and remove them. There was no moral ill in believing the earth was flat like a trencher, any more than there was moral virtue in believing it was round like a globe; neither was there any moral ill in believing that the Creator made no other world than this, any more than there was moral virtue in believing that he made millions, and that the infinity of space is filled with worlds. But when a system of religion is made to grow out of a supposed system of creation that is not true, and to unite itself therewith in a manner almost inseparable therefrom, the case assumes an entirely different ground. It is then that errors, not morally bad, become fraught with the same mischiefs as if they were. It is then that the truth, though otherwise indifferent itself, becomes an essential, by becoming the criterion that either confirms by corresponding evidence, or denies by contradictory evidence, the reality of the religion itself. In this view of the case it is the moral duty of man to obtain every possible evidence that the structure of the heavens, or any other part of creation affords, with respect to systems of religion. But this, the supporters or partizans of the christian system, as if dreading the result, incessantly opposed, and not only rejected the sciences, but persecuted the professors. Had Newton or Descartes lived three or four hundred years ago, and pursued their studies as they did, it is most probable they would not have lived to finish them; and had Franklin drawn lightning from the clouds at the same time, it would have been at the hazard of expiring for it in flames.

Later times have laid all the blame upon the Goths and Vandals, but, however unwilling the partizans of the Christian system may be to believe or to acknowledge it, it is nevertheless true, that the age of ignorance commenced with the Christian system. There was more knowledge in the world before that period, than for many centuries afterwards; and as to religious knowledge, the Christian system, as already said, was only another species of mythology; and the mythology to which it succeeded, was a corruption of an ancient system of theism. [NOTE by Paine: It is impossible for us now to know at what time the heathen mythology began; but it is certain, from the internal evidence that it carries, that it did not begin in the same state or condition in which it ended. All the gods of that mythology, except Saturn, were of modern invention. The supposed reign of Saturn was prior to that which is called the heathen mythology, and was so far a species of theism that it admitted the belief of only one God. Saturn is supposed to have abdicated the government in favour of his three sons and one daughter, Jupiter, Pluto, Neptune, and Juno; after this, thousands of other gods and demigods were imaginarily created, and the calendar of gods increased as fast as the calendar of saints and the calendar of courts have increased since.

All the corruptions that have taken place, in theology and in religion have been produced by admitting of what man calls 'revealed religion.' The mythologists pretended to more revealed religion than the christians do. They had their oracles and their priests, who were supposed to receive and deliver the word of God verbally on almost all occasions.

Since then all corruptions down from Moloch to modern predestinarianism, and the human sacrifices of the heathens to the christian sacrifice of the Creator, have been produced by admitting of what is called revealed religion, the most effectual means to prevent all such evils and impositions is, not to admit of any other revelation than that which is manifested in the book of Creation., and to contemplate the Creation as the only true and real word of God that ever did or ever will exist; and every thing else called the word of God is fable and imposition.—Author.]

It is owing to this long interregnum of science, and to no other cause, that we have now to look back through a vast chasm of many hundred years to the respectable characters we call the Ancients. Had the progression of knowledge gone on proportionably with the stock that before existed, that chasm would have been filled up with characters rising superior in knowledge to each other; and those Ancients we now so much admire would have appeared respectably in the background of the scene. But the christian system laid all waste; and if we take our stand about the beginning of the sixteenth century, we look back through that long chasm, to the times of the Ancients, as over a vast sandy desert, in which not a shrub appears to intercept the vision to the fertile hills beyond.

It is an inconsistency scarcely possible to be credited, that any thing should exist, under the name of a religion, that held it to be irreligious to study and contemplate the structure of the universe that God had made. But the fact is too well established to be denied. The event that served more than any other to break the first link in this long chain of despotic ignorance, is that known by the name of the Reformation by Luther. From that time, though it does not appear to have made any part of the intention of Luther, or of those who are called Reformers, the Sciences began to revive, and Liberality, their natural associate, began to appear. This was the only public good the Reformation did; for, with respect to religious good, it might as well not have taken place. The mythology still continued the same; and a multiplicity of National Popes grew out of the downfall of the Pope of Christendom.

CHAPTER XIII - COMPARISON OF CHRISTIANISM WITH THE RELIGIOUS IDEAS

INSPIRED BY NATURE.

HAVING thus shewn, from the internal evidence of things, the cause that produced a change in the state of learning, and the motive for substituting the study of the dead languages, in the place of the Sciences, I proceed, in addition to the several observations already made in the former part of this work, to compare, or rather to confront, the evidence that the structure of the universe affords, with the christian system of religion. But as I cannot begin this part better than by referring to the ideas that occurred to me at an early part of life, and which I doubt not have occurred in some degree to almost every other person at one time or other, I shall state what those ideas were, and add thereto such other matter as shall arise out of the subject, giving to the whole, by way of preface, a short introduction.

My father being of the quaker profession, it was my good fortune to have an exceedingly good moral education, and a tolerable stock of useful learning. Though I went to the grammar school, I did not learn Latin, not only because I had no inclination to learn languages, but because of the objection the quakers have against the books in which the language is taught. But this did not prevent me from being acquainted with the subjects of all the Latin books used in the school.

The natural bent of my mind was to science. I had some turn, and I believe some talent for poetry; but this I rather repressed than encouraged, as leading too much into the field of imagination. As soon as I was able, I purchased a pair of globes, and attended the philosophical lectures of Martin and Ferguson, and became afterwards acquainted with Dr. Bevis, of the society called the Royal Society, then living in the Temple, and an excellent astronomer.

I had no disposition for what was called politics. It presented to my mind no other idea than is contained in the word jockeyship. When, therefore, I turned my thoughts towards matters of government, I had to form a system for myself, that accorded with the moral and philosophic principles in which I had been educated. I saw, or at least I thought I saw, a vast scene opening itself to the world in the affairs of America; and it appeared to me, that unless the Americans changed the plan they were then pursuing, with respect to the government of England, and declared themselves independent, they would not only involve themselves in a multiplicity of new difficulties, but shut out the prospect that was then offering itself to mankind through their means. It was from these motives that I published the work known by the name of Common Sense, which is the first work I ever did publish, and so far as I can judge of myself, I believe I should never have been known in the world as an author on any subject whatever, had it not been for the affairs of America. I wrote Common Sense the latter end of the year 1775, and published it the first of January, 1776. Independence was declared the fourth of July following. [NOTE: The pamphlet Common Sense was first advertised, as "just published," on January 10, 1776. His plea for the Officers of Excise, written before leaving England, was printed, but not published until 1793. Despite his reiterated assertion that Common Sense was the first work he ever published the notion that he was "junius" still finds some believers. An indirect comment on our Paine-Junians may be found in Part 2 of this work where Paine says a man capable of writing Homer "would not have thrown away his own fame by giving it to another." It is probable that Paine ascribed the Letters of Junius to Thomas Hollis. His friend F. Lanthenas, in his translation of the Age of Reason (1794) advertises his translation of the Letters of Junius from the English "(Thomas Hollis)." This he could hardly have done without consultation with Paine. Unfortunately this translation of Junius cannot be found either in the Bibliotheque Nationale or the British Museum, and it cannot be said whether it contains any attempt at an identification of Junius—Editor.]

Any person, who has made observations on the state and progress of the human mind, by observing his own, can not but have observed, that there are two distinct classes of what are called Thoughts; those that we produce in ourselves by reflection and the act of thinking, and those that bolt into the mind of their own accord. I have always made it a rule to treat those voluntary visitors with civility, taking care to examine, as well as I was able, if they were worth entertaining; and it is from them I have acquired almost all the knowledge that I have. As to the learning that any person gains from school education, it serves only, like a small capital, to put him in the way of beginning learning for himself afterwards. Every person of learning is finally his own teacher; the reason of which is, that principles, being of a distinct quality to circumstances, cannot be impressed upon the memory; their place of mental residence is the understanding, and they are never so lasting as when they begin by conception. Thus much for the introductory part.

From the time I was capable of conceiving an idea, and acting upon it by reflection, I either doubted the truth of the christian system, or thought it to be a strange affair; I scarcely knew which it was: but I well remember, when about seven or eight years of age, hearing a sermon read by a relation of mine, who was a great devotee of the church, upon the subject of what is called Redemption by the death of the Son of God. After the sermon was ended, I went into the garden, and as I was going down the garden steps (for I perfectly recollect the spot) I revolted at the recollection of what I had heard, and thought to myself that it was making God Almighty act like a passionate man, that killed his son, when he could not revenge himself any other way; and as I was sure a man would be hanged that did such a thing, I could not see for what purpose they preached such sermons. This was not one of those kind of thoughts that had any thing in it of childish levity; it was to me a serious reflection, arising from the idea I had that God was too good to do such an action, and also too almighty to be under any necessity of doing it. I believe in the same manner to this moment; and I moreover believe, that any system of religion that has anything in it that shocks the mind of a child, cannot be a true system.

It seems as if parents of the christian profession were ashamed to tell their children any thing about the principles of their religion. They sometimes instruct them in morals, and talk to them of the goodness of what they call Providence; for the Christian mythology has five deities: there is God the Father, God the Son, God the Holy Ghost, the God Providence, and the Goddess Nature. But the christian story of God the Father putting his son to death, or employing people to do it, (for that is the plain language of the story,) cannot be told by a parent to a child; and to tell him that it was done to make mankind happier and better, is making the story still worse; as if mankind could be improved by the example of murder; and to tell him that all this is a mystery, is only making an excuse for the incredibility of it.

How different is this to the pure and simple profession of Deism! The true deist has but one Deity; and his religion consists in contemplating the power, wisdom, and benignity of the Deity in his works, and in endeavouring to imitate him in every thing moral, scientifical, and mechanical.

The religion that approaches the nearest of all others to true Deism, in the moral and benign part thereof, is that professed by the quakers: but they have contracted themselves too much by leaving the works of God out of their system. Though I reverence their philanthropy, I can not help smiling at the conceit, that if the taste of a quaker could have been consulted at the creation, what a silent and drab-colored creation it would have been! Not a flower would have blossomed its gaieties, nor a bird been permitted to sing.

Quitting these reflections, I proceed to other matters. After I had made myself master of the use of the globes, and of the orrery, [NOTE by Paine: As this book may fall into the bands of persons who do not know what an orrery is, it is for their information I add this note, as the name gives no idea of the uses of the thing. The orrery has its name from the person who invented it. It is a machinery of clock-work, representing the universe in miniature: and in which the revolution of the earth round itself and round the sun, the revolution of the moon round the earth, the revolution of the planets round the sun, their relative distances from the sun, as the center of the whole system, their relative distances from each other, and their different magnitudes, are represented as they really exist in what we call the heavens.—Author.] and conceived an idea of the infinity of space, and of the eternal divisibility of matter, and obtained, at least, a general knowledge of what was called natural philosophy, I began to compare, or, as I have before said, to confront, the internal evidence those things afford with the christian system of faith.

Though it is not a direct article of the christian system that this world that we inhabit is the whole of the habitable creation, yet it is so worked up therewith, from what is called the Mosaic account of the creation, the story of Eve and the apple, and the counterpart of that story, the death of the Son of God, that to believe otherwise, that is, to believe that God created a plurality of worlds, at least as numerous as what we call stars, renders the christian system of faith at once little and ridiculous; and scatters it in the mind like feathers in the air. The two beliefs can not be held together in the same mind; and he who thinks that he believes both, has thought but little of either.

Though the belief of a plurality of worlds was familiar to the ancients, it is only within the last three centuries that the extent and dimensions of this globe that we inhabit have been ascertained. Several vessels, following the tract of the ocean, have sailed entirely round the world, as a man may march in a circle, and come round by the contrary side of the circle to the spot he set out from. The circular dimensions of our world, in the widest part, as a man would measure the widest round of an apple, or a ball, is only twenty-five thousand and twenty English miles, reckoning sixty-nine miles and an half to an equatorial degree, and may be sailed round in the space of about three years. [NOTE by Paine: Allowing a ship to sail, on an average, three miles in an hour, she would sail entirely round the world in less than one year, if she could sail in a direct circle, but she is obliged to follow the course of the ocean.—Author.]

A world of this extent may, at first thought, appear to us to be great; but if we compare it with the immensity of space in which it is suspended, like a bubble or a balloon in the air, it is infinitely less in proportion than the smallest grain of sand is to the size of the world, or the finest particle of dew to the whole ocean, and is therefore but small; and, as will be hereafter shown, is only one of a system of worlds, of which the universal creation is composed.

It is not difficult to gain some faint idea of the immensity of space in which this and all the other worlds are suspended, if we follow a progression of ideas. When we think of the size or dimensions of, a room, our ideas limit themselves to the walls, and there they stop. But when our eye, or our imagination darts into space, that is, when it looks upward into what we call the open air, we cannot conceive any walls or boundaries it can have; and if for the sake of resting our ideas we suppose a boundary, the question immediately renews itself, and asks, what is beyond that boundary? and in the same manner, what beyond the next boundary? and so on till the fatigued imagination returns and says, there is no end. Certainly, then, the Creator was not pent for room when he made this world no larger than it is; and we have to seek the reason in something else.

If we take a survey of our own world, or rather of this, of which the Creator has given us the use as our portion in the immense system of creation, we find every part of it, the earth, the waters, and the air that surround it, filled, and as it were crowded with life, down from the largest animals that we know of to the smallest insects the naked eye can behold, and from thence to others still smaller, and totally invisible without the assistance of the microscope. Every tree, every plant, every leaf, serves not only as an habitation, but as a world to some numerous race, till animal existence becomes so exceedingly refined, that the effluvia of a blade of grass would be food for thousands.

Since then no part of our earth is left unoccupied, why is it to be supposed that the immensity of space is a naked void, lying in eternal waste? There is room for millions of worlds as large or larger than ours, and each of them millions of miles apart from each other.

Having now arrived at this point, if we carry our ideas only one thought further, we shall see, perhaps, the true reason, at least a very good reason for our happiness, why the Creator, instead of making one immense world, extending over an immense quantity of space, has preferred dividing that quantity of matter into several distinct and separate worlds, which we call planets, of which our earth is one. But before I explain my ideas upon this subject, it is necessary (not for the sake of those that already know, but for those who do not) to show what the system of the universe is.

CHAPTER XIV - SYSTEM OF THE UNIVERSE.

THAT part of the universe that is called the solar system (meaning the system of worlds to which our earth belongs, and of which Sol, or in English language, the Sun, is the center) consists, besides the Sun, of six distinct orbs, or planets, or worlds, besides the secondary bodies, called the satellites, or moons, of which our earth has one that attends her in her annual revolution round the Sun, in like manner as the other satellites or moons, attend the planets or worlds to which they severally belong, as may be seen by the assistance of the telescope.

The Sun is the center round which those six worlds or planets revolve at different distances therefrom, and in circles concentric to each other. Each world keeps constantly in nearly the same tract round the Sun, and continues at the same time turning round itself, in nearly an upright position, as a top turns round itself when it is spinning on the ground, and leans a little sideways.

It is this leaning of the earth (23 1/2 degrees) that occasions summer and winter, and the different length of days and nights. If the earth turned round itself in a position perpendicular to the plane or level of the circle it moves in round the Sun, as a top turns round when it stands erect on the ground, the days and nights would be always of the same length, twelve hours day and twelve hours night, and the season would be uniformly the same throughout the year.

Every time that a planet (our earth for example) turns round itself, it makes what we call day and night; and every time it goes entirely round the Sun, it makes what we call a year, consequently our world turns three hundred and sixty-five times round itself, in going once round the Sun.

The names that the ancients gave to those six worlds, and which are still called by the same names, are Mercury, Venus, this world that we call ours, Mars, Jupiter, and Saturn. They appear larger to the eye than the stars, being many million miles nearer to our earth than any of the stars are. The planet Venus is that which is called the evening star, and sometimes the morning star, as she happens to set after, or rise before the Sun, which in either case is never more than three hours.

The Sun as before said being the center, the planet or world nearest the Sun is Mercury; his distance from the Sun is thirty-four million miles, and he moves round in a circle always at that distance from the Sun, as a top may be supposed to spin round in the tract in which a horse goes in a mill. The second world is Venus; she is fifty-seven million miles distant from the Sun, and consequently moves round in a circle much greater than that of Mercury. The third world is this that we inhabit, and which is eighty-eight million miles distant from the Sun, and consequently moves round in a circle greater than that of Venus. The fourth world is Mars; he is distant from the sun one hundred and thirty-four million miles, and consequently moves round in a circle greater than that of our earth. The fifth is Jupiter; he is distant from the Sun five hundred and fifty-seven million miles, and consequently moves round in a circle greater than that of Mars. The sixth world is Saturn; he is distant from the Sun seven hundred and sixty-three million miles, and consequently moves round in a circle that surrounds the circles or orbits of all the other worlds or planets.

The space, therefore, in the air, or in the immensity of space, that our solar system takes up for the several worlds to perform their revolutions in round the Sun, is of the extent in a strait line of the whole diameter of the orbit or circle in which Saturn moves round the Sun, which being double his distance from the Sun, is fifteen hundred and twenty-six million miles; and its circular extent is nearly five thousand million; and its globical content is almost three thousand five hundred million times three thousand five hundred million square miles. [NOTE by Paine: If it should be asked, how can man know these things? I have one plain answer to give, which is, that man knows how to calculate an eclipse, and also how to calculate to a minute of time when the planet Venus, in making her revolutions round the Sun, will come in a strait line between our earth and the Sun, and will appear to us about the size of a large pea passing across the face of the Sun. This happens but twice in about a hundred years, at the distance of about eight years from each other, and has happened twice in our time, both of which were foreknown by calculation. It can also be known when they will happen again for a thousand years to come, or to any other portion of time. As therefore, man could not be able to do these things if he did not understand the solar system, and the manner in which the revolutions of the several planets or worlds are performed, the fact of calculating an eclipse, or a transit of Venus, is a proof in point that the knowledge exists; and as to a few thousand, or even a few million miles, more or less, it makes scarcely any sensible difference in such immense distances.—Author.]

But this, immense as it is, is only one system of worlds. Beyond this, at a vast distance into space, far beyond all power of calculation, are the stars called the fixed stars. They are called fixed, because they have no revolutionary motion, as the six worlds or planets have that I have been describing. Those fixed stars continue always at the same distance from each other, and always in the same place, as the Sun does in the center of our system. The probability, therefore, is that each of those fixed stars is also a Sun, round which another system of worlds or planets, though too remote for us to discover, performs its revolutions, as our system of worlds does round our central Sun. By this easy progression of ideas, the immensity of space will appear to us to be filled with systems of worlds; and that no part of space lies at waste, any more than any part of our globe of earth and water is left unoccupied.

Having thus endeavoured to convey, in a familiar and easy manner, some idea of the structure of the universe, I return to explain what I before alluded to, namely, the great benefits arising to man in consequence of the Creator having made a Plurality of worlds, such as our system is, consisting of a central Sun and six worlds, besides satellites, in preference to that of creating one world only of a vast extent.

CHAPTER XV – ADVANTAGES OF THE EXISTENCE OF MANY WORLDS IN EACH SOLAR SYSTEM

IT is an idea I have never lost sight of, that all our knowledge of science is derived from the revolutions (exhibited to our eye and from thence to our understanding) which those several planets or worlds of which our system is composed make in their circuit round the Sun.

Had then the quantity of matter which these six worlds contain been blended into one solitary globe, the consequence to us would have been, that either no revolutionary motion would have existed, or not a sufficiency of it to give us the ideas and the knowledge of science we now have; and it is from the sciences that all the mechanical arts that contribute so much to our earthly felicity and comfort are derived.

As therefore the Creator made nothing in vain, so also must it be believed that he organized the structure of the universe in the most advantageous manner for the benefit of man; and as we see, and from experience feel, the benefits we derive from the structure of the universe, formed as it is, which benefits we should not have had the opportunity of enjoying if the structure, so far as relates to our system, had been a solitary globe, we can discover at least one reason why a plurality of worlds has been made, and that reason calls forth the devotional gratitude of man, as well as his admiration.

But it is not to us, the inhabitants of this globe, only, that the benefits arising from a plurality of worlds are limited. The inhabitants of each of the worlds of which our system is composed, enjoy the same opportunities of knowledge as we do. They behold the revolutionary motions of our earth, as we behold theirs. All the planets revolve in sight of each other; and, therefore, the same universal school of science presents itself to all.

Neither does the knowledge stop here. The system of worlds next to us exhibits, in its revolutions, the same principles and school of science, to the inhabitants of their system, as our system does to us, and in like manner throughout the immensity of space.

Our ideas, not only of the almightiness of the Creator, but of his wisdom and his beneficence, become enlarged in proportion as we contemplate the extent and the structure of the universe. The solitary idea of a solitary world, rolling or at rest in the immense ocean of space, gives place to the cheerful idea of a society of worlds, so happily contrived as to administer, even by their motion, instruction to man. We see our own earth filled with abundance; but we forget to consider how much of that abundance is owing to the scientific knowledge the vast machinery of the universe has unfolded.

CHAPTER XVI - APPLICATION OF THE PRECEDING TO THE SYSTEM OF THE

CHRISTIANS.

BUT, in the midst of those reflections, what are we to think of the christian system of faith that forms itself upon the idea of only one world, and that of no greater extent, as is before shown, than twenty-five thousand miles. An extent which a man, walking at the rate of three miles an hour for twelve hours in the day, could he keep on in a circular direction, would walk entirely round in less than two years. Alas! what is this to the mighty ocean of space, and the almighty power of the Creator!

From whence then could arise the solitary and strange conceit that the Almighty, who had millions of worlds equally dependent on his protection, should quit the care of all the rest, and come to die in our world, because, they say, one man and one woman had eaten an apple! And, on the other hand, are we to suppose that every world in the boundless creation had an Eve, an apple, a serpent, and a redeemer? In this case, the person who is irreverently called the Son of God, and sometimes God himself, would have nothing else to do than to travel from world to world, in an endless succession of death, with scarcely a momentary interval of life.

It has been by rejecting the evidence, that the word, or works of God in the creation, affords to our senses, and the action of our reason upon that evidence, that so many wild and whimsical systems of faith, and of religion, have been fabricated and set up. There may be many systems of religion that so far from being morally bad are in many respects morally good: but there can be but ONE that is true; and that one necessarily must, as it ever will, be in all things consistent with the ever existing word of God that we behold in his works. But such is the strange construction of the christian system of faith, that every evidence the heavens affords to man, either directly contradicts it or renders it absurd.

It is possible to believe, and I always feel pleasure in encouraging myself to believe it, that there have been men in the world who persuaded themselves that what is called a pious fraud, might, at least under particular circumstances, be productive of some good. But the fraud being once established, could not afterwards be explained; for it is with a pious fraud as with a bad action, it begets a calamitous necessity of going on.

The persons who first preached the christian system of faith, and in some measure combined with it the morality preached by Jesus Christ, might persuade themselves that it was better than the heathen mythology that then prevailed. From the first preachers the fraud went on to the second, and to the third, till the idea of its being a pious fraud became lost in the belief of its being true; and that belief became again encouraged by the interest of those who made a livelihood by preaching it.

But though such a belief might, by such means, be rendered almost general among the laity, it is next to impossible to account for the continual persecution carried on by the church, for several hundred years, against the sciences, and against the professors of science, if the church had not some record or tradition that it was originally no other than a pious fraud, or did not foresee that it could not be maintained against the evidence that the structure of the universe afforded.

CHAPTER XVII – OF THE MEANS EMPLOYED IN ALL TIME, AND ALMOST

UNIVERSALLY, TO DECEIVE THE PEOPLES.

HAVING thus shown the irreconcilable inconsistencies between the real word of God existing in the universe, and that which is called the word of God, as shown to us in a printed book that any man might make, I proceed to speak of the three principal means that have been employed in all ages, and perhaps in all countries, to impose upon mankind.

Those three means are Mystery, Miracle, and Prophecy, The first two are incompatible with true religion, and the third ought always to be suspected.

With respect to Mystery, everything we behold is, in one sense, a mystery to us. Our own existence is a mystery: the whole vegetable world is a mystery. We cannot account how it is that an acorn, when put into the ground, is made to develop itself and become an oak. We know not how it is that the seed we sow unfolds and multiplies itself, and returns to us such an abundant interest for so small a capital.

The fact however, as distinct from the operating cause, is not a mystery, because we see it; and we know also the means we are to use, which is no other than putting the seed in the ground. We know, therefore, as much as is necessary for us to know; and that part of the operation that we do not know, and which if we did, we could not perform, the Creator takes upon himself and performs it for us. We are, therefore, better off than if we had been let into the secret, and left to do it for ourselves.

But though every created thing is, in this sense, a mystery, the word mystery cannot be applied to moral truth, any more than obscurity can be applied to light. The God in whom we believe is a God of moral truth, and not a God of mystery or obscurity. Mystery is the antagonist of truth. It is a fog of human invention that obscures truth, and represents it in distortion. Truth never envelops itself in mystery; and the mystery in which it is at any time enveloped, is the work of its antagonist, and never of itself.

Religion, therefore, being the belief of a God, and the practice of moral truth, cannot have connection with mystery. The belief of a God, so far from having any thing of mystery in it, is of all beliefs the most easy, because it arises to us, as is before observed, out of necessity. And the practice of moral truth, or, in other words, a practical imitation of the moral goodness of God, is no other than our acting towards each other as he acts benignly towards all. We cannot serve God in the manner we serve those who cannot do without such service; and, therefore, the only idea we can have of serving God, is that of contributing to the happiness of the living creation that God has made. This cannot be done by retiring ourselves from the society of the world, and spending a recluse life in selfish devotion.

The very nature and design of religion, if I may so express it, prove even to demonstration that it must be free from every thing of mystery, and unincumbered with every thing that is mysterious. Religion, considered as a duty, is incumbent upon every living soul alike, and, therefore, must be on a level to the understanding and comprehension of all. Man does not learn religion as he learns the secrets and mysteries of a trade. He learns the theory of religion by reflection. It arises out of the action of his own mind upon the things which he sees, or upon what he may happen to hear or to read, and the practice joins itself thereto.

When men, whether from policy or pious fraud, set up systems of religion incompatible with the word or works of God in the creation, and not only above but repugnant to human comprehension, they were under the necessity of inventing or adopting a word that should serve as a bar to all questions, inquiries and speculations. The word mystery answered this purpose, and thus it has happened that religion, which is in itself without mystery, has been corrupted into a fog of mysteries.

As mystery answered all general purposes, miracle followed as an occasional auxiliary. The former served to bewilder the mind, the latter to puzzle the senses. The one was the lingo, the other the legerdemain.

But before going further into this subject, it will be proper to inquire what is to be understood by a miracle.

In the same sense that every thing may be said to be a mystery, so also may it be said that every thing is a miracle, and that no one thing is a greater miracle than another. The elephant, though larger, is not a greater miracle than a mite: nor a mountain a greater miracle than an atom. To an almighty power it is no more difficult to make the one than the other, and no more difficult to make a million of worlds than to make one. Every thing, therefore, is a miracle, in one sense; whilst, in the other sense, there is no such thing as a miracle. It is a miracle when compared to our power, and to our comprehension. It is not a miracle compared to the power that performs it. But as nothing in this description conveys the idea that is affixed to the word miracle, it is necessary to carry the inquiry further.

Mankind have conceived to themselves certain laws, by which what they call nature is supposed to act; and that a miracle is something contrary to the operation and effect of those laws. But unless we know the whole extent of those laws, and of what are commonly called the powers of nature, we are not able to judge whether any thing that may appear to us wonderful or miraculous, be within, or be beyond, or be contrary to, her natural power of acting.

The ascension of a man several miles high into the air, would have everything in it that constitutes the idea of a miracle, if it were not known that a species of air can be generated several times lighter than the common atmospheric air, and yet possess elasticity enough to prevent the balloon, in which that light air is inclosed, from being compressed into as many times less bulk, by the common air that surrounds it. In like manner, extracting flashes or sparks of fire from the human body, as visibly as from a steel struck with a flint, and causing iron or steel to move without any visible agent, would also give the idea of a miracle, if we were not acquainted with electricity and magnetism; so also would many other experiments in natural philosophy, to those who are not acquainted with the subject. The restoring persons to life who are to appearance dead as is practised upon drowned persons, would also be a miracle, if it were not known that animation is capable of being suspended without being extinct.

Besides these, there are performances by slight of hand, and by persons acting in concert, that have a miraculous appearance, which, when known, are thought nothing of. And, besides these, there are mechanical and optical deceptions. There is now an exhibition in Paris of ghosts or spectres, which, though it is not imposed upon the spectators as a fact, has an astonishing appearance. As, therefore, we know not the extent to which either nature or art can go, there is no criterion to determine what a miracle is; and mankind, in giving credit to appearances, under the idea of their being miracles, are subject to be continually imposed upon.

Since then appearances are so capable of deceiving, and things not real have a strong resemblance to things that are, nothing can be more inconsistent than to suppose that the Almighty would make use of means, such as are called miracles, that would subject the person who performed them to the suspicion of being an impostor, and the person who related them to be suspected of lying, and the doctrine intended to be supported thereby to be suspected as a fabulous invention.

Of all the modes of evidence that ever were invented to obtain belief to any system or opinion to which the name of religion has been given, that of miracle, however successful the imposition may have been, is the most inconsistent. For, in the first place, whenever recourse is had to show, for the purpose of procuring that belief (for a miracle, under any idea of the word, is a show) it implies a lameness or weakness in the doctrine that is preached. And, in the second place, it is degrading the Almighty into the character of a show-man, playing tricks to amuse and make the people stare and wonder. It is also the most equivocal sort of evidence that can be set up; for the belief is not to depend upon the thing called a miracle, but upon the credit of the reporter, who says that he saw it; and, therefore, the thing, were it true, would have no better chance of being believed than if it were a lie.

Suppose I were to say, that when I sat down to write this book, a hand presented itself in the air, took up the pen and wrote every word that is herein written; would any body believe me? Certainly they would not. Would they believe me a whit the more if the thing had been a fact? Certainly they would not. Since then a real miracle, were it to happen, would be subject to the same fate as the falsehood, the inconsistency becomes the greater of supposing the Almighty would make use of means that would not answer the purpose for which they were intended, even if they were real.

If we are to suppose a miracle to be something so entirely out of the course of what is called nature, that she must go out of that course to accomplish it, and we see an account given of such a miracle by the person who said he saw it, it raises a question in the mind very easily decided, which is,—Is it more probable that nature should go out of her course, or that a man should tell a lie? We have never seen, in our time, nature go out of her course; but we have good reason to believe that millions of lies have been told in the same time; it is, therefore, at least millions to one, that the reporter of a miracle tells a lie.

The story of the whale swallowing Jonah, though a whale is large enough to do it, borders greatly on the marvellous; but it would have approached nearer to the idea of a miracle, if Jonah had swallowed the whale. In this, which may serve for all cases of miracles, the matter would decide itself as before stated, namely, Is it more probable that a man should have, swallowed a whale, or told a lie?

But suppose that Jonah had really swallowed the whale, and gone with it in his belly to Nineveh, and to convince the people that it was true have cast it up in their sight, of the full length and size of a whale, would they not have believed him to have been the devil instead of a prophet? or if the whale had carried Jonah to Nineveh, and cast him up in the same public manner, would they not have believed the whale to have been the devil, and Jonah one of his imps?

The most extraordinary of all the things called miracles, related in the New Testament, is that of the devil flying away with Jesus Christ, and carrying him to the top of a high mountain; and to the top of the highest pinnacle of the temple, and showing him and promising to him all the kingdoms of the world. How happened it that he did not discover America? or is it only with kingdoms that his sooty highness has any interest.

I have too much respect for the moral character of Christ to believe that he told this whale of a miracle himself: neither is it easy to account for what purpose it could have been fabricated, unless it were to impose upon the connoisseurs of miracles, as is sometimes practised upon the connoisseurs of Queen Anne's farthings, and collectors of relics and antiquities; or to render the belief of miracles ridiculous, by outdoing miracle, as Don Quixote outdid chivalry; or to embarrass the belief of miracles, by making it doubtful by what power, whether of God or of the devil, any thing called a miracle was performed. It requires, however, a great deal of faith in the devil to believe this miracle.

In every point of view in which those things called miracles can be placed and considered, the reality of them is improbable, and their existence unnecessary. They would not, as before observed, answer any useful purpose, even if they were true; for it is more difficult to obtain belief to a miracle, than to a principle evidently moral, without any miracle. Moral principle speaks universally for itself. Miracle could be but a thing of the moment, and seen but by a few; after this it requires a transfer of faith from God to man to believe a miracle upon man's report. Instead, therefore, of admitting the recitals of miracles as evidence of any system of religion being true, they ought to be considered as symptoms of its being fabulous. It is necessary to the full and upright character of truth that it rejects the crutch; and it is consistent with the character of fable to seek the aid that truth rejects. Thus much for Mystery and Miracle.

As Mystery and Miracle took charge of the past and the present, Prophecy took charge of the future, and rounded the tenses of faith. It was not sufficient to know what had been done, but what would be done. The supposed prophet was the supposed historian of times to come; and if he happened, in shooting with a long bow of a thousand years, to strike within a thousand miles of a mark, the ingenuity of posterity could make it point-blank; and if he happened to be directly wrong, it was only to suppose, as in the case of Jonah and Nineveh, that God had repented himself and changed his mind. What a fool do fabulous systems make of man!

It has been shewn, in a former part of this work, that the original meaning of the words prophet and prophesying has been changed, and that a prophet, in the sense of the word as now used, is a creature of modern invention; and it is owing to this change in the meaning of the words, that the flights and metaphors of the Jewish poets, and phrases and expressions now rendered obscure by our not being acquainted with the local circumstances to which they applied at the time they were used, have been erected into prophecies, and made to bend to explanations at the will and whimsical conceits of sectaries, expounders, and commentators. Every thing unintelligible was prophetical, and every thing insignificant was typical. A blunder would have served for a prophecy; and a dish-clout for a type.

If by a prophet we are to suppose a man to whom the Almighty communicated some event that would take place in future, either there were such men, or there were not. If there were, it is consistent to believe that the event so communicated would be told in terms that could be understood, and not related in such a loose and obscure manner as to be out of the comprehension of those that heard it, and so equivocal as to fit almost any circumstance that might happen afterwards. It is conceiving very irreverently of the Almighty, to suppose he would deal in this jesting manner with mankind; yet all the things called prophecies in the book called the Bible come under this description.

But it is with Prophecy as it is with Miracle. It could not answer the purpose even if it were real. Those to whom a prophecy should be told could not tell whether the man prophesied or lied, or whether it had been revealed to him, or whether he conceited it; and if the thing that he prophesied, or pretended to prophesy, should happen, or some thing like it, among the multitude of things that are daily happening, nobody could again know whether he foreknew it, or guessed at it, or whether it was accidental. A prophet, therefore, is a character useless and unnecessary; and the safe side of the case is to guard against being imposed upon, by not giving credit to such relations.

Upon the whole, Mystery, Miracle, and Prophecy, are appendages that belong to fabulous and not to true religion. They are the means by which so many Lo heres! and Lo theres! have been spread about the world, and religion been made into a trade. The success of one impostor gave encouragement to another, and the quieting salvo of doing some good by keeping up a pious fraud protected them from remorse.

RECAPITULATION.

HAVING now extended the subject to a greater length than I first intended, I shall bring it to a close by abstracting a summary from the whole.

First, That the idea or belief of a word of God existing in print, or in writing, or in speech, is inconsistent in itself for the reasons already assigned. These reasons, among many others, are the want of an universal language; the mutability of language; the errors to which translations are subject, the possibility of totally suppressing such a word; the probability of altering it, or of fabricating the whole, and imposing it upon the world.

Secondly, That the Creation we behold is the real and ever existing word of God, in which we cannot be deceived. It proclaimeth his power, it demonstrates his wisdom, it manifests his goodness and beneficence.

Thirdly, That the moral duty of man consists in imitating the moral goodness and beneficence of God manifested in the creation towards all his creatures. That seeing as we daily do the goodness of God to all men, it is an example calling upon all men to practise the same towards each other; and, consequently, that every thing of persecution and revenge between man and man, and every thing of cruelty to animals, is a violation of moral duty.

I trouble not myself about the manner of future existence. I content myself with believing, even to positive conviction, that the power that gave me existence is able to continue it, in any form and manner he pleases, either with or without this body; and it appears more probable to me that I shall continue to exist hereafter than that I should have had existence, as I now have, before that existence began.

It is certain that, in one point, all nations of the earth and all religions agree. All believe in a God. The things in which they disgrace are the redundancies annexed to that belief; and therefore, if ever an universal religion should prevail, it will not be believing anything new, but in getting rid of redundancies, and believing as man believed at first. ["In the childhood of the world," according to the first (French) version; and the strict translation of the final sentence is: "Deism was the religion of Adam, supposing him not an imaginary being; but none the less must it be left to all men to follow, as is their right, the religion and worship they prefer."—Editor.] Adam, if ever there was such a man, was created a Deist; but in the mean time, let every man follow, as he has a right to do, the religion and worship he prefers.

END OF PART I

* * *

3.2 - THE AGE OF REASON - PART II

PREFACE

I HAVE mentioned in the former part of The Age of Reason that it had long been my intention to publish my thoughts upon Religion; but that I had originally reserved it to a later period in life, intending it to be the last work I should undertake. The circumstances, however, which existed in France in the latter end of the year 1793, determined me to delay it no longer. The just and humane principles of the Revolution which Philosophy had first diffused, had been departed from. The Idea, always dangerous to Society as it is derogatory to the Almighty,—that priests could forgive sins,—though it seemed to exist no longer, had blunted the feelings of humanity, and callously prepared men for the commission of all crimes. The intolerant spirit of church persecution had transferred itself into politics; the tribunals, stiled Revolutionary, supplied the place of an Inquisition; and the Guillotine of the Stake. I saw many of my most intimate friends destroyed; others daily carried to prison; and I had reason to believe, and had also intimations given me, that the same danger was approaching myself.

Under these disadvantages, I began the former part of the Age of Reason; I had, besides, neither Bible nor Testament [It must be borne in mind that throughout this work Paine generally means by "Bible" only the Old Testament, and speaks of the New as the "Testament."—Editor.] to refer to, though I was writing against both; nor could I procure any; notwithstanding which I have produced a work that no Bible Believer, though writing at his ease and with a Library of Church Books about him, can refute. Towards the latter end of December of that year, a motion was made and carried, to exclude foreigners from the Convention. There were but two, Anacharsis Cloots and myself; and I saw I was particularly pointed at by Bourdon de l'Oise, in his speech on that motion.

Conceiving, after this, that I had but a few days of liberty, I sat down and brought the work to a close as speedily as possible; and I had not finished it more than six hours, in the state it has since appeared, [This is an allusion to the essay which Paine wrote at an earlier part of 1793. See Introduction.—Editor.] before a guard came there, about three in the morning, with an order signed by the two Committees of Public Safety and Surety General, for putting me in arrestation as a foreigner, and conveying me to the prison of the Luxembourg. I contrived, in my way there, to call on Joel Barlow, and I put the Manuscript of the work into his hands, as more safe than in my possession in prison; and not knowing what might be the fate in France either of the writer or the work, I addressed it to the protection of the citizens of the United States.

It is justice that I say, that the guard who executed this order, and the interpreter to the Committee of General Surety, who accompanied them to examine my papers, treated me not only with civility, but with respect. The keeper of the 'Luxembourg, Benoit, a man of good heart, shewed to me every friendship in his power, as did also all his family, while he continued in that station. He was removed from it, put into arrestation, and carried before the tribunal upon a malignant accusation, but acquitted.

After I had been in Luxembourg about three weeks, the Americans then in Paris went in a body to the Convention to reclaim me as their countryman and friend; but were answered by the President, Vadier, who was also President of the Committee of Surety General, and had signed the order for my arrestation, that I was born in England. [These excited Americans do not seem to have understood or reported the most important item in Vadeer's reply, namely that their application was "unofficial," i.e. not made through or sanctioned by Gouverneur Morris, American Minister. For the detailed history of all this see vol. iii.—Editor.] I heard no more, after this, from any person out of the walls of the prison, till the fall of Robespierre, on the 9th of Thermidor—July 27, 1794.

About two months before this event, I was seized with a fever that in its progress had every symptom of becoming mortal, and from the effects of which I am not recovered. It was then that I remembered with renewed satisfaction, and congratulated myself most sincerely, on having written the former part of The Age of Reason. I had then but little expectation of surviving, and those about me had less. I know therefore by experience the conscientious trial of my own principles.

I was then with three chamber comrades: Joseph Vanheule of Bruges, Charles Bastfni, and Michael Robyns of Louvain. The unceasing and anxious attention of these three friends to me, by night and day, I remember with gratitude and mention with pleasure. It happened that a physician (Dr. Graham) and a surgeon, (Mr. Bond,) part of the suite of General O'Hara, [The officer who at Yorktown, Virginia, carried out the sword of Cornwallis for surrender, and satirically offered it to Rochambeau instead of Washington. Paine loaned him 300 pounds when he (O'Hara) left the prison, the money he had concealed in the lock of his cell-door.—Editor.] were then in the Luxembourg: I ask not myself whether it be convenient to them, as men under the English Government, that I express to them my thanks; but I should reproach myself if I did not; and also to the physician of the Luxembourg, Dr. Markoski.

I have some reason to believe, because I cannot discover any other, that this illness preserved me in existence. Among the papers of Robespierre that were examined and reported upon to the Convention by a Committee of Deputies, is a note in the hand writing of Robespierre, in the following words:

"Demander que Thomas Paine soit decrete d'accusation, pour l'interet de l'Amerique autant que de la France."

[Demand that Thomas Paine be decreed of accusation, for the interest of America, as well as of France.] From what cause it was that the intention was not put in execution, I know not, and cannot inform myself; and therefore I ascribe it to impossibility, on account of that illness.

The Convention, to repair as much as lay in their power the injustice I had sustained, invited me publickly and unanimously to return into the Convention, and which I accepted, to shew I could bear an injury without permitting it to injure my principles or my disposition. It is not because right principles have been violated, that they are to be abandoned.

I have seen, since I have been at liberty, several publications written, some in America, and some in England, as answers to the former part of "The Age of Reason." If the authors of these can amuse themselves by so doing, I shall not interrupt them, They may write against the work, and against me, as much as they please; they do me more service than they intend, and I can have no objection that they write on. They will find, however, by this Second Part, without its being written as an answer to them, that they must return to their work, and spin their cobweb over again. The first is brushed away by accident.

They will now find that I have furnished myself with a Bible and Testament; and I can say also that I have found them to be much worse books than I had conceived. If I have erred in any thing, in the former part of the Age of Reason, it has been by speaking better of some parts than they deserved.

I observe, that all my opponents resort, more or less, to what they call Scripture Evidence and Bible authority, to help them out. They are so little masters of the subject, as to confound a dispute about authenticity with a dispute about doctrines; I will, however, put them right, that if they should be disposed to write any more, they may know how to begin.

THOMAS PAINE. October, 1795.

CHAPTER I - THE OLD TESTAMENT

IT has often been said that any thing may be proved from the Bible; but before any thing can be admitted as proved by Bible, the Bible itself must be proved to be true; for if the Bible be not true, or the truth of it be doubtful, it ceases to have authority, and cannot be admitted as proof of any thing.

It has been the practice of all Christian commentators on the Bible, and of all Christian priests and preachers, to impose the Bible on the world as a mass of truth, and as the word of God; they have disputed and wrangled, and have anathematized each other about the supposeable meaning of particular parts and passages therein; one has said and insisted that such a passage meant such a thing, another that it meant directly the contrary, and a third, that it meant neither one nor the other, but something different from both; and this they have called understanding the Bible.

It has happened, that all the answers that I have seen to the former part of 'The Age of Reason' have been written by priests: and these pious men, like their predecessors, contend and wrangle, and understand the Bible; each understands it differently, but each understands it best; and they have agreed in nothing but in telling their readers that Thomas Paine understands it not.

Now instead of wasting their time, and heating themselves in fractious disputations about doctrinal points drawn from the Bible, these men ought to know, and if they do not it is civility to inform them, that the first thing to be understood is, whether there is sufficient authority for believing the Bible to be the word of God, or whether there is not?

There are matters in that book, said to be done by the express command of God, that are as shocking to humanity, and to every idea we have of moral justice, as any thing done by Robespierre, by Carrier, by Joseph le Bon, in France, by the English government in the East Indies, or by any other assassin in modern times. When we read in the books ascribed to Moses, Joshua, etc., that they (the Israelites) came by stealth upon whole nations of people, who, as the history itself shews, had given them no offence; that they put all those nations to the sword; that they spared neither age nor infancy; that they utterly destroyed men, women and children; that they left not a soul to breathe; expressions that are repeated over and over again in those books, and that too with exulting ferocity; are we sure these things are facts? are we sure that the Creator of man commissioned those things to be done? Are we sure that the books that tell us so were written by his authority?

It is not the antiquity of a tale that is an evidence of its truth; on the contrary, it is a symptom of its being fabulous; for the more ancient any history pretends to be, the more it has the resemblance of a fable. The origin of every nation is buried in fabulous tradition, and that of the Jews is as much to be suspected as any other.

To charger the commission of things upon the Almighty, which in their own nature, and by every rule of moral justice, are crimes, as all assassination is, and more especially the assassination of infants, is matter of serious concern. The Bible tells us, that those assassinations were done by the express command of God. To believe therefore the Bible to be true, we must unbelieve all our belief in the moral justice of God; for wherein could crying or smiling infants offend? And to read the Bible without horror, we must undo every thing that is tender, sympathising, and benevolent in the heart of man. Speaking for myself, if I had no other evidence that the Bible is fabulous, than the sacrifice I must make to believe it to be true, that alone would be sufficient to determine my choice.

But in addition to all the moral evidence against the Bible, I will, in the progress of this work, produce such other evidence as even a priest cannot deny; and show, from that evidence, that the Bible is not entitled to credit, as being the word of God.

But, before I proceed to this examination, I will show wherein the Bible differs from all other ancient writings with respect to the nature of the evidence necessary to establish its authenticity; and this is is the more proper to be done, because the advocates of the Bible, in their answers to the former part of 'The Age of Reason,' undertake to say, and they put some stress thereon, that the authenticity of the Bible is as well established as that of any other ancient book: as if our belief of the one could become any rule for our belief of the other.

I know, however, but of one ancient book that authoritatively challenges universal consent and belief, and that is Euclid's Elements of Geometry; [Euclid, according to chronological history, lived three hundred years before Christ, and about one hundred before Archimedes; he was of the city of Alexandria, in Egypt.—Author.] and the reason is, because it is a book of self-evident demonstration, entirely independent of its author, and of every thing relating to time, place, and circumstance. The matters contained in that book would have the same authority they now have, had they been written by any other person, or had the work been anonymous, or had the author never been known; for the identical certainty of who was the author makes no part of our belief of the matters contained in the book. But it is quite otherwise with respect to the books ascribed to Moses, to Joshua, to Samuel, etc.: those are books of testimony, and they testify of things naturally incredible; and therefore the whole of our belief, as to the authenticity of those books, rests, in the first place, upon the certainty that they were written by Moses, Joshua, and Samuel; secondly, upon the credit we give to their testimony. We may believe the first, that is, may believe the certainty of the authorship, and yet not the testimony; in the same manner that we may believe that a certain person gave evidence upon a case, and yet not believe the evidence that he gave. But if it should be found that the books ascribed to Moses, Joshua, and Samuel, were not written by Moses, Joshua, and Samuel, every part of the authority and authenticity of those books is gone at once; for there can be no such thing as forged or invented testimony; neither can there be anonymous testimony, more especially as to things naturally incredible; such as that of talking with God face to face, or that of the sun and moon standing still at the command of a man.

The greatest part of the other ancient books are works of genius; of which kind are those ascribed to Homer, to Plato, to Aristotle, to Demosthenes, to Cicero, etc. Here again the author is not an essential in the credit we give to any of those works; for as works of genius they would have the same merit they have now, were they anonymous. Nobody believes the Trojan story, as related by Homer, to be true; for it is the poet only that is admired, and the merit of the poet will remain, though the story be fabulous. But if we disbelieve the matters related by the Bible authors (Moses for instance) as we disbelieve the things related by Homer, there remains nothing of Moses in our estimation, but an imposter. As to the ancient historians, from Herodotus to Tacitus, we credit them as far as they relate things probable and credible, and no further: for if we do, we must believe the two miracles which Tacitus relates were performed by Vespasian, that of curing a lame man, and a blind man, in just the same manner as the same things are told of Jesus Christ by his historians. We must also believe the miracles cited by Josephus, that of the sea of Pamphilia opening to let Alexander and his army pass, as is related of the Red Sea in Exodus. These miracles are quite as well authenticated as the Bible miracles, and yet we do not believe them; consequently the degree of evidence necessary to establish our belief of things naturally incredible, whether in the Bible or elsewhere, is far greater than that which obtains our belief to natural and probable things; and therefore the advocates for the Bible have no claim to our belief of the Bible because that we believe things stated in other ancient writings; since that we believe the things stated in those writings no further than they are probable and credible, or because they are self-evident, like Euclid; or admire them because they are elegant, like Homer; or approve them because they are sedate, like Plato; or judicious, like Aristotle.

Having premised these things, I proceed to examine the authenticity of the Bible; and I begin with what are called the five books of Moses, Genesis, Exodus, Leviticus, Numbers, and Deuteronomy. My intention is to shew that those books are spurious, and that Moses is not the author of them; and still further, that they were not written in the time of Moses nor till several hundred years afterwards; that they are no other than an attempted history of the life of Moses, and of the times in which he is said to have lived, and also of the times prior thereto, written by some very ignorant and stupid pretenders to authorship, several hundred years after the death of Moses; as men now write histories of things that happened, or are supposed to have happened, several hundred or several thousand years ago.

The evidence that I shall produce in this case is from the books themselves; and I will confine myself to this evidence only. Were I to refer for proofs to any of the ancient authors, whom the advocates of the Bible call prophane authors, they would controvert that authority, as I controvert theirs: I will therefore meet them on their own ground, and oppose them with their own weapon, the Bible.

In the first place, there is no affirmative evidence that Moses is the author of those books; and that he is the author, is altogether an unfounded opinion, got abroad nobody knows how. The style and manner in which those books are written give no room to believe, or even to suppose, they were written by Moses; for it is altogether the style and manner of another person speaking of Moses. In Exodus, Leviticus and Numbers, (for every thing in Genesis is prior to the times of Moses and not the least allusion is made to him therein,) the whole, I say, of these books is in the third person; it is always, the Lord said unto Moses, or Moses said unto the Lord; or Moses said unto the people, or the people said unto Moses; and this is the style and manner that historians use in speaking of the person whose lives and actions they are writing. It may be said, that a man may speak of himself in the third person, and, therefore, it may be supposed that Moses did; but supposition proves nothing; and if the advocates for the belief that Moses wrote those books himself have nothing better to advance than supposition, they may as well be silent.

But granting the grammatical right, that Moses might speak of himself in the third person, because any man might speak of himself in that manner, it cannot be admitted as a fact in those books, that it is Moses who speaks, without rendering Moses truly ridiculous and absurd:—for example, Numbers xii. 3: "Now the man Moses was very MEEK, above all the men which were on the face of the earth." If Moses said this of himself, instead of being the meekest of men, he was one of the most vain and arrogant coxcombs; and the advocates for those books may now take which side they please, for both sides are against them: if Moses was not the author, the books are without authority; and if he was the author, the author is without credit, because to boast of meekness is the reverse of meekness, and is a lie in sentiment.

In Deuteronomy, the style and manner of writing marks more evidently than in the former books that Moses is not the writer. The manner here used is dramatical; the writer opens the subject by a short introductory discourse, and then introduces Moses as in the act of speaking, and when he has made Moses finish his harrangue, he (the writer) resumes his own part, and speaks till he brings Moses forward again, and at last closes the scene with an account of the death, funeral, and character of Moses.

This interchange of speakers occurs four times in this book: from the first verse of the first chapter, to the end of the fifth verse, it is the writer who speaks; he then introduces Moses as in the act of making his harrangue, and this continues to the end of the 40th verse of the fourth chapter; here the writer drops Moses, and speaks historically of what was done in consequence of what Moses, when living, is supposed to have said, and which the writer has dramatically rehearsed.

The writer opens the subject again in the first verse of the fifth chapter, though it is only by saying that Moses called the people of Israel together; he then introduces Moses as before, and continues him as in the act of speaking, to the end of the 26th chapter. He does the same thing at the beginning of the 27th chapter; and continues Moses as in the act of speaking, to the end of the 28th chapter. At the 29th chapter the writer speaks again through the whole of the first verse, and the first line of the second verse, where he introduces Moses for the last time, and continues him as in the act of speaking, to the end of the 33d chapter.

The writer having now finished the rehearsal on the part of Moses, comes forward, and speaks through the whole of the last chapter: he begins by telling the reader, that Moses went up to the top of Pisgah, that he saw from thence the land which (the writer says) had been promised to Abraham, Isaac, and Jacob; that he, Moses, died there in the land of Moab, that he buried him in a valley in the land of Moab, but that no man knoweth of his sepulchre unto this day, that is unto the time in which the writer lived who wrote the book of Deuteronomy. The writer then tells us, that Moses was one hundred and ten years of age when he died—that his eye was not dim, nor his natural force abated; and he concludes by saying, that there arose not a prophet since in Israel like unto Moses, whom, says this anonymous writer, the Lord knew face to face.

Having thus shewn, as far as grammatical evidence implies, that Moses was not the writer of those books, I will, after making a few observations on the inconsistencies of the writer of the book of Deuteronomy, proceed to shew, from the historical and chronological evidence contained in those books, that Moses was not, because he could not be, the writer of them; and consequently, that there is no authority for believing that the inhuman and horrid butcheries of men, women, and children, told of in those books, were done, as those books say they were, at the command of God. It is a duty incumbent on every true deist, that he vindicates the moral justice of God against the calumnies of the Bible.

The writer of the book of Deuteronomy, whoever he was, for it is an anonymous work, is obscure, and also contradictory with himself in the account he has given of Moses.

After telling that Moses went to the top of Pisgah (and it does not appear from any account that he ever came down again) he tells us, that Moses died there in the land of Moab, and that he buried him in a valley in the land of Moab; but as there is no antecedent to the pronoun he, there is no knowing who he was, that did bury him. If the writer meant that he (God) buried him, how should he (the writer) know it? or why should we (the readers) believe him? since we know not who the writer was that tells us so, for certainly Moses could not himself tell where he was buried.

The writer also tells us, that no man knoweth where the sepulchre of Moses is unto this day, meaning the time in which this writer lived; how then should he know that Moses was buried in a valley in the land of Moab? for as the writer lived long after the time of Moses, as is evident from his using the expression of unto this day, meaning a great length of time after the death of Moses, he certainly was not at his funeral; and on the other hand, it is impossible that Moses himself could say that no man knoweth where the sepulchre is unto this day. To make Moses the speaker, would be an improvement on the play of a child that hides himself and cries nobody can find me; nobody can find Moses.

This writer has no where told us how he came by the speeches which he has put into the mouth of Moses to speak, and therefore we have a right to conclude that he either composed them himself, or wrote them from oral tradition. One or other of these is the more probable, since he has given, in the fifth chapter, a table of commandments, in which that called the fourth commandment is different from the fourth commandment in the twentieth chapter of Exodus. In that of Exodus, the reason given for keeping the seventh day is, because (says the commandment) God made the heavens and the earth in six days, and rested on the seventh; but in that of Deuteronomy, the reason given is, that it was the day on which the children of Israel came out of Egypt, and therefore, says this commandment, the Lord thy God commanded thee to kee the sabbath-day This makes no mention of the creation, nor that of the coming out of Egypt. There are also many things given as laws of Moses in this book, that are not to be found in any of the other books; among which is that inhuman and brutal law, xxi. 18, 19, 20, 21, which authorizes parents, the father and the mother, to bring their own children to have them stoned to death for what it pleased them to call stubbornness.—But priests have always been fond of preaching up Deuteronomy, for Deuteronomy preaches up tythes; and it is from this book, xxv. 4, they have taken the phrase, and applied it to tything, that "thou shalt not muzzle the ox when he treadeth

Out the corn:" and that this might not escape observation, they have noted it in the table of contents at the head of the chapter, though it is only a single verse of less than two lines. O priests! priests! ye are willing to be compared to an ox, for the sake of tythes. [An elegant pocket edition of Paine's Theological Works (London. R. Carlile, 1822) has in its title a picture of Paine, as a Moses in evening dress, unfolding the two tables of his "Age of Reason" to a farmer from whom the Bishop of Llandaff (who replied to this work) has taken a sheaf and a lamb which he is carrying to a church at the summit of a well stocked hill.—Editor.]—Though it is impossible for us to know identically who the writer of Deuteronomy was, it is not difficult to discover him professionally, that he was some Jewish priest, who lived, as I shall shew in the course of this work, at least three hundred and fifty years after the time of Moses.

I come now to speak of the historical and chronological evidence. The chronology that I shall use is the Bible chronology; for I mean not to go out of the Bible for evidence of any thing, but to make the Bible itself prove historically and chronologically that Moses is not the author of the books ascribed to him. It is therefore proper that I inform the readers (such an one at least as may not have the opportunity of knowing it) that in the larger Bibles, and also in some smaller ones, there is a series of chronology printed in the margin of every page for the purpose of showing how long the historical matters stated in each page happened, or are supposed to have happened, before Christ, and consequently the distance of time between one historical circumstance and another.

I begin with the book of Genesis.—In Genesis xiv., the writer gives an account of Lot being taken prisoner in a battle between the four kings against five, and carried off; and that when the account of Lot being taken came to Abraham, that he armed all his household and marched to rescue Lot from the captors; and that he pursued them unto Dan. (ver. 14.)

To shew in what manner this expression of Pursuing them unto Dan applies to the case in question, I will refer to two circumstances, the one in America, the other in France. The city now called New York, in America, was originally New Amsterdam; and the town in France, lately called Havre Marat, was before called Havre-de-Grace. New Amsterdam was changed to New York in the year 1664; Havre-de-Grace to Havre Marat in the year 1793. Should, therefore, any writing be found, though without date, in which the name of New-York should be mentioned, it would be certain evidence that such a writing could not have been written before, and must have been written after New Amsterdam was changed to New York, and consequently not till after the year 1664, or at least during the course of that year. And in like manner, any dateless writing, with the name of Havre Marat, would be certain evidence that such a writing must have been written after Havre-de-Grace became Havre Marat, and consequently not till after the year 1793, or at least during the course of that year.

I now come to the application of those cases, and to show that there was no such place as Dan till many years after the death of Moses; and consequently, that Moses could not be the writer of the book of Genesis, where this account of pursuing them unto Dan is given.

The place that is called Dan in the Bible was originally a town of the Gentiles, called Laish; and when the tribe of Dan seized upon this town, they changed its name to Dan, in commemoration of Dan, who was the father of that tribe, and the great grandson of Abraham.

To establish this in proof, it is necessary to refer from Genesis to chapter xviii. of the book called the Book of judges. It is there said (ver. 27) that "they (the Danites) came unto Laish to a people that were quiet and secure, and they smote them with the edge of the sword [the Bible is filled with murder] and burned the city with fire; and they built a city, (ver. 28,) and dwelt therein, and [ver. 29,] they called the name of the city Dan, after the name of Dan, their father; howbeit the name of the city was Laish at the first."

This account of the Danites taking possession of Laish and changing it to Dan, is placed in the book of Judges immediately after the death of Samson. The death of Samson is said to have happened B.C. 1120 and that of Moses B.C. 1451; and, therefore, according to the historical arrangement, the place was not called Dan till 331 years after the death of Moses.

There is a striking confusion between the historical and the chronological arrangement in the book of judges. The last five chapters, as they stand in the book, 17, 18, 19, 20, 21, are put chronologically before all the preceding chapters; they are made to be 28 years before the 16th chapter, 266 before the 15th, 245 before the 13th, 195 before the 9th, 90 before the 4th, and 15 years before the 1st chapter. This shews the uncertain and fabulous state of the Bible. According to the chronological arrangement, the taking of Laish, and giving it the name of Dan, is made to be twenty years after the death of Joshua, who was the successor of Moses; and by the historical order, as it stands in the book, it is made to be 306 years after the death of Joshua, and 331 after that of Moses; but they both exclude Moses from being the writer of Genesis, because, according to either of the statements, no such a place as Dan existed in the time of Moses; and therefore the writer of Genesis must have been some person who lived after the town of Laish had the name of Dan; and who that person was nobody knows, and consequently the book of Genesis is anonymous, and without authority.

I come now to state another point of historical and chronological evidence, and to show therefrom, as in the preceding case, that Moses is not the author of the book of Genesis.

In Genesis xxxvi. there is given a genealogy of the sons and descendants of Esau, who are called Edomites, and also a list by name of the kings of Edom; in enumerating of which, it is said, verse 31, "And these are the kings that reigned in Edom, before there reigned any king over the children of Israel."

Now, were any dateless writing to be found, in which, speaking of any past events, the writer should say, these things happened before there was any Congress in America, or before there was any Convention in France, it would be evidence that such writing could not have been written before, and could only be written after there was a Congress in America or a Convention in France, as the case might be; and, consequently, that it could not be written by any person who died before there was a Congress in the one country, or a Convention in the other.

Nothing is more frequent, as well in history as in conversation, than to refer to a fact in the room of a date: it is most natural so to do, because a fact fixes itself in the memory better than a date; secondly, because the fact includes the date, and serves to give two ideas at once; and this manner of speaking by circumstances implies as positively that the fact alluded to is past, as if it was so expressed. When a person in speaking upon any matter, says, it was before I was married, or before my son was born, or before I went to America, or before I went to France, it is absolutely understood, and intended to be understood, that he has been married, that he has had a son, that he has been in America, or been in France. Language does not admit of using this mode of expression in any other sense; and whenever such an expression is found anywhere, it can only be understood in the sense in which only it could have been used.

The passage, therefore, that I have quoted—that "these are the kings that reigned in Edom, before there reigned any king over the children of Israel," could only have been written after the first king began to reign over them; and consequently that the book of Genesis, so far from having been written by Moses, could not have been written till the time of Saul at least. This is the positive sense of the passage; but the expression, any king, implies more kings than one, at least it implies two, and this will carry it to the time of David; and, if taken in a general sense, it carries itself through all times of the Jewish monarchy.

Had we met with this verse in any part of the Bible that professed to have been written after kings began to reign in Israel, it would have been impossible not to have seen the application of it. It happens then that this is the case; the two books of Chronicles, which give a history of all the kings of Israel, are professedly, as well as in fact, written after the Jewish monarchy began; and this verse that I have quoted, and all the remaining verses of Genesis xxxvi. are, word for word, In 1 Chronicles i., beginning at the 43d verse.

It was with consistency that the writer of the Chronicles could say as he has said, 1 Chron. i. 43, "These are the kings that reigned in Edom, before there reigned any king ever the children of Israel," because he was going to give, and has given, a list of the kings that had reigned in Israel; but as it is impossible that the same expression could have been used before that period, it is as certain as any thing can be proved from historical language, that this part of Genesis is taken from Chronicles, and that Genesis is not so old as Chronicles, and probably not so old as the book of Homer, or as AEsop's Fables; admitting Homer to have been, as the tables of chronology state, contemporary with David or Solomon, and AEsop to have lived about the end of the Jewish monarchy.

Take away from Genesis the belief that Moses was the author, on which only the strange belief that it is the word of God has stood, and there remains nothing of Genesis but an anonymous book of stories, fables, and traditionary or invented absurdities, or of downright lies. The story of Eve and the serpent, and of Noah and his ark, drops to a level with the Arabian Tales, without the merit of being entertaining, and the account of men living to eight and nine hundred years becomes as fabulous as the immortality of the giants of the Mythology.

Besides, the character of Moses, as stated in the Bible, is the most horrid that can be imagined. If those accounts be true, he was the wretch that first began and carried on wars on the score or on the pretence of religion; and under that mask, or that infatuation, committed the most unexampled atrocities that are to be found in the history of any nation. Of which I will state only one instance:

When the Jewish army returned from one of their plundering and murdering excursions, the account goes on as follows (Numbers xxxi. 13): "And Moses, and Eleazar the priest, and all the princes of the congregation, went forth to meet them without the camp; and Moses was wroth with the officers of the host, with the captains over thousands, and captains over hundreds, which came from the battle; and Moses said unto them, 'Have ye saved all the women alive?' behold, these caused the children of Israel, through the counsel of Balaam, to commit trespass against the Lord in the matter of Peor, and there was a plague among the congregation of the Lord. Now therefore, 'kill every male among the little ones, and kill every woman that hath known a man by lying with him; but all the women-children that have not known a man by lying with him, keep alive for Yourselves.'"

Among the detestable villains that in any period of the world have disgraced the name of man, it is impossible to find a greater than Moses, if this account be true. Here is an order to butcher the boys, to massacre the mothers, and debauch the daughters.

Let any mother put herself in the situation of those mothers, one child murdered, another destined to violation, and herself in the hands of an executioner: let any daughter put herself in the situation of those daughters, destined as a prey to the murderers of a mother and a brother, and what will be their feelings? It is in vain that we attempt to impose upon nature, for nature will have her course, and the religion that tortures all her social ties is a false religion.

After this detestable order, follows an account of the plunder taken, and the manner of dividing it; and here it is that the profaneings of priestly hypocrisy increases the catalogue of crimes. Verse 37, "And the Lord's tribute of the sheep was six hundred and threescore and fifteen; and the beeves were thirty and six thousand, of which the Lord's tribute was threescore and twelve; and the asses were thirty thousand, of which the Lord's tribute was threescore and one; and the persons were sixteen thousand, of which the Lord's tribute was thirty and two." In short, the matters contained in this chapter, as well as in many other parts of the Bible, are too horrid for humanity to read, or for decency to hear; for it appears, from the 35th verse of this chapter, that the number of women-children consigned to debauchery by the order of Moses was thirty-two thousand.

People in general know not what wickedness there is in this pretended word of God. Brought up in habits of superstition, they take it for granted that the Bible is true, and that it is good; they permit themselves not to doubt of it, and they carry the ideas they form of the benevolence of the Almighty to the book which they have been taught to believe was written by his authority. Good heavens! it is quite another thing, it is a book of lies, wickedness, and blasphemy; for what can be greater blasphemy, than to ascribe the wickedness of man to the orders of the Almighty!

But to return to my subject, that of showing that Moses is not the author of the books ascribed to him, and that the Bible is spurious. The two instances I have already given would be sufficient, without any additional evidence, to invalidate the authenticity of any book that pretended to be four or five hundred years more ancient than the matters it speaks of, refers to, them as facts; for in the case of pursuing them unto Dan, and of the kings that reigned over the children of Israel; not even the flimsy pretence of prophecy can be pleaded. The expressions are in the preter tense, and it would be downright idiotism to say that a man could prophecy in the preter tense.

But there are many other passages scattered throughout those books that unite in the same point of evidence. It is said in Exodus, (another of the books ascribed to Moses,) xvi. 35: "And the children of Israel did eat manna until they came to a land inhabited; they did eat manna until they came unto the borders of the land of Canaan."

Whether the children of Israel ate manna or not, or what manna was, or whether it was anything more than a kind of fungus or small mushroom, or other vegetable substance common to that part of the country, makes no part of my argument; all that I mean to show is, that it is not Moses that could write this account, because the account extends itself beyond the life time of Moses. Moses, according to the Bible, (but it is such a book of lies and contradictions there is no knowing which part to believe, or whether any) died in the wilderness, and never came upon the borders of 'the land of Canaan; and consequently, it could not be he that said what the children of Israel did, or what they ate when they came there. This account of eating manna, which they tell us was written by Moses, extends itself to the time of Joshua, the successor of Moses, as appears by the account given in the book of Joshua, after the children of Israel had passed the river Jordan, and came into the borders of the land of Canaan. Joshua, v. 12: "And the manna ceased on the morrow, after they had eaten of the old corn of the land; neither had the children of Israel manna any more, but they did eat of the fruit of the land of Canaan that year."

But a more remarkable instance than this occurs in Deuteronomy; which, while it shows that Moses could not be the writer of that book, shows also the fabulous notions that prevailed at that time about giants' In Deuteronomy iii. 11, among the conquests said to be made by Moses, is an account of the taking of Og, king of Bashan: "For only Og, king of Bashan, remained of the race of giants; behold, his bedstead was a bedstead of iron; is it not in Rabbath of the children of Ammon? nine cubits was the length thereof, and four cubits the breadth of it, after the cubit of a man." A cubit is 1 foot 9 888/1000 inches; the length therefore of the bed was 16 feet 4 inches, and the breadth 7 feet 4 inches: thus much for this giant's bed. Now for the historical part, which, though the evidence is not so direct and positive as in the former cases, is nevertheless very presumable and corroborating evidence, and is better than the best evidence on the contrary side.

The writer, by way of proving the existence of this giant, refers to his bed, as an ancient relick, and says, is it not in Rabbath (or Rabbah) of the children of Ammon? meaning that it is; for such is frequently the bible method of affirming a thing. But it could not be Moses that said this, because Moses could know nothing about Rabbah, nor of what was in it. Rabbah was not a city belonging to this giant king, nor was it one of the cities that Moses took. The knowledge therefore that this bed was at Rabbah, and of the particulars of its dimensions, must be referred to the time when Rabbah was taken, and this was not till four hundred years after the death of Moses; for which, see 2 Sam. xii. 26: "And Joab [David's general] fought against Rabbah of the children of Ammon, and took the royal city," etc.

As I am not undertaking to point out all the contradictions in time, place, and circumstance that abound in the books ascribed to Moses, and which prove to demonstration that those books could not be written by Moses, nor in the time of Moses, I proceed to the book of Joshua, and to shew that Joshua is not the author of that book, and that it is anonymous and without authority. The evidence I shall produce is contained in the book itself: I will not go out of the Bible for proof against the supposed authenticity of the Bible. False testimony is always good against itself.

Joshua, according to Joshua i., was the immediate successor of Moses; he was, moreover, a military man, which Moses was not; and he continued as chief of the people of Israel twenty-five years; that is, from the time that Moses died, which, according to the Bible chronology, was B.C. 1451, until B.C. 1426, when, according to the same chronology, Joshua died. If, therefore, we find in this book, said to have been written by Joshua, references to facts done after the death of Joshua, it is evidence that Joshua could not be the author; and also that the book could not have been written till after the time of the latest fact which it records. As to the character of the book, it is horrid; it is a military history of rapine and murder, as savage and brutal as those recorded of his predecessor in villainy and hypocrisy, Moses; and the blasphemy consists, as in the former books, in ascribing those deeds to the orders of the Almighty.

In the first place, the book of Joshua, as is the case in the preceding books, is written in the third person; it is the historian of Joshua that speaks, for it would have been absurd and vainglorious that Joshua should say of himself, as is said of him in the last verse of the sixth chapter, that "his fame was noised throughout all the country."—I now come more immediately to the proof.

In Joshua xxiv. 31, it is said "And Israel served the Lord all the days of Joshua, and all the days of the elders that over-lived Joshua." Now, in the name of common sense, can it be Joshua that relates what people had done after he was dead? This account must not only have been written by some historian that lived after Joshua, but that lived also after the elders that out-lived Joshua.

There are several passages of a general meaning with respect to time, scattered throughout the book of Joshua, that carries the time in which the book was written to a distance from the time of Joshua, but without marking by exclusion any particular time, as in the passage above quoted. In that passage, the time that intervened between the death of Joshua and the death of the elders is excluded descriptively and absolutely, and the evidence substantiates that the book could not have been written till after the death of the last.

But though the passages to which I allude, and which I am going to quote, do not designate any particular time by exclusion, they imply a time far more distant from the days of Joshua than is contained between the death of Joshua and the death of the elders. Such is the passage, x. 14, where, after giving an account that the sun stood still upon Gibeon, and the moon in the valley of Ajalon, at the command of Joshua, (a tale only fit to amuse children) [NOTE: This tale of the sun standing still upon Motint Gibeon, and the moon in the valley of Ajalon, is one of those fables that detects itself. Such a circumstance could not have happened without being known all over the world. One half would have wondered why the sun did not rise, and the other why it did not set; and the tradition of it would be universal; whereas there is not a nation in the world that knows anything about it. But why must the moon stand still? What occasion could there be for moonlight in the daytime, and that too whilst the sun shined? As a poetical figure, the whole is well enough; it is akin to that in the song of Deborah and Barak, The stars in their courses fought against Sisera; but it is inferior to the figurative declaration of Mahomet to the persons who came to expostulate with him on his goings on, Wert thou, said he, to come to me with the sun in thy right hand and the moon in thy left, it should not alter my career. For Joshua to have exceeded Mahomet, he should have put the sun and moon, one in each pocket, and carried them as Guy Faux carried his dark lanthorn, and taken them out to shine as he might happen to want them. The sublime and the ridiculous are often so nearly related that it is difficult to class them separately. One step above the sublime makes the ridiculous, and one step above the ridiculous makes the sublime again; the account, however, abstracted from the poetical fancy, shews the ignorance of Joshua, for he should have commanded the earth to have stood still.—Author.] the passage says: "And there was no day like that, before it, nor after it, that the Lord hearkened to the voice of a man."

The time implied by the expression after it, that is, after that day, being put in comparison with all the time that passed before it, must, in order to give any expressive signification to the passage, mean a great length of time:—for example, it would have been ridiculous to have said so the next day, or the next week, or the next month, or the next year; to give therefore meaning to the passage, comparative with the wonder it relates, and the prior time it alludes to, it must mean centuries of years; less however than one would be trifling, and less than two would be barely admissible.

A distant, but general time is also expressed in chapter viii.; where, after giving an account of the taking the city of Ai, it is said, ver. 28th, "And Joshua burned Ai, and made it an heap for ever, a desolation unto this day;" and again, ver. 29, where speaking of the king of Ai, whom Joshua had hanged, and buried at the entering of the gate, it is said, "And he raised thereon a great heap of stones, which remaineth unto this day," that is, unto the day or time in which the writer of the book of Joshua lived. And again, in chapter x. where, after speaking of the five kings whom Joshua had hanged on five trees, and then thrown in a cave, it is said, "And he laid great stones on the cave's mouth, which remain unto this very day."

In enumerating the several exploits of Joshua, and of the tribes, and of the places which they conquered or attempted, it is said, xv. 63, "As for the Jebusites, the inhabitants of Jerusalem, the children of Judah could not drive them out; but the Jebusites dwell with the children of Judah AT JERUSALEM unto this day." The question upon this passage is, At what time did the Jebusites and the children of Judah dwell together at Jerusalem? As this matter occurs again in judges i. I shall reserve my observations till I come to that part.

Having thus shewn from the book of Joshua itself, without any auxiliary evidence whatever, that Joshua is not the author of that book, and that it is anonymous, and consequently without authority, I proceed, as before-mentioned, to the book of Judges.

The book of Judges is anonymous on the face of it; and, therefore, even the pretence is wanting to call it the word of God; it has not so much as a nominal voucher; it is altogether fatherless.

This book begins with the same expression as the book of Joshua. That of Joshua begins, chap i. 1, Now after the death of Moses, etc., and this of the Judges begins, Now after the death of Joshua, etc. This, and the similarity of stile between the two books, indicate that they are the work of the same author; but who he was, is altogether unknown; the only point that the book proves is that the author lived long after the time of Joshua; for though it begins as if it followed immediately after his death, the second chapter is an epitome or abstract of the whole book, which, according to the Bible chronology, extends its history through a space of 306 years; that is, from the death of Joshua, B.C. 1426 to the death of Samson, B.C. 1120, and only 25 years before Saul went to seek his father's asses, and was made king. But there is good reason to believe, that it was not written till the time of David, at least, and that the book of Joshua was not written before the same time.

In Judges i., the writer, after announcing the death of Joshua, proceeds to tell what happened between the children of Judah and the native inhabitants of the land of Canaan. In this statement the writer, having abruptly mentioned Jerusalem in the 7th verse, says immediately after, in the 8th verse, by way of explanation, "Now the children of Judah had fought against Jerusalem, and taken it;" consequently this book could not have been written before Jerusalem had been taken. The reader will recollect the quotation I have just before made from Joshua xv. 63, where it said that the Jebusites dwell with the children of Judah at Jerusalem at this day; meaning the time when the book of Joshua was written.

The evidence I have already produced to prove that the books I have hitherto treated of were not written by the persons to whom they are ascribed, nor till many years after their death, if such persons ever lived, is already so abundant, that I can afford to admit this passage with less weight than I am entitled to draw from it. For the case is, that so far as the Bible can be credited as an history, the city of Jerusalem was not taken till the time of David; and consequently, that the book of Joshua, and of Judges, were not written till after the commencement of the reign of David, which was 370 years after the death of Joshua.

The name of the city that was afterward called Jerusalem was originally Jebus, or Jebusi, and was the capital of the Jebusites. The account of David's taking this city is given in 2 Samuel, v. 4, etc.; also in 1 Chron. xiv. 4, etc. There is no mention in any part of the Bible that it was ever taken before, nor any account that favours such an opinion. It is not said, either in Samuel or in Chronicles, that they "utterly destroyed men, women and children, that they left not a soul to breathe," as is said of their other conquests; and the silence here observed implies that it was taken by capitulation; and that the Jebusites, the native inhabitants, continued to live in the place after it was taken. The account therefore, given in Joshua, that "the Jebusites dwell with the children of Judah" at Jerusalem at this day, corresponds to no other time than after taking the city by David.

Having now shown that every book in the Bible, from Genesis to Judges, is without authenticity, I come to the book of Ruth, an idle, bungling story, foolishly told, nobody knows by whom, about a strolling country-girl creeping slily to bed to her cousin Boaz. [The text of Ruth does not imply the unpleasant sense Paine's words are likely to convey.—Editor.] Pretty stuff indeed to be called the word of God. It is, however, one of the best books in the Bible, for it is free from murder and rapine.

I come next to the two books of Samuel, and to shew that those books were not written by Samuel, nor till a great length of time after the death of Samuel; and that they are, like all the former books, anonymous, and without authority.

To be convinced that these books have been written much later than the time of Samuel, and consequently not by him, it is only necessary to read the account which the writer gives of Saul going to seek his father's asses, and of his interview with Samuel, of whom Saul went to enquire about those lost asses, as foolish people now-a-days go to a conjuror to enquire after lost things.

The writer, in relating this story of Saul, Samuel, and the asses, does not tell it as a thing that had just then happened, but as an ancient story in the time this writer lived; for he tells it in the language or terms used at the time that Samuel lived, which obliges the writer to explain the story in the terms or language used in the time the writer lived.

Samuel, in the account given of him in the first of those books, chap. ix. 13 called the seer; and it is by this term that Saul enquires after him, ver. 11, "And as they [Saul and his servant] went up the hill to the city, they found young maidens going out to draw water; and they said unto them, Is the seer here?" Saul then went according to the direction of these maidens, and met

Samuel without knowing him, and said unto him, ver. 18, "Tell me, I pray thee, where the seer's house is? and Samuel answered Saul, and said, I am the seer."

As the writer of the book of Samuel relates these questions and answers, in the language or manner of speaking used in the time they are said to have been spoken, and as that manner of speaking was out of use when this author wrote, he found it necessary, in order to make the story understood, to explain the terms in which these questions and answers are spoken; and he does this in the 9th verse, where he says, "Before-time in Israel, when a man went to enquire of God, thus he spake, Come let us go to the seer; for he that is now called a prophet, was before-time called a seer." This proves, as I have before said, that this story of Saul, Samuel, and the asses, was an ancient story at the time the book of Samuel was written, and consequently that Samuel did not write it, and that the book is without authenticity.

But if we go further into those books the evidence is still more positive that Samuel is not the writer of them; for they relate things that did not happen till several years after the death of Samuel. Samuel died before Saul; for i Samuel, xxviii. tells, that Saul and the witch of Endor conjured Samuel up after he was dead; yet the history of matters contained in those books is extended through the remaining part of Saul's life, and to the latter end of the life of David, who succeeded Saul. The account of the death and burial of Samuel (a thing which he could not write himself) is related in i Samuel xxv.; and the chronology affixed to this chapter makes this to be B.C. 1060; yet the history of this first book is brought down to B.C. 1056, that is, to the death of Saul, which was not till four years after the death of Samuel.

The second book of Samuel begins with an account of things that did not happen till four years after Samuel was dead; for it begins with the reign of David, who succeeded Saul, and it goes on to the end of David's reign, which was forty-three years after the death of Samuel; and, therefore, the books are in themselves positive evidence that they were not written by Samuel.

I have now gone through all the books in the first part of the Bible, to which the names of persons are affixed, as being the authors of those books, and which the church, styling itself the Christian church, have imposed upon the world as the writings of Moses, Joshua and Samuel; and I have detected and proved the falsehood of this imposition.—And now ye priests, of every description, who have preached and written against the former part of the 'Age of Reason,' what have ye to say? Will ye with all this mass of evidence against you, and staring you in the face, still have the assurance to march into your pulpits, and continue to impose these books on your congregations, as the works of inspired penmen and the word of God? when it is as evident as demonstration can make truth appear, that the persons who ye say are the authors, are not the authors, and that ye know not who the authors are. What shadow of pretence have ye now to produce for continuing the blasphemous fraud? What have ye still to offer against the pure and moral religion of deism, in support of your system of falsehood, idolatry, and pretended revelation? Had the cruel and murdering orders, with which the Bible is filled, and the numberless torturing executions of men, women, and children, in consequence of those orders, been ascribed to some friend, whose memory you revered, you would have glowed with satisfaction at detecting the falsehood of the charge, and gloried in defending his injured fame. It is because ye are sunk in the cruelty of superstition, or feel no interest in the honour of your Creator, that ye listen to the horrid tales of the Bible, or hear them with callous indifference. The evidence I have produced, and shall still produce in the course of this work, to prove that the Bible is without authority, will, whilst it wounds the stubbornness of a priest, relieve and tranquillize the minds of millions: it will free them from all those hard thoughts of the Almighty which priestcraft and the Bible had infused into their minds, and which stood in everlasting opposition to all their ideas of his moral justice and benevolence.

I come now to the two books of Kings, and the two books of Chronicles.—Those books are altogether historical, and are chiefly confined to the lives and actions of the Jewish kings, who in general were a parcel of rascals: but these are matters with which we have no more concern than we have with the Roman emperors, or Homer's account of the Trojan war. Besides which, as those books are anonymous, and as we know nothing of the writer, or of his character, it is impossible for us to know what degree of credit to give to the matters related therein. Like all other ancient histories, they appear to be a jumble of fable and of fact, and of probable and of improbable things, but which distance of time and place, and change of circumstances in the world, have rendered obsolete and uninteresting.

The chief use I shall make of those books will be that of comparing them with each other, and with other parts of the Bible, to show the confusion, contradiction, and cruelty in this pretended word of God.

The first book of Kings begins with the reign of Solomon, which, according to the Bible chronology, was B.C. 1015; and the second book ends B.C. 588, being a little after the reign of Zedekiah, whom Nebuchadnezzar, after taking Jerusalem and conquering the Jews, carried captive to Babylon. The two books include a space of 427 years.

The two books of Chronicles are an history of the same times, and in general of the same persons, by another author; for it would be absurd to suppose that the same author wrote the history twice over. The first book of Chronicles (after giving the genealogy from Adam to Saul, which takes up the first nine chapters) begins with the reign of David; and the last book ends, as in the last book of Kings, soon, after the reign of Zedekiah, about B.C. 588. The last two verses of the last chapter bring the history 52 years more forward, that is, to 536. But these verses do not belong to the book, as I shall show when I come to speak of the book of Ezra.

The two books of Kings, besides the history of Saul, David, and Solomon, who reigned over all Israel, contain an abstract of the lives of seventeen kings, and one queen, who are stiled kings of Judah; and of nineteen, who are stiled kings of Israel; for the Jewish nation, immediately on the death of Solomon, split into two parties, who chose separate kings, and who carried on most rancorous wars against each other.

These two books are little more than a history of assassinations, treachery, and wars. The cruelties that the Jews had accustomed themselves to practise on the Canaanites, whose country they had savagely invaded, under a pretended gift from God, they afterwards practised as furiously on each other. Scarcely half their kings died a natural death, and in some instances whole families were destroyed to secure possession to the successor, who, after a few years, and sometimes only a few months, or less, shared the same fate. In 2 Kings x., an account is given of two baskets full of children's heads, seventy in number, being exposed at the entrance of the city; they were the children of Ahab, and were murdered by the orders of Jehu, whom Elisha, the pretended man of God, had anointed to be king over Israel, on purpose to commit this bloody deed, and assassinate his predecessor. And in the account of the reign of Menahem, one of the kings of Israel who had murdered Shallum, who had reigned but one month, it is said, 2 Kings xv. 16, that Menahem smote the city of Tiphsah, because they opened not the city to him, and all the women therein that were with child he ripped up.

Could we permit ourselves to suppose that the Almighty would distinguish any nation of people by the name of his chosen people, we must suppose that people to have been an example to all the rest of the world of the purest piety and humanity, and not such a nation of ruffians and cut-throats as the ancient Jews were,—a people who, corrupted by and copying after such monsters and imposters as Moses and Aaron, Joshua, Samuel, and David, had distinguished themselves above all others on the face of the known earth for barbarity and wickedness. If we will not stubbornly shut our eyes and steel our hearts it is impossible not to see, in spite of all that long-established superstition imposes upon the mind, that the flattering appellation of his chosen people is no other than a LIE which the priests and leaders of the Jews had invented to cover the baseness of their own characters; and which Christian priests sometimes as corrupt, and often as cruel, have professed to believe.

The two books of Chronicles are a repetition of the same crimes; but the history is broken in several places, by the author leaving out the reign of some of their kings; and in this, as well as in that of Kings, there is such a frequent transition from kings of Judah to kings of Israel, and from kings of Israel to kings of Judah, that the narrative is obscure in the reading. In the same book the history sometimes contradicts itself: for example, in 2 Kings, i. 17, we are told, but in rather ambiguous terms, that after the death of Ahaziah, king of Israel, Jehoram, or Joram, (who was of the house of Ahab), reigned in his stead in the second Year of Jehoram, or Joram, son of Jehoshaphat, king of Judah; and in viii. 16, of the same book, it is said, "And in the fifth year of Joram, the son of Ahab, king of Israel, Jehoshaphat being then king of Judah, Jehoram, the son of Jehoshaphat king of judah, began to reign." That is, one chapter says Joram of Judah began to reign in the second year of Joram of Israel; and the other chapter says, that Joram of Israel began to reign in the fifth year of Joram of Judah.

Several of the most extraordinary matters related in one history, as having happened during the reign of such or such of their kings, are not to be found in the other, in relating the reign of the same king: for example, the two first rival kings, after the death of Solomon, were Rehoboam and Jeroboam; and in i Kings xii. and xiii. an account is given of Jeroboam making an offering of burnt incense, and that a man, who is there called a man of God, cried out against the altar (xiii. 2): "O altar, altar! thus saith the Lord: Behold, a child shall be born unto the house of David, Josiah by name, and upon thee shall he offer the priests of the high places that burn incense upon thee, and men's bones shall be burned upon thee." Verse 4: "And it came to pass, when king Jeroboam heard the saying of the man of God, which had cried against the altar in Bethel, that he put forth his hand from the altar, saying, Lay hold on him; and his hand which he put out against him dried up so that he could not pull it again to him."

One would think that such an extraordinary case as this, (which is spoken of as a judgement,) happening to the chief of one of the parties, and that at the first moment of the separation of the Israelites into two nations, would, if it,. had been true, have been recorded in both histories. But though men, in later times, have believed all that the prophets have said unto them, it does appear that those prophets, or historians, disbelieved each other: they knew each other too well.

A long account also is given in Kings about Elijah. It runs through several chapters, and concludes with telling, 2 Kings ii. 11, "And it came to pass, as they (Elijah and Elisha) still went on, and talked, that, behold, there appeared a chariot of fire and horses of fire, and parted them both asunder, and Elijah went up by a whirlwind into heaven." Hum! this the author of Chronicles, miraculous as the story is, makes no mention of, though he mentions Elijah by name; neither does he say anything of the story related in the second chapter of the same book of Kings, of a parcel of children calling Elisha bald head; and that this man of God (ver. 24) "turned back, and looked upon them, and cursed them in the name of the Lord; and there came forth two she-bears out of the wood, and tare forty and two children of them." He also passes over in silence the story told, 2 Kings xiii., that when they were burying a man in the sepulchre where Elisha had been buried, it happened that the dead man, as they were letting him down, (ver. 21) "touched the bones of Elisha, and he (the dead man) revived, and stood up on his feet." The story does not tell us whether they buried the man, notwithstanding he revived and stood upon his feet, or drew him up again. Upon all these stories the writer of the Chronicles is as silent as any writer of the present day, who did not chose to be accused of lying, or at least of romancing, would be about stories of the same kind.

But, however these two historians may differ from each other with respect to the tales related by either, they are silent alike with respect to those men styled prophets whose writings fill up the latter part of the Bible. Isaiah, who lived in the time of Hezekiab, is mentioned in Kings, and again in Chronicles, when these histories are speaking of that reign; but except in one or two instances at most, and those very slightly, none of the rest are so much as spoken of, or even their existence hinted at; though, according to the Bible chronology, they lived within the time those histories were written; and some of them long before. If those prophets, as they are called, were men of such importance in their day, as the compilers of the Bible, and priests and commentators have since represented them to be, how can it be accounted for that not one of those histories should say anything about them?

The history in the books of Kings and of Chronicles is brought forward, as I have already said, to the year B.C. 588; it will, therefore, be proper to examine which of these prophets lived before that period.

Here follows a table of all the prophets, with the times in which they lived before Christ, according to the chronology affixed to the first chapter of each of the books of the prophets; and also of the number of years they lived before the books of Kings and Chronicles were written:

TABLE of the Prophets, with the time in which they lived before Christ, and also before the books of Kings and Chronicles were written:

NAMES.	Years before Christ.	Years before Kings and Chronicles.	Observations.
Isaiah	760	172	mentioned.
Jeremiah	629	41	(mentioned only in the last [two] chapters of Chronicles.
Ezekiel	595	7	not mentioned.
Daniel	607	19	not mentioned.
Hosea	785	97	not mentioned.
Joel	800	212	not mentioned.
Amos	789	199	not mentioned.
Obadiah	789	199	not mentioned.
Jonah	862	274	see the note.
Micah	750	162	not mentioned.
Nahum	713	125	not mentioned.
Habakkuk	620	38	not mentioned.
Zepbaniah	630	42	not mentioned.

Haggai Zechariah all three after the year 588 Medachi [NOTE In 2 Kings xiv. 25, the name of Jonah is mentioned on account of the restoration of a tract of land by Jeroboam; but nothing further is said of him, nor is any allusion made to the book of Jonah, nor to his expedition to Nineveh, nor to his encounter with the whale.—Author.]

This table is either not very honourable for the Bible historians, or not very honourable for the Bible prophets; and I leave to priests and commentators, who are very learned in little things, to settle the point of etiquette between the two; and to assign a reason, why the authors of Kings and of Chronicles have treated those prophets, whom, in the former part of the 'Age of Reason,' I have considered as poets, with as much degrading silence as any historian of the present day would treat Peter Pindar.

I have one more observation to make on the book of Chronicles; after which I shall pass on to review the remaining books of the Bible.

In my observations on the book of Genesis, I have quoted a passage from xxxvi. 31, which evidently refers to a time, after that kings began to reign over the children of Israel; and I have shown that as this verse is verbatim the same as in 1 Chronicles i. 43, where it stands consistently with the order of history, which in Genesis it does not, that the verse in Genesis, and a great part of the 36th chapter, have been taken from Chronicles; and that the book of Genesis, though it is placed first in the Bible, and ascribed to Moses, has been manufactured by some unknown person, after the book of Chronicles was written, which was not until at least eight hundred and sixty years after the time of Moses.

The evidence I proceed by to substantiate this, is regular, and has in it but two stages. First, as I have already stated, that the passage in Genesis refers itself for time to Chronicles; secondly, that the book of Chronicles, to which this passage refers itself, was not begun to be written until at least eight hundred and sixty years after the time of Moses. To prove this, we have only to look into 1 Chronicles iii. 15, where the writer, in giving the genealogy of the descendants of David, mentions Zedekiah; and it was in the time of Zedekiah that Nebuchadnezzar conquered Jerusalem, B.C. 588, and consequently more than 860 years after Moses. Those who have superstitiously boasted of the antiquity of the Bible, and particularly of the books ascribed to Moses, have done it without examination, and without any other authority than that of one credulous man telling it to another: for, so far as historical and chronological evidence applies, the very first book in the Bible is not so ancient as the book of Homer, by more than three hundred years, and is about the same age with AEsop's Fables.

I am not contending for the morality of Homer; on the contrary, I think it a book of false glory, and tending to inspire immoral and mischievous notions of honour; and with respect to AEsop, though the moral is in general just, the fable is often cruel; and the cruelty of the fable does more injury to the heart, especially in a child, than the moral does good to the judgment.

Having now dismissed Kings and Chronicles, I come to the next in course, the book of Ezra.

As one proof, among others I shall produce to shew the disorder in which this pretended word of God, the Bible, has been put together, and the uncertainty of who the authors were, we have only to look at the first three verses in Ezra, and the last two in 2 Chronicles; for by what kind of cutting and shuffling has it been that the first three verses in Ezra should be the last two verses in 2 Chronicles, or that the last two in 2 Chronicles should be the first three in Ezra? Either the authors did not know their own works or the compilers did not know the authors.

Last Two Verses of 2 Chronicles.

Ver. 22. Now in the first year of Cyrus, King of Persia, that the word of the Lord, spoken by the mouth of Jeremiah, might be accomplished, the Lord stirred up the spirit of Cyrus, king of Persia, that he made a proclamation throughout all his kingdom, and put it also in writing, saying.

earth hath the Lord God of heaven given me; and he hath charged me to build him an house in Jerusalem which is in Judah. Who is there among you of all his people? the Lord his God be with him, and let him go up. ***

First Three Verses of Ezra.

Ver. 1. Now in the first year of Cyrus, king of Persia, that the word of the Lord, by the mouth of Jeremiah, might be fulfilled, the Lord stirred up the spirit of Cyrus, king of Persia, that he made a proclamation throughout all his kingdom, and put it also in writing, saying.

2. Thus saith Cyrus, king of Persia, The Lord God of heaven hath given me all the kingdoms of the earth; and he hath charged me to build him an house at Jerusalem, which is in Judah.

3. Who is there among you of all his people? his God be with him, and let him go up to Jerusalem, which is in Judah, and build the house of the Lord God of Israel (he is the God) which is in Jerusalem.

*** The last verse in Chronicles is broken abruptly, and ends in the middle of the phrase with the word 'up' without signifying to what place. This abrupt break, and the appearance of the same verses in different books, show as I have already said, the disorder and ignorance in which the Bible has been put together, and that the compilers of it had no authority for what they were doing, nor we any authority for believing what they have done. [NOTE I observed, as I passed along, several broken and senseless passages in the Bible, without thinking them of consequence enough to be introduced in the body of the work; such as that, 1 Samuel xiii. 1, where it is said, "Saul reigned one year; and when he had reigned two years over Israel, Saul chose him three thousand men," &c. The first part of the verse, that Saul reigned one year has no sense, since it does not tell us what Saul did, nor say any thing of what happened at the end of that one year; and it is, besides, mere absurdity to say he reigned one year, when the very next phrase says he had reigned two for if he had reigned two, it was impossible not to have reigned one.

Another instance occurs in Joshua v. where the writer tells us a story of an angel (for such the table of contents at the head of the chapter calls him) appearing unto Joshua; and the story ends abruptly, and without any conclusion. The story is as follows:— Ver. 13. "And it came to pass, when Joshua was by Jericho, that he lifted up his eyes and looked, and behold there stood a man over against him with his sword drawn in his hand; and Joshua went unto him and said unto him, Art thou for us, or for our adversaries?" Verse 14, "And he said, Nay; but as captain of the host of the Lord am I now come. And Joshua fell on his face to the earth, and did worship and said unto him, What saith my Lord unto his servant?" Verse 15, "And the captain of the Lord's host said unto Joshua, Loose thy shoe from off thy foot; for the place whereon thou standeth is holy. And Joshua did so."—And what then? nothing: for here the story ends, and the chapter too.

Either this story is broken off in the middle, or it is a story told by some Jewish humourist in ridicule of Joshua's pretended mission from God, and the compilers of the Bible, not perceiving the design of the story, have told it as a serious matter. As a story of humour and ridicule it has a great deal of point; for it pompously introduces an angel in the figure of a man, with a drawn sword in his hand, before whom Joshua falls on his face to the earth, and worships (which is contrary to their second commandment;) and then, this most important embassy from heaven ends in telling Joshua to pull off his shoe. It might as well have told him to pull up his breeches.

It is certain, however, that the Jews did not credit every thing their leaders told them, as appears from the cavalier manner in which they speak of Moses, when he was gone into the mount. As for this Moses, say they, we wot not what is become of him. Exod. xxxii. 1.—Author.

The only thing that has any appearance of certainty in the book of Ezra is the time in which it was written, which was immediately after the return of the Jews from the Babylonian captivity, about B.C. 536. Ezra (who, according to the Jewish commentators, is the same person as is called Esdras in the Apocrypha) was one of the persons who returned, and who, it is probable, wrote the account of that affair. Nebemiah, whose book follows next to Ezra, was another of the returned persons; and who, it is also probable, wrote the account of the same affair, in the book that bears his name. But those accounts are nothing to us, nor to any other person, unless it be to the Jews, as a part of the history of their nation; and there is just as much of the word of God in those books as there is in any of the histories of France, or Rapin's history of England, or the history of any other country.

But even in matters of historical record, neither of those writers are to be depended upon. In Ezra ii., the writer gives a list of the tribes and families, and of the precise number of souls of each, that returned from Babylon to Jerusalem; and this enrolment of the persons so returned appears to have been one of the principal objects for writing the book; but in this there is an error that destroys the intention of the undertaking.

The writer begins his enrolment in the following manner (ii. 3): "The children of Parosh, two thousand one hundred seventy and four." Ver. 4, "The children of Shephatiah, three hundred seventy and two." And in this manner he proceeds through all the families; and in the 64th verse, he makes a total, and says, the whole congregation together was forty and two thousand three hundred and threescore.

But whoever will take the trouble of casting up the several particulars, will find that the total is but 29,818; so that the error is 12,542. What certainty then can there be in the Bible for any thing?

[Here Mr. Paine includes the long list of numbers from the Bible of all the children listed and the total thereof. This can be had directly from the Bible.]

Nehemiah, in like manner, gives a list of the returned families, and of the number of each family. He begins as in Ezra, by saying (vii. 8): "The children of Parosh, two thousand three hundred and seventy-two;" and so on through all the families. (The list differs in several of the particulars from that of Ezra.) In ver. 66, Nehemiah makes a total, and says, as Ezra had said, "The whole congregation together was forty and two thousand three hundred and threescore." But the particulars of this list make a total but of 31,089, so that the error here is 11,271. These writers may do well enough for Bible-makers, but not for any thing where truth and exactness is necessary.

The next book in course is the book of Esther. If Madam Esther thought it any honour to offer herself as a kept mistress to Ahasuerus, or as a rival to Queen Vashti, who had refused to come to a drunken king in the midst of a drunken company, to be made a show of, (for the account says, they had been drinking seven days, and were merry,) let Esther and Mordecai look to that, it is no business of ours, at least it is none of mine; besides which, the story has a great deal the appearance of being fabulous, and is also anonymous. I pass on to the book of Job.

The book of Job differs in character from all the books we have hitherto passed over. Treachery and murder make no part of this book; it is the meditations of a mind strongly impressed with the vicissitudes of human life, and by turns sinking under, and struggling against the pressure. It is a highly wrought composition, between willing submission and involuntary discontent; and shows man, as he sometimes is, more disposed to be resigned than he is capable of being. Patience has but a small share in the character of the person of whom the book treats; on the contrary, his grief is often impetuous; but he still endeavours to keep a guard upon it, and seems determined, in the midst of accumulating ills, to impose upon himself the hard duty of contentment.

I have spoken in a respectful manner of the book of Job in the former part of the 'Age of Reason,' but without knowing at that time what I have learned since; which is, that from all the evidence that can be collected, the book of Job does not belong to the Bible.

I have seen the opinion of two Hebrew commentators, Abenezra and Spinoza, upon this subject; they both say that the book of Job carries no internal evidence of being an Hebrew book; that the genius of the composition, and the drama of the piece, are not Hebrew; that it has been translated from another language into Hebrew, and that the author of the book was a Gentile; that the character represented under the name of Satan (which is the first and only time this name is mentioned in the Bible) [In a later work Paine notes that in "the Bible" (by which he always means the Old Testament alone) the word Satan occurs also in 1 Chron. xxi. 1, and remarks that the action there ascribed to Satan is in 2 Sam. xxiv. 1, attributed to Jehovah ("Essay on Dreams"). In these places, however, and in Ps. cix. 6, Satan means "adversary," and is so translated (A.S. version) in 2 Sam. xix. 22, and 1 Kings v. 4, xi. 25. As a proper name, with the article, Satan appears in the Old Testament only in Job and in Zech. iii. 1, 2. But the authenticity of the passage in Zechariah has been questioned, and it may be that in finding the proper name of Satan in Job alone, Paine was following some opinion met with in one of the authorities whose comments are condensed in his paragraph.—Editor.] does not correspond to any Hebrew idea; and that the two convocations which the Deity is supposed to have made of those whom the poem calls sons of God, and the familiarity which this supposed Satan is stated to have with the Deity, are in the same case.

It may also be observed, that the book shows itself to be the production of a mind cultivated in science, which the Jews, so far from being famous for, were very ignorant of. The allusions to objects of natural philosophy are frequent and strong, and are of a different cast to any thing in the books known to be Hebrew. The astronomical names, Pleiades, Orion, and Arcturus, are Greek and not Hebrew names, and it does not appear from any thing that is to be found in the Bible that the Jews knew any thing of astronomy, or that they studied it, they had no translation of those names into their own language, but adopted the names as they found them in the poem. [Paine's Jewish critic, David Levi, fastened on this slip ("Defence of the Old Testament," 1797, p. 152). In the original the names are Ash (Arcturus), Kesil' (Orion), Kimah' (Pleiades), though the identifications of the constellations in the A.S.V. have been questioned.—Editor.]

That the Jews did translate the literary productions of the Gentile nations into the Hebrew language, and mix them with their own, is not a matter of doubt; Proverbs xxxi. i, is an evidence of this: it is there said, The word of king Lemuel, the prophecy which his mother taught him. This verse stands as a preface to the proverbs that follow, and which are not the proverbs of Solomon, but of Lemuel; and this Lemuel was not one of the kings of Israel, nor of Judah, but of some other country, and consequently a Gentile. The Jews however have adopted his proverbs; and as they cannot give any account who the author of the book of Job was, nor how they came by the book, and as it differs in character from the Hebrew writings, and stands totally unconnected with every other book and chapter in the Bible before it and after it, it has all the circumstantial evidence of being originally a book of the Gentiles. [The prayer known by the name of Agur's Prayer, in Proverbs xxx.,—immediately preceding the proverbs of Lemuel,—and which is the only sensible, well-conceived, and well-expressed prayer in the Bible, has much the appearance of being a prayer taken from the Gentiles. The name of Agur occurs on no other occasion than this; and he is introduced, together with the prayer ascribed to him, in the same manner, and nearly in the same words, that Lemuel and his proverbs are introduced in the chapter that follows. The first verse says, "The words of Agur, the son of Jakeh, even the prophecy:" here the word prophecy is used with the same application it has in the following chapter of Lemuel, unconnected with anything of prediction. The prayer of Agur is in the 8th and 9th verses, "Remove far from me vanity and lies; give me neither riches nor poverty, but feed me with food convenient for me; lest I be full and deny thee and say, Who is the Lord? or lest I be poor and steal, and take the name of my God in vain." This has not any of the marks of being a Jewish prayer, for the Jews never prayed but when they were in trouble, and never for anything but victory, vengeance, or riches.—Author. (Prov. xxx. 1, and xxxi. 1) the word "prophecy" in these verses is translated "oracle" or "burden" (marg.) in the revised version.—The prayer of Agur was quoted by Paine in his plea for the officers of Excise, 1772.—Editor.]

The Bible-makers, and those regulators of time, the Bible chronologists, appear to have been at a loss where to place and how to dispose of the book of Job; for it contains no one historical circumstance, nor allusion to any, that might serve to determine its place in the Bible. But it would not have answered the purpose of these men to have informed the world of their ignorance; and, therefore, they have affixed it to the aera of B.C. 1520, which is during the time the Israelites were in Egypt, and for which they have just as much authority and no more than I should have for saying it was a thousand years before that period. The probability however is, that it is older than any book in the Bible; and it is the only one that can be read without indignation or disgust.

We know nothing of what the ancient Gentile world (as it is called) was before the time of the Jews, whose practice has been to calumniate and blacken the character of all other nations; and it is from the Jewish accounts that we have learned to call them heathens. But, as far as we know to the contrary, they were a just and moral people, and not addicted, like the Jews, to cruelty and revenge, but of whose profession of faith we are unacquainted. It appears to have been their custom to personify both virtue and vice by statues and images, as is done now-a-days both by statuary and by painting; but it does not follow from this that they worshipped them any more than we do.—I pass on to the book of,

Psalms, of which it is not necessary to make much observation. Some of them are moral, and others are very revengeful; and the greater part relates to certain local circumstances of the Jewish nation at the time they were written, with which we have nothing to do. It is, however, an error or an imposition to call them the Psalms of David; they are a collection, as song-books are now-a-days, from different song-writers, who lived at different times. The 137th Psalm could not have been written till more than 400 years after the time of David, because it is written in commemoration of an event, the captivity of the Jews in Babylon, which did not happen till that distance of time. "By the rivers of Babylon we sat down; yea, we wept when we remembered Zion. We hanged our harps upon the willows, in the midst thereof; for there they that carried us away captive required of us a song, saying, sing us one of the songs of Zion." As a man would say to an American, or to a Frenchman, or to an Englishman, sing us one of your American songs, or your French songs, or your English songs. This remark, with respect to the time this psalm was written, is of no other use than to show (among others already mentioned) the general imposition the world has been under with respect to the authors of the Bible. No regard has been paid to time, place, and circumstance; and the names of persons have been affixed to the several books which it was as impossible they should write, as that a man should walk in procession at his own funeral.

The Book of Proverbs. These, like the Psalms, are a collection, and that from authors belonging to other nations than those of the Jewish nation, as I have shewn in the observations upon the book of Job; besides which, some of the Proverbs ascribed to Solomon did not appear till two hundred and fifty years after the death of Solomon; for it is said in xxv. i, "These are also proverbs of Solomon which the men of Hezekiah, king of Judah, copied out." It was two hundred and fifty years from the time of Solomon to the time of Hezekiah. When a man is famous and his name is abroad he is made the putative father of things he never said or did; and this, most probably, has been the case with Solomon. It appears to have been the fashion of that day to make proverbs, as it is now to make jest-books, and father them upon those who never saw them. [A "Tom Paine's Jest Book" had appeared in London with little or nothing of Paine in it.—Editor.]

The book of Ecclesiastes, or the Preacher, is also ascribed to Solomon, and that with much reason, if not with truth. It is written as the solitary reflections of a worn-out debauchee, such as Solomon was, who looking back on scenes he can no longer enjoy, cries out All is Vanity! A great deal of the metaphor and of the sentiment is obscure, most probably by translation; but enough is left to show they were strongly pointed in the original. [Those that look out of the window shall be darkened, is an obscure figure in translation for loss of sight.—Author.] From what is transmitted to us of the character of Solomon, he was witty, ostentatious, dissolute, and at last melancholy. He lived fast, and died, tired of the world, at the age of fifty-eight years.

Seven hundred wives, and three hundred concubines, are worse than none; and, however it may carry with it the appearance of heightened enjoyment, it defeats all the felicity of affection, by leaving it no point to fix upon; divided love is never happy. This was the case with Solomon; and if he could not, with all his pretensions to wisdom, discover it beforehand, he merited, unpitied, the mortification he afterwards endured. In this point of view, his preaching is unnecessary, because, to know the consequences, it is only necessary to know the cause. Seven hundred wives, and three hundred concubines would have stood in place of the whole book. It was needless after this to say that all was vanity and vexation of spirit; for it is impossible to derive happiness from the company of those whom we deprive of happiness.

To be happy in old age it is necessary that we accustom ourselves to objects that can accompany the mind all the way through life, and that we take the rest as good in their day. The mere man of pleasure is miserable in old age; and the mere drudge in business is but little better: whereas, natural philosophy, mathematical and mechanical science, are a continual source of tranquil pleasure, and in spite of the gloomy dogmas of priests, and of superstition, the study of those things is the study of the true theology; it teaches man to know and to admire the Creator, for the principles of science are in the creation, and are unchangeable, and of divine origin.

Those who knew Benjamin Franklin will recollect, that his mind was ever young; his temper ever serene; science, that never grows grey, was always his mistress. He was never without an object; for when we cease to have an object we become like an invalid in an hospital waiting for death.

Solomon's Songs, amorous and foolish enough, but which wrinkled fanaticism has called divine.—The compilers of the Bible have placed these songs after the book of Ecclesiastes; and the chronologists have affixed to them the aera of B.C. 1014, at which time Solomon, according to the same chronology, was nineteen years of age, and was then forming his seraglio of wives and concubines. The Bible-makers and the chronologists should have managed this matter a little better, and either have said nothing about the time, or chosen a time less inconsistent with the supposed divinity of those songs; for Solomon was then in the honey-moon of one thousand debaucheries.

It should also have occurred to them, that as he wrote, if he did write, the book of Ecclesiastes, long after these songs, and in which he exclaims that all is vanity and vexation of spirit, that he included those songs in that description. This is the more probable, because he says, or somebody for him, Ecclesiastes ii. 8, I got me men-singers, and women-singers [most probably to sing those songs], and musical instruments of all sorts; and behold (Ver. ii), "all was vanity and vexation of spirit." The compilers however have done their work but by halves; for as they have given us the songs they should have given us the tunes, that we might sing them.

The books called the books of the Prophets fill up all the remaining part of the Bible; they are sixteen in number, beginning with Isaiah and ending with Malachi, of which I have given a list in the observations upon Chronicles. Of these sixteen prophets, all of whom except the last three lived within the time the books of Kings and Chronicles were written, two only, Isaiah and Jeremiah, are mentioned in the history of those books. I shall begin with those two, reserving, what I have to say on the general character of the men called prophets to another part of the work.

Whoever will take the trouble of reading the book ascribed to Isaiah, will find it one of the most wild and disorderly compositions ever put together; it has neither beginning, middle, nor end; and, except a short historical part, and a few sketches of history in the first two or three chapters, is one continued incoherent, bombastical rant, full of extravagant metaphor, without application, and destitute of meaning; a school-boy would scarcely have been excusable for writing such stuff; it is (at least in translation) that kind of composition and false taste that is properly called prose run mad.

The historical part begins at chapter xxxvi., and is continued to the end of chapter xxxix. It relates some matters that are said to have passed during the reign of Hezekiah, king of Judah, at which time Isaiah lived. This fragment of history begins and ends abruptly; it has not the least connection with the chapter that precedes it, nor with that which follows it, nor with any other in the book. It is probable that Isaiah wrote this fragment himself, because he was an actor in the circumstances it treats of; but except this part there are scarcely two chapters that have any connection with each other. One is entitled, at the beginning of the first verse, the burden of Babylon; another, the burden of Moab; another, the burden of Damascus; another, the burden of Egypt; another, the burden of the Desert of the Sea; another, the burden of the Valley of Vision: as you would say the story of the Knight of the Burning Mountain, the story of Cinderella, or the glassen slipper, the story of the Sleeping Beauty in the Wood, etc., etc.

I have already shown, in the instance of the last two verses of 2 Chronicles, and the first three in Ezra, that the compilers of the Bible mixed and confounded the writings of different authors with each other; which alone, were there no other cause, is sufficient to destroy the authenticity of an compilation, because it is more than presumptive evidence that the compilers are ignorant who the authors were. A very glaring instance of this occurs in the book ascribed to Isaiah: the latter part of the 44th chapter, and the beginning of the 45th, so far from having been written by Isaiah, could only have been written by some person who lived at least an hundred and fifty years after Isaiah was dead.

These chapters are a compliment to Cyrus, who permitted the Jews to return to Jerusalem from the Babylonian captivity, to rebuild Jerusalem and the temple, as is stated in Ezra. The last verse of the 44th chapter, and the beginning of the 45th [Isaiah] are in the following words: "That saith of Cyrus, he is my shepherd, and shall perform all my pleasure; even saying to Jerusalem, thou shalt be built; and to the temple thy foundations shall be laid: thus saith the Lord to his enointed, to Cyrus, whose right hand I have holden to subdue nations before him, and I will loose the loins of kings to open before him the two-leaved gates, and the gates shall not be shut; I will go before thee," etc.

What audacity of church and priestly ignorance it is to impose this book upon the world as the writing of Isaiah, when Isaiah, according to their own chronology, died soon after the death of Hezekiah, which was B.C. 698; and the decree of Cyrus, in favour of the Jews returning to Jerusalem, was, according to the same chronology, B.C. 536; which is a distance of time between the two of 162 years. I do not suppose that the compilers of the Bible made these books, but rather that they picked up some loose, anonymous essays, and put them together under the names of such authors as best suited their purpose. They have encouraged the imposition, which is next to inventing it; for it was impossible but they must have observed it.

When we see the studied craft of the scripture-makers, in making every part of this romantic book of school-boy's eloquence bend to the monstrous idea of a Son of God, begotten by a ghost on the body of a virgin, there is no imposition we are not justified in suspecting them of. Every phrase and circumstance are marked with the barbarous hand of superstitious torture, and forced into meanings it was impossible they could have. The head of every chapter, and the top of every page, are blazoned with the names of Christ and the Church, that the unwary reader might suck in the error before he began to read.

Behold a virgin shall conceive, and bear a son (Isa. vii. 14), has been interpreted to mean the person called Jesus Christ, and his mother Mary, and has been echoed through christendom for more than a thousand years; and such has been the rage of this opinion, that scarcely a spot in it but has been stained with blood and marked with desolation in consequence of it. Though it is not my intention to enter into controversy on subjects of this kind, but to confine myself to show that the Bible is spurious,—and thus, by taking away the foundation, to overthrow at once the whole structure of superstition raised thereon,—I will however stop a moment to expose the fallacious application of this passage.

Whether Isaiah was playing a trick with Ahaz, king of Judah, to whom this passage is spoken, is no business of mine; I mean only to show the misapplication of the passage, and that it has no more reference to Christ and his mother, than it has to me and my mother. The story is simply this:

The king of Syria and the king of Israel (I have already mentioned that the Jews were split into two nations, one of which was called Judah, the capital of which was Jerusalem, and the other Israel) made war jointly against Ahaz, king of Judah, and marched their armies towards Jerusalem. Ahaz and his people became alarmed, and the account says (Is. vii. 2), Their hearts were moved as the trees of the wood are moved with the wind.

In this situation of things, Isaiah addresses himself to Ahaz, and assures him in the name of the Lord (the cant phrase of all the prophets) that these two kings should not succeed against him; and to satisfy Ahaz that this should be the case, tells him to ask a sign. This, the account says, Ahaz declined doing; giving as a reason that he would not tempt the Lord; upon which Isaiah, who is the speaker, says, ver. 14, "Therefore the Lord himself shall give you a sign; behold a virgin shall conceive and bear a son;" and the 16th verse says, "And before this child shall know to refuse the evil, and choose the good, the land which thou abhorrest or dreadest [meaning Syria and the kingdom of Israel] shall be forsaken of both her kings." Here then was the sign, and the time limited for the completion of the assurance or promise; namely, before this child shall know to refuse the evil and choose the good.

Isaiah having committed himself thus far, it became necessary to him, in order to avoid the imputation of being a false prophet, and the consequences thereof, to take measures to make this sign appear. It certainly was not a difficult thing, in any time of the world, to find a girl with child, or to make her so; and perhaps Isaiah knew of one beforehand; for I do not suppose that the prophets of that day were any more to be trusted than the priests of this: be that, however, as it may, he says in the next chapter, ver. 2, "And I took unto me faithful witnesses to record, Uriah the priest, and Zechariah the son of Jeberechiah, and I went unto the prophetess, and she conceived and bare a son."

Here then is the whole story, foolish as it is, of this child and this virgin; and it is upon the barefaced perversion of this story that the book of Matthew, and the impudence and sordid interest of priests in later times, have founded a theory, which they call the gospel; and have applied this story to signify the person they call Jesus Christ; begotten, they say, by a ghost, whom they call holy, on the body of a woman engaged in marriage, and afterwards married, whom they call a virgin, seven hundred years after this foolish story was told; a theory which, speaking for myself, I hesitate not to believe, and to say, is as fabulous and as false as God is true. [In Is. vii. 14, it is said that the child should be called Immanuel; but this name was not given to either of the children, otherwise than as a character, which the word signifies. That of the prophetess was called Maher-shalalhash-baz, and that of Mary was called Jesus.—Author.]

But to show the imposition and falsehood of Isaiah we have only to attend to the sequel of this story; which, though it is passed over in silence in the book of Isaiah, is related in 2 Chronicles, xxviii; and which is, that instead of these two kings failing in their attempt against Ahaz, king of Judah, as Isaiah had pretended to foretel in the name of the Lord, they succeeded: Ahaz was defeated and destroyed; an hundred and twenty thousand of his people were slaughtered; Jerusalem was plundered, and two hundred thousand women and sons and daughters carried into captivity. Thus much for this lying prophet and imposter Isaiah, and the book of falsehoods that bears his name. I pass on to the book of Jeremiah. This prophet, as he is called, lived in the time that Nebuchadnezzar besieged Jerusalem, in the reign of Zedekiah, the last king of Judah; and the suspicion was strong against him that he was a traitor in the interest of Nebuchadnezzar. Every thing relating to Jeremiah shows him to have been a man of an equivocal character: in his metaphor of the potter and the clay, (ch. xviii.) he guards his prognostications in such a crafty manner as always to leave himself a door to escape by, in case the event should be contrary to what he had predicted. In the 7th and 8th verses he makes the Almighty to say, "At what instant I shall speak concerning a nation, and concerning a kingdom, to pluck up, and to pull down, and destroy it, if that nation, against whom I have pronounced, turn from their evil, I will repent me of the evil that I thought to do unto them." Here was a proviso against one side of the case: now for the other side. Verses 9 and 10, "At what instant I shall speak concerning a nation, and concerning a kingdom, to build and to plant it, if it do evil in my sight, that it obey not my voice, then I will repent me of the good wherewith I said I would benefit them." Here is a proviso against the other side; and, according to this plan of prophesying, a prophet could never be wrong, however mistaken the Almighty might be. This sort of absurd subterfuge, and this manner of speaking of the Almighty, as one would speak of a man, is consistent with nothing but the stupidity of the Bible.

As to the authenticity of the book, it is only necessary to read it in order to decide positively that, though some passages recorded therein may have been spoken by Jeremiah, he is not the author of the book. The historical parts, if they can be called by that name, are in the most confused condition; the same events are several times repeated, and that in a manner different, and sometimes in contradiction to each other; and this disorder runs even to the last chapter, where the history, upon which the greater part of the book has been employed, begins anew, and ends abruptly. The book has all the appearance of being a medley of unconnected anecdotes respecting persons and things of that time, collected together in the same rude manner as if the various and contradictory accounts that are to be found in a bundle of newspapers, respecting persons and things of the present day, were put together without date, order, or explanation. I will give two or three examples of this kind.

It appears, from the account of chapter xxxvii. that the army of Nebuchadnezzer, which is called the army of the Chaldeans, had besieged Jerusalem some time; and on their hearing that the army of Pharaoh of Egypt was marching against them, they raised the siege and retreated for a time. It may here be proper to mention, in order to understand this confused history, that Nebuchadnezzar had besieged and taken Jerusalem during the reign of Jehoakim, the redecessor of Zedekiah; and that it was Nebuchadnezzar who had make Zedekiah king, or rather viceroy; and that this second siege, of which the book of Jeremiah treats, was in consequence of the revolt of Zedekiah against Nebuchadnezzar. This will in some measure account for the suspicion that affixes itself to Jeremiah of being a traitor, and in the interest of Nebuchadnezzar,—whom Jeremiah calls, xliii. 10, the servant of God.

Chapter xxxvii. 11-13, says, "And it came to pass, that, when the army of the Chaldeans was broken up from Jerusalem, for fear of Pharaoh's army, that Jeremiah went forth out of Jerusalem, to go (as this account states) into the land of Benjamin, to separate himself thence in the midst of the people; and when he was in the gate of Benjamin a captain of the ward was there, whose name was Irijah... and he took Jeremiah the prophet, saying, Thou fallest away to the Chaldeans; then Jeremiah said, It is false; I fall not away to the Chaldeans." Jeremiah being thus stopt and accused, was, after being examined, committed to prison, on suspicion of being a traitor, where he remained, as is stated in the last verse of this chapter.

But the next chapter gives an account of the imprisonment of Jeremiah, which has no connection with this account, but ascribes his imprisonment to another circumstance, and for which we must go back to chapter xxi. It is there stated, ver. 1, that Zedekiah sent Pashur the son of Malchiah, and Zephaniah the son of Maaseiah the priest, to Jeremiah, to enquire of him concerning Nebuchadnezzar, whose army was then before Jerusalem; and Jeremiah said to them, ver. 8, "Thus saith the Lord, Behold I set before you the way of life, and the way of death; he that abideth in this city shall die by the sword and by the famine, and by the pestilence; but he that goeth out and falleth to the Chaldeans that besiege you, he shall live, and his life shall be unto him for a prey."

This interview and conference breaks off abruptly at the end of the 10th verse of chapter xxi.; and such is the disorder of this book that we have to pass over sixteen chapters upon various subjects, in order to come at the continuation and event of this conference; and this brings us to the first verse of chapter xxxviii., as I have just mentioned. The chapter opens with saying, "Then Shaphatiah, the son of Mattan, Gedaliah the son of Pashur, and Jucal the son of Shelemiah, and Pashur the son of Malchiah, (here are more persons mentioned than in chapter xxi.) heard the words that Jeremiah spoke unto all the people, saying, Thus saith the Lord, He that remaineth in this city, shall die by the sword, by famine, and by the pestilence; but he that goeth forth to the Chaldeans shall live; for he shall have his life for a prey, and shall live"; [which are the words of the conference;] therefore, (say they to Zedekiah,) "We beseech thee, let this man be put to death, for thus he weakeneth the hands of the men of war that remain in this city, and the hands of all the people, in speaking such words unto them; for this man seeketh not the welfare of the people, but the hurt:" and at the 6th verse it is said, "Then they took Jeremiah, and put him into the dungeon of Malchiah."

These two accounts are different and contradictory. The one ascribes his imprisonment to his attempt to escape out of the city; the other to his preaching and prophesying in the city; the one to his being seized by the guard at the gate; the other to his being accused before Zedekiah by the conferees. [I observed two chapters in I Samuel (xvi. and xvii.) that contradict each other with respect to David, and the manner he became acquainted with Saul; as Jeremiah xxxvii. and xxxviii. contradict each other with respect to the cause of Jeremiah's imprisonment.

In 1 Samuel, xvi., it is said, that an evil spirit of God troubled Saul, and that his servants advised him (as a remedy) "to seek out a man who was a cunning player upon the harp." And Saul said, ver. 17, "Provide me now a man that can play well, and bring him to me. Then answered one of his servants, and said, Behold, I have seen a son of Jesse, the Bethlehemite, that is cunning in playing, and a mighty man, and a man of war, and prudent in matters, and a comely person, and the Lord is with him; wherefore Saul sent messengers unto Jesse, and said, Send me David, thy son. And (verse 21) David came to Saul, and stood before him, and he loved him greatly, and he became his armour-bearer; and when the evil spirit from God was upon Saul, (verse 23) David took his harp, and played with his hand, and Saul was refreshed, and was well."

But the next chapter (xvii.) gives an account, all different to this, of the manner that Saul and David became acquainted. Here it is ascribed to David's encounter with Goliah, when David was sent by his father to carry provision to his brethren in the camp. In the 55th verse of this chapter it is said, "And when Saul saw David go forth against the Philistine (Goliah) he said to Abner, the captain of the host, Abner, whose son is this youth? And Abner said, As thy soul liveth, 0 king, I cannot tell. And the king said, Enquire thou whose son the stripling is. And as David returned from the slaughter of the Philistine, Abner took him and brought him before Saul, with the head of the Philistine in his hand; and Saul said unto him, Whose son art thou, thou young man? And David answered, I am the son of thy servant, Jesse, the Betblehemite," These two accounts belie each other, because each of them supposes Saul and David not to have known each other before. This book, the Bible, is too ridiculous for criticism.—Author.]

In the next chapter (Jer. xxxix.) we have another instance of the disordered state of this book; for notwithstanding the siege of the city by Nebuchadnezzar has been the subject of several of the preceding chapters, particularly xxxvii. and xxxviii., chapter xxxix. begins as if not a word had been said upon the subject, and as if the reader was still to be informed of every particular respecting it; for it begins with saying, ver. 1, "In the ninth year of Zedekiah king of Judah, in the tenth month, came Nebuchadnezzar king of Babylon, and all his army, against Jerusalem, and besieged it," etc.

But the instance in the last chapter (lii.) is still more glaring; for though the story has been told over and over again, this chapter still supposes the reader not to know anything of it, for it begins by saying, ver. i, "Zedekiah was one and twenty years old when he began to reign, and he reigned eleven years in Jerusalem, and his mother's name was Hamutal, the daughter of Jeremiah of Libnah." (Ver. 4,) "And it came to pass in the ninth year of his reign, in the tenth month, that Nebuchadnezzar king of Babylon came, he and all his army, against Jerusalem, and pitched against it, and built forts against it," etc.

It is not possible that any one man, and more particularly Jeremiah, could have been the writer of this book. The errors are such as could not have been committed by any person sitting down to compose a work. Were I, or any other man, to write in such a disordered manner, no body would read what was written, and every body would suppose that the writer was in a state of insanity. The only way, therefore, to account for the disorder is, that the book is a medley of detached unauthenticated anecdotes, put together by some stupid book-maker, under the name of Jeremiah; because many of them refer to him, and to the circumstances of the times he lived in.

Of the duplicity, and of the false predictions of Jeremiah, I shall mention two instances, and then proceed to review the remainder of the Bible.

It appears from chapter xxxviii. that when Jeremiah was in prison, Zedekiah sent for him, and at this interview, which was private, Jeremiah pressed it strongly on Zedekiah to surrender himself to the enemy. "If," says he, (ver. 17,) "thou wilt assuredly go forth unto the king of Babylon's princes, then thy soul shall live," etc. Zedekiah was apprehensive that what passed at this conference should be known; and he said to Jeremiah, (ver. 25,) "If the princes [meaning those of Judah] hear that I have talked with thee, and they come unto thee, and say unto thee, Declare unto us now what thou hast said unto the king; hide it not from us, and we will not put thee to death; and also what the king said unto thee; then thou shalt say unto them, I presented my supplication before the king that he would not cause me to return to Jonathan's house, to die there. Then came all the princes unto Jeremiah, and asked him, and "he told them according to all the words the king had commanded." Thus, this man of God, as he is called, could tell a lie, or very strongly prevaricate, when he supposed it would answer his purpose; for certainly he did not go to Zedekiah to make this supplication, neither did he make it; he went because he was sent for, and he employed that opportunity to advise Zedekiah to surrender himself to Nebuchadnezzar.

In chapter xxxiv. 2-5, is a prophecy of Jeremiah to Zedekiah in these words: "Thus saith the Lord, Behold I will give this city into the hand of the king of Babylon, and he will burn it with fire; and thou shalt not escape out of his hand, but thou shalt surely be taken, and delivered into his hand; and thine eyes shall behold the eyes of the king of Babylon, and he shall speak with thee mouth to mouth, and thou shalt go to Babylon. Yet hear the word of the Lord; O Zedekiah, king, of Judah, thus saith the Lord,

Thou shalt not die by the sword, but thou shalt die in Peace; and with the burnings of thy fathers, the former kings that were before thee, so shall they burn odours for thee, and they will lament thee, saying, Ah, Lord! for I have pronounced the word, saith the Lord."

Now, instead of Zedekiah beholding the eyes of the king of Babylon, and speaking with him mouth to mouth, and dying in peace, and with the burning of odours, as at the funeral of his fathers, (as Jeremiah had declared the Lord himself had pronounced,) the reverse, according to chapter Iii., 10, 11 was the case; it is there said, that the king of Babylon slew the sons of Zedekiah before his eyes: then he put out the eyes of Zedekiah, and bound him in chains, and carried him to Babylon, and put him in prison till the day of his death.

What then can we say of these prophets, but that they are impostors and liars?

As for Jeremiah, he experienced none of those evils. He was taken into favour by Nebuchadnezzar, who gave him in charge to the captain of the guard (xxxix, 12), "Take him (said he) and look well to him, and do him no harm; but do unto him even as he shall say unto thee." Jeremiah joined himself afterwards to Nebuchadnezzar, and went about prophesying for him against the Egyptians, who had marched to the relief of Jerusalem while it was besieged. Thus much for another of the lying prophets, and the book that bears his name.

I have been the more particular in treating of the books ascribed to Isaiah and Jeremiah, because those two are spoken of in the books of Kings and Chronicles, which the others are not. The remainder of the books ascribed to the men called prophets I shall not trouble myself much about; but take them collectively into the observations I shall offer on the character of the men styled prophets.

In the former part of the 'Age of Reason,' I have said that the word prophet was the Bible-word for poet, and that the flights and metaphors of Jewish poets have been foolishly erected into what are now called prophecies. I am sufficiently justified in this opinion, not only because the books called the prophecies are written in poetical language, but because there is no word in the Bible, except it be the word prophet, that describes what we mean by a poet. I have also said, that the word signified a performer upon musical instruments, of which I have given some instances; such as that of a company of prophets, prophesying with psalteries, with tabrets, with pipes, with harps, etc., and that Saul prophesied with them, 1 Sam. x., 5. It appears from this passage, and from other parts in the book of Samuel, that the word prophet was confined to signify poetry and music; for the person who was supposed to have a visionary insight into concealed things, was not a prophet but a seer, [I know not what is the Hebrew word that corresponds to the word seer in English; but I observe it is translated into French by Le Voyant, from the verb voir to see, and which means the person who sees, or the seer.—Author.]

[The Hebrew word for Seer, in 1 Samuel ix., transliterated, is chozeh, the gazer, it is translated in Is. xlvii. 13, "the stargazers."—Editor.] (i Sam, ix. 9;) and it was not till after the word seer went out of use (which most probably was when Saul banished those he called wizards) that the profession of the seer, or the art of seeing, became incorporated into the word prophet.

According to the modern meaning of the word prophet and prophesying, it signifies foretelling events to a great distance of time; and it became necessary to the inventors of the gospel to give it this latitude of meaning, in order to apply or to stretch what they call the prophecies of the Old Testament, to the times of the New. But according to the Old Testament, the prophesying of the seer, and afterwards of the prophet, so far as the meaning of the word "seer" was incorporated into that of prophet, had reference only to things of the time then passing, or very closely connected with it; such as the event of a battle they were going to engage in, or of a journey, or of any enterprise they were going to undertake, or of any circumstance then pending, or of any difficulty they were then in; all of which had immediate reference to themselves (as in the case already mentioned of Ahaz and Isaiah with respect to the expression, Behold a virgin shall conceive and bear a son,) and not to any distant future time. It was that kind of prophesying that corresponds to what we call fortune-telling; such as casting nativities, predicting riches, fortunate or unfortunate marriages, conjuring for lost goods, etc.; and it is the fraud of the Christian church, not that of the Jews, and the ignorance and the superstition of modern, not that of ancient times, that elevated those poetical, musical, conjuring, dreaming, strolling gentry, into the rank they have since had.

But, besides this general character of all the prophets, they had also a particular character. They were in parties, and they prophesied for or against, according to the party they were with; as the poetical and political writers of the present day write in defence of the party they associate with against the other.

After the Jews were divided into two nations, that of Judah and that of Israel, each party had its prophets, who abused and accused each other of being false prophets, lying prophets, impostors, etc.

The prophets of the party of Judah prophesied against the prophets of the party of Israel; and those of the party of Israel against those of Judah. This party prophesying showed itself immediately on the separation under the first two rival kings, Rehoboam and Jeroboam. The prophet that cursed, or prophesied against the altar that Jeroboam had built in Bethel, was of the party of Judah, where Rehoboam was king; and he was way-laid on his return home by a prophet of the party of Israel, who said unto him (i Kings xiii.) "Art thou the man of God that came from Judah? and he said, I am." Then the prophet of the party of Israel said to him "I am a prophet also, as thou art, [signifying of Judah,] and an angel spake unto me by the word of the Lord, saying, Bring him back with thee unto thine house, that he may eat bread and drink water; but (says the 18th verse) he lied unto him." The event, however, according to the story, is, that the prophet of Judah never got back to Judah; for he was found dead on the road by the contrivance of the prophet of Israel, who no doubt was called a true prophet by his own party, and the prophet of Judah a lying prophet.

In 2 Kings, iii., a story is related of prophesying or conjuring that shews, in several particulars, the character of a prophet. Jehoshaphat king of Judah, and Joram king of Israel, had for a while ceased their party animosity, and entered into an alliance; and these two, together with the king of Edom, engaged in a war against the king of Moab. After uniting and marching their armies, the story says, they were in great distress for water, upon which Jehoshaphat said, "Is there not here a prophet of the Lord, that we may enquire of the Lord by him? and one of the servants of the king of Israel said here is Elisha. [Elisha was of the party of Judah.] And Jehoshaphat the king of Judah said, The word of the Lord is with him." The story then says, that these three kings went down to Elisha; and when Elisha [who, as I have said, was a Judahmite prophet] saw the King of Israel, he said unto him, "What have I to do with thee, get thee to the prophets of thy father and the prophets of thy mother. Nay but, said the king of Israel, the Lord hath called these three kings together, to deliver them into the hands of the king of Moab," (meaning because of the distress they were in for water;) upon which Elisha said, "As the Lord of hosts liveth before whom I stand, surely, were it not that I regard the presence of Jehoshaphat, king of Judah, I would not look towards thee nor see thee." Here is all the venom and vulgarity of a party prophet. We are now to see the performance, or manner of prophesying.

Ver. 15. "'Bring me,' (said Elisha), 'a minstrel'; and it came to pass, when the minstrel played, that the hand of the Lord came upon him." Here is the farce of the conjurer. Now for the prophecy: "And Elisha said, [singing most probably to the tune he was playing], Thus saith the Lord, Make this valley full of ditches;" which was just telling them what every countryman could have told them without either fiddle or farce, that the way to get water was to dig for it.

> But as every conjuror is not famous alike for the same thing, so neither were those prophets; for though all of them, at least those I have spoken of, were famous for lying, some of them excelled in cursing. Elisha, whom I have just mentioned, was a chief in this branch of prophesying; it was he that cursed the forty-two children in the name of the Lord, whom the two she-bears came and devoured. We are to suppose that those children were of the party of Israel; but as those who will curse will lie, there is just as much credit to be given to this story of Elisha's two she-bears as there is to that of the Dragon of Wantley, of whom it is said:
>
> Poor children three devoured be,
> That could not with him grapple;
> And at one sup he eat them up,
> As a man would eat an apple.

There was another description of men called prophets, that amused themselves with dreams and visions; but whether by night or by day we know not. These, if they were not quite harmless, were but little mischievous. Of this class are,

EZEKIEL and DANIEL; and the first question upon these books, as upon all the others, is, Are they genuine? that is, were they written by Ezekiel and Daniel?

Of this there is no proof; but so far as my own opinion goes, I am more inclined to believe they were, than that they were not. My reasons for this opinion are as follows: First, Because those books do not contain internal evidence to prove they were not written by Ezekiel and Daniel, as the books ascribed to Moses, Joshua, Samuel, etc., prove they were not written by Moses, Joshua, Samuel, etc.

Secondly, Because they were not written till after the Babylonish captivity began; and there is good reason to believe that not any book in the bible was written before that period; at least it is proveable, from the books themselves, as I have already shown, that they were not written till after the commencement of the Jewish monarchy.

Thirdly, Because the manner in which the books ascribed to Ezekiel and Daniel are written, agrees with the condition these men were in at the time of writing them.

Had the numerous commentators and priests, who have foolishly employed or wasted their time in pretending to expound and unriddle those books, been carred into captivity, as Ezekiel and Daniel were, it would greatly have improved their intellects in comprehending the reason for this mode of writing, and have saved them the trouble of racking their invention, as they have done to no purpose; for they would have found that themselves would be obliged to write whatever they had to write, respecting their own affairs, or those of their friends, or of their country, in a concealed manner, as those men have done.

These two books differ from all the rest; for it is only these that are filled with accounts of dreams and visions: and this difference arose from the situation the writers were in as prisoners of war, or prisoners of state, in a foreign country, which obliged them to convey even the most trifling information to each other, and all their political projects or opinions, in obscure and metaphorical terms. They pretend to have dreamed dreams, and seen visions, because it was unsafe for them to speak facts or plain language. We ought, however, to suppose, that the persons to whom they wrote understood what they meant, and that it was not intended anybody else should. But these busy commentators and priests have been puzzling their wits to find out what it was not intended they should know, and with which they have nothing to do.

Ezekiel and Daniel were carried prisoners to Babylon, under the first captivity, in the time of Jehoiakim, nine years before the second captivity in the time of Zedekiah. The Jews were then still numerous, and had considerable force at Jerusalem; and as it is natural to suppose that men in the situation of Ezekiel and Daniel would be meditating the recovery of their country, and their own deliverance, it is reasonable to suppose that the accounts of dreams and visions with which these books are filled, are no other than a disguised mode of correspondence to facilitate those objects: it served them as a cypher, or secret alphabet. If they are not this, they are tales, reveries, and nonsense; or at least a fanciful way of wearing off the wearisomeness of captivity; but the presumption is, they are the former.

Ezekiel begins his book by speaking of a vision of cherubims, and of a wheel within a wheel, which he says he saw by the river Chebar, in the land of his captivity. Is it not reasonable to suppose that by the cherubims he meant the temple at Jerusalem, where they had figures of cherubims? and by a wheel within a wheel (which as a figure has always been understood to signify political contrivance) the project or means of recovering Jerusalem? In the latter part of his book he supposes himself transported to Jerusalem, and into the temple; and he refers back to the vision on the river Chebar, and says, (xliii- 3,) that this last vision was like the vision on the river Chebar; which indicates that those pretended dreams and visions had for their object the recovery of Jerusalem, and nothing further.

As to the romantic interpretations and applications, wild as the dreams and visions they undertake to explain, which commentators and priests have made of those books, that of converting them into things which they call prophecies, and making them bend to times and circumstances as far remote even as the present day, it shows the fraud or the extreme folly to which credulity or priestcraft can go.

Scarcely anything can be more absurd than to suppose that men situated as Ezekiel and Daniel were, whose country was over-run, and in the possession of the enemy, all their friends and relations in captivity abroad, or in slavery at home, or massacred, or in continual danger of it; scarcely any thing, I say, can be more absurd than to suppose that such men should find nothing to do but that of employing their time and their thoughts about what was to happen to other nations a thousand or two thousand years after they were dead; at the same time nothing more natural than that they should meditate the recovery of Jerusalem, and their own deliverance; and that this was the sole object of all the obscure and apparently frantic writing contained in those books.

In this sense the mode of writing used in those two books being forced by necessity, and not adopted by choice, is not irrational; but, if we are to use the books as prophecies, they are false. In Ezekiel xxix. 11., speaking of Egypt, it is said, "No foot of man shall pass through it, nor foot of beast pass through it; neither shall it be inhabited for forty years." This is what never came to pass, and consequently it is false, as all the books I have already reviewed are.—I here close this part of the subject.

In the former part of 'The Age of Reason' I have spoken of Jonah, and of the story of him and the whale.—A fit story for ridicule, if it was written to be believed; or of laughter, if it was intended to try what credulity could swallow; for, if it could swallow Jonah and the whale it could swallow anything.

But, as is already shown in the observations on the book of Job and of Proverbs, it is not always certain which of the books in the Bible are originally Hebrew, or only translations from the books of the Gentiles into Hebrew; and, as the book of Jonah, so far from treating of the affairs of the Jews, says nothing upon that subject, but treats altogether of the Gentiles, it is more probable that it is a book of the Gentiles than of the Jews, [I have read in an ancient Persian poem (Saadi, I believe, but have mislaid the reference) this phrase: "And now the whale swallowed Jonah: the sun set."—Editor.] and that it has been written as a fable to expose the nonsense, and satyrize the vicious and malignant character, of a Bible-prophet, or a predicting priest.

Jonah is represented, first as a disobedient prophet, running away from his mission, and taking shelter aboard a vessel of the Gentiles, bound from Joppa to Tarshish; as if he ignorantly supposed, by such a paltry contrivance, he could hide himself where God could not find him. The vessel is overtaken by a storm at sea; and the mariners, all of whom are Gentiles, believing it to be a judgement on account of some one on board who had committed a crime, agreed to cast lots to discover the offender; and the lot fell upon Jonah. But before this they had cast all their wares and merchandise over-board to lighten the vessel, while Jonah, like a stupid fellow, was fast asleep in the hold.

After the lot had designated Jonah to be the offender, they questioned him to know who and what he was? and he told them he was an Hebrew; and the story implies that he confessed himself to be guilty. But these Gentiles, instead of sacrificing him at once without pity or mercy, as a company of Bible-prophets or priests would have done by a Gentile in the same case, and as it is related Samuel had done by Agag, and Moses by the women and children, they endeavoured to save him, though at the risk of their own lives: for the account says, "Nevertheless [that is, though Jonah was a Jew and a foreigner, and the cause of all their misfortunes, and the loss of their cargo] the men rowed hard to bring the boat to land, but they could not, for the sea wrought and was tempestuous against them." Still however they were unwilling to put the fate of the lot into execution; and they cried, says the account, unto the Lord, saying, "We beseech thee, O Lord, let us not perish for this man's life, and lay not upon us innocent blood; for thou, O Lord, hast done as it pleased thee." Meaning thereby, that they did not presume to judge Jonah guilty, since that he might be innocent; but that they considered the lot that had fallen upon him as a decree of God, or as it pleased God. The address of this prayer shows that the Gentiles worshipped one Supreme Being, and that they were not idolaters as the Jews represented them to be. But the storm still continuing, and the danger encreasing, they put the fate of the lot into execution, and cast Jonah in the sea; where, according to the story, a great fish swallowed him up whole and alive!

We have now to consider Jonah securely housed from the storm in the fish's belly. Here we are told that he prayed; but the prayer is a made-up prayer, taken from various parts of the Psalms, without connection or consistency, and adapted to the distress, but not at all to the condition that Jonah was in. It is such a prayer as a Gentile, who might know something of the Psalms, could copy out for him. This circumstance alone, were there no other, is sufficient to indicate that the whole is a made-up story. The prayer, however, is supposed to have answered the purpose, and the story goes on, (taking-off at the same time the cant language of a Bible-prophet,) saying, "The Lord spake unto the fish, and it vomited out Jonah upon dry land."

Jonah then received a second mission to Nineveh, with which he sets out; and we have now to consider him as a preacher. The distress he is represented to have suffered, the remembrance of his own disobedience as the cause of it, and the miraculous escape he is supposed to have had, were sufficient, one would conceive, to have impressed him with sympathy and benevolence in the execution of his mission; but, instead of this, he enters the city with denunciation and malediction in his mouth, crying, "Yet forty days, and Nineveh shall be overthrown."

We have now to consider this supposed missionary in the last act of his mission; and here it is that the malevolent spirit of a Bible-prophet, or of a predicting priest, appears in all that blackness of character that men ascribe to the being they call the devil.

Having published his predictions, he withdrew, says the story, to the east side of the city.—But for what? not to contemplate in retirement the mercy of his Creator to himself or to others, but to wait, with malignant impatience, the destruction of Nineveh. It came to pass, however, as the story relates, that the Ninevites reformed, and that God, according to the Bible phrase, repented him of the evil he had said he would do unto them, and did it not. This, saith the first verse of the last chapter, displeased Jonah exceedingly and he was very angry. His obdurate heart would rather that all Nineveh should be destroyed, and every soul, young and old, perish in its ruins, than that his prediction should not be fulfilled. To expose the character of a prophet still more, a gourd is made to grow up in the night, that promises him an agreeable shelter from the heat of the sun, in the place to which he is retired; and the next morning it dies.

Here the rage of the prophet becomes excessive, and he is ready to destroy himself. "It is better, said he, for me to die than to live." This brings on a supposed expostulation between the Almighty and the prophet; in which the former says, "Doest thou well to be angry for the gourd? And Jonah said, I do well to be angry even unto death. Then said the Lord, Thou hast had pity on the gourd, for which thou hast not laboured, neither madest it to grow, which came up in a night, and perished in a night; and should not I spare Nineveh, that great city, in which are more than threescore thousand persons, that cannot discern between their right hand and their left?"

Here is both the winding up of the satire, and the moral of the fable. As a satire, it strikes against the character of all the Bible-prophets, and against all the indiscriminate judgements upon men, women and children, with which this lying book, the bible, is crowded; such as Noah's flood, the destruction of the cities of Sodom and Gomorrah, the extirpation of the Canaanites, even to suckling infants, and women with child; because the same reflection 'that there are more than threescore thousand persons that cannot discern between their right hand and their left,' meaning young children, applies to all their cases. It satirizes also the supposed partiality of the Creator for one nation more than for another.

As a moral, it preaches against the malevolent spirit of prediction; for as certainly as a man predicts ill, he becomes inclined to wish it. The pride of having his judgment right hardens his heart, till at last he beholds with satisfaction, or sees with disappointment, the accomplishment or the failure of his predictions.—This book ends with the same kind of strong and well-directed point against prophets, prophecies and indiscriminate judgements, as the chapter that Benjamin Franklin made for the Bible, about Abraham and the stranger, ends against the intolerant spirit of religious persecutions—Thus much for the book Jonah. [The story of Abraham and the Fire-worshipper, ascribed to Franklin, is from Saadi. (See my "Sacred Anthology," p. 61.) Paine has often been called a "mere scoffer," but he seems to have been among the first to treat with dignity the book of Jonah, so especially liable to the ridicule of superficial readers, and discern in it the highest conception of Deity known to the Old Testament.—Editor.]

Of the poetical parts of the Bible, that are called prophecies, I have spoken in the former part of 'The Age of Reason,' and already in this, where I have said that the word for prophet is the Bible-word for Poet, and that the flights and metaphors of those poets, many of which have become obscure by the lapse of time and the change of circumstances, have been ridiculously erected into things called prophecies, and applied to purposes the writers never thought of. When a priest quotes any of those passages, he unriddles it agreeably to his own views, and imposes that explanation upon his congregation as the meaning of the writer. The whore of Babylon has been the common whore of all the priests, and each has accused the other of keeping the strumpet; so well do they agree in their explanations.

There now remain only a few books, which they call books of the lesser prophets; and as I have already shown that the greater are impostors, it would be cowardice to disturb the repose of the little ones. Let them sleep, then, in the arms of their nurses, the priests, and both be forgotten together.

I have now gone through the Bible, as a man would go through a wood with an axe on his shoulder, and fell trees. Here they lie; and the priests, if they can, may replant them. They may, perhaps, stick them in the ground, but they will never make them grow.—I pass on to the books of the New Testament.

CHAPTER II - THE NEW TESTAMENT

THE New Testament, they tell us, is founded upon the prophecies of the Old; if so, it must follow the fate of its foundation.

As it is nothing extraordinary that a woman should be with child before she was married, and that the son she might bring forth should be executed, even unjustly, I see no reason for not believing that such a woman as Mary, and such a man as Joseph, and Jesus, existed; their mere existence is a matter of indifference, about which there is no ground either to believe or to disbelieve, and which comes under the common head of, It may be so, and what then? The probability however is that there were such persons, or at least such as resembled them in part of the circumstances, because almost all romantic stories have been suggested by some actual circumstance; as the adventures of Robinson Crusoe, not a word of which is true, were suggested by the case of Alexander Selkirk.

It is not then the existence or the non-existence, of the persons that I trouble myself about; it is the fable of Jesus Christ, as told in the New Testament, and the wild and visionary doctrine raised thereon, against which I contend. The story, taking it as it is told, is blasphemously obscene. It gives an account of a young woman engaged to be married, and while under this engagement, she is, to speak plain language, debauched by a ghost, under the impious pretence, (Luke i. 35,) that "the Holy Ghost shall come upon thee, and the power of the Highest shall overshadow thee." Notwithstanding which, Joseph afterwards marries her, cohabits with her as his wife, and in his turn rivals the ghost. This is putting the story into intelligible language, and when told in this manner, there is not a priest but must be ashamed to own it. [Mary, the supposed virgin, mother of Jesus, had several other children, sons and daughters. See Matt. xiii. 55, 56.—Author.]

Obscenity in matters of faith, however wrapped up, is always a token of fable and imposture; for it is necessary to our serious belief in God, that we do not connect it with stories that run, as this does, into ludicrous interpretations. This story is, upon the face of it, the same kind of story as that of Jupiter and Leda, or Jupiter and Europa, or any of the amorous adventures of Jupiter; and shews, as is already stated in the former part of 'The Age of Reason,' that the Christian faith is built upon the heathen Mythology.

As the historical parts of the New Testament, so far as concerns Jesus Christ, are confined to a very short space of time, less than two years, and all within the same country, and nearly to the same spot, the discordance of time, place, and circumstance, which detects the fallacy of the books of the Old Testament, and proves them to be impositions, cannot be expected to be found here in the same abundance. The New Testament compared with the Old, is like a farce of one act, in which there is not room for very numerous violations of the unities. There are, however, some glaring contradictions, which, exclusive of the fallacy of the pretended prophecies, are sufficient to show the story of Jesus Christ to be false.

I lay it down as a position which cannot be controverted, first, that the agreement of all the parts of a story does not prove that story to be true, because the parts may agree, and the whole may be false; secondly, that the disagreement of the parts of a story proves the whole cannot be true. The agreement does not prove truth, but the disagreement proves falsehood positively.

The history of Jesus Christ is contained in the four books ascribed to Matthew, Mark, Luke, and John.—The first chapter of Matthew begins with giving a genealogy of Jesus Christ; and in the third chapter of Luke there is also given a genealogy of Jesus Christ. Did these two agree, it would not prove the genealogy to be true, because it might nevertheless be a fabrication; but as they contradict each other in every particular, it proves falsehood absolutely. If Matthew speaks truth, Luke speaks falsehood; and if Luke speaks truth, Matthew speaks falsehood: and as there is no authority for believing one more than the other, there is no authority for believing either; and if they cannot be believed even in the very first thing they say, and set out to prove, they are not entitled to be believed in any thing they say afterwards. Truth is an uniform thing; and as to inspiration and revelation, were we to admit it, it is impossible to suppose it can be contradictory. Either then the men called apostles were imposters, or the books ascribed to them have been written by other persons, and fathered upon them, as is the case in the Old Testament.

The book of Matthew gives (i. 6), a genealogy by name from David, up, through Joseph, the husband of Mary, to Christ; and makes there to be twent eight generations. The book of Luke gives also a genealogy by name from Christ, through Joseph the husband of Mary, down to David, and makes there to be forty-three generations; besides which, there is only the two names of David and Joseph that are alike in the two lists.—I here insert both genealogical lists, and for the sake of perspicuity and comparison, have placed them both in the same direction, that is, from Joseph down to David.

Genealogy, according to   *Genealogy, according to*

Matthew.	Luke.
Christ	Christ
2 Joseph	2 Joseph
3 Jacob	3 Heli
4 Matthan	4 Matthat
5 Eleazer	5 Levi
6 Eliud	6 Melchl
7 Achim	7 Janna
8 Sadoc	8 Joseph
9 Azor	9 Mattathias
10 Eliakim	10 Amos
11 Abiud	11 Naum
12 Zorobabel	12 Esli
13 Salathiel	13 Nagge
14 Jechonias	14 Maath
15 Josias	15 Mattathias
16 Amon	16 Semei
17 Manasses	17 Joseph
18 Ezekias	18 Juda
19 Achaz	19 Joanna
20 Joatham	20 Rhesa
21 Ozias	21 Zorobabel
22 Joram	22 Salathiel
23 Josaphat	23 Neri
24 Asa	24 Melchi
25 Abia	25 Addi
26 Roboam	26 Cosam
27 Solomon	27 Elmodam
28 David *	28 Er
29 Jose	
30 Eliezer	
31 Jorim	
32 Matthat	
33 Levi	
34 Simeon	
35 Juda	
36 Joseph	
37 Jonan	
38 Eliakim	
39 Melea	
40 Menan	
41 Mattatha	
42 Nathan	
43 David	

[NOTE: * From the birth of David to the birth of Christ is upwards of 1080 years; and as the life-time of Christ is not included, there are but 27 full generations. To find therefore the average age of each person mentioned in the list, at the time his first son was born, it is only necessary to divide 1080 by 27, which gives 40 years for each person. As the life-time of man was then but of the same extent it is now, it is an absurdity to suppose, that 27 following generations should all be old bachelors, before they married; and the more so, when we are told that Solomon, the next in succession to David, had a house full of wives and mistresses before he was twenty-one years of age. So far from this genealogy being a solemn truth, it is not even a reasonable lie. The list of Luke gives about twenty-six years for the average age, and this is too much.—Author.]

Now, if these men, Matthew and Luke, set out with a falsehood between them (as these two accounts show they do) in the very commencement of their history of Jesus Christ, and of who, and of what he was, what authority (as I have before asked) is there left for believing the strange things they tell us afterwards? If they cannot be believed in their account of his natural genealogy, how are we to believe them when they tell us he was the son of God, begotten by a ghost; and that an angel announced this in secret to his mother? If they lied in one genealogy, why are we to believe them in the other? If his natural genealogy be manufactured, which it certainly is, why are we not to suppose that his celestial genealogy is manufactured also, and that the whole is fabulous? Can any man of serious reflection hazard his future happiness upon the belief of a story naturally impossible, repugnant to every idea of decency, and related by persons already detected of falsehood? Is it not more safe that we stop ourselves at the plain, pure, and unmixed belief of one God, which is deism, than that we commit ourselves on an ocean of improbable, irrational, indecent, and contradictory tales?

The first question, however, upon the books of the New Testament, as upon those of the Old, is, Are they genuine? were they written by the persons to whom they are ascribed? For it is upon this ground only that the strange things related therein have been credited. Upon this point, there is no direct proof for or against; and all that this state of a case proves is doubtfulness; and doubtfulness is the opposite of belief. The state, therefore, that the books are in, proves against themselves as far as this kind of proof can go.

But, exclusive of this, the presumption is that the books called the Evangelists, and ascribed to Matthew, Mark, Luke, and John, were not written by Matthew, Mark, Luke, and John; and that they are impositions. The disordered state of the history in these four books, the silence of one book upon matters related in the other, and the disagreement that is to be found among them, implies that they are the productions of some unconnected individuals, many years after the things they pretend to relate, each of whom made his own legend; and not the writings of men living intimately together, as the men called apostles are supposed to have done: in fine, that they have been manufactured, as the books of the Old Testament have been, by other persons than those whose names they bear.

The story of the angel announcing what the church calls the immaculate conception, is not so much as mentioned in the books ascribed to Mark, and John; and is differently related in Matthew and Luke. The former says the angel, appeared to Joseph; the latter says, it was to Mary; but either Joseph or Mary was the worst evidence that could have been thought of; for it was others that should have testified for them, and not they for themselves. Were any girl that is now with child to say, and even to swear it, that she was gotten with child by a ghost, and that an angel told her so, would she be believed? Certainly she would not. Why then are we to believe the same thing of another girl whom we never saw, told by nobody knows who, nor when, nor where? How strange and inconsistent is it, that the same circumstance that would weaken the belief even of a probable story, should be given as a motive for believing this one, that has upon the face of it every token of absolute impossibility and imposture.

The story of Herod destroying all the children under two years old, belongs altogether to the book of Matthew; not one of the rest mentions anything about it. Had such a circumstance been true, the universality of it must have made it known to all the writers, and the thing would have been too striking to have been omitted by any. This writer tell us, that Jesus escaped this slaughter, because Joseph and Mary were warned by an angel to flee with him into Egypt; but he forgot to make provision for John [the Baptist], who was then under two years of age. John, however, who staid behind, fared as well as Jesus, who fled; and therefore the story circumstantially belies itself.

Not any two of these writers agree in reciting, exactly in the same words, the written inscription, short as it is, which they tell us was put over Christ when he was crucified; and besides this, Mark says, He was crucified at the third hour, (nine in the morning;) and John says it was the sixth hour, (twelve at noon.) [According to John, (xix. 14) the sentence was not passed till about the sixth hour (noon,) and consequently the execution could not be till the afternoon; but Mark (xv. 25) Says expressly that he was crucified at the third hour, (nine in the morning,)—Author.]

The inscription is thus stated in those books:

Matthew—This is Jesus the king of the Jews. Mark—The king of the Jews. Luke—This is the king of the Jews. John—Jesus of Nazareth the king of the Jews.

We may infer from these circumstances, trivial as they are, that those writers, whoever they were, and in whatever time they lived, were not present at the scene. The only one of the men called apostles who appears to have been near to the spot was Peter, and when he was accused of being one of Jesus's followers, it is said, (Matthew xxvi. 74,) "Then Peter began to curse and to swear, saying, I know not the man:" yet we are now called to believe the same Peter, convicted, by their own account, of perjury. For what reason, or on what authority, should we do this?

The accounts that are given of the circumstances, that they tell us attended the crucifixion, are differently related in those four books.

The book ascribed to Matthew says 'there was darkness over all the land from the sixth hour unto the ninth hour—that the veil of the temple was rent in twain from the top to the bottom—that there was an earthquake—that the rocks rent—that the graves opened, that the bodies of many of the saints that slept arose and came out of their graves after the resurrection, and went into the holy city and appeared unto many.' Such is the account which this dashing writer of the book of Matthew gives, but in which he is not supported by the writers of the other books.

The writer of the book ascribed to Mark, in detailing the circumstances of the crucifixion, makes no mention of any earthquake, nor of the rocks rending, nor of the graves opening, nor of the dead men walking out. The writer of the book of Luke is silent also upon the same points. And as to the writer of the book of John, though he details all the circumstances of the crucifixion down to the burial of Christ, he says nothing about either the darkness—the veil of the temple—the earthquake—the rocks—the graves—nor the dead men.

Now if it had been true that these things had happened, and if the writers of these books had lived at the time they did happen, and had been the persons they are said to be—namely, the four men called apostles, Matthew, Mark, Luke, and John,—it was not possible for them, as true historians, even without the aid of inspiration, not to have recorded them. The things, supposing them to have been facts, were of too much notoriety not to have been known, and of too much importance not to have been told. All these supposed apostles must have been witnesses of the earthquake, if there had been any, for it was not possible for them to have been absent from it: the opening of the graves and resurrection of the dead men, and their walking about the city, is of still greater importance than the earthquake. An earthquake is always possible, and natural, and proves nothing; but this opening of the graves is supernatural, and directly in point to their doctrine, their cause, and their apostleship. Had it been true, it would have filled up whole chapters of those books, and been the chosen theme and general chorus of all the writers; but instead of this, little and trivial things, and mere prattling conversation of 'he said this and she said that' are often tediously detailed, while this most important of all, had it been true, is passed off in a slovenly manner by a single dash of the pen, and that by one writer only, and not so much as hinted at by the rest.

It is an easy thing to tell a lie, but it is difficult to support the lie after it is told. The writer of the book of Matthew should have told us who the saints were that came to life again, and went into the city, and what became of them afterwards, and who it was that saw them; for he is not hardy enough to say that he saw them himself;—whether they came out naked, and all in natural buff, he-saints and she-saints, or whether they came full dressed, and where they got their dresses; whether they went to their former habitations, and reclaimed their wives, their husbands, and their property, and how they were received; whether they entered ejectments for the recovery of their possessions, or brought actions of crim. con. against the rival interlopers; whether they remained on earth, and followed their former occupation of preaching or working; or whether they died again, or went back to their graves alive, and buried themselves.

Strange indeed, that an army of saints should return to life, and nobody know who they were, nor who it was that saw them, and that not a word more should be said upon the subject, nor these saints have any thing to tell us! Had it been the prophets who (as we are told) had formerly prophesied of these things, they must have had a great deal to say. They could have told us everything, and we should have had posthumous prophecies, with notes and commentaries upon the first, a little better at least than we have now. Had it been Moses, and Aaron, and Joshua, and Samuel, and David, not an unconverted Jew had remained in all Jerusalem. Had it been John the Baptist, and the saints of the times then present, everybody would have known them, and they would have out-preached and out-famed all the other apostles. But, instead of this, these saints are made to pop up, like Jonah's gourd in the night, for no purpose at all but to wither in the morning.—Thus much for this part of the story.

The tale of the resurrection follows that of the crucifixion; and in this as well as in that, the writers, whoever they were, disagree so much as to make it evident that none of them were there.

The book of Matthew states, that when Christ was put in the sepulchre the Jews applied to Pilate for a watch or a guard to be placed over the septilchre, to prevent the body being stolen by the disciples; and that in consequence of this request the sepulchre was made sure, sealing the stone that covered the mouth, and setting a watch. But the other books say nothing about this application, nor about the sealing, nor the guard, nor the watch; and according to their accounts, there were none. Matthew, however, follows up this part of the story of the guard or the watch with a second part, that I shall notice in the conclusion, as it serves to detect the fallacy of those books.

The book of Matthew continues its account, and says, (xxviii. 1,) that at the end of the Sabbath, as it began to dawn, towards the first day of the week, came Mary Magdalene and the other Mary, to see the sepulchre. Mark says it was sun-rising, and John says it was dark. Luke says it was Mary Magdalene and Joanna, and Mary the mother of James, and other women, that came to the sepulchre; and John states that Mary Magdalene came alone. So well do they agree about their first evidence! They all, however, appear to have known most about Mary Magdalene; she was a woman of large acquaintance, and it was not an ill conjecture that she might be upon the stroll. [The Bishop of Llandaff, in his famous "Apology," censured Paine severely for this insinuation against Mary Magdalene, but the censure really falls on our English version, which, by a chapter-heading (Luke vii.), has unwarrantably identified her as the sinful woman who anointed Jesus, and irrevocably branded her.—Editor.]

The book of Matthew goes on to say (ver. 2): "And behold there was a great earthquake, for the angel of the Lord descended from heaven, and came and rolled back the stone from the door, and sat upon it" But the other books say nothing about any earthquake, nor about the angel rolling back the stone, and sitting upon it and, according to their account, there was no angel sitting there. Mark says the angel [Mark says "a young man," and Luke "two men."—Editor.] was within the sepulchre, sitting on the right side. Luke says there were two, and they were both standing up; and John says they were both sitting down, one at the head and the other at the feet.

Matthew says, that the angel that was sitting upon the stone on the outside of the sepulchre told the two Marys that Christ was risen, and that the women went away quickly. Mark says, that the women, upon seeing the stone rolled away, and wondering at it, went into the sepulchre, and that it was the angel that was sitting within on the right side, that told them so. Luke says, it was the two angels that were Standing up; and John says, it was Jesus Christ himself that told it to Mary Magdalene; and that she did not go into the sepulchre, but only stooped down and looked in.

Now, if the writers of these four books had gone into a court of justice to prove an alibi, (for it is of the nature of an alibi that is here attempted to be proved, namely, the absence of a dead body by supernatural means,) and had they given their evidence in the same contradictory manner as it is here given, they would have been in danger of having their ears cropt for perjury, and would have justly deserved it. Yet this is the evidence, and these are the books, that have been imposed upon the world as being given by divine inspiration, and as the unchangeable word of God.

The writer of the book of Matthew, after giving this account, relates a story that is not to be found in any of the other books, and which is the same I have just before alluded to. "Now," says he, [that is, after the conversation the women had had with the angel sitting upon the stone,] "behold some of the watch [meaning the watch that he had said had been placed over the sepulchre] came into the city, and shawed unto the chief priests all the things that were done; and when they were assembled with the elders and had taken counsel, they gave large money unto the soldiers, saying, Say ye, that his disciples came by night, and stole him away while we slept; and if this come to the governor's ears, we will persuade him, and secure you. So they took the money, and did as they were taught; and this saying [that his disciples stole him away] is commonly reported among the Jews until this day."

The expression, until this day, is an evidence that the book ascribed to Matthew was not written by Matthew, and that it has been manufactured long after the times and things of which it pretends to treat; for the expression implies a great length of intervening time. It would be inconsistent in us to speak in this manner of any thing happening in our own time. To give, therefore, intelligible meaning to the expression, we must suppose a lapse of some generations at least, for this manner of speaking carries the mind back to ancient time.

The absurdity also of the story is worth noticing; for it shows the writer of the book of Matthew to have been an exceeding weak and foolish man. He tells a story that contradicts itself in point of possibility; for though the guard, if there were any, might be made to say that the body was taken away while they were asleep, and to give that as a reason for their not having prevented it, that same sleep must also have prevented their knowing how, and by whom, it was done; and yet they are made to say that it was the disciples who did it. Were a man to tender his evidence of something that he should say was done, and of the manner of doing it, and of the person who did it, while he was asleep, and could know nothing of the matter, such evidence could not be received: it will do well enough for Testament evidence, but not for any thing where truth is concerned.

I come now to that part of the evidence in those books, that respects the pretended appearance of Christ after this pretended resurrection.

The writer of the book of Matthew relates, that the angel that was sitting on the stone at the mouth of the sepulchre, said to the two Marys (xxviii. 7), "Behold Christ is gone before you into Galilee, there ye shall see him; lo, I have told you." And the same writer at the next two verses (8, 9,) makes Christ himself to speak to the same purpose to these women immediately after the angel had told it to them, and that they ran quickly to tell it to the disciples; and it is said (ver. 16), "Then the eleven disciples went away into Galilee, into a mountain where Jesus had appointed them; and, when they saw him, they worshipped him."

But the writer of the book of John tells us a story very different to this; for he says (xx. 19) "Then the same day at evening, being the first day of the week, [that is, the same day that Christ is said to have risen,] when the doors were shut, where the disciples were assembled, for fear of the Jews, came Jesus and stood in the midst of them."

According to Matthew the eleven were marching to Galilee, to meet Jesus in a mountain, by his own appointment, at the very time when, according to John, they were assembled in another place, and that not by appointment, but in secret, for fear of the Jews.

The writer of the book of Luke xxiv. 13, 33-36, contradicts that of Matthew more pointedly than John does; for he says expressly, that the meeting was in Jerusalem the evening of the same day that he (Christ) rose, and that the eleven were there.

Now, it is not possible, unless we admit these supposed disciples the right of wilful lying, that the writers of these books could be any of the eleven persons called disciples; for if, according to Matthew, the eleven went into Galilee to meet Jesus in a mountain by his own appointment, on the same day that he is said to have risen, Luke and John must have been two of that eleven; yet the writer of Luke says expressly, and John implies as much, that the meeting was that same day, in a house in

Jerusalem; and, on the other hand, if, according to Luke and John, the eleven were assembled in a house in Jerusalem, Matthew must have been one of that eleven; yet Matthew says the meeting was in a mountain in Galilee, and consequently the evidence given in those books destroy each other.

The writer of the book of Mark says nothing about any meeting in Galilee; but he says (xvi. 12) that Christ, after his resurrection, appeared in another form to two of them, as they walked into the country, and that these two told it to the residue, who would not believe them. [This belongs to the late addition to Mark, which originally ended with xvi. 8.—Editor.] Luke also tells a story, in which he keeps Christ employed the whole of the day of this pretended resurrection, until the evening, and which totally invalidates the account of going to the mountain in Galilee. He says, that two of them, without saying which two, went that same day to a village called Emmaus, three score furlongs (seven miles and a half) from Jerusalem, and that Christ in disguise went with them, and stayed with them unto the evening, and supped with them, and then vanished out of their sight, and reappeared that same evening, at the meeting of the eleven in Jerusalem.

This is the contradictory manner in which the evidence of this pretended reappearance of Christ is stated: the only point in which the writers agree, is the skulking privacy of that reappearance; for whether it was in the recess of a mountain in Galilee, or in a shut-up house in Jerusalem, it was still skulking. To what cause then are we to assign this skulking? On the one hand, it is directly repugnant to the supposed or pretended end, that of convincing the world that Christ was risen; and, on the other hand, to have asserted the publicity of it would have exposed the writers of those books to public detection; and, therefore, they have been under the necessity of making it a private affair.

As to the account of Christ being seen by more than five hundred at once, it is Paul only who says it, and not the five hundred who say it for themselves. It is, therefore, the testimony of but one man, and that too of a man, who did not, according to the same account, believe a word of the matter himself at the time it is said to have happened. His evidence, supposing him to have been the writer of Corinthians xv., where this account is given, is like that of a man who comes into a court of justice to swear that what he had sworn before was false. A man may often see reason, and he has too always the right of changing his opinion; but this liberty does not extend to matters of fact.

I now come to the last scene, that of the ascension into heaven.—Here all fear of the Jews, and of every thing else, must necessarily have been out of the question: it was that which, if true, was to seal the whole; and upon which the reality of the future mission of the disciples was to rest for proof. Words, whether declarations or promises, that passed in private, either in the recess of a mountain in Galilee, or in a shut-up house in Jerusalem, even supposing them to have been spoken, could not be evidence in public; it was therefore necessary that this last scene should preclude the possibility of denial and dispute; and that it should be, as I have stated in the former part of 'The Age of Reason,' as public and as visible as the sun at noon-day; at least it ought to have been as public as the crucifixion is reported to have been.—But to come to the point.

In the first place, the writer of the book of Matthew does not say a syllable about it; neither does the writer of the book of John. This being the case, is it possible to suppose that those writers, who affect to be even minute in other matters, would have been silent upon this, had it been true? The writer of the book of Mark passes it off in a careless, slovenly manner, with a single dash of the pen, as if he was tired of romancing, or ashamed of the story. So also does the writer of Luke. And even between these two, there is not an apparent agreement, as to the place where this final parting is said to have been. [The last nine verses of Mark being ungenuine, the story of the ascension rests exclusively on the words in Luke xxiv. 51, "was carried up into heaven,"—words omitted by several ancient authorities.—Editor.]

The book of Mark says that Christ appeared to the eleven as they sat at meat, alluding to the meeting of the eleven at Jerusalem: he then states the conversation that he says passed at that meeting; and immediately after says (as a school-boy would finish a dull story,) "So then, after the Lord had spoken unto them, he was received up into heaven, and sat on the right hand of God." But the writer of Luke says, that the ascension was from Bethany; that he (Christ) led them out as far as Bethany, and was parted from them there, and was carried up into heaven. So also was Mahomet: and, as to Moses, the apostle Jude says, ver. 9. That 'Michael and the devil disputed about his body.' While we believe such fables as these, or either of them, we believe unworthily of the Almighty.

I have now gone through the examination of the four books ascribed to Matthew, Mark, Luke and John; and when it is considered that the whole space of time, from the crucifixion to what is called the ascension, is but a few days, apparently not more than three or four, and that all the circumstances are reported to have happened nearly about the same spot, Jerusalem, it is, I believe, impossible to find in any story upon record so many and such glaring absurdities, contradictions, and falsehoods, as are in those books. They are more numerous and striking than I had any expectation of finding, when I began this examination, and far more so than I had any idea of when I wrote the former part of 'The Age of Reason.' I had then neither Bible nor Testament to refer to, nor could I procure any. My own situation, even as to existence, was becoming every day more precarious;

and as I was willing to leave something behind me upon the subject, I was obliged to be quick and concise. The quotations I then made were from memory only, but they are correct; and the opinions I have advanced in that work are the effect of the most clear and long-established conviction,—that the Bible and the Testament are impositions upon the world;—that the fall of man, the account of Jesus Christ being the Son of God, and of his dying to appease the wrath of God, and of salvation by that strange means, are all fabulous inventions, dishonourable to the wisdom and power of the Almighty;—that the only true religion is deism, by which I then meant and now mean the belief of one God, and an imitation of his moral character, or the practice of what are called moral virtues;—and that it was upon this only (so far as religion is concerned) that I rested all my hopes of happiness hereafter. So say I now—and so help me God.

But to return to the subject.—Though it is impossible, at this distance of time, to ascertain as a fact who were the writers of those four books (and this alone is sufficient to hold them in doubt, and where we doubt we do not believe) it is not difficult to ascertain negatively that they were not written by the persons to whom they are ascribed. The contradictions in those books demonstrate two things:

First, that the writers cannot have been eye-witnesses and ear-witnesses of the matters they relate, or they would have related them without those contradictions; and, consequently that the books have not been written by the persons called apostles, who are supposed to have been witnesses of this kind.

Secondly, that the writers, whoever they were, have not acted in concerted imposition, but each writer separately and individually for himself, and without the knowledge of the other.

The same evidence that applies to prove the one, applies equally to prove both cases; that is, that the books were not written by the men called apostles, and also that they are not a concerted imposition. As to inspiration, it is altogether out of the question; we may as well attempt to unite truth and falsehood, as inspiration and contradiction.

If four men are eye-witnesses and ear-witnesses to a scene, they will without any concert between them, agree as to time and place, when and where that scene happened. Their individual knowledge of the thing, each one knowing it for himself, renders concert totally unnecessary; the one will not say it was in a mountain in the country, and the other at a house in town; the one will not say it was at sunrise, and the other that it was dark. For in whatever place it was and whatever time it was, they know it equally alike.

And on the other hand, if four men concert a story, they will make their separate relations of that story agree and corroborate with each other to support the whole. That concert supplies the want of fact in the one case, as the knowledge of the fact supersedes, in the other case, the necessity of a concert. The same contradictions, therefore, that prove there has been no concert, prove also that the reporters had no knowledge of the fact, (or rather of that which they relate as a fact,) and detect also the falsehood of their reports. Those books, therefore, have neither been written by the men called apostles, nor by imposters in concert.—How then have they been written?

I am not one of those who are fond of believing there is much of that which is called wilful lying, or lying originally, except in the case of men setting up to be prophets, as in the Old Testament; for prophesying is lying professionally. In almost all other cases it is not difficult to discover the progress by which even simple supposition, with the aid of credulity, will in time grow into a lie, and at last be told as a fact; and whenever we can find a charitable reason for a thing of this kind, we ought not to indulge a severe one.

The story of Jesus Christ appearing after he was dead is the story of an apparition, such as timid imaginations can always create in vision, and credulity believe. Stories of this kind had been told of the assassination of Julius Caesar not many years before, and they generally have their origin in violent deaths, or in execution of innocent persons. In cases of this kind, compassion lends its aid, and benevolently stretches the story. It goes on a little and a little farther, till it becomes a most certain truth. Once start a ghost, and credulity fills up the history of its life, and assigns the cause of its appearance; one tells it one way, another another way, till there are as many stories about the ghost, and about the proprietor of the ghost, as there are about Jesus Christ in these four books.

The story of the appearance of Jesus Christ is told with that strange mixture of the natural and impossible, that distinguishes legendary tale from fact. He is represented as suddenly coming in and going out when the doors are shut, and of vanishing out of sight, and appearing again, as one would conceive of an unsubstantial vision; then again he is hungry, sits down to meat, and eats his supper. But as those who tell stories of this kind never provide for all the cases, so it is here: they have told us, that when he arose he left his grave-clothes behind him; but they have forgotten to provide other clothes for him to appear in afterwards, or to tell us what he did with them when he ascended; whether he stripped all off, or went up clothes and all. In the case of Elijah, they have been careful enough to make him throw down his mantle; how it happened not to be burnt in the chariot of fire, they also have not told us; but as imagination supplies all deficiencies of this kind, we may suppose if we please that it was made of salamander's wool.

Those who are not much acquainted with ecclesiastical history, may suppose that the book called the New Testament has existed ever since the time of Jesus Christ, as they suppose that the books ascribed to Moses have existed ever since the time of Moses. But the fact is historically otherwise; there was no such book as the New Testament till more than three hundred years after the time that Christ is said to have lived.

At what time the books ascribed to Matthew, Mark, Luke and John, began to appear, is altogether a matter of uncertainty. There is not the least shadow of evidence of who the persons were that wrote them, nor at what time they were written; and they might as well have been called by the names of any of the other supposed apostles as by the names they are now called. The originals are not in the possession of any Christian Church existing, any more than the two tables of stone written on, they pretend, by the finger of God, upon Mount Sinai, and given to Moses, are in the possession of the Jews. And even if they were, there is no possibility of proving the hand-writing in either case. At the time those four books were written there was no printing, and consequently there could be no publication otherwise than by written copies, which any man might make or alter at pleasure, and call them originals. Can we suppose it is consistent with the wisdom of the Almighty to commit himself and his will to man upon such precarious means as these; or that it is consistent we should pin our faith upon such uncertainties? We cannot make nor alter, nor even imitate, so much as one blade of grass that he has made, and yet we can make or alter words of God as easily as words of man. [The former part of the 'Age of Reason' has not been published two years, and there is already an expression in it that is not mine. The expression is: The book of Luke was carried by a majority of one voice only. It may be true, but it is not I that have said it. Some person who might know of that circumstance, has added it in a note at the bottom of the page of some of the editions, printed either in England or in America; and the printers, after that, have erected it into the body of the work, and made me the author of it. If this has happened within such a short space of time, notwithstanding the aid of printing, which prevents the alteration of copies individually, what may not have happened in a much greater length of time, when there was no printing, and when any man who could write could make a written copy and call it an original by Matthew, Mark, Luke, or John?—Author.]

[The spurious addition to Paine's work alluded to in his footnote drew on him a severe criticism from Dr. Priestley ("Letters to a Philosophical Unbeliever," p. 75), yet it seems to have been Priestley himself who, in his quotation, first incorporated into Paine's text the footnote added by the editor of the American edition (1794). The American added: "Vide Moshiem's (sic) Ecc. History," which Priestley omits. In a modern American edition I notice four verbal alterations introduced into the above footnote.—Editor.]

About three hundred and fifty years after the time that Christ is said to have lived, several writings of the kind I am speaking of were scattered in the hands of divers individuals; and as the church had begun to form itself into an hierarchy, or church government, with temporal powers, it set itself about collecting them into a code, as we now see them, called 'The New Testament.' They decided by vote, as I have before said in the former part of the Age of Reason, which of those writings, out of the collection they had made, should be the word of God, and which should not. The Robbins of the Jews had decided, by vote, upon the books of the Bible before.

As the object of the church, as is the case in all national establishments of churches, was power and revenue, and terror the means it used, it is consistent to suppose that the most miraculous and wonderful of the writings they had collected stood the best chance of being voted. And as to the authenticity of the books, the vote stands in the place of it; for it can be traced no higher.

Disputes, however, ran high among the people then calling themselves Christians, not only as to points of doctrine, but as to the authenticity of the books. In the contest between the person called St. Augustine, and Fauste, about the year 400, the latter says, "The books called the Evangelists have been composed long after the times of the apostles, by some obscure men, who, fearing that the world would not give credit to their relation of matters of which they could not be informed, have published them under the names of the apostles; and which are so full of sottishness and discordant relations, that there is neither agreement nor connection between them."

And in another place, addressing himself to the advocates of those books, as being the word of God, he says, "It is thus that your predecessors have inserted in the scriptures of our Lord many things which, though they carry his name, agree not with his doctrine." This is not surprising, since that we have often proved that these things have not been written by himself, nor by his apostles, but that for the greatest part they are founded upon tales, upon vague reports, and put together by I know not what half-Jews, with but little agreement between them; and which they have nevertheless published under the name of the apostles of our Lord, and have thus attributed to them their own errors and their lies. [I have taken these two extracts from Boulanger's

Life of Paul, written in French; Boulanger has quoted them from the writings of Augustine against Fauste, to which he refers.—Author.]

This Bishop Faustus is usually styled "The Manichaeum," Augustine having entitled his book, Contra Frustum Manichaeum Libri xxxiii., in which nearly the whole of Faustus' very able work is quoted.—Editor.]

The reader will see by those extracts that the authenticity of the books of the New Testament was denied, and the books treated as tales, forgeries, and lies, at the time they were voted to be the word of God. But the interest of the church, with the assistance of the faggot, bore down the opposition, and at last suppressed all investigation. Miracles followed upon miracles, if we will believe them, and men were taught to say they believed whether they believed or not. But (by way of throwing in a thought) the French Revolution has excommunicated the church from the power of working miracles; she has not been able, with the assistance of all her saints, to work one miracle since the revolution began; and as she never stood in greater need than now, we may, without the aid of divination, conclude that all her former miracles are tricks and lies. [Boulanger in his life of Paul, has collected from the ecclesiastical histories, and the writings of the fathers as they are called, several matters which show the opinions that prevailed among the different sects of Christians, at the time the Testament, as we now see it, was voted to be the word of God. The following extracts are from the second chapter of that work:

[The Marcionists (a Christian sect) asserted that the evangelists were filled with falsities. The Manichaeans, who formed a very numerous sect at the commencement of Christianity, rejected as false all the New Testament, and showed other writings quite different that they gave for authentic. The Corinthians, like the Marcionists, admitted not the Acts of the Apostles. The Encratites and the Sevenians adopted neither the Acts, nor the Epistles of Paul. Chrysostom, in a homily which he made upon the Acts of the Apostles, says that in his time, about the year 400, many people knew nothing either of the author or of the book. St. Irene, who lived before that time, reports that the Valentinians, like several other sects of the Christians, accused the scriptures of being filled with imperfections, errors, and contradictions. The Ebionites, or Nazarenes, who were the first Christians, rejected all the Epistles of Paul, and regarded him as an impostor. They report, among other things, that he was originally a Pagan; that he came to Jerusalem, where he lived some time; and that having a mind to marry the daughter of the high priest, he had himself been circumcised; but that not being able to obtain her, he quarrelled with the Jews and wrote against circumcision, and against the observation of the Sabbath, and against all the legal ordinances.—Author.] [Much abridged from the Exam. Crit. de la Vie de St. Paul, by N.A. Boulanger, 1770.—Editor.]

When we consider the lapse of more than three hundred years intervening between the time that Christ is said to have lived and the time the New Testament was formed into a book, we must see, even without the assistance of historical evidence, the exceeding uncertainty there is of its authenticity. The authenticity of the book of Homer, so far as regards the authorship, is much better established than that of the New Testament, though Homer is a thousand years the most ancient. It was only an exceeding good poet that could have written the book of Homer, and, therefore, few men only could have attempted it; and a man capable of doing it would not have thrown away his own fame by giving it to another. In like manner, there were but few that could have composed Euclid's Elements, because none but an exceeding good geometrician could have been the author of that work.

But with respect to the books of the New Testament, particularly such parts as tell us of the resurrection and ascension of Christ, any person who could tell a story of an apparition, or of a man's walking, could have made such books; for the story is most wretchedly told. The chance, therefore, of forgery in the Testament is millions to one greater than in the case of Homer or Euclid. Of the numerous priests or parsons of the present day, bishops and all, every one of them can make a sermon, or translate a scrap of Latin, especially if it has been translated a thousand times before; but is there any amongst them that can write poetry like Homer, or science like Euclid? The sum total of a parson's learning, with very few exceptions, is a, b, ab, and hic, haec, hoc; and their knowledge of science is, three times one is three; and this is more than sufficient to have enabled them, had they lived at the time, to have written all the books of the New Testament.

As the opportunities of forgery were greater, so also was the inducement. A man could gain no advantage by writing under the name of Homer or Euclid; if he could write equal to them, it would be better that he wrote under his own name; if inferior, he could not succeed. Pride would prevent the former, and impossibility the latter. But with respect to such books as compose the New Testament, all the inducements were on the side of forgery. The best imagined history that could have been made, at the distance of two or three hundred years after the time, could not have passed for an original under the name of the real writer; the only chance of success lay in forgery; for the church wanted pretence for its new doctrine, and truth and talents were out of the question.

But as it is not uncommon (as before observed) to relate stories of persons walking after they are dead, and of ghosts and apparitions of such as have fallen by some violent or extraordinary means; and as the people of that day were in the habit of believing such things, and of the appearance of angels, and also of devils, and of their getting into people's insides, and shaking them like a fit of an ague, and of their being cast out again as if by an emetic—(Mary Magdalene, the book of Mark tells us had brought up, or been brought to bed of seven devils;) it was nothing extraordinary that some story of this kind should get abroad of the person called Jesus Christ, and become afterwards the foundation of the four books ascribed to Matthew, Mark, Luke, and John. Each writer told a tale as he heard it, or thereabouts, and gave to his book the name of the saint or the apostle whom tradition had given as the eye-witness. It is only upon this ground that the contradictions in those books can be accounted for; and if this be not the case, they are downright impositions, lies, and forgeries, without even the apology of credulity.

That they have been written by a sort of half Jews, as the foregoing quotations mention, is discernible enough. The frequent references made to that chief assassin and impostor Moses, and to the men called prophets, establishes this point; and, on the other hand, the church has complimented the fraud, by admitting the Bible and the Testament to reply to each other. Between the Christian-Jew and the Christian-Gentile, the thing called a prophecy, and the thing prophesied of, the type and the thing typified, the sign and the thing signified, have been industriously rummaged up, and fitted together like old locks and pick-lock keys. The story foolishly enough told of Eve and the serpent, and naturally enough as to the enmity between men and serpents (for the serpent always bites about the heel, because it cannot reach higher, and the man always knocks the serpent about the head, as the most effectual way to prevent its biting;) ["It shall bruise thy head, and thou shalt bruise his heel." Gen. iii. 15.—Author.] this foolish story, I say, has been made into a prophecy, a type, and a promise to begin with; and the lying imposition of Isaiah to Ahaz, 'That a virgin shall conceive and bear a son,' as a sign that Ahaz should conquer, when the event was that he was defeated (as already noticed in the observations on the book of Isaiah), has been perverted, and made to serve as a winder up.

Jonah and the whale are also made into a sign and type. Jonah is Jesus, and the whale is the grave; for it is said, (and they have made Christ to say it of himself, Matt. xii. 40), "For as Jonah was three days and three nights in the whale's belly, so shall the Son of man be three days and three nights in the heart of the earth." But it happens, awkwardly enough, that Christ, according to their own account, was but one day and two nights in the grave; about 36 hours instead of 72; that is, the Friday night, the Saturday, and the Saturday night; for they say he was up on the Sunday morning by sunrise, or before. But as this fits quite as well as the bite and the kick in Genesis, or the virgin and her son in Isaiah, it will pass in the lump of orthodox things.—Thus much for the historical part of the Testament and its evidences.

Epistles of Paul—The epistles ascribed to Paul, being fourteen in number, almost fill up the remaining part of the Testament. Whether those epistles were written by the person to whom they are ascribed is a matter of no great importance, since that the writer, whoever he was, attempts to prove his doctrine by argument. He does not pretend to have been witness to any of the scenes told of the resurrection and the ascension; and he declares that he had not believed them.

The story of his being struck to the ground as he was journeying to Damascus, has nothing in it miraculous or extraordinary; he escaped with life, and that is more than many others have done, who have been struck with lightning; and that he should lose his sight for three days, and be unable to eat or drink during that time, is nothing more than is common in such conditions. His companions that were with him appear not to have suffered in the same manner, for they were well enough to lead him the remainder of the journey; neither did they pretend to have seen any vision.

The character of the person called Paul, according to the accounts given of him, has in it a great deal of violence and fanaticism; he had persecuted with as much heat as he preached afterwards; the stroke he had received had changed his thinking, without altering his constitution; and either as a Jew or a Christian he was the same zealot. Such men are never good moral evidences of any doctrine they preach. They are always in extremes, as well of action as of belief.

The doctrine he sets out to prove by argument, is the resurrection of the same body: and he advances this as an evidence of immortality. But so much will men differ in their manner of thinking, and in the conclusions they draw from the same premises, that this doctrine of the resurrection of the same body, so far from being an evidence of immortality, appears to me to be an evidence against it; for if I have already died in this body, and am raised again in the same body in which I have died, it is presumptive evidence that I shall die again. That resurrection no more secures me against the repetition of dying, than an ague-fit, when past, secures me against another. To believe therefore in immortality, I must have a more elevated idea than is contained in the gloomy doctrine of the resurrection.

Besides, as a matter of choice, as well as of hope, I had rather have a better body and a more convenient form than the present. Every animal in the creation excels us in something. The winged insects, without mentioning doves or eagles, can pass over more space with greater ease in a few minutes than man can in an hour. The glide of the smallest fish, in proportion to its bulk, exceeds us in motion almost beyond comparison, and without weariness. Even the sluggish snail can ascend from the bottom of a dungeon, where man, by the want of that ability, would perish; and a spider can launch itself from the top, as a playful amusement. The personal powers of man are so limited, and his heavy frame so little constructed to extensive enjoyment, that there is nothing to induce us to wish the opinion of Paul to be true. It is too little for the magnitude of the scene, too mean for the sublimity of the subject.

But all other arguments apart, the consciousness of existence is the only conceivable idea we can have of another life, and the continuance of that consciousness is immortality. The consciousness of existence, or the knowing that we exist, is not necessarily confined to the same form, nor to the same matter, even in this life.

We have not in all cases the same form, nor in any case the same matter, that composed our bodies twenty or thirty years ago; and yet we are conscious of being the same persons. Even legs and arms, which make up almost half the human frame, are not necessary to the consciousness of existence. These may be lost or taken away and the full consciousness of existence remain; and were their place supplied by wings, or other appendages, we cannot conceive that it could alter our consciousness of existence. In short, we know not how much, or rather how little, of our composition it is, and how exquisitely fine that little is, that creates in us this consciousness of existence; and all beyond that is like the pulp of a peach, distinct and separate from the vegetative speck in the kernel.

Who can say by what exceeding fine action of fine matter it is that a thought is produced in what we call the mind? and yet that thought when produced, as I now produce the thought I am writing, is capable of becoming immortal, and is the only production of man that has that capacity.

Statues of brass and marble will perish; and statues made in imitation of them are not the same statues, nor the same workmanship, any more than the copy of a picture is the same picture. But print and reprint a thought a thousand times over, and that with materials of any kind, carve it in wood, or engrave it on stone, the thought is eternally and identically the same thought in every case. It has a capacity of unimpaired existence, unaffected by change of matter, and is essentially distinct, and of a nature different from every thing else that we know of, or can conceive. If then the thing produced has in itself a capacity of being immortal, it is more than a token that the power that produced it, which is the self-same thing as consciousness of existence, can be immortal also; and that as independently of the matter it was first connected with, as the thought is of the printing or writing it first appeared in. The one idea is not more difficult to believe than the other; and we can see that one is true.

That the consciousness of existence is not dependent on the same form or the same matter, is demonstrated to our senses in the works of the creation, as far as our senses are capable of receiving that demonstration. A very numerous part of the animal creation preaches to us, far better than Paul, the belief of a life hereafter. Their little life resembles an earth and a heaven, a present and a future state; and comprises, if it may be so expressed, immortality in miniature.

The most beautiful parts of the creation to our eye are the winged insects, and they are not so originally. They acquire that form and that inimitable brilliancy by progressive changes. The slow and creeping caterpillar worm of to day, passes in a few days to a torpid figure, and a state resembling death; and in the next change comes forth in all the miniature magnificence of life, a splendid butterfly. No resemblance of the former creature remains; every thing is changed; all his powers are new, and life is to him another thing. We cannot conceive that the consciousness of existence is not the same in this state of the animal as before;

why then must I believe that the resurrection of the same body is necessary to continue to me the consciousness of existence hereafter?

In the former part of 'The Agee of Reason.' I have called the creation the true and only real word of God; and this instance, or this text, in the book of creation, not only shows to us that this thing may be so, but that it is so; and that the belief of a future state is a rational belief, founded upon facts visible in the creation: for it is not more difficult to believe that we shall exist hereafter in a better state and form than at present, than that a worm should become a butterfly, and quit the dunghill for the atmosphere, if we did not know it as a fact.

As to the doubtful jargon ascribed to Paul in 1 Corinthians xv., which makes part of the burial service of some Christian sectaries, it is as destitute of meaning as the tolling of a bell at the funeral; it explains nothing to the understanding, it illustrates nothing to the imagination, but leaves the reader to find any meaning if he can. "All flesh," says he, "is not the same flesh. There is one flesh of men, another of beasts, another of fishes, and another of birds." And what then? nothing. A cook could have said as much. "There are also," says he, "bodies celestial and bodies terrestrial; the glory of the celestial is one and the glory of the terrestrial is the other." And what then? nothing. And what is the difference? nothing that he has told. "There is," says he, "one glory of the sun, and another glory of the moon, and another glory of the stars." And what then? nothing; except that he says that one star differeth from another star in glory, instead of distance; and he might as well have told us that the moon did not shine so bright as the sun. All this is nothing better than the jargon of a conjuror, who picks up phrases he does not understand to confound the credulous people who come to have their fortune told. Priests and conjurors are of the same trade.

Sometimes Paul affects to be a naturalist, and to prove his system of resurrection from the principles of vegetation. "Thou fool" says he, "that which thou sowest is not quickened except it die." To which one might reply in his own language, and say, Thou fool, Paul, that which thou sowest is not quickened except it die not; for the grain that dies in the ground never does, nor can vegetate. It is only the living grains that produce the next crop. But the metaphor, in any point of view, is no simile. It is succession, and [not] resurrection.

The progress of an animal from one state of being to another, as from a worm to a butterfly, applies to the case; but this of a grain does not, and shows Paul to have been what he says of others, a fool.

Whether the fourteen epistles ascribed to Paul were written by him or not, is a matter of indifference; they are either argumentative or dogmatical; and as the argument is defective, and the dogmatical part is merely presumptive, it signifies not who wrote them. And the same may be said for the remaining parts of the Testament. It is not upon the Epistles, but upon what is called the Gospel, contained in the four books ascribed to Matthew, Mark, Luke, and John, and upon the pretended prophecies, that the theory of the church, calling itself the Christian Church, is founded. The Epistles are dependant upon those, and must follow their fate; for if the story of Jesus Christ be fabulous, all reasoning founded upon it, as a supposed truth, must fall with it.

We know from history, that one of the principal leaders of this church, Athanasius, lived at the time the New Testament was formed; [Athanasius died, according to the Church chronology, in the year 371—Author.] and we know also, from the absurd jargon he has left us under the name of a creed, the character of the men who formed the New Testament; and we know also from the same history that the authenticity of the books of which it is composed was denied at the time. It was upon the vote of such as Athanasius that the Testament was decreed to be the word of God; and nothing can present to us a more strange idea than that of decreeing the word of God by vote. Those who rest their faith upon such authority put man in the place of God, and have no true foundation for future happiness. Credulity, however, is not a crime, but it becomes criminal by resisting conviction. It is strangling in the womb of the conscience the efforts it makes to ascertain truth. We should never force belief upon ourselves in any thing.

I here close the subject on the Old Testament and the New. The evidence I have produced to prove them forgeries, is extracted from the books themselves, and acts, like a two-edge sword, either way. If the evidence be denied, the authenticity of the Scriptures is denied with it, for it is Scripture evidence: and if the evidence be admitted, the authenticity of the books is disproved. The contradictory impossibilities, contained in the Old Testament and the New, put them in the case of a man who swears for and against. Either evidence convicts him of perjury, and equally destroys reputation.

Should the Bible and the Testament hereafter fall, it is not that I have done it. I have done no more than extracted the evidence from the confused mass of matters with which it is mixed, and arranged that evidence in a point of light to be clearly seen and easily comprehended; and, having done this, I leave the reader to judge for himself, as I have judged for myself.

CHAPTER III - CONCLUSION

IN the former part of 'The Age of Reason' I have spoken of the three frauds, mystery, miracle, and Prophecy; and as I have seen nothing in any of the answers to that work that in the least affects what I have there said upon those subjects, I shall not encumber this Second Part with additions that are not necessary.

I have spoken also in the same work upon what is celled revelation, and have shown the absurd misapplication of that term to the books of the Old Testament and the New; for certainly revelation is out of the question in reciting any thing of which man has been the actor or the witness. That which man has done or seen, needs no revelation to tell him he has done it, or seen it—for he knows it already—nor to enable him to tell it or to write it. It is ignorance, or imposition, to apply the term revelation in such cases; yet the Bible and Testament are classed under this fraudulent description of being all revelation.

Revelation then, so far as the term has relation between God and man, can only be applied to something which God reveals of his will to man; but though the power of the Almighty to make such a communication is necessarily admitted, because to that power all things are possible, yet, the thing so revealed (if any thing ever was revealed, and which, by the bye, it is impossible to prove) is revelation to the person only to whom it is made. His account of it to another is not revelation; and whoever puts faith in that account, puts it in the man from whom the account comes; and that man may have been deceived, or may have dreamed it; or he may be an impostor and may lie. There is no possible criterion whereby to judge of the truth of what he tells; for even the morality of it would be no proof of revelation. In all such cases, the proper answer should be, "When it is revealed to me, I will believe it to be revelation; but it is not and cannot be incumbent upon me to believe it to be revelation before; neither is it proper that I should take the word of man as the word of God, and put man in the place of God." This is the manner in which I have spoken of revelation in the former part of The Age of Reason; and which, whilst it reverentially admits revelation as a possible thing, because, as before said, to the Almighty all things are possible, it prevents the imposition of one man upon another, and precludes the wicked use of pretended revelation.

But though, speaking for myself, I thus admit the possibility of revelation, I totally disbelieve that the Almighty ever did communicate any thing to man, by any mode of speech, in any language, or by any kind of vision, or appearance, or by any means which our senses are capable of receiving, otherwise than by the universal display of himself in the works of the creation, and by that repugnance we feel in ourselves to bad actions, and disposition to good ones. [A fair parallel of the then unknown aphorism of Kant: "Two things fill the soul with wonder and reverence, increasing evermore as I meditate more closely upon them: the starry heavens above me and the moral law within me." (Kritik derpraktischen Vernunfe, 1788). Kant's religious utterances at the beginning of the French Revolution brought on him a royal mandate of silence, because he had worked out from "the moral law within" a principle of human equality precisely similar to that which Paine had derived from his Quaker doctrine of the "inner light" of every man. About the same time Paine's writings were suppressed in England. Paine did not understand German, but Kant, though always independent in the formation of his opinions, was evidently well acquainted with the literature of the Revolution, in America, England, and France.—Editor.]

The most detestable wickedness, the most horrid cruelties, and the greatest miseries, that have afflicted the human race have had their origin in this thing called revelation, or revealed religion. It has been the most dishonourable belief against the character of the divinity, the most destructive to morality, and the peace and happiness of man, that ever was propagated since man began to exist. It is better, far better, that we admitted, if it were possible, a thousand devils to roam at large, and to preach publicly the doctrine of devils, if there were any such, than that we permitted one such impostor and monster as Moses, Joshua, Samuel, and the Bible prophets, to come with the pretended word of God in his mouth, and have credit among us.

Whence arose all the horrid assassinations of whole nations of men, women, and infants, with which the Bible is filled; and the bloody persecutions, and tortures unto death and religious wars, that since that time have laid Europe in blood and ashes; whence arose they, but from this impious thing called revealed religion, and this monstrous belief that God has spoken to man? The lies of the Bible have been the cause of the one, and the lies of the Testament [of] the other.

Some Christians pretend that Christianity was not established by the sword; but of what period of time do they speak? It was impossible that twelve men could begin with the sword: they had not the power; but no sooner were the professors of Christianity sufficiently powerful to employ the sword than they did so, and the stake and faggot too; and Mahomet could not do it sooner. By the same spirit that Peter cut off the ear of the high priest's servant (if the story be true) he would cut off his head, and the head of his master, had he been able. Besides this, Christianity grounds itself originally upon the [Hebrew] Bible, and the Bible was established altogether by the sword, and that in the worst use of it—not to terrify, but to extirpate. The Jews made no converts: they butchered all. The Bible is the sire of the [New] Testament, and both are called the word of God. The Christians read both books; the ministers preach from both books; and this thing called Christianity is made up of both. It is then false to say that Christianity was not established by the sword.

The only sect that has not persecuted are the Quakers; and the only reason that can be given for it is, that they are rather Deists than Christians. They do not believe much about Jesus Christ, and they call the scriptures a dead letter. [This is an interesting and correct testimony as to the beliefs of the earlier Quakers, one of whom was Paine's father.—Editor.] Had they called them by a worse name, they had been nearer the truth.

It is incumbent on every man who reverences the character of the Creator, and who wishes to lessen the catalogue of artificial miseries, and remove the cause that has sown persecutions thick among mankind, to expel all ideas of a revealed religion as a dangerous heresy, and an impious fraud. What is it that we have learned from this pretended thing called revealed religion? Nothing that is useful to man, and every thing that is dishonourable to his Maker. What is it the Bible teaches us?—repine, cruelty, and murder. What is it the Testament teaches us?—to believe that the Almighty committed debauchery with a woman engaged to be married; and the belief of this debauchery is called faith.

As to the fragments of morality that are irregularly and thinly scattered in those books, they make no part of this pretended thing, revealed religion. They are the natural dictates of conscience, and the bonds by which society is held together, and without which it cannot exist; and are nearly the same in all religions, and in all societies. The Testament teaches nothing new upon this subject, and where it attempts to exceed, it becomes mean and ridiculous. The doctrine of not retaliating injuries is much better expressed in Proverbs, which is a collection as well from the Gentiles as the Jews, than it is in the Testament. It is there said, (Xxv. 2 I) "If thine enemy be hungry, give him bread to eat; and if he be thirsty, give him water to drink:" [According to what is called Christ's sermon on the mount, in the book of Matthew, where, among some other [and] good things, a great deal of this feigned morality is introduced, it is there expressly said, that the doctrine of forbearance, or of not retaliating injuries, was not any part of the doctrine of the Jews; but as this doctrine is found in "Proverbs," it must, according to that statement, have been copied from the Gentiles, from whom Christ had learned it. Those men whom Jewish and Christian idolators have abusively called heathen, had much better and clearer ideas of justice and morality than are to be found in the Old Testament, so far as it is Jewish, or in the New. The answer of Solon on the question, "Which is the most perfect popular government," has never been exceeded by any man since his time, as containing a maxim of political morality, "That," says he, "where the least injury done to the meanest individual, is considered as an insult on the whole constitution." Solon lived about 500 years before Christ.—Author.] but when it is said, as in the Testament, "If a man smite thee on the right cheek, turn to him the other also," it is assassinating the dignity of forbearance, and sinking man into a spaniel.

Loving, of enemies is another dogma of feigned morality, and has besides no meaning. It is incumbent on man, as a moralist, that he does not revenge an injury; and it is equally as good in a political sense, for there is no end to retaliation; each retaliates on the other, and calls it justice: but to love in proportion to the injury, if it could be done, would be to offer a premium for a crime. Besides, the word enemies is too vague and general to be used in a moral maxim, which ought always to be clear and defined, like a proverb. If a man be the enemy of another from mistake and prejudice, as in the case of religious opinions, and sometimes in politics, that man is different to an enemy at heart with a criminal intention; and it is incumbent upon us, and it contributes also to our own tranquillity, that we put the best construction upon a thing that it will bear. But even this erroneous motive in him makes no motive for love on the other part; and to say that we can love voluntarily, and without a motive, is morally and physically impossible.

Morality is injured by prescribing to it duties that, in the first place, are impossible to be performed, and if they could be would be productive of evil; or, as before said, be premiums for crime. The maxim of doing as we would be done unto does not include this strange doctrine of loving enemies; for no man expects to be loved himself for his crime or for his enmity.

Those who preach this doctrine of loving their enemies, are in general the greatest persecutors, and they act consistently by so doing; for the doctrine is hypocritical, and it is natural that hypocrisy should act the reverse of what it preaches. For my own part, I disown the doctrine, and consider it as a feigned or fabulous morality; yet the man does not exist that can say I have persecuted him, or any man, or any set of men, either in the American Revolution, or in the French Revolution; or that I have, in any case, returned evil for evil. But it is not incumbent on man to reward a bad action with a good one, or to return good for evil; and wherever it is done, it is a voluntary act, and not a duty. It is also absurd to suppose that such doctrine can make any part of a revealed religion. We imitate the moral character of the Creator by forbearing with each other, for he forbears with all; but this doctrine would imply that he loved man, not in proportion as he was good, but as he was bad.

If we consider the nature of our condition here, we must see there is no occasion for such a thing as revealed religion. What is it we want to know? Does not the creation, the universe we behold, preach to us the existence of an Almighty power, that governs and regulates the whole? And is not the evidence that this creation holds out to our senses infinitely stronger than any thing we can read in a book, that any imposter might make and call the word of God? As for morality, the knowledge of it exists in every man's conscience.

Here we are. The existence of an Almighty power is sufficiently demonstrated to us, though we cannot conceive, as it is impossible we should, the nature and manner of its existence. We cannot conceive how we came here ourselves, and yet we know for a fact that we are here. We must know also, that the power that called us into being, can if he please, and when he pleases, call us to account for the manner in which we have lived here; and therefore without seeking any other motive for the belief, it is rational to believe that he will, for we know beforehand that he can. The probability or even possibility of the thing is all that we ought to know; for if we knew it as a fact, we should be the mere slaves of terror; our belief would have no merit, and our best actions no virtue.

Deism then teaches us, without the possibility of being deceived, all that is necessary or proper to be known. The creation is the Bible of the deist. He there reads, in the hand-writing of the Creator himself, the certainty of his existence, and the immutability of his power; and all other Bibles and Testaments are to him forgeries. The probability that we may be called to account hereafter, will, to reflecting minds, have the influence of belief; for it is not our belief or disbelief that can make or unmake the fact. As this is the state we are in, and which it is proper we should be in, as free agents, it is the fool only, and not the philosopher, nor even the prudent man, that will live as if there were no God.

But the belief of a God is so weakened by being mixed with the strange fable of the Christian creed, and with the wild adventures related in the Bible, and the obscurity and obscene nonsense of the Testament, that the mind of man is bewildered as in a fog. Viewing all these things in a confused mass, he confounds fact with fable; and as he cannot believe all, he feels a disposition to reject all. But the belief of a God is a belief distinct from all other things, and ought not to be confounded with any. The notion of a Trinity of Gods has enfeebled the belief of one God. A multiplication of beliefs acts as a division of belief; and in proportion as anything is divided, it is weakened.

Religion, by such means, becomes a thing of form instead of fact; of notion instead of principle: morality is banished to make room for an imaginary thing called faith, and this faith has its origin in a supposed debauchery; a man is preached instead of a God; an execution is an object for gratitude; the preachers daub themselves with the blood, like a troop of assassins, and pretend to admire the brilliancy it gives them; they preach a humdrum sermon on the merits of the execution; then praise Jesus Christ for being executed, and condemn the Jews for doing it.

A man, by hearing all this nonsense lumped and preached together, confounds the God of the Creation with the imagined God of the Christians, and lives as if there were none.

Of all the systems of religion that ever were invented, there is none more derogatory to the Almighty, more unedifying to man, more repugnant to reason, and more contradictory in itself, than this thing called Christianity. Too absurd for belief, too impossible to convince, and too inconsistent for practice, it renders the heart torpid, or produces only atheists and fanatics. As an engine of power, it serves the purpose of despotism; and as a means of wealth, the avarice of priests; but so far as respects the good of man in general, it leads to nothing here or hereafter.

The only religion that has not been invented, and that has in it every evidence of divine originality, is pure and simple deism. It must have been the first and will probably be the last that man believes. But pure and simple deism does not answer the purpose of despotic governments. They cannot lay hold of religion as an engine but by mixing it with human inventions, and making their own authority a part; neither does it answer the avarice of priests, but by incorporating themselves and their functions with it, and becoming, like the government, a party in the system. It is this that forms the otherwise mysterious connection of church and state; the church human, and the state tyrannic.

Were a man impressed as fully and strongly as he ought to be with the belief of a God, his moral life would be regulated by the force of belief; he would stand in awe of God, and of himself, and would not do the thing that could not be concealed from either. To give this belief the full opportunity of force, it is necessary that it acts alone. This is deism.

But when, according to the Christian Trinitarian scheme, one part of God is represented by a dying man, and another part, called the Holy Ghost, by a flying pigeon, it is impossible that belief can attach itself to such wild conceits. [The book called the book of Matthew, says, (iii. 16,) that the Holy Ghost descended in the shape of a dove. It might as well have said a goose; the creatures are equally harmless, and the one is as much a nonsensical lie as the other. Acts, ii. 2, 3, says, that it descended in a mighty rushing wind, in the shape of cloven tongues: perhaps it was cloven feet. Such absurd stuff is fit only for tales of witches and wizards.—Author.]

It has been the scheme of the Christian church, and of all the other invented systems of religion, to hold man in ignorance of the Creator, as it is of government to hold him in ignorance of his rights. The systems of the one are as false as those of the other, and are calculated for mutual support. The study of theology as it stands in Christian churches, is the study of nothing; it is founded on nothing; it rests on no principles; it proceeds by no authorities; it has no data; it can demonstrate nothing; and admits of no conclusion. Not any thing can be studied as a science without our being in possession of the principles upon which it is founded; and as this is not the case with Christian theology, it is therefore the study of nothing.

Instead then of studying theology, as is now done, out of the Bible and Testament, the meanings of which books are always controverted, and the authenticity of which is disproved, it is necessary that we refer to the Bible of the creation. The principles we discover there are eternal, and of divine origin: they are the foundation of all the science that exists in the world, and must be the foundation of theology.

We can know God only through his works. We cannot have a conception of any one attribute, but by following some principle that leads to it. We have only a confused idea of his power, if we have not the means of comprehending something of its immensity. We can have no idea of his wisdom, but by knowing the order and manner in which it acts. The principles of science lead to this knowledge; for the Creator of man is the Creator of science, and it is through that medium that man can see God, as it were, face to face.

Could a man be placed in a situation, and endowed with power of vision to behold at one view, and to contemplate deliberately, the structure of the universe, to mark the movements of the several planets, the cause of their varying appearances, the unerring order in which they revolve, even to the remotest comet, their connection and dependence on each other, and to know the system of laws established by the Creator, that governs and regulates the whole; he would then conceive, far beyond what any church theology can teach him, the power, the wisdom, the vastness, the munificence of the Creator. He would then see that all the knowledge man has of science, and that all the mechanical arts by which he renders his situation comfortable here, are derived from that source: his mind, exalted by the scene, and convinced by the fact, would increase in gratitude as it increased in knowledge: his religion or his worship would become united with his improvement as a man: any employment he followed that had connection with the principles of the creation,—as everything of agriculture, of science, and of the mechanical arts, has,— would teach him more of God, and of the gratitude he owes to him, than any theological Christian sermon he now hears. Great objects inspire great thoughts; great munificence excites great gratitude; but the grovelling tales and doctrines of the Bible and the Testament are fit only to excite contempt.

Though man cannot arrive, at least in this life, at the actual scene I have described, he can demonstrate it, because he has knowledge of the principles upon which the creation is constructed. We know that the greatest works can be represented in model, and that the universe can be represented by the same means. The same principles by which we measure an inch or an acre of ground will measure to millions in extent. A circle of an inch diameter has the same geometrical properties as a circle that would circumscribe the universe. The same properties of a triangle that will demonstrate upon paper the course of a ship, will do it on the ocean; and, when applied to what are called the heavenly bodies, will ascertain to a minute the time of an eclipse, though those bodies are millions of miles distant from us. This knowledge is of divine origin; and it is from the Bible of the creation that man has learned it, and not from the stupid Bible of the church, that teaches man nothing. [The Bible-makers have undertaken to give us, in the first chapter of Genesis, an account of the creation; and in doing this they have demonstrated nothing but their ignorance. They make there to have been three days and three nights, evenings and mornings, before there was any sun; when it is the presence or absence of the sun that is the cause of day and night—and what is called his rising and setting that of morning and evening. Besides, it is a puerile and pitiful idea, to suppose the Almighty to say, "Let there be light." It is the imperative manner of speaking that a conjuror uses when he says to his cups and balls, Presto, be gone—and most probably has been taken from it, as Moses and his rod is a conjuror and his wand. Longinus calls this expression the sublime; and by the same rule the conjurer is sublime too; for the manner of speaking is expressively and grammatically the same. When authors and critics talk of the sublime, they see not how nearly it borders on the ridiculous. The sublime of the critics, like some parts of Edmund Burke's sublime and beautiful, is like a windmill just visible in a fog, which imagination might distort into a flying mountain, or an archangel, or a flock of wild geese.—Author.]

All the knowledge man has of science and of machinery, by the aid of which his existence is rendered comfortable upon earth, and without which he would be scarcely distinguishable in appearance and condition from a common animal, comes from the great machine and structure of the universe. The constant and unwearied observations of our ancestors upon the movements and revolutions of the heavenly bodies, in what are supposed to have been the early ages of the world, have brought this knowledge upon earth. It is not Moses and the prophets, nor Jesus Christ, nor his apostles, that have done it. The Almighty is the great mechanic of the creation, the first philosopher, and original teacher of all science. Let us then learn to reverence our master, and not forget the labours of our ancestors.

Had we, at this day, no knowledge of machinery, and were it possible that man could have a view, as I have before described, of the structure and machinery of the universe, he would soon conceive the idea of constructing some at least of the mechanical works we now have; and the idea so conceived would progressively advance in practice. Or could a model of the universe, such as is called an orrery, be presented before him and put in motion, his mind would arrive at the same idea. Such an object and such a subject would, whilst it improved him in knowledge useful to himself as a man and a member of society, as well as entertaining, afford far better matter for impressing him with a knowledge of, and a belief in the Creator, and of the reverence and gratitude that man owes to him, than the stupid texts of the Bible and the Testament, from which, be the talents of the preacher; what they may, only stupid sermons can be preached. If man must preach, let him preach something that is edifying, and from the texts that are known to be true.

The Bible of the creation is inexhaustible in texts. Every part of science, whether connected with the geometry of the universe, with the systems of animal and vegetable life, or with the properties of inanimate matter, is a text as well for devotion as for philosophy—for gratitude, as for human improvement. It will perhaps be said, that if such a revolution in the system of religion takes place, every preacher ought to be a philosopher. Most certainly, and every house of devotion a school of science.

It has been by wandering from the immutable laws of science, and the light of reason, and setting up an invented thing called "revealed religion," that so many wild and blasphemous conceits have been formed of the Almighty. The Jews have made him the assassin of the human species, to make room for the religion of the Jews. The Christians have made him the murderer of himself, and the founder of a new religion to supersede and expel the Jewish religion. And to find pretence and admission for these things, they must have supposed his power or his wisdom imperfect, or his will changeable; and the changeableness of the will is the imperfection of the judgement. The philosopher knows that the laws of the Creator have never changed, with respect either to the principles of science, or the properties of matter. Why then is it to be supposed they have changed with respect to man?

I here close the subject. I have shown in all the foregoing parts of this work that the Bible and Testament are impositions and forgeries; and I leave the evidence I have produced in proof of it to be refuted, if any one can do it; and I leave the ideas that are suggested in the conclusion of the work to rest on the mind of the reader; certain as I am that when opinions are free, either in matters of government or religion, truth will finally and powerfully prevail.

END OF PART II

* * *